To ~ ~ ~ ~
Don't let the ~~ ~
eat this one.

Diane & Neil

THE GENUS
CYPRIPEDIUM

CARSON WHITLOW

515 993-4841

A BOTANICAL MAGAZINE MONOGRAPH

The Genus
CYPRIPEDIUM

Phillip Cribb

Illustrations by
Mary Bates, Eleanor Catherine, William Curtis,
Miss Drake, Walter Fitch, Conrad Gesner, Valerie Price,
Susie Ray, Pandora Sellars, Matilda Smith, Lilian Snelling,
James Sowerby, and Florence Woolward

Edited by Peter Green

Series Editor—Brian Mathew

Published in association with
The Royal Botanic Gardens, Kew

Timber Press
Portland, Oregon

Published in 1997 by
Timber Press, Inc.
133 S.W. Second Avenue, Suite 450
Portland, Oregon 97204, U.S.A.

Reprinted 1999

Printed in Hong Kong

Library of Congress Cataloging-in-Publication Data

Cribb, Phillip.
    The genus Cypripedium / Phillip Cribb ; illustrations by Mary
Bates . . . et al.] ; edited by Peter Green.
        p.   cm.
    "The Royal Botanic Gardens, Kew, in association with Timber
Press."
    "A Botanical magazine monograph."
    Includes bibliographical references (p.   ) and index.
    ISBN 0-88192-403-2
    1. Cypripedium. 2. Cypripedium—Classification. I. Green, Peter.
II. Royal Botanic Gardens, Kew. III. Title.
QK495.064C74   1997
584'.4—dc21   96-30083
                                                                    CIP

Reprint errata

page 102: for "10 sections" read "11 sections."
page 176: the legends for the distribution map are transposed.
page 269: for "R. M. Brown" read "P. M. Brown."
page 271: for "*colombianum*" read "*columbianum*," and for "Colombia"
    read "Columbia."
page 272: for "*manschuricum*" read "*manchuricum*."

Plate 113: caption should read "*Cypripedium tibeticum*, Temo La Pass,
    Tibet. Photo by A. Chambers."
Plate 115: caption should read "*Cypripedium tibeticum*, Huang-long,
    Sichuan, China. Photo by P. J. Cribb."
Plate 116: caption should read "*Cypripedium tibeticum*, Balangshan Pass,
    Sichuan, China. Photo by C. Grey-Wilson."

Cypripediums—The grandest and most august of the Orchidaceae, one great race which is supreme alike in the open and under cover, deserves full treatment by itself.

—Reginald Farrer (1919) in *The English Rock Garden*

CONTENTS

Colour plates 1–26 follow page 144.
Colour plates 27–124 follow page 224.

ACKNOWLEDGEMENTS

I would like to thank Professor Simon Owens, the Keeper of the Herbarium, and his predecessor, Professor Gren Lucas, for letting me use the facilities of the Herbarium and Library of the Royal Botanic Gardens, Kew; the following colleagues for discussions on *Cypripedium:* Sandra Bell, Mark Chase, Tony Cox, Chris Grey-Wilson, Tony Hall, Gren Lucas, Brian Mathew, Alec Pridgeon, Alan Radcliffe-Smith, Margaret Ramsay, Marianne Syrylak Sandison, David Simpson, William Stearn, Sarah Thomas, and Jeffrey Wood. I have benefitted enormously from the combined wisdom and help of many friends and correspondents: John Atwood, Dr. Leonid Averyanov, Chris Bailes, Fred Case, Dr. Chen Sing-chi, Joan and Brian Cooper, Peter Corkhill, Kath Dryden, W. Evertse, Werner Frosch, Leslie Garay, Dora Gerhardt, Eric Hágsater, Professor Iwatsuki, J. Kawahara, Professor Hal Koopowitz, Emil Lueckel, Carlyle Luer, Luo Yi Bin, H. Okuyama, Holger Perner, J. Petersen, Jany Renz, Gustavo Romero, Gerardo Salazar, Charles (Chuck) Sheviak, Miguel Soto, Samuel Sprunger, Joyce Stewart, Barry Tattersall, Peter Taylor, Carson Whitlow, Dr. Yamaguchi, and Y. Z. Xi.

The superb and new colour illustrations are the work of Mary Bates in Edinburgh, Pandora Sellars and Susie Ray at Kew. The use of selected watercolours by William Curtis, Walter Hood Fitch, Matilda Smith, and Lilian Snelling from the Kew archive is gratefully acknowledged to the Director, Professor Sir Ghillean Prance, and Chief Librarian, Miss Sylvia Fitzgerald. The painting by James Sowerby is courtesy of the Director of the Natural History Museum. The publishers of the recent facsimile of Gesner's drawings in Zoller, Steinmann, and Schmidt (1973–1980) have kindly allowed the reproduction of the exceptional watercolour illustration of *Cypripedium calceolus* by Conrad Gesner. Michael and Jane Ancram have kindly given permission for the use of the Florence Woolward plate of *C. calceolus*.

The exquisite line drawings are the work of Eleanor Catherine, and I am grateful for her enthusiasm and endurance in preparing them. The illustrations of *Cypripedium molle* and *C. dickinsonianum* were prepared by Rolando Jiménez, and I am grateful to Eric Hágsater of AMO for their use. The maps were prepared at Kew by the Media Resources Unit. Colour photographs have been lent to me by John Atwood, Anne Chambers, Joan and Brian Cooper, Jill Cowley, W. Evertse, Werner Frosch, Ed Greenwood, Chris Grey-Wilson, Eric Hágsater, J. Kawahara, David Lang, Carl Luer, David Menzies, Sabine Miehe, Yevgeni Mokhov, Holger Perner, David Tennant, and others.

I am particularly grateful to Holger Perner for preparing the chapter on cultivation. He was given detailed information on methods used by several growers but especially Kath Dryden, Werner Frosch, Charles Sheviak, and Barry Tattersall. Peter Green, formerly Deputy Director of the Royal Botanic Gardens, Kew, has kindly and constructively edited my text. Brian Mathew, editor of *Curtis's Botanical Magazine,* has kindly seen the book through to publication.

I have travelled widely hunting cypripediums in the wild. In Mexico I was looked after by Eric Hágsater, Gerardo Salazar, and Miguel Soto; in the United States by Leslie Garay, Carl Luer, and the late Herman Sweet; in Europe by Jany Renz and Samuel Sprunger; in China by S. C. Chen, CITS, and my many companions. I should not forget my fellow members, especially Peter Corkhill, David Harberd and Edgar Milne-Redhead, of what is now English Nature's Cypripedium Committee in the United Kingdom. Joining this committee, when I started at Kew over 20 years ago, first brought the lady's slipper orchids to my attention.

I would like to thank the curators of the following herbaria for their assistance on my visits to examine material of *Cypripedium:* AMES, BM, E, G, KUN, P, PE, SEL, W, Z. I have also received material on loan from these, S and UPS.

Most of all I would like to thank my wife, Marianne, who has encouraged me in this work and with whom I have enjoyed many hours slipper orchid hunting around the world.

INTRODUCTION

Orchids have always been popular with horticulturists. The earliest records we have of orchid growing date back over 500 years before Christ to the time of Confucius in China. Modern orchid growing is, however, more recent and European in origin, dating back to early Victorian times when the Industrial Revolution gave people the time and resources to build glasshouses in which to grow exotic plants. Orchids were the group that benefitted most. The introduction of tropical species at this time saw the start of an obsession that became a mania by late Victorian times. The influx of orchids into European nurseries and orchid collections resulted in the description of many new species, especially from the tropics. Novelties were sought after in the wild on a massive scale, leading some species to the verge of extinction.

Ever since, the lady's slippers have been among the most popular of orchids. The earliest record we have of their cultivation is that of John Gerard (1597). Philip Miller in 1731 grew the native lady's slipper orchid at the Chelsea Physic Garden. Nowadays, no collection is complete without its selection of slipper orchids, although the tropical species have outshone the temperate ones, which have acquired a reputation of being difficult to grow for any length of time.

Slipper orchids have fascinated generations of botanists as well. They have features that set them apart from other orchids, notably the prominent slipper-shaped lip, the strange column with two anthers rather than one, and a shield-shaped sterile anther called the staminode. Consequently, they have been considered to be "primitive" orchids. Their pollination biology was first studied by no less an eminence than Charles Darwin. They are also considered rare and indeed the only British species is our rarest plant, having been collected by gardeners, over the decades, to the point of extinction.

In this monograph I have considered the history, biology, evolution, conservation, cultivation, and classification of the temperate slipper orchids of the genus *Cypripedium*. It is a companion to my account of the tropical Asiatic genus *Paphiopedilum*, which appeared in 1987 in the Kew Magazine Monograph Series. I have spent the

11

last twenty-three years as a botanist intrigued by slipper orchids, and I hope that this fascination is in some way communicated to those who read this account.

HISTORY

Linnaeus first used the name *Cypripedium* in 1737 in his *Flora Lapponica* in describing the European species as *Cypripedium foliis ovatolanceolatis,* the name *Cypripedium* alluding to Cyprus, the island that was the mythological birthplace of Aphrodite (Venus), and *pedilum,* a shoe or slipper, in allusion to the popular name of lady's slipper. In 1753 he named and described two species, *C. calceolus* and *C. bulbosum.* The former concept included the well-known European *C. calceolus* and the North American species now treated as *C. parviflorum* (var. β), *C. acaule* (var. γ), and *C. guttatum* (var. δ). The latter is now considered to belong to the distinct and unrelated genus *Calypso.*

Linnaeus was by no means the first to describe slipper orchids. Conrad Gesner (or Gessner) (1561) provided the earliest description of a slipper orchid in his *Horti Germaniae,* where he described *"Alismatis species, ut quidam putant, Calceolus diuae virginis vulgo dictus . . .".* Rembert Dodoens (1568) published the earliest illustration (Fig. 1) in his *Florum, et coroniariarium odoratarumque nonnullarum herbarium historia.* His illustration of *Damasonium nothum* or "Papen schoen", a one-flowered plant of *Cypripedium calceolus* complete with rhizome and roots, was simple but accurate and clearly identifiable. The drawing was sent to him by Joannes Vreccomtus of Brussels, who had flowered the illustrated plant in his garden, the earliest record of its cultivation.

Mathias de L'Obel (1576) reproduced Dodoens's illustration in his *Plantarum seu stirpium historia,* while Dodoens used it again in his *Stirpium historiae pemptades sex* of 1583 together with a more refined illustration of a plant with a branched rhizome with several shoots, one of which bears two flowers and the other two seed pods. The latter originated in the contemporary herbal *Rariorum aliquot stirpium . . .* of Charles de L'Ecluse (1583), also known as Clusius. Dodoens used the name *Calceolus Marianus,* "Pfaffen schuh", "Papen schoen", and *Calceolus Sacerdotis,* while Clusius, referring to it as "Marienschuh", placed it next to the helleborines, "Elleborine". Dodoens stated that it was found in *Helvetiorum, & Norici, ac*

Recentiorū
CALCEOLVS
Mariæ. Ad-
uerf.p 1.127.
Damaſoniū
nothū Dod.

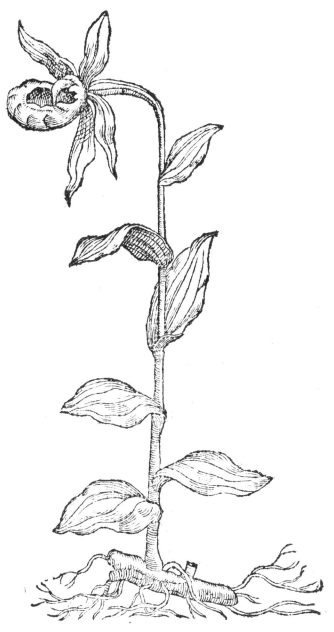

Figure 1. Cypripedium calceolus. From R. Dodoens, *Florum, et coroniariarium odoratarumque nonnullarum herbarium historia* (1568).

Pannoniae superioris sive Austriae montibus. Clusius had seen the plant in the wild in Austria and Hungary and it seems likely that his illustration was based on a wild plant seen on his travels. The woodcut would then have been produced for his own work but shared with Dodoens who was a good friend (Arber 1986). Another early illustration was that by Jacques Daleschamp (1586) in his *Historiae Generalis Plantarum,* where he illustrated *C. calceolus* under the name *Elleborine ferruginea Daleschampii* (Fig. 2).

Dodoens's plate reappeared in several later herbals, notably in John Gerard's (1597) *The Herball* and in John Parkinson's (1629) *Paradisi in sole paradisus terrestris.* Large chunks of Dodoens's work were used in translation in Gerard's *The Herball.* However, this was an accepted methodology of the day and Gerard did add notes on plants with which he was familiar. He called *Cypripedium calceolus* "Our Ladies shooe or slipper" and noted that it "groweth upon the mountains of Germanie, Hungarie, and Poland". He grew a plant given to him by his friend the Apothecary Master Garret and this is the earliest reference I can trace of the cultivation of the species in the British Isles. It is interesting that Gerard was unaware that it was a native British species. Its recognition as such was left to John Parkinson (1629), who called it *Helleborine vel Elleborine maior, sive Calceolus Mariae.*

Parkinson (1629) recorded *Cypripedium calceolus* as growing in

Lancashire, neare the border of Yorkshire, in a wood or place called the Helkes, which is three miles from Ingleborough, the higest Hill in England, and not farre from Ingleton, as I am informed by a couteous Gentlewoman, called Mistris Thomasin Turnstall, who dwelleth at Bull-banke, near Hornby Castle. . . . [she] hathe often sent mee up the rootes to London which have faire flowers in my Garden.

The lady's slipper survived in that area until into the twentieth century, and Parkinson's only mistake was his suggestion that Ingleborough is the highest hill in England. Parkinson was indeed an astute observer and noted that the seed of *C. calceolus* "is very small, very like unto the seede of the Orchides or Satyrions, and contained in such like long pods, but bigger." As far as I can determine, he was the first to connect *Cypripedium* with the orchids and to note their tiny seeds. Michel Adanson (1763) was the first botanist to formally include slipper orchids in the orchid family.

14

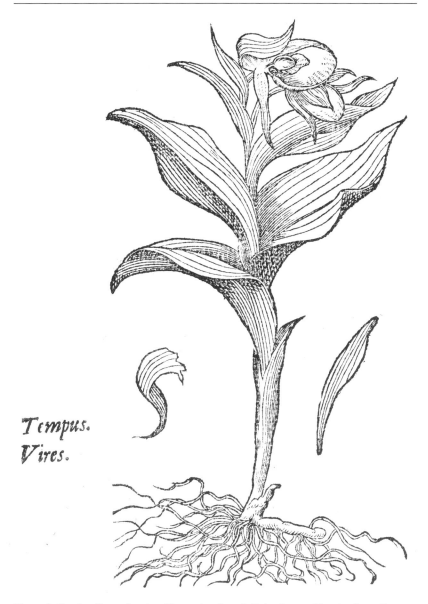

Tempus.
Vires.

Figure 2. Cypripedium calceolus. Illustration from J. Daleschamp, *Historiae Generalis Plantarum* (1586).

The earliest known colour illustration of *Cypripedium calceolus* is that by Conrad Gesner dating from 1541, a watercolour of a plant from Mt. Saleu near Geneva in Switzerland (see Frontispiece). It is an accomplished likeness, far superior to the later woodcuts in the herbals of L'Obel, Dodoens, and Clusius, while in botanical accuracy and detail of the rhizome, fruit, and column it was not matched for another two hundred or more years. Gesner died from plague before he was able to publish his botanical illustrations. Schmiedel (1751, 1759–1771) published part of Gesner's botanical work for the first time as *Opera Botanica* and included the coloured illustration and account of *C. calceolus* as *Calceolus Mariae*. These have recently been reproduced in facsimile by Zoller et al. (1973–1980). A useful list of early descriptions and illustrations of slipper orchids is included.

Another early colour illustration of *Cypripedium calceolus* is that by Daniel Rabel (1578–1638), recently reproduced in the second edition of Blunt and Stearn (1994). The original is in the Bibliothèque Nationale in Paris and was probably painted in 1631 or 1632.

Parkinson (1640) returned to the theme of "Our Ladyes Slipper or the great wilde Helleborine" in his *Theatrum botanicum*. There he recorded a North American species, undoubtedly *Cypripedium reginae*, as a "sort thereof . . . brought from the North parts of America, differing onely in being greater both in stalkes, leaves and flowers, which are not yellow but white, with reddish strakes through the bellies of them". An earlier reference to a North American species, however, is that of J. P. Cornut (1635) in his *Canadensium Plantarum Historia*, where he listed and illustrated *Calceolus marianus canadensis*, a reference to *Cypripedium reginae*.

Cypripedium reginae and three other North American taxa, *C. acaule*, *C. parviflorum* var. *parviflorum* (*Calceolus . . . flore luteo minore*), and *C. parviflorum* var. *pubescens*, were described by Leonard Plukenet (1696, 1700), the first two and the last being illustrated by him in 1705 in his *Almatheum botanicum* (Fig. 3). These line illustrations are the earliest representations of North American slipper orchids. The earliest coloured illustration of a North American species is that of *Calceolus flore maximo rubente* (*C. acaule*) by Mark Catesby (1754) in *The Natural History of Carolina, Florida and the Bahama Islands*.

The first edition of Philip Miller's *Gardeners Dictionary*, published in 1731, included three species of hardy slipper orchid: the European species as *Helleborine; flore rotundo, sive Calceolus* and two North

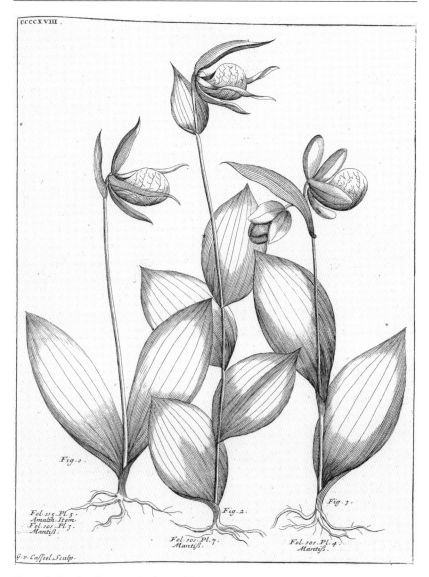

Figure 3. Cypripedium acaule, C. parviflorum var. **pubescens,** and **C. reginae.** From L. Plukenet, *Almatheum botanicum,* t. 418 (1705).

American species *Helleborine; Virginiana, flore rotundo luteo*, one of the varieties of *Cypripedium parviflorum*, and *Helleborine; Canadensis, sive calceolus mariae*, probably *C. reginae*. He commented that "all (are) Natives of Woody and shady Places". The first is "found in the woods of Yorkshire, Lancashire and other Northern Counties of England . . . so the only Expense is in the first procuring them, which is easily effected in many Parts of England". How times have changed! In the seventh edition of the *Gardeners Dictionary* in 1757, he noted that "[a]ll these Sorts are with Difficulty preserved in the Gardens; they must be planted in a loamy soil, and in a situation where they may have the Morning Sun only". He provided a coloured illustration in his *Figures of the most beautiful, useful and uncommon plants figured in the Gardeners Dictionary* published in 1758. This illustration may, indeed, be the first of a British plant as Miller reiterates that it was "found in some Parts of England; particularly in Helkeswood, by Ingleborough in Yorkshire; and in the Park of the late Robert Fenwick Esq. at Borough Hall, near Kirby Lonsdale, in Lancashire" and also mentions flowering it at Chelsea where, no doubt, the coloured illustration by R. Lancake was made.

Linnaeus (1753) apparently overlooked Parkinson's and Miller's references to North American species, but included Cornut and Morison's names within *Cypripedium calceolus*, the European species which must have been familiar to him in his native Sweden.

William Aiton (1789) listed three species in his *Hortus Kewensis:* the European *Cypripedium calceolus* and the North American *C. reginae* (as *C. album*) (Plate 22) and *C. acaule* as being grown at Kew. *Cypripedium reginae* had been introduced by William Hamilton in 1786 and *C. acaule* by William Young in 1770.

Another early published illustration of a native British plant of *Cypripedium calceolus* is that by James Sowerby (1790), the first plate in the first volume of *English Botany*. The fascination of this beautiful plant is summed up by Sowerby's words:

> If the beauty or scarcity of a plant, or the singularity of its structure entitle it to our notice, the Ladies Slipper certainly merits the first place in a work on British Plants. It may indeed be reckoned the queen of all the European Orchideae. Accordingly it has not only been and cherished by the scientific botanist, but it has been among gardeners always been sold at the highest price of any British Vegetable.

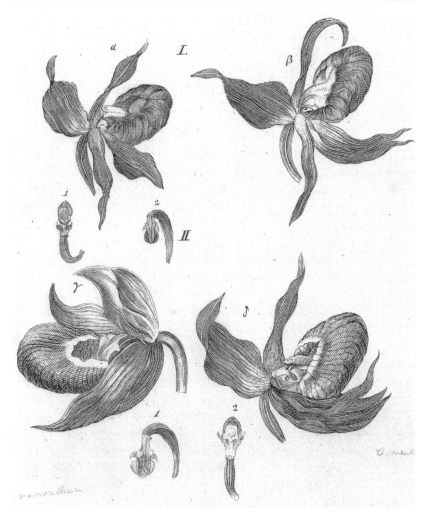

Figure 4. Cypripedium calceolus (α & β), **C. macranthos** (γ), and **C.** × **ventricosum** (δ).
From J. Gmelin, *Flora Sibirica* (1747).

Amman (1739) and Gmelin (1747–1749) published the first descriptions and illustrations of the Siberian slipper orchids. Amman illustrated *Cypripedium macranthos* as *Calceolus purpureus speciosus* and *C. guttatum* as *Calceolus minor flore vario*. Gmelin figured *C. calceolus*, *C. ventricosum*, and *C. macranthos*, the last as *Calceolus purpureis speciosus* (Fig. 4). Swartz (1800) based the names *C. ventricosum* and *C. macranthos* on Gmelin's collections.

Sessé and Moçiño collected the first Central American *Cypripedium* species in Mexico between 1787 and 1803. Their collections are in the herbarium of the Royal Botanic Garden, Madrid. They collected two species to which they gave the manuscript names *C. turgidum* (Fig. 5) and *C. acuminatum*. The former name was eventually published posthumously in 1890 (by which time it had already been described by La Llave and Lexarza as *C. irapeanum*). The latter name, referable to Lindley's *C. molle*, has never been published. Contemporary coloured illustrations of the two Sessé and Moçiño species are preserved in the Hunt Institute collection in Pittsburgh, Pennsylvania (Cribb and Soto Arenas 1993).

Linnaeus's pupil Carl Peter Thunberg was the first Western botanist to visit Japan. He collected and described *Cypripedium japonicum* and *C. macranthos* (as *C. calceolus*) in his *Flora Japonica* (1784). His illustration of the former appeared in 1794 in his *Icones Plantarum Japonicarum* (Fig. 6). The earliest Japanese illustrations of native slipper orchids I have traced are those of *C. japonicum*, *C. debile*, and *C. macranthos* in Yokusai Iinuma's *Sintei Somoku Dzusetsu* of 1874. However, Ludovic Savatier's watercolours of *C. japonicum* and *C. macranthos* made between 1856 and 1866 survive in the Kew collection. Most of the species in the Far East remained unknown for nearly a century more until botanists began to penetrate into mountainous western China.

The first hint of the rich array of western Chinese species was the collection in 1864 by Père David of the yellow-flowered *Cypripedium luteum* (now *C. flavum*) at Moupin in what is now western Sichuan. However, the diversity of the Chinese cypripediums was not apparent until the last few years of the nineteenth century. From 1894 onwards, the indefatigable French missionaries, Delavay, Soulie, Maire, Monbeig, and Farges, based in Yunnan and Sichuan, began to send back large numbers of collections to Paris, some to be described as new to science by the French botanist Franchet. By the turn of the century the British collectors Augustine Henry in Hubei, Sichuan, and Yunnan and E. H. Wilson in Sichuan and Hubei had

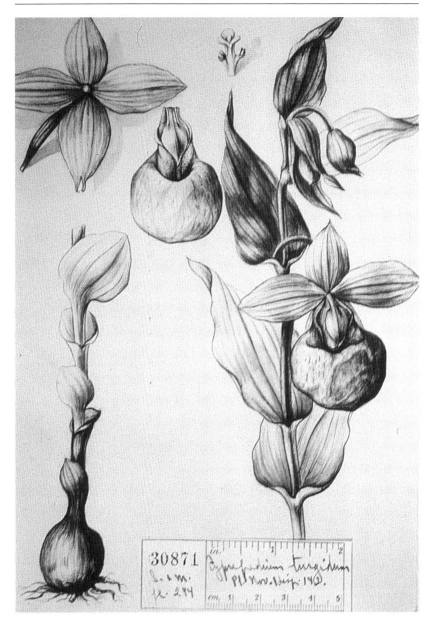

Figure 5. Cypripedium irapeanum (as **C. turgidum**). Illustration by unknown artist for Sessé & Moçiño's unpublished *Icones Florae Mexicanae*, t. 294. Courtesy of the Director of the Missouri Botanical Gardens.

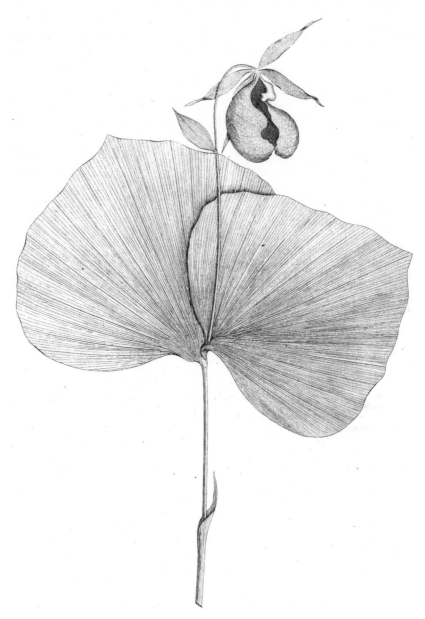

Figure 6. Cypripedium japonicum. From C. Thunberg, *Icones Plantarum Japonicarum*, t. 1 (1795).

added further species. Wilson was probably the first to send back living material of western Chinese cypripediums, *C. flavum* and *C. tibeticum* being successfully cultivated at the Arnold Arboretum in 1911. New Chinese species have continued to be discovered and described this century (Tang and Wang 1951, Chen and Lang 1986, Cribb 1992, Cribb and Chen 1994).

A gradual understanding of the variation in *Cypripedium* can be traced from Linnaeus (1753), who recognised one species (four taxa), through Rolfe (1896) and Pfitzer (1886, 1903), who included 28 in their treatments of the genus, to the present account where 45 species are recognised.

THE CYPRIPEDIOIDEAE

Linnaeus (1753) placed his genus *Cypripedium* in order Diandria of the class Gynandreae, recognising that the slipper orchids have two anthers. The taxonomic significance of anther number in the orchids was recognised by Olof Swartz (1800), who placed the slipper orchids in his 'Orchider med tuå Antherer'. Lindley (1838) also used the name Diandrae for these orchids.

The slipper orchids form a distinct, well-defined group within the Orchidaceae distinguished by the flowers which have lateral sepals joined to form a synsepal, a pouched ventral petal termed the lip, two fertile lateral anthers of the inner whorl, a sterile more or less shield-shaped staminode at the apex of the column, and a stalked trilobed stigma that lies ventrally on the column behind the staminode. Most recent authors have recognised the slipper orchids as a distinct subfamily, the Cypripedioideae, within the Orchidaceae (Dressler 1981, 1993). Their inclusion within the orchids has been debated (for a summary see Dressler 1981), and some authors (Rasmussen 1985) have treated the slipper orchids as a distinct family, the Cypripediaceae. Their possession of an endotrophic mycorrhiza, seeds lacking endosperm, fusion of the male and female reproductive organs into a column, and reduction in anther number seem sufficient to include this group in the orchids. Characters such as a synsepal, a slipper-shaped lip, and two fertile anthers are found elsewhere in the family. Furthermore, recent molecular and embryological studies have placed Cypripedioideae within the orchid clade (Chase et al. 1994, Clements 1995).

THE DELIMITATION OF CYPRIPEDIUM

All slipper orchids were included in the genus *Cypripedium* for almost a century after the name was established by Linnaeus. The first to recognise the diversity within the slipper orchids was C. S. Rafinesque (1819, 1838), who knew the hardy American species at first hand. He established the genera *Sacodon, Stimegas, Cordula, Menophora,* and *Criosanthes,* but his work was largely ignored by his contemporaries because it was published in obscure and little-circulated works and he was less than clear himself about the status of his taxa. Of these names, *Sacodon* and *Criosanthes* refer to species now included in *Cypripedium,* while the rest refer to species now included in *Paphiopedilum,* which has been conserved over *Cordula, Menophora,* and *Stimegas* (Farr et al. 1979).

H. G. Reichenbach (1854) established the genus *Selenipedium* for the tropical American species that have a trilocular ovary. Blume (1858–1859) discounted this character because he found that unilocular ovaries of some species were trilocular towards each end. However, Bentham and Hooker (1883) followed Reichenbach in dividing the slipper orchids into two genera: *Cypripedium* for the north temperate and Asiatic species with unilocular ovaries, *Selenipedium* for the tropical American species with trilocular ovaries.

Ernst Pfitzer (1886) prepared the ground for the modern generic treatment of the slipper orchids by recognising the correlation of leaf type with perianth persistence. He established the genus *Paphiopedilum* for the tropical Asiatic and American species with hard leaves and a deciduous perianth, leaving the plicate-leaved northern temperate species with a persistent perianth in *Cypripedium* and the tropical American ones in *Selenipedium.*

Pfitzer's publications (1886, 1889, 1894) tackled the problem of the slipper orchids in a piecemeal manner, and it was left to Robert Rolfe (1896) to revise all the known species, placing them in their appropriate taxa, generally revising their nomenclature, and providing keys to the genera and species. Rolfe placed the New World hard-leaved species in a new genus *Phragmipedium* based on their leaf type, valvate imbrication of the sepals, and distribution. The genus *Paphiopedilum* was restricted to the Old World hard-leaved species with imbricate imbrication. The use of *Cypripedium* and *Selenipedium* followed that of Pfitzer. Rolfe listed 28 *Cypripedium* species, including 11 restricted to the New World, 14 to eastern Asia, and 3 widespread species.

MORPHOLOGY

HABIT

Detailed accounts of the vegetative morphology of slipper orchids are provided by Pfitzer (1889) and Stoutamire (1990). All cypripediums are terrestrial and have much in common in their habit with other terrestrial rhizomatous orchids. They do, however, exhibit a considerable diversity in habit. Most species have a short but stout and seldom-branching rhizome, comprising a chain of annually produced growths buried 1–2 cm in the soil, adding new annual growths at the anterior end and dying at the posterior end. In a few species, such as *Cypripedium guttatum* and *C. margaritaceum* and their allies, the rhizome is elongate with the growths borne at intervals of several centimetres. The rhizome survives the dormant period with the bud occupying a terminal position. The roots emerge from the rhizome behind the shoot and are usually slender and elongate, rarely branching. In many species the roots are hairy, but in some species they appear glabrous, at least when mature.

The erect leaf-bearing stem emerges from the terminal bud of the rhizome, which is protected by a number of foliar bracts. In most species the stem is elongate, bearing leaves along its length or towards the apex. However, in a number of species, notably those allied to *Cypripedium acaule*, *C. fasciculatum*, and *C. margaritaceum*, the stem is short and subterranean and the leaves are consequently borne at ground level. To varying degrees, the stems of most species are hairy or glandular, the hairs and glands being multicellular. The species allied to *C. calceolus* have glandular stems, while *C. subtropicum* has both multicellular hairs and glands on its stem. A few species such as *C. debile* have glabrous stems. In many species the stem is sheathed by foliar bracts and sheathing leaf bases.

Most species of *Cypripedium* have three to several leaves borne along the stem. The blades are ovate, elliptic, or lanceolate leaves pleated longitudinally with prominent veins. They are often hairy, particularly on the veins and margins. In a few species the number of leaves is reduced to two or even one. *Cypripedium guttatum* has two spreading, obovate, plicate leaves borne near the top of the stem. The leaves of others are, however, even more distinctive. *Cypripedium formosanum* and *C. japonicum* have two subopposite, fan-shaped, and heavily pleated leaves at the stem apex. Their veins radiate to the margin but are, on closer inspection, seen to be joined by a delicate marginal vein. *Cypripedium debile, C. elegans,* and *C. palangshanense* also have two terminal leaves, but these are only faintly pleated, glabrous, and ovate to cordate in outline. The leaves of *C. debile* and *C. palangshanense* have three prominent longitudinal veins.

The species of section *Trigonopedia* are the most extraordinary in the genus. They apparently have two more or less prostrate leaves. The upper of these must, however, be interpreted as a foliar bract despite its position on the plant. Of the species in this section, the leaves of *Cypripedium fargesii, C. forrestii, C. lichiangense, C. margaritaceum,* and *C. wumengense* are spotted on their upper surface with black marks which, under magnification, are seen to be papillose. The allied species *C. bardolphianum* and *C. micranthum* lack spotting and have a purplish margin.

INFLORESCENCE

All cypripediums have a racemose or almost spicate inflorescence. The rhachis may be pubescent, glandular, or glabrous. Bracts are, in most species, leaf-like but smaller than the leaves. The exceptional case of *Cypripedium margaritaceum* and allied species has been mentioned already. In *C. debile* the bract is reduced to a slender ligule quite unlike the heart-shaped leaves.

Flower number varies from one to twelve according to species, the most floriferous being *Cypripedium californicum,* which can have up to twelve flowers in its inflorescence, the flowers opening more or less simultaneously. The Central American *C. irapeanum, C. molle,* and *C. dickinsonianum,* and the Chinese *C. subtropicum,* also have several-flowered inflorescences, but their flowers are produced consecutively. Most species bear one to three flowers. Several, including *C. acaule, C. cordigerum, C. debile, C. guttatum, C. himalaicum, C. macranthos, C. margaritaceum, C. reginae,* and their allies, are usually one-flowered, but can occasionally produce a second flower from a terminal bud that usually aborts. Species such as *C. henryi* and *C. calceolus* are commonly two- or even three-flowered, while *C. fasciculatum* occasionally has as many as four flowers.

FLOWER

Cypripediums have resupinate flowers with the lip lowermost in position, produced as a result of twisting of the ovary through 180 degrees during development. The structure of the *Cypripedium* flower is remarkably similar to that of the other genera of slipper orchids, the most distinctive features being the slipper-shaped lip, fused lateral sepals, column with a terminal staminode, two lateral anthers of the inner staminal whorl, and a stalked tripartite stigma. R. Brown (1831) and Darwin (1877) have given detailed discussions of the homologies of orchid flowers and of *Cypripedium* in particular. Current views agree with most of their interpretation. However, more recent authorities suggest that the lip is petaloid rather than comprising the median petal and two of the staminodes of the outer whorl (Pfitzer 1889, Dressler 1981).

The flower has a trilocular ovary that is either almost sessile or borne on a short pedicel in the axil of a bract. The pedicel is obscure in most species, but in *Cypripedium margaritaceum* and its allies is longer than the ovary and elongates rapidly after fertilisation to lift the capsule well clear of the leaves. The ovary may be hairy, glandular, hairy and glandular, or glabrous. Hairy ovaries are found in species such as *C. franchetii, C. passerinum, C. reginae,* and *C. subtropicum;* glandular ovaries in *C. calceolus* and its allies; hairy and glandular ovaries in *C. irapeanum* and allies; and glabrous ovaries in *C. debile, C. macranthos,* and some related species.

The outermost floral whorl consists of the sepals. *Cypripedium arietinum* and *C. plectrochilum* have three sepals, the dorsal suberect and the lateral slender and dependent. In all other species the lateral sepals are fused for at least the basal half and often to near the apex or even completely. The resulting structure is termed a "synsepal" in informal conversation and "synsepalum" in botanical descriptions. In some species, notably *C. shanxiense* and *C. passerinum,* the sepals may be joined for only half their length. Plants in which there is little or no fusion of the lateral sepals have occasionally been found in some other species such as *C. macranthos* and *C. calceolus,* which normally have a more or less entire synsepal.

The second floral whorl comprises three organs, two being petals and the third a deeply pouched lip. The petals can vary in shape from elliptic to linear or even subpandurate, depending on the species. The Central American species have spreading elliptic or oblong-elliptic petals. *Cypripedium fasciculatum* has incurving ovate-acute petals. In *C. reginae* and its allies the petals are narrowly oblong and blunt. *Cypripedium guttatum* also has distinctive blunt petals, which are subpandurate and which have an almost spathulate tip. The species allied to *C. margaritaceum* have very strange petals that curve forwards and grasp the lip closely. However, most species have tapering acute or acuminate petals that spread at a 20- to 45-degree angle below the horizontal. Some of these species, such as *C. calceolus, C. candidum, C. fasciolatum,* and *C. montanum* are characterised by having spirally twisted petals.

In many species the petals are basally hairy on the inner side and ciliate on the margins. However, in *Cypripedium irapeanum* and its allies, and in *C. lichiangense* and *C. fargesii,* the petals are hairy all over. In *C. margaritaceum* the hairs on the petals are confined to the veins on the outer side. A few species such as *C. debile* and *C. guttatum* have glabrous petals.

Flower colour can also be diagnostically useful in the genus. Species such as *Cypripedium flavum, C. irapeanum,* and *C. macranthos* have essentially concolorous flowers, but it is far more common for the sepals and petals to be similarly coloured and different from the lip, the common *C. calceolus* being a good example. *Cypripedium passerinum,* in contrast, has similarly coloured white petals and lip and greenish sepals. *Cypripedium fargesii, C. forrestii, C. lichiangense, C. margaritaceum,* and *C. wumengense* have yellowish-brown flowers that are variously spotted and streaked on the segments with maroon and brown. *Cypripedium guttatum* also has spotted flowers with a white or pale yellow-green background and rose-purple or reddish-brown spotting. The inside of the lip of several species is spotted with purple or red. In some plants of *C. flavum* the usually yellow lip can be more or less spotted with red on the outside.

The lip is a distinctive feature of the slipper orchid flower and *Cypripedium* is no exception. In the genus five distinctive lip types can be found, which I shall refer to as the "arietinum", "calceolus", "guttatum", "japonicum", and "margaritaceum" types. These correspond to those outlined by Xi and Chen (1991), except that they include the "japonicum" type in the "calceolus" type and recognise the "debile" type, which I include in the "calceolus" type, as distinct.

The "arietinum" type of lip, found only in *C. arietinum* and the closely allied *C. plectrochilum,* is obliquely obconical with a small subcircular mouth that has an incurved margin and a hairy margin and front. The "calceolus" type is by far the most widespread and is obovoid to ellipsoidal with incurved side lobes that have a distinct basal crease and an incurved apical margin. The mouth of the lip is usually circular, subcircular, or elliptic. In addition to *C. calceolus*, this lip shape is found in species as diverse as *C. debile*, *C. irapeanum*, *C. reginae*, and *C. subtropicum*. The "guttatum" type, which is very distinctive and only found in *C. guttatum* and *C. yatabeanum*, is urn-shaped with a slightly flared circular mouth. In this type the margins are incurved but only very narrowly so, and the margin around the mouth is sharp-edged as if it had been crimped. The "japonicum" type is found in *C. acaule*, *C. formosanum*, and *C. japonicum*, although the inclusion of *C. acaule* here is debatable and it may warrant its own type. The lip of these species is obovoid and very inflated and is characterised by an elongated slit-like to subpandurate mouth. The final type, characteristic of *C. margaritaceum* and its allies, is dorsiventrally flattened but also more or less subcircular in outline from above.

The lip of the slipper orchid facilitates cross-pollination by trapping insects that are attracted to the flower. It lacks nectar. The staminode and lip margins usually have slippery sides, and an insect that falls into the lip cannot escape easily through the mouth because of the infolded slippery margins and infolded side lobes. The lip is, however, furnished with hairs on the inner surface that form a ladder to the small orifices at the base on each side of the column. If the insect takes this escape route it will pass in turn under the stigma and one of the anthers, transmitting or picking up pollen on its way.

The central part of the flowers is a short-stalked column that comprises the much reduced and fused fertile structures of the monocotyledon flower. The stamens are reduced to two lateral fertile anthers and a single terminal sterile one, the staminode. The lateral anthers are stalked and bear two locules, the filament often extending past the anther as a blunt to pointed stalk. The pollen of all species that have been examined is rather uniform (Xi and Chen 1991). The pollen grains are in monads and are characterised by one to three (rarely four) sulculi, an imperforate, microperforate, or sometimes microrugulate or scabrate tectum lacking ornamentation, an absence of the foot layer, and a distinct exine. The pollen masses are viscid and can be drawn out in sticky threads when touched. The staminode, diagnostic in many species, is usually a shield-shaped structure that blocks the mouth of the lip where the side lobes meet. The staminode shape varies with the species as does the way it is presented, either flat, convex, or conduplicate.

The surface varies from sparsely pubescent or papillose to glabrous depending upon the species. Staminodes are usually coloured, often matching the lip, and may be spotted with red in a number of species.

The stigma is hidden on the ventral side of the column behind and below the staminode, which effectively isolates it from the approach of insects from above. It is stalked and the surface is oblique, facing towards the base of the lip. The tripartite nature of the stigma is readily seen in many species, its surface being papillate to a greater or lesser degree. Asa Gray (1862) remarked that the stigma surface is beset with "minute, rigid, sharp pointed papillae, all directed forwards, which are excellently adapted to brush off the pollen from an insect's head or back".

SEED

Cypripediums have seeds that are in most respects typical of those of most orchids. The seed has a firm brown fusiform testa with an opening at one end where the micropyle of the ovule was situated. The marginal cells have a stiffened rim suited to keeping the aperture open. The outer surface of the testa is not easily wettable and the seed floats in water. Liquid enters the seed through the testa aperture. The embryo is spherical to oval and the cells are isodyametric and little differentiated. The embryo is firmly enclosed in an impermeable sheath that develops from the inner integument. This layer matures after about eight weeks from fertilization, and the greatest success with asymbiotic seed germination is achieved before this layer has matured when the embryo is about two-thirds to three-quarters fully developed.

The development of the seed has been outlined by Lucke (1982). Fertilisation of the ovule occurs about four weeks after pollination. The embryo begins to develop in the fifth week after fertilisation. One of the two generative pollen nuclei fertilises the egg cell inside the micropylar part of the inner integument of the ovum, and the embryo starts to grow. In the process the outer integument develops into the testa of the seed, the inner integument into the seed coat. After a period of growth the cell contents of both integuments die off. The testa is still colourless seven weeks from pollination and starts to colour between 49 and 56 days after pollination. After the eighth week it becomes increasingly dark brown. By this stage the inner integument forms an impermeable container around the embryo. Germination of mature seed can only occur if this barrier is penetrated. The germinating embryo develops into a protocorm from which shoot and roots develop.

PROTOCORM

The protocorm of *Cypripedium* species begins top-shaped, but develops into an achlorophyllous rhizomatous structure. Rhizoids are few, as are fungal symbionts, and it seems likely that the mycorrhizal association functions only in early seedling growth. The shoot develops from the apex of the protocorm and the roots are scattered along the structure (Clements 1995). The rhizome and roots elongate rapidly to form an extensive underground system even when the shoot and leaves are relatively small. The development of cypripediums from germination to flowering can take many years. Summerhayes (1968) cites 16 years in the case of *C. calceolus*. However, in culture some *Cypripedium* hybrids raised by Frosch (pers. comm.) have flowered three years from sowing of the seed.

LIFE HISTORY

GERMINATION AND DEVELOPMENT

The germination and growth of *Cypripedium* has been summarised by Hanne Rasmussen (1995), and the following account is based largely on her synopsis. Hardy terrestrial orchids, such as cypripediums, have small seeds weighing about 1 to 2 µg and ranging from 0.11 to 1.97 mm long and 0.07 to 0.4 mm across. *Cypripedium* seeds are fusiform in shape and undoubtedly wind-dispersed. The seeds of *C. acaule* have been calculated to weigh about 1.9 µg (Stoutamire 1964). The embryo consists of a few dozen cells and is surrounded by an impermeable coat of suberised cells, which are derived from the ovule's inner integument and testa of dead cells, which in turn are derived from the outer integument. Orchid seeds do not have any endosperm and rely for nutrition upon an intimate association with a mycorrhizal fungus.

The seeds mature between three to four months after fertilisation and disperse through slits in the capsule that develop as it turns brown and dries out. Germination for most species probably occurs in the spring or early summer (Fuchs and Ziegenspeck 1926, Curtis 1943) although Irmisch (1853) recorded small protocorms of *Cypripedium calceolus* in December. Germination occurs in the dark in the soil, probably some 2–5 cm or so below the surface. The protocorm of *C. calceolus* is greenish in colour and produces long rhizoids, which become infected with mycorrhizal hyphae. In the first autumn a root emerges behind the shoot apex and continues to grow during the winter and following spring. The rhizomatous protocorm elongates throughout the second year and produces a further root in the autumn. The first leaf appears in the second, third, or fourth spring in the few species so far examined (Ziegenspeck 1936, Curtis 1943, Böckel 1972). The first root, which contains little xylem but copious phloem, is covered in rhizoids and is mycotrophic from the start. The cortex is densely infected with fungal pelotons. However, later roots are progressively less infected and by the fifth, the roots are characteristically slender with well-developed xylem and a lack of pelotons.

In mature plants the bud containing the leaves and inflorescence for the following year develops during the summer. The new rhizome begins to develop even before flowering has finished and finishes developing by the start of winter. The new roots emerge about a fortnight after the rhizome starts to grow, and the old leaves wither in the autumn during September and October.

Flowering occurs in late spring in some species such as *Cypripedium formosanum, C. kentuckiense,* and *C. plectrochilum,* but in early to mid summer in most species. June is the peak month for many species, but *C. irapeanum* flowers in July and August in Mexico. Flowers last for between two and five weeks and, on dying, are deciduous.

Although unusual, there is good evidence to suggest that cypripediums can become dormant, surviving for a season or more without producing aerial shoots (Sheviak 1974, Gill 1989).

POLLINATION

The distinctive flowers of *Cypripedium* and other slipper orchids are marked by the inflated slipper- or shoe-shaped lip that lies ventrally in the open flower. The lip has a large opening on its upper surface enclosed by the incurved margins of the lip. The staminode blocks the opening at the base of the lip, leaving just two small openings or orifices, one on each side of the column at its base. The inside of the lip is covered with hairs, particularly in the basal part. On the column the staminode is the most prominent organ in most species. The stalked staminode lies behind it on the ventral side of the column, and an anther lies just behind the stigma on each side. Based on his knowledge of the flower, Darwin (1862), in his hugely influential account of orchid pollination, suggested that pollination of *C. calceolus* was effected by an insect sitting on the outside of the lip and reaching the pollen by inserting its mouthparts through the basal orifices of the lip.

The first scientist to study the pollination of *Cypripedium* in nature was Asa Gray (1862), who examined the pollination syndrome of three American species. Gray noted that bees entered the lip of these species through the large opening on its upper surface, but he did not observe effective pollination. Müller (1868, 1873) observed bee pollination of *C. calceolus* in the wild and confirmed

Delpino's (1867) theory that pollination occurred when the bees crawled out of the lip through the small openings set either side of the column. Darwin (1877) also confirmed it by placing a small *Andrena* bee in the lip of a flower of *C. calceolus*. It failed to escape the way it had entered because of the infolded lip margins and eventually crawled out through one of the openings at the base of the column and lip. When it was then examined. the bee was found to be smeared with the glutinous pollen. Gray had noted that the stigmatic surfaces of most cypripediums were covered by "minute, rigid, sharp-pointed papillae, all directed forwards, which are excellently adapted to brush off the pollen from the insect's head or back". He also noted that *C. acaule* has drier, rather granular pollen and a slightly concave stigma that is viscid.

Of the many observations on the pollination of *Cypripedium calceolus*, those in the study of Nilsson (1979), working on the Swedish island of Öland, have been the most detailed. He studied seasonal and diurnal activity, approach, alighting, entering, and escape of different insects visiting the orchid's flowers over a four-year period. Several visiting insects, notably bees and hover flies, were found to enter the lip. They were attracted by flower colour, by the floral fragrance which is rich in acetates that appear to mimic pheromone secretions of some bees, and also by the spotting patterns of the staminode and lip which are false nectar guides. He suggested that the fragrance chemicals might upset the landing control pheromones of bees alighting on the lip, thereby increasing the likelihood of them slipping into the pouched lip.

The presence or absence of food in the lip has been much debated. Darwin (1862) was intrigued by the flower's attraction and noted that the hairs within the lip secreted little drops of a slightly viscid fluid. He observed that this liquid formed a brittle crust on the summits of the hairs and suggested that if this were sweet or nutritious it would explain the attraction of the flowers for bees. The occurrence of "nectar" in the lip has been widely and erroneously reported (Müller 1869, Summerhayes 1951, Procter and Yeo 1973) and has been interpreted as food for pollinators. Nilsson (1979) refutes this because the hairs contain oil not nectar. According to Ziegenspeck (1936) and Daumann (1968), the hairs within the lip are not eaten or chewed, but Stoutamire (1967) reported chewed hairs. Overall, it seems probable that pollinators are attracted by deceit to the trap flowers of *Cypripedium*.

Once inside the lip the insects seldom escape by the route

through which they entered. Rather, they exit, if at all, out of the base of the lip through the basal orifices. The expanded stigma acts as the essential support to allow pollinators to bend down the lip and thence pass under the anthers and out through the basal orifices. Only bees of the right size, neither too large nor too small, can pass out of the lip this way to effect pollination. Nilsson (1979) found that the most frequent and regular pollen vectors were female bees of *Andrena haemorrhoa* (F.), but that other species can also occasionally pollinate flowers.

The lips of many cypripediums have areas of unpigmented tissue, so called "windows", in the lateral part of the posterior region of the lip. These have been suggested as inducing phototaxis in pollinators to lead them out the correct way (Webster 1886, Troll 1951). However, the evidence for this is inconclusive (Nilsson 1979).

Although the pollination of *Cypripedium calceolus* in Europe has attracted most attention, that of other species has also been studied or observed, particularly in North America. Stoutamire (1967) and Catling (1985) have provided summaries of these observations. Stoutamire commented that the sizes of the lip mouth and basal orifices and of the escape route under the stigma and anthers determined the likely pollinators.

Bee pollination has been suggested as typical of the pollination syndrome of *Cypripedium* by van der Pijl and Dodson (1966). Certainly, observations on most North American species have confirmed that bees are the most frequent pollinators: *C. acaule* is pollinated by *Bombus vagans* (Stoutamire 1967); *C. arietinum* by *Dialictus* sp. (Stoutamire 1967); *C. candidum* by *Andrena placida* and other short-tongued bees in the Andrenidae and Halictidae (Stoutamire 1967, Catling and Knerer 1980); *C. parviflorum* var. *pubescens* by *Ceratina calcarata* males (Stoutamire 1967); and *C. reginae* by *Megachile melanophaea* and *M. centuncularis* (Guignard 1886).

Stoutamire (1967) suggested that the widespread *Cypripedium debile* from China, Japan, and Taiwan, which has flowers with a mushroom scent, may be fly-pollinated. Certainly the flowers of the Chinese *C. lichiangense*, *C. margaritaceum*, and their allies have a colouration and fragrance that suggests fly pollination, and I have seen flies apparently attracted to the flowers and approaching the lip of both species.

Catling (1985) reported self-pollination in *Cypripedium passerinum*. This has also been suggested for the Mexican species *C. dickinsonianum* by Hágsater (1984). Averyanov and Perner (pers.

comm.) reported *C. shanxiense* to be self-pollinating in the Primorsky region of eastern Siberia. The pollen is like treacle and oozes onto the stigma directly from the anthers.

Natural hybridization has been reported on several occasions between various species: *Cypripedium calceolus* and *C. macranthos* (Stoutamire 1967, Slyusarenko 1981); *C. guttatum* and *C. yatabeanum* (Luer 1975, P. M. Brown 1995a); *C. parviflorum* and *C. candidum* (Klier et al. 1991); and *C. parviflorum* var. *pubescens* and *C. montanum* (Sheviak 1992).

CYTOLOGY

The earliest study of the cytology of *Cypripedium* was by Pace (1907). He examined the fertilization and embryology of *C. candidum, C. parviflorum, C. pubescens* (*C. parviflorum* var. *pubescens*), and *C. spectabile* (*C. reginae*), citing the base chromosome number as n = 11. Belling (1924) found a base number of n = 10 in *C. acaule*, and subsequent work suggests that this is the basic number for *Cypripedium*. Aneuploidy has, however, been recorded by Vij and Mehra (1974) for *C. cordigerum* and by Karasawa and Aoyama (1986) for *C. macranthos* var. *speciosum*. Recent summaries of chromosome number have been provided by Tanaka and Kamemoto (1974, 1984), counts from twenty taxa being given in the latter (see Table 1).

More recently, Karasawa and Aoyama (1986) have studied the chromosome morphology of nine taxa comprising six species, *Cypripedium debile, C. formosanum, C. japonicum, C. macranthos* (three varieties), *C. segawai*, and *C. yatabeanum* (as *C. guttatum* var. *yatabeanum*). The base number for all the taxa was n = 10, although both diploid and triploid clones of *C. formosanum* were reported. A count of 2n = 21 was made for *C. macranthos* var. *speciosum*, but the other varieties of that species examined were found to have 2n = 20. The clone of var. *speciosum* counted is most likely an aneuploid with an additional B-chromosome or chromosome fragment. Two different types of resting nucleus, dark type and complex chromocentre type, were identified in *Cypripedium*. The authors suggest that the differences in the karyotypes of the species examined corresponded to the infrageneric classification of Brieger (1973). Species in subgenus *Cypripedium* had 16 or 17 metacentric chromosomes and three or four telocentric ones; subgenera *Gultata* (*C. yatabeanum*) and *Retinervia* (*C. debile*) had 20 metacentrics; subgenus *Flabellinervia* (*C. formosanum, C. japonicum*) had 12 metacentrics and eight telocentrics.

Because of the wide occurrence of 2n = 20 in *Cypripedium* and *Phragmipedium*, Atwood (1984) suggested that the karyology of the plicate-leaved slipper orchids is conservative relative to that of the conduplicate-leaved ones.

Table 1. Chromosome numbers in *Cypripedium*.

Taxon	Chromosome no. (2n)	Earliest authority
C. acaule	20	Belling 1924
C. × andrewsii	20	Duncan 1959
C. arietinum	20	Löve and Simon 1968
C. calceolus	20	Humphrey 1932
	22	Francini 1931
C. candidum	20	Humphrey 1932
	22	Pace 1907
C. cordigerum	20	Mehra and Bawa 1970
C. debile	20	Miduno 1955
C. fasciculatum	20	Löve and Simon 1968
C. formosanum	20, 30	Karasawa and Aoyama 1986
C. guttatum	20	Sokolovskaya 1966
	30	Balaeva and Siplivinski 1975
C. japonicum	20	Ohno 1954
C. kentuckiense	20	Karasawa and Atwood 1988
C. macranthos	20	Sokolovskaya 1966
C. macranthos (as var. *hotei-atsumorianum*)	20	Karasawa and Aoyama 1986
C. macranthos (as var. *rebunense*)	20	Karasawa and Aoyama 1986
C. macranthos (as var. *speciosum*)	21	Karasawa and Aoyama 1986
C. macranthos (as var. *taiwanianum*)	20	Karasawa and Aoyama 1986
C. parviflorum var. *parviflorum*	20	Carlson 1945
	22	Pace 1907
C. parviflorum var. *pubescens* (as *C. pubescens*)	20	Humphrey 1932
	22	Pace 1907
C. passerinum	20	Löve and Löve 1965
C. reginae (as *C. spectabile*)	20	Humphrey 1933
	22	Pace 1907
C. segawai	20	Karasawa and Aoyama 1986
C. yatabeanum	20	Karasawa and Aoyama 1986

PHYLOGENETIC RELATIONSHIPS AND BIOGEOGRAPHY

Swartz (1800, 1805) was the first to include the lady's slippers amongst the orchids, treating them as a separate group, the Diantherae, characterised by the presence of two anthers and a slipper-shaped lip. The only other orchids with two or three anthers are *Apostasia* and *Neuwiedia*, but these have a petaloid lip or one that is only slightly differentiated from the lateral petals. They are considered by most authors to form the basal subfamily Apostasioideae. Since then most authors (e.g., Lindley 1826, 1840, Schlechter 1926, Garay 1960, 1972, Vermeulen 1966, Dressler 1981, 1993) have included the slipper orchids within the orchids, usually at subfamilial rank. Of recent accounts, only Rasmussen (1985) has separated them as the family Cypripediaceae Lindl. (1833) and, likewise, has separated *Apostasia* and *Neuwiedia* as the Apostasiaceae Lindl. (1835).

More light has been thrown on this question recently by the work of Clements (1995). His data derive from extensive morphological, embryological, protocorm, and seedling studies. Clements concludes that 13 character states are common to apostasioids, cypripedioids, and orchids, notably amongst these, lack of endosperm in the seed, lack of vascularization of the funiculus, protocorm formation, the presence of a column, and reduction in the number of anthers. I agree that the features held in common by these taxa lend strong support to the inclusion of the apostasioids and cypripedioids within the Orchidaceae.

RELATIONSHIPS OF THE SLIPPER ORCHID GENERA

Rolfe (1896) provided a detailed treatment of all known slipper orchids (see discussion in the chapter on taxonomy). He retained *Cypripedium* for the northern temperate plicate-leaved species and followed Pfitzer (1886, 1887, 1889) in recognizing the conduplicate-leaved Asiatic species in the genus *Paphiopedilum*. He divided the tropical American species into *Phragmipedium* for the conduplicate-leaved species and *Selenipedium* for the plicate-leaved ones.

Atwood (1984) analysed morphological, anatomical, and cytological data from the slipper orchids and assessed relationships by using the Wagner Groundplan-divergence method. He suggested that *Selenipedium* grades into *Cypripedium* via *C. irapeanum* and *C. californicum*, postulating that reduced vegetative features in *Cypripedium* are correlated with increasing latitude and reduced temperature climates. He resurrected the genus *Criosanthes* for *Cypripedium arietinum*, based on the lack of fusion of its lateral sepals, interpreting this as an ancestral condition. In his analysis *C. parviflorum* and its allies, designated "most Cypripedium", follow *C. irapeanum*, whereas *C. acaule* and *C. guttatum* have most derived characters.

Albert and Chase (1992) established the genus *Mexipedium* based upon an aberrant species from southern Mexico described as *Phragmipedium xerophyticum* by Soto et al. (1990). Albert and Chase distinguished it from *Phragmipedium* because of its unilocular ovary, a character that has been considered diagnostic of *Paphiopedilum* among the conduplicate-leaved slipper orchids.

Albert (1994) has examined the relationships of the slipper orchids based on analyses of morphological, anatomical, and molecular evidence. Eight species of *Cypripedium*, seven of *Paphiopedilum*, four of *Phragmipedium*, and one each of *Selenipedium* and *Mexipedium* were included in the analyses. *Apostasia* and *Neuwiedia* were selected as the outgroup taxa. He confirmed that *Mexipedium* is sister to *Phragmipedium*. Its inclusion in *Phragmipedium*, however, is still debatable because the clade including *Mexipedium* and *Phragmipedium* is sister to *Paphiopedilum*. The extreme view recently promoted by Albert and Petterson (1994) that the two tropical American genera should be sunk into *Paphiopedilum* has been widely dismissed. The molecular evidence could be argued either way, but the cytological and hybridization evidence suggests that the American and Asiatic genera should be kept distinct.

In conclusion, *Selenipedium* is, as expected, basal in slipper orchid phylogeny. It has plesiomorphic features such as elongate stems, many pubescent plicate leaves, lateral and terminal inflorescences, and seeds with a sclerotic testa that set it apart from the other genera. *Cypripedium*, *Phragmipedium*, *Paphiopedilum*, and *Mexipedium* are demonstrably monophyletic, with *Cypripedium* sister to the conduplicate-leaved genera.

RELATIONSHIPS WITHIN CYPRIPEDIUM

Atwood (1984) addressed the question of relationships within *Cypripedium* as part of his analysis of the relationships of the Cypripedioideae. Based on morphological, anatomical, and cytological evidence of twelve, mainly American species, he suggested that *C. arietinum* formed the sister clade to the other *Cypripedium* species, and therefore recommended the re-establishment of Rafinesque's genus *Criosanthes* for this species.

Two recent phylogenetic analyses of 44 taxa by Cribb and Simpson (in prep.) and of 30 taxa by Cox (1995) have contradicted this view. In both cases *Selenipedium* was chosen as the outgroup.

The morphological analysis (Fig. 7) includes *Cypripedium subtropicum*, considered by Chen and Lang (1986) to have many features in common with *Selenipedium*, the little-known *C. wardii* from southwestern China, and other rarities such as *C. bardolphianum, C. dickinsonianum, C. elegans, C. fargesii, C. farreri, C. fasciolatum, C. micranthum, C. molle,* and *C. palangshanense,* none of which was available for the molecular analysis.

In the cladogram, *Cypripedium subtropicum* and *C. wardii* are sister to each other and to all the other taxa. When it was first described by Chen and Lang (1986), *C. subtropicum* had been suggested as the most primitive species in the genus because of its similarity to *Selenipedium. Cypripedium wardii,* considered by Pradhan (1976) to be a variety of *C. guttatum* and by Chen and Xi (1987) to be close to *C. flavum,* is sister to *C. subtropicum.*

The Mexican species *Cypripedium dickinsonianum, C. irapeanum,* and *C. molle* are morphologically very closely related and comprise one clade. Section *Irapeana,* as understood here, appears to be monophyletic. *Cypripedium californicum,* which I have included, is sister to the Mexican species. *Cypripedium fasciculatum,* of the monotypic section *Enantiopedilum,* is sister to the remaining species.

The resolution of the clades including respectively *Cypripedium calceolus, C. macranthos,* and *C. himalaicum* is less certain. The species of section *Cypripedium* comprise two clades whose relationships are unresolved. The basal branch comprises *C. macranthos* and its allies in section *Cypripedium* subsection *Macrantha. Cypripedium calceolus* and its allies in subsection *Cypripedium* appear to be sister to section *Obtusipetalum.* The position of *Cypripedium himalaicum* is unresolved and not with *C. macranthos* with which it has been traditionally been placed. The two species of section *Arietinum* form a sister clade to *C.*

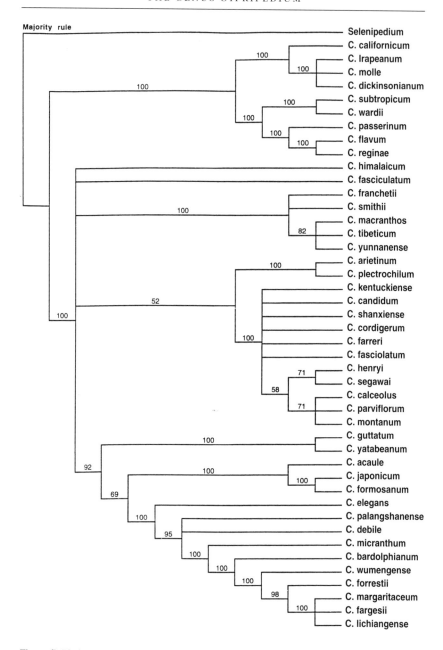

Figure 7. Phylogenetic analysis of *Cypripedium* based on 42 morphological characters.

calceolus and its allies, but it does nest within *Cypripedium* and, therefore, its status as a distinct genus *Criosanthes* (Atwood 1984) is not supported.

There is more resolution among the one- and two-leaved species. Sections *Acaulia, Bifolia, Flabellinervia,* and *Trigonopedia* are all monophyletic. *Cypripedium guttatum* and *C. yatabeanum* in section *Bifolia* are sister to the remaining clades. *Cypripedium acaule* is sister to *C. japonicum* and *C. formosanum.* The resolution of section *Retinervia* is poor, and although *C. debile, C. elegans,* and *C. palangshanense* cluster together in the cladogram, they do not form a monophyletic clade. Section *Trigonopedia* is monophyletic and forms the terminal clade.

The latter study by Cox (Fig. 8) is based on molecular data from the nuclear 5 s r-DNA gene and covers less than three-quarters of the species, critically missing the rare taxa that are basal in the morphological study. As with the morphological analysis, section *Arietinum* is firmly nested within *Cypripedium.* The molecular data set places the clade comprising *C. irapeanum* and *C. californicum* as sister to all the others. The remainder of the species fall into two clades: the first including all the species assigned to section *Cypripedium* (*C. calceolus* and *C. macranthos* and their allies); the other includes all the remaining species in sections *Acaulia, Arietinum, Bifolia, Enantiopedilum, Flabellinervia, Obtusipetala, Retinervia,* and *Trigonopedia.* The latter clade includes all the morphologically unusual species with one or two leaves.

These analyses confirm the view of Atwood that, by and large, evolution in the genus has proceeded by reduction in vegetative features and flower number, and that this has probably been associated with latitudinal, altitudinal, and climatic changes.

BIOGEOGRAPHY

Albert (1994) suggested that the current distribution of the Cypripedioideae represents a relict distribution. *Selenipedium* is confined to northern South America as far north as Panama; *Cypripedium,* although mainly temperate, is found throughout the Northern Hemisphere as far south as the Himalayas in Asia and Guatemala and Honduras in the Americas; *Phragmipedium* is found in tropical South and Central America as far north as southern Mexico; *Mexipedium* is known only from southern Mexico; and *Paphiopedilum*

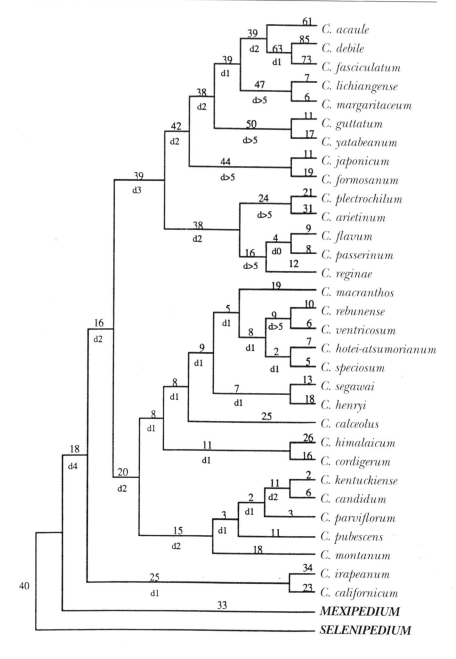

Figure 8. Phylogenetic analysis of *Cypripedium* based on the nuclear 5s r-DNA gene. From Cox 1995.

ranges from southern India across to southern China and south through the Malay Archipelago and the Philippines to New Guinea and the Solomon Islands.

The wide distribution of *Cypripedium* is more or less continuous, and one species, *C. guttatum*, is found in both the Old and New World. Several species pairs also bridge this gap, namely, *C. flavum* and *C. reginae / C. passerinum; C. plectrochilum* and *C. arietinum;* and *C. calceolus* and *C. parviflorum*. Of those species of *Cypripedium* at the base of the morphological cladogram, *C. subtropicum* and *C. wardii* are found in southwestern China; *C. irapeanum* is found in Mexico, Honduras, and Guatemala; and *C. molle* and *C. dickinsonianum* are found in southern Mexico, further evidence of a relict distribution.

Based on nucleotide sequence divergence data, Albert (1994) suggested that the Cypripedioideae may have branched from the Apostasioideae in the late Cretaceous or early Eocene. He postulated that the *Selenipedium* lineage was once more widespread in Asia and the Americas and that its present restricted distribution represents a contraction brought about as temperatures cooled in the late Oligocene to early Miocene. *Cypripedium* diverged from it at this time and further speciation occurred in the late Miocene. However, the divergence of closely related species such as *C. japonicum* and *C. formosanum; C. henryi* and *C. segawai, C. montanum* and *C. parviflorum,* and *C. margaritaceum, C. lichiangense,* and *C. fargesii,* is likely to have been much later, probably concurrent with the Quaternary expansions and contractions of the ice sheets in the Northern Hemisphere.

ECOLOGY

Detailed ecological observations and analyses are lacking for most species of *Cypripedium*, but the general ecological preferences of several species have been recorded. Most species grow in colonies. The colonies are small in some species, such as *C. elegans*, *C. lichiangense*, and *C. margaritaceum*, but can be extensive, covering hundreds of hectares, in species such as *C. macranthos* and *C. tibeticum*. Much depends upon the extent of suitable habitat, because most species seem to have rather specific edaphic, climatic, and shade requirements.

MYCORRHIZAL ASSOCIATIONS

The critical element in the extent of a colony may be the limiting factors that control the distribution of suitable mycorrhizal symbionts in the soil rather than more obvious climatic or ecological factors. Sheviak (1983) provided an illustration of *Cypripedium acaule* growing in a fairy ring, strongly suggesting that the fairy ring fungus was the mycorrhizal symbiont for the orchid.

SEASONALITY

All temperate slipper orchids are found in climates with a distinct seasonality, growing in the spring, flowering in early to mid summer, and setting seed in the autumn. They survive dormancy by storing food reserves in their fleshy rhizomes, and the dormant shoot lies with its tip at or just below the soil surface. Growth commences as the weather improves in early spring, increasing warmth and moisture being critical factors. Most species flower in May, June, and early July, but flowering can be as early as April in species such as *Cypripedium formosanum* and *C. kentuckiense*. On the other hand, *C. irapeanum* and *C. molle* can be found in flower in July and August.

Several Asian species, such as *Cypripedium guttatum, C. himalaicum,* and *C. tibeticum,* are found most commonly in montane grassland and meadows. All grow at elevations of up to 4000 m or more, and the grassland is covered by deep snow in the winter and early spring. As the snow melts in May, *C. tibeticum* emerges among the brown grasses, flowering as its young leaves develop.

HABITATS

Temperate slipper orchids are found over an extensive latitudinal range, extending from north of the Arctic Circle (about 70° North) in Alaska to 25° North in southwestern China and even further south (about 14° North) in Central America. In the northern part of their distribution slipper orchids are found from sea level into the lower hills, usually denizens of coniferous forests, mixed deciduous woodlands, bogs, fens, grasslands, or prairies. Further south they usually inhabit montane woodlands and grasslands at higher altitude. *Cypripedium himalaicum* has been reported from as high as 4900 m in the Himalayas.

Cypripediums most usually grow in light, moderate, or deep shade. *Cypripedium tibeticum* can thrive in full sun but, in contrast, Griesbach and Asher (1983) reported that *C. acaule, C. arietinum,* and *C. parviflorum* var. *parviflorum* grow in deep shade on raised acid bogs and their margins. However, in other woodland species, forest clearance may allow temperate slipper orchids to persist in more open situations, although reproductive success may be much reduced. Few species thrive in full sun, but *C. candidum* is a species of the North American prairies. *Cypripedium guttatum* and *C. tibeticum* are also commonly found in high altitude grasslands in Asia. Some species grow in bogs, fens, or along the sides of streams. *Cypripedium parviflorum* var. *parviflorum* and *C. reginae* are characteristic plants of the calcareous fens of North America. *Cypripedium californicum* grows along turbulent mountain streams in northern California and southern Oregon and must have its rhizomes in moist soil most of the growing season.

Perner (pers. comm.) examined the distribution of *Cypripedium calceolus, C. macranthos,* and *C. shanxiense* in Primorskiy Kray in Siberia. He noted that *C. calceolus* and *C. shanxiense* grew in slightly drier sites than *C. macranthos. Cypripedium shanxiense* grows in more shaded situations than *C. calceolus.*

47

SUBSTRATE AND pH

In Europe, *Cypripedium calceolus* is a well-known calcicole, growing in alkaline or rarely neutral soils. In England its former localities were on Oolitic and Magnesian Limestone on north-facing slopes in light shade of oak and hazel woodland (Summerhayes 1968). However, Perner (pers. comm.) reports that he found it growing in slightly acidic conditions (pH 6) in eastern Siberia. In central Europe it grows in conifer forest and on the edges of mixed deciduous woods, often in flat or sloping sites, to an altitude of 2000 m or more. In places it forms large colonies with individual plants bearing many shoots. Other plants, often in the same habitat, can comprise a single shoot, the propensity to produce clumps being related to the branching of the rhizome.

Many other Eurasian species are apparently calcicoles, the extensive limestone regions of eastern Asia being host to many *Cypripedium* species. Species such as *C. debile, C. flavum, C. forrestii, C. henryi, C. lichiangense,* and *C. margaritaceum* grow in mixed deciduous woods of poplar, birch, pine, fir, and larch. The substrate is hard limestone and the soils are thin, comprising leaf litter and humus derived from the leaves of the forest trees with its understorey dominated by rhododendron. It would be a mistake to suggest that such soils are alkaline, and I have measured a pH of 5.5 to 7. That the habitats often sustain a rich ericaceous flora confirms this. More work is needed to establish the effects of substrate on the ecology of Asiatic species. Perner (pers. comm.) measured the pH of soils where *C. macranthos* and *C. shanxiense* grow in eastern Siberia and found the soils ranged from neutral to slightly acidic (pH 6).

The ecological preferences of the North American species have been catalogued by several authors (e.g., Morris and Eames 1929, Correll 1950, Luer 1975, Sheviak 1983, Griesbach and Asher 1983, Case 1987). Several species grow in acidic conditions, but Case (1987) made the point that some of these grow in other habitats as well. For example, *Cypripedium acaule* is recorded from acidic, mineral-poor *Larix-* to *Picea*-dominated bogs and other marshy habitats, but also in pine-barrens on deep dry sands; *C. parviflorum* var. *pubescens* can grow in neutral or alkaline bogs, in acidic sterile damp sandy soil with little vegetation, or in neutral to alkaline soils in deciduous woods and beach flats. Sheviak (1983) considered that soil chemistry is the most critical factor in establishment of orchids because of its effect on the mycorrhizal fungi. The solubility of nutrients is particularly affected by pH, and levels of critical nutrients may allow a species to grow in both acidic and alkaline habitats, but not in neutral ones where elements such as phosphorus, manganese, and boron are present in higher concentrations. Griesbach and Asher (1983) noted that *C. reginae* grows equally well in slightly acid (pH 6.3) or slightly alkaline soils (pH 7.8). Steady soil temperates during the growing season may also be a limiting factor.

RAINFALL AND MOISTURE

All temperate slipper orchids need adequate moisture during the growing season, but their tolerance of moisture in the substrate can vary substantially. *Cypripedium acaule* is recorded from both very wet habitats such as sphagnum bogs and dry deep sands. Sharp drainage is a feature of most substrates that slipper orchids occupy. Adequate water supply during the growing season is essential, but too much moisture during dormancy may lead to shoot rot, as many growers have found to their cost. Cold is not the killer, but cold allied with damp conditions often can be fatal.

SUCCESSION

The effects of vegetational succession can be dramatic on temperate slipper orchid populations. Case (1987) reported that a thriving colony of *Cypripedium reginae* growing in a balsam fir–cedar bog declined dramatically when deer grazing was reduced. The deer heavily grazed the cedar, creating open, lightly shaded or sunny glades in the forest where, in 1946, more than 2000 plants flourished. By 1957 the reduction of the deer population by hunting had led to the regeneration of cedar and the shading of the glades. By 1960 most of the plants had disappeared or become spindly, almost like seedlings. Clearance of cedar by hand, allowing more light into the forest, resulted in the reappearance of flowering plants by 1962.

It is not unusual to find areas where a few old clumps of *Cypripedium acaule, C. calceolus,* or *C. parviflorum* var. *pubescens* survive in old woodland but with no or little sign of young seedlings. Conversely, in neighbouring areas where older trees have been cleared, seedlings may be common but large plants absent. Habitat management has been successful in restoring slipper orchid habitats to

49

optimal level. In Europe I have seen several sites of *C. calceolus* in Germany and Switzerland that are carefully managed to maintain orchid populations at high levels. Clearance of heavily shaded areas improves light levels and provides bare soil where seed germination and seedling growth is encouraged. In North America prairie management regimes have increased the populations of the rare *C. candidum* in several Middle American states.

Our knowledge of the ecology of most slipper orchids is still poor. This is particularly true of Asiatic and Mexican species, including those which are most narrowly endemic. The current vogues in many countries for habitat restoration and management, and for reintroduction of rare species, has emphasised the need for more information to provide optimal conditions for reintroduction.

USES

Interest in growing hardy slipper orchids is increasing dramatically at present, particularly as seedlings are becoming more readily available, as asymbiotic germination techniques improve. Most will always remain, I think, a subject for the specialist, but some of the more easily grown species and the newly available hybrids may well be grown more widely in the future.

The horticultural interest in slipper orchids has tended to overshadow other aspects of their use. However, the herbal use of *Cypripedium* in North America has been well documented (Rafinesque 1828, Bown 1995). The orchid most frequently cited is *C. parviflorum* var. *pubescens*, the rhizomes being "collected in the fall, or early in the spring, carefully dried and reduced to a powder" and administered as "a teaspoon of powder, diluted in sugar water, or any other convenient form" (Rafinesque 1828). Nowadays, a tincture (one part orchid rhizome to five parts of an ethanol/water mixture) is extracted from the dried rhizomes. The tincture can be stored indefinitely and used to treat several disorders such as insomnia, anxiety, headache, neuralgia, emotional tension, palpitations, tremors, irritable bowel syndrome, delirium, and convulsions due to fever. It generally has a sedative, nervine, anodyne, or antispasmodic effect. The Cherokee Indians used it to cure worms in children. It has also been reported as being used by native North Americans in childbirth and as a sedative in serious illness, having the relaxing capabilities of opium without the side effects. The ingredients of the tincture are glycosides, volatile oil, tannin, and resin. Care has to be taken because overdosing can cause hallucinations, while harvesting the plant can cause contact dermatitis.

In North America other taxa such as *Cypripedium parviflorum* var. *parviflorum, C. acaule, C. reginae,* and *C. candidum,* with decreasing efficacy, have also been reported as being collected for this use. Modern herbals tend to emphasise that plants must not be collected from the wild and that generally other plants with similar properties can be successfully substituted for species of *Cypripedium* (Bown 1995).

Cypripediums are also used in northeastern China (Zhu 1989). *Cypripedium guttatum* has many uses. The stems, rhizomes, and flowers can be used medicinally. A soup of the stems has the effect of dilating the blood vessels, stimulating appetite, and curing gastritis. A tincture of the flowers is a strong sedative, effective in various neurological and mental disorders, and especially effective for epilepsy. It is also effective against childhood convulsions, caused by high fever, headaches, and pain in the upper abdomen. It has uses as a diuretic and diaphoretic. There are rumours that it has also been effectively used against cancer.

The rhizomes, stems, and leaves of *Cypripedium macranthos* are also used medicinally in China as a diuretic, detumescent, for removing blood clots, improving circulation, and for relieving rheumatic pains. The species has been used for curing dropsy, oedema of the legs, leucorrhoea, gonorrhoea, dysentery, rheumatic pains of the back and legs, fractures, and internal lesions caused by overexertion. The recommended dosage is 10–15 g boiled in water or as a tincture. For dysentery, it should be taken three to four times a day in tablet form, each containing 2 g of dried powdered plant. A powder made of the dried flowers can be used to stop bleeding. A chemical analysis of *C. macranthos* has identified phenolics, sterol-3-terpin, carbohydrate, a small amount of alkaloid in the stems and leaves, and vitamin C and large amounts of potassium oxalate in the leaves.

CONSERVATION

Cypripediums are the showiest and most sought after hardy orchids, collected and grown by orchid and alpine plant enthusiasts alike. They are, or have been, used medicinally in North America and the Far East for centuries. The major source of plants has been from the wild and, consequently, many of the more accessible populations of many species have declined through overcollection. In addition, habitat destruction, particularly logging and agricultural improvement, and drainage of habitats, especially in Europe and North America, have been factors. The current conservation status of the European, Japanese, and North American species is relatively well known, but that of the Asiatic species is still poorly appreciated.

Concern about the conservation status of hardy slipper orchids is not a recent phenomenon. Farrer (1919) made a pointed jibe at overcollection of *Cypripedium calceolus* in northern England that even then had brought it to the verge of extinction as a native species (see "The Lady's Slipper Orchid in the British Isles"). Concern in continental Europe is equally high over the future of this lovely orchid, most sites being protected as nature reserves. The European Union has placed *C. calceolus* on its Habitats Directive, providing protection equivalent to that of placing it on Appendix I of CITES (Convention on Trade in Endangered Species). In North America, nearly every article written about the native slipper orchids mentions their decline in accessible habitats through overcollection or habitat change. Most concern, however, has been expressed about local populations of widespread species. I would like to consider here the global status of *Cypripedium* species and whether any useful information can be gleaned from examination of herbarium specimens and the through the field work undertaken for this study.

For want of better information I have counted the number of herbarium specimens of each of the 47 taxa covered in this monograph. Of these, 11 taxa are known from four or fewer wild-collected specimens, 9 of these being represented by only one or two specimens. A further 11 taxa are represented by 15 or fewer

Table 2. Herbarium collections of *Cypripedium*.

		No. of specimens		
1	2	3	4	<15
C. BARDOLPHIANUM var. ZHONGDIANENSE	C. dickinsonianum	C. WARDII	C. MICRANTHUM	C. BARDOLPHIANUM var. BARDOLPHIANUM
C. LUDLOWII	C. FARRERI			C. californicum
C. SUBTROPICUM	C. FORRESTII			C. FARGESII
C. WUMENGENSE	C. PALANGSHANENSE			C. fasciculatum
	C. SEGAWAI			C. FORMOSANUM
				C. kentuckiense
				C. LICHIANGENSE
				C. MARGARITACEUM
				C. molle
				C. SMITHII
				C. yatabeanum

Names in boldface indicate taxa in cultivation.
Names in small caps indicate Chinese taxa.

wild-collected specimens. These figures are given with the proviso that the North American taxa are underrepresented in my sample because I have not seen material from many of the smaller American herbaria. The Asiatic species are also probably underestimated because of the relative inaccessibility of the localities, mostly in western and southwestern China. Nevertheless, these figures suggest that many taxa are rather narrowly endemic, amongst the Asiatic species confined often to a single mountain or mountain range. Whether any of the rarest eight taxa are restricted to a single locality is doubtful, although *Cypripedium bardolphianum* var. *zhongdianense, C. dickinsonianum, C. ludlowii, C. palangshanense, C. segawai, C. subtropicum,* and *C. wumengense* are the best candidates.

Of the 22 taxa listed in Table 2, 16 are Chinese (including Taiwan), 3 North American, and 2 Mexican. Only *Cypripedium yatabeanum* is found in both the Old and New Worlds, being recorded from Russia, Japan, and Alaska. The narrow endemicity of many of the Chinese species is probably accurate and not merely an artifact of undercollecting. These regions are relatively poorly collected in comparison with North America and Europe, Japan and the Himalayas, but hardy slipper orchids are not easily overlooked and are indeed sought out by collectors because of their exotic flowers.

A comparison of the listed species with the phylogeny suggested by the cladogram based on morphological data (see Figure 7) suggests that most of the rare taxa are either primitive species that might be considered to have a relictual distribution or are among the most recently evolved species. Thus *Cypripedium subtropicum* and *C. wardii,* the two most basal species, both have very limited distributions in northwestern Yunnan and adjacent southeastern Xizang (Tibet); *C. forrestii, C. lichiangense,* and *C. wumengense* are all restricted to southwestern China. Of the species occupying the middle of the phylogeny, *C. segawai* from Taiwan is a variant of the more widespread *C. henryi,* while *C. dickinsonianum* is an autogamous species closely related to *C. molle* and *C. irapeanum.*

Few of the species in Table 2 are in cultivation. Of the rarest 11 taxa, only *Cypripedium segawai* is relatively frequently seen in collections. *Cypripedium farreri* has also begun to appear in collections in Japan, Germany, the Netherlands, and the United States. *Cypripedium dickinsonianum* has been grown by Sterling Dickinson in Mexico in soil dug up around the plant, but it did not survive long. I have no doubt that *C. forrestii, C. subtropicum,* and *C. wumengense* would be welcome additions to collections if they were available.

Of the other 11 species listed, *Cypripedium californicum, C. formosanum,* and *C. yatabeanum* are relatively frequent in cultivation, desirable plants by any standard. *Cypripedium formosanum* has been propagated in some quantity; fortunately this lovely orchid divides easily and is one of the easiest species to grow from seed. *Cypripedium bardolphianum* var. *bardolphianum, C. fasciculatum, C. kentuckiense, C. lichiangense, C. margaritaceum,* and *C. yatabeanum* have been grown in recent years, in all cases, as far as I know, from wild-collected material. *Cypripedium kentuckiense* and possibly some of the other species have been germinated but too recently for nursery-raised material to be available. Currently the only source of 21 of the 22 taxa listed is from the wild, but current developments in raising hardy slipper orchids from seed suggests that this may not long be the case.

Cribb and Sandison (in press) have assessed the conservation status of the listed taxa accordingly to the most recently published IUCN criteria. The available, if scanty, evidence suggests that seven species, all but *Cypripedium dickinsonianum* being Chinese, can be considered to be Critically Endangered, eight Endangered, and the remaining eight Vulnerable. Somewhat surprisingly, the species most often referred to in the literature as endangered such as *C. calceolus* and *C. reginae* must be considered among the more common and more widespread species. The threats to these are largely of a regional or more local nature.

In conclusion, it is evident that more data, particularly of slipper orchid populations and demography, are needed to properly assess the current status of species of *Cypripedium* in the wild. The lack of information on Chinese species, where little work of this nature has been attempted, is a major, but not the only, lacuna in our knowledge. However, even where we have more information, as in Europe and North America, it is of a local or regional nature and this severely limits the formulation and implementation of conservation measures to protect the species as a whole.

THE LADY'S SLIPPER
ORCHID IN THE
BRITISH ISLES

"Native; north-facing grassy slope on limestone; 1 locality . . . , formerly widespread on limestone in N.En.[gland]".

This terse, depressing statement is to be found in the latest account of Britain's wild plants, Clive Stace's (1991) *New Flora of the British Isles*. It is, sadly, as close as most of us will get these days to Britain's most beautiful wild flower, the lady's slipper orchid, *Cypripedium calceolus*.

Few plants have had the public attention and press in this country afforded to the lady's slipper orchid. It has all the attributes of a star (Plate 4). It is beautiful (Farrer called it the "grandest and most august of Orchidaceae"), it is and always has been desirable to collectors both horticultural and botanical, and it is our greatest rarity. In the British Isles the lady's slipper orchid has been reduced in its range to a single known locality and, tragically, to a single plant. This clump has survived alone in its protected and guarded site in northern England for more than fifty years. Yet the lady's slipper was common enough in the area in the nineteenth century to be collected for table decorations in a local hostelry and to be dug up to adorn many a garden in the region.

The earliest record of the lady's slipper as a British plant can be traced to John Parkinson (1629) in his *Paradisus terrestris*. He called it "Calceolus Mariae" and later (1640), in his *Theatricum botanicum*, "Our Ladyes slipper". He was sent plants for his garden by Mrs. Thomasin Tunstall from "Lancashire, near the border of Yorkshire, in a wood called the Helkes, which is 3 miles from Ingleborough, the highest hill in England, and not farre from Ingleton". Reginald Farrer (1919), who lived nearby, acerbically commented that "that worthy gentlewoman and great—even, excessive—lover of these delights, quarried it so piteously to send to Parkinson".

The first coloured illustration of a British plant is probably that by James Sowerby in his *English Botany* (1790), but he gives no locality. However, recently I have been shown a watercolour painting of *Cypripedium calceolus* by Nicholas Wickham Irvine, which was painted by his ancestor, Harriet Wickham. This is probably the earliest illustration of a genuine British plant from a known locality. The handwritten caption states that the plant came from "Helms wood near Ingleborough in Yorkshire—this drawing taken from a plant in the garden at Cottingley May 25th 1798".

Farrer (1919) in *The English Rock Garden* wrote of *Cypripedium calceolus* that it "still lingers in the upland roughs of Craven here and there, nor has even been afraid to erect its head once more after many centuries". From a historical distribution that stretched from the Peak District in the south to Northumberland in the northeast and across to the vicinity of Kendle in the northwest, this spectacular orchid has been reduced to the verge of extinction by collection, mainly for horticulture but also for the herbarium.

The lady's slipper orchid has survived as a native plant because it has received protection from local botanists for many years. Twice a year a committee of interested parties from English Nature, local universities, the County Naturalists Trust, and the Royal Botanic Gardens, Kew, meet to discuss a variety of topics related to the plant such as its welfare, how protection measures are coping, and how the plant can be propagated for reintroduction. For many years until recently, the committee outnumbered the plants left in the wild. The costs of running the committee and of protecting the plant by having a warden camping at the site have been immense.

The question has to be asked whether it is worth all the effort and money that has been spent on one plant when dozens of other species are also declining and are likewise threatened with extinction from the British flora. I have to declare here an interest as a member of that committee and also because of the endangered British orchid micropropagation project at Kew. I do strongly believe that the lady's slipper orchid is worth saving as a native plant, both for its aesthetic appeal and as a powerful symbol of what is happening to or could befall much of our native flora besieged on all sides by the encroachment of suburbia, changing agricultural practice, mining, forestry, tourism, and acid rain amongst others. I also firmly believe that individuals can turn the tide and that rarities such as the lady's slipper orchid can be saved and its populations increased by sensible management, protection, and appropriate reintroduction programmes. In the case of this orchid the careful management of the site and restriction of access that is possible, because the plant grows on private land, together with Kew's micropropagation programme, leaves me with great hope for the future. In particular I look forward to seeing in my lifetime a healthy population in the known locality and its reintroduction into sites from which it has become extinct but which are otherwise unchanged, there being several in the region.

Reintroduction is a sensitive issue and one that has generated heated debate both in plant and animal circles. I do not subscribe to the purist approach that says to leave Nature alone and, if a plant is going extinct, then to let Nature take its course. Humankind after all brought the lady's slipper to its present parlous state in this country and has the ability to restore matters, if only to a limited degree. Our single native plant produces few viable seeds when selfed but, when crossed with garden plants of undoubted British origin, does better. Fortunately, there are a few surviving garden plants whose origins are well documented. The committee would, nevertheless, be pleased to hear of any more that might survive. The micropropagation and reintroduction programme depends for its success on working from the broadest genetic base.

Work has been undertaken at Kew to understand the germination, development, and horticulture of the lady's slipper orchid. For this experimental work, seed from Continental plants has been used. The results are very promising, and native seedlings are now being successfully raised for the programme. Who knows, but in a few years time we may all be able once again to see a hillside of our most distinctive and celebrated native plant.

CULTIVATION

by Holger Perner

Hardy slipper orchids have fascinated gardeners for almost four centuries. The earliest record of the cultivation of a hardy slipper orchid is that of *Cypripedium calceolus* by John Gerard in 1597, but it was only late in the nineteenth century that growers such as Edward Leeds of Longford-Bridge, England and Charles Clément of Switzerland were able to report sustained success with their cultivation. The latter grew the plants in a ferny rockery situated in the Jura Mountains at an altitude of 745 m and had attained a proficiency in growing cypripediums that has only recently been emulated.

Hardy slipper orchids were offered by many of the great orchid nurseries of the nineteenth century. Every autumn or early spring quantities of cypripediums from Siberia, North America and, in later years, the Himalayas, were sent to Europe. Even the extremely difficult *Cypripedium irapeanum* from Mexico was sold in some quantity. Most customers bought the plants with the intention of bringing an exotic flair to their gardens, unaware of the demanding conditions needed by the plants for their successful cultivation. Consequently, most cypripediums died in their first season, to be replaced by fresh collections the following year. However, if the basic demands of the more easily grown species are provided, they will survive and even thrive in cultivation. More is needed for the successful cultivation of many of the species. To succeed with them the grower must appreciate their cultural requirements. If these are met it will result in increasing numbers of shoots from year to year and possibly in the spontaneous development of *Cypripedium* seedlings in the garden.

Over the past 10 or 12 years *Cypripedium* cultivation has made great strides, which have seen, in 1987, the registration of the first artificial hybrid, *Cypripedium* Genesis (*C. reginae* × *C. pubescens*), registered by the North American grower Carson E. Whitlow. He and the German *Cypripedium* specialist Werner Frosch have registered about 17 artificial hybrids, with more crosses to be registered in near future.

New selections of natural hybrids of cypripediums introduced from the Russian Far East by a German-Russian Expedition in 1994 have flowers that show better colour, shape, and size comparable with those of many tropical slipper orchids. In future years artificially produced seedlings and new hybrids from legally collected plants from there and elsewhere will enrich the increasing market for horticulturally propagated hardy slipper orchids. Unfortunately, the market for illegally collected cypripediums is also growing. Every responsible grower should resist the temptation to buy these plants. However, a moral obligation, even clearly supported by existing laws, is not as powerful as customer's behaviour: growers simply get better quality plants if they buy nursery produced plants. Cypripediums removed from nature are usually difficult to establish and because of inadequate handling, often become infected by pathogenic fungi or even viruses. Also, many of these wild-collected plants have disappointing flower quality and vigor. Buying wild-collected cypripediums usually means a waste of money for the grower, inexcusable support for the destruction of nature, and additional weight to the opinion that cypripediums are difficult to grow, simply because of the high mortality rate of the smuggled plants.

The production of a reliable range of *Cypripedium* species and hybrids by micropropagation is no longer fiction, but underway in Europe and North America. Flowering *C. reginae* from seed is routine for many orchidists in North America and Europe today, and from Denmark it is rumoured that even mericlones from this species have been produced!

GENERAL REQUIREMENTS

Cypripediums are adapted to the temperate and cold climates of the Northern Hemisphere. Their delicate leaves cannot stand high temperatures and low humidity for long. Most species prefer open shade with some sun during part of the day. Usually sunnier sites give more stems and more flowers, but these tend to be smaller and more compact than in shadier situations. Full sky light (north side of a building with nothing blocking the sky) is very good, with direct sunlight only in the early morning and evening. The soil should stay cool and the humidity high (not below 50 percent for long periods), while air movement is essential to prevent rotting. Too strong a wind can bend the stems over. To avoid this and to support the ambient microclimate, companion plants, such as ferns, are helpful. However, these plants must not overcrowd the cypripediums. Sites must be well drained, but watered as necessary for the species. Bog and fen species do not need to be wet, and overly wet conditions are dangerous.

When in full dormancy, only very few species are unable to withstand severe frosts in winter. They require a cold, constant winter. The more that dormancy is disturbed by warm spells initiating growth, the more difficult it is to overwinter cypripediums. A Mediterranean climate with mild wet winters and dry hot summers is disadvantageous for cultivating them. The grower has to correct such conditions with sophisticated technical equipment in an artificial environment. However, in the climate zones colder than the Mediterranean, the grower will find adequate conditions if the summers are not too dry and hot. In the United States *Cypripedium parviflorum* var. *pubescens* can be grown as far south as northern Louisiana, while *C. irapeanum* grows as far south as Central America. When warm spells occur in winter, plants adapted to a constant continental winter (i.e., species from the Himalayas and its ridges, from Siberia and boreal North America) should be protected from the warmth by a cover that is to be removed immediately when the frost returns. If such warm spells are frequent in a given area, it would be easier to grow these plants in pots that are plunged in a bed or open frame during summer and stored in a cold room between 0° and 4°C or in a closed frame (protected from sunshine and rain), in winter. Species from temperate northeastern North America and coastal eastern Asia can usually withstand these warm spells and do not need a special treatment in winter, at least if they are established.

In spring, late frosts may harm the developing growth. The more the growth has developed, the more harmful is frost. Flower buds and flowers are usually killed by even the slightest frost. At this period, the grower should watch the weather forecast and protect the plants overnight if a frosty night is announced.

In summer the average temperature should not be far above 20°C during the day, and the humidity not too far below 50 percent for a long period. In particular around noon the plants should be protected from direct sun. Good air movement is necessary to prevent rotting.

The beginning of dormancy in autumn differs within the genus, but can also be disrupted by low moisture in combination with high temperature in the latter part of the season, producing the same results as early frost. The plants should be encouraged to stay green as long as possible.

For most species it is not necessary to give any special protection in winter if the plants are well established. A slight mulching with pine needles, fresh fallen beech leaf litter, or other materials is sufficient. If the mulch is too deep it can become too compact or it may occasionally attract pests such as mice. In late winter and early spring an airy cover of spruce twigs can be beneficial with some species such as *Cypripedium formosanum, C. henryi,* or *C. macranthos.* Some growers prefer to clean the bed of the dead growths as a precaution against pests and diseases. It should be done after the stems are completely dead. If the soil is frozen the old stems can be pulled out; when soil is not frozen it is necessary and better to cut the dead and dried stems. The dead material should not be composted but placed with the domestic rubbish for disposal. Other growers usually leave the stems of healthy plants until spring, to use them as a natural protection that also helps to keep some mulch in place. However, with the emergence of the new growths the old stems should be removed.

CULTIVATION UNDER LIGHTS

Cypripediums can be grown in fully artificial conditions with a controlled climate under lights. A room in the basement, or any other room, with good insulation and not effected by summer heat can be used. Requirements for light and moisture correspond to those of other herbs from cool-temperate climate zones. It is reasonable to grow cypripediums under lights if the plants are very tiny and liable to be easily destroyed in the garden (and no sufficient greenhouse is available) or if the plants arrive during a frosty period in winter and cannot be planted out. In subtropical and tropical climates it is the only way to grow cypripediums.

The plants should be grown in pots or other containers, preferably in mix J (see Table 3 under "Compost"). For a bench 1 m wide, nine lines of fluorescent tubes (a mixture of cool-white and wide spectrum gao-lux or warm white) are necessary. The plants have to be placed under the tubes with the growth tips separated 15–25 cm from the tubes. The humidity should be controlled with an optimum between 70 and 80 percent RH. However, experience has shown that even without this control the plants can grow in humidity oscillating between 30 and 70 percent. In the lower ranges the obligatory fans should be turned down to avoid desiccation of the leaves and should be used to blow away the warm air from the tubes. In the growing season the temperature should be adjusted to between 17° and 20°C during the day with a decline of 5–10°C at night. About six months after initiation of growth, dormancy should be initiated by reducing watering and dropping the temperature below 10°C. For at least three months the plants have to be stored at about 4°C. Do not freeze the plants. They should be kept in the cold until they begin to grow, but some only start to grow when temperatures have risen beforehand.

The day-length should be about 12 hours at the start of growth, rising to 16 hours in the main growing period and dropping to 10 hours before dormancy.

CULTIVATION UNDER GLASS

Species or clones that are adapted to alpine or arctic climates, that is, long constant winters without warm spells, short springs, and cool damp summers, are suitable subjects for a greenhouse that provides cool conditions. Here the growing conditions can be controlled better than in the garden. Also, any other species of *Cypripedium* that can be grown in the garden can also be grown in these conditions. However, in suitable climates there is no better place to grow most cypripediums than the open air. This can be the garden, an open frame house, or a shadehouse that ideally unites the advantages of greenhouse and garden.

An Alpine House

An alpine house is necessary to grow cypripediums successfully under glass. A location providing shade around noon and good shading of the house itself is important to keep temperatures low in summer. Ideal temperatures are 18–20°C, maximum 25°C, by day in summer with a humidity of 60 to 80 percent. At night the temperature should fall about 10°C. Good air movement is important for cultivation in the glasshouse, so sufficient fans are essential. In winter the temperature should be around 0°C, that is, it should not rise above 5°C and not fall under −2°C. Direct sunlight not only heats up the glasshouse, but also the pots and substrates in it. A general requirement is to keep the compost cool. Besides sufficiently shading the glasshouse, plunging the pots in raised sand beds can be helpful. However, pathogenic fungi are likely to occur in glasshouse cultivation, and they can spread rapidly from pot to pot if these are plunged.

A Shadehouse

A shadehouse is probably the safest way to grow cypripediums. The plants are protected from most climatic hazards. In summer the walls consist of wire netting or screen wire, allowing a full exchange of air, while pests are excluded. In winter the walls can be closed for better temperature control. The roof should be made of polycarbonate or glass, with sufficient shading from late spring until autumn. Ideally plants are grown in beds at ground level or in suitable pots and containers placed on benches in summer, then plunged in sand beds in winter to protect roots and rhizomes from too much frost. The shadehouse is often used by commercial growers.

A Cold Frame

A reliable compromise for the amateur is a cold frame. In many respects it is similar to a shadehouse. Protection from digging animals, hailstorms, late frosts, and so forth is easily given in a frame, and it provides overwintering even for delicate species. A frame can cover a growing bed for plants or a sand bed into which pots and containers are plunged. Usually there is room, even in the smallest backyard, for a frame. The right spot for one is the north wall of a house or any other place that provides relatively cool and humid conditions. The frame should only be closed during frost. With higher temperatures the cover should be lifted but not removed, providing protection from sun and rain and avoiding stagnant air. In summer the cover should be removed completely (except for hailstorms and so forth) and, if necessary, only shading should be attached.

CULTIVATION OUTDOORS

In suitable climates the best method of growing cypripediums is in the open garden. Nowhere are wind, temperature changes, and ultraviolet light—all necessary to promote robustness and health of the plants—provided in such abundance as in the open. Certainly the shadehouse is better if it should become too chilly, but nothing matches the aesthetics of a lady's slipper in flower under the open sky. If in late spring a frost is announced for the night, the grower can simply place a bucket over an exposed plant in the evening and remove it the next morning to save the flowers and leaves.

For garden cultivation there is also the choice of growing cypripediums in pots or a bed. Pots are recommended if the garden soil is unsuitable and the grower does not want to prepare a special bed, or if the hardiness of a given species of *Cypripedium* is suspect in the local climate. In late autumn pots can easily be removed from the garden and put in a sheltered place (e.g., an unheated room in the basement). If digging rodents are a problem, growing cypripediums in plunged pots can help to protect the rhizomes and roots.

The most vigorous and prolific specimens are usually produced in specially prepared beds where the plants can grow undisturbed for many years, provided the compost is still open and not exhausted. A few robust species such as *Cypripedium parviflorum* var. *pubescens* and most clones of var. *parviflorum* can grow in any decent garden soil, as long as it is loose and open, with much air and not overwatered. However, for a given species such treatment is satisfactory only for regions with a suitable climate. There is good reason to expect that in the coming years more selected clones of species and hybrids, suitable to thrive in the border or woodland bed with other perennials, will become available. However, a specially prepared bed is recommended for most cypripediums. It should be situated in a north-, northeast-, or east-facing situation, protected by shrubs, ferns, or open trees, but not overcrowded. A microclimate that provides cool soil, fresh air, humidity, and open shade with some sun in the morning or evening is suitable for most species. The bed should be dug out to about 40 cm, then filled with a 10-cm layer of drainage material such as pebbles or coarse gravel. If the ground is free-draining it is enough to dig only to a depth of 30 cm and not provide extra drainage. If the surrounding soil is open, light, and not very different in its chemical composition to the growing compost, it is not necessary to insulate the walls of the bed with plastic or other materials. Otherwise this should be done. After filling the bed with prepared compost to about 2 or 3 cm above the level of the surrounding soil, it is ready for planting. After planting the surface should be mulched with pine needles to prevent the compost from becoming compressed by rain or by watering. It also helps to keep away blackbirds or cats. A cover with living moss (a common moss found under shrubs or on tree stumps, such as *Brachythecium* or *Eurhynchium,* but not *Sphagnum*) is a good alternative to mulch. It acts as an excellent indicator of the correct humidity, but it attracts blackbirds, which will destroy an unprotected moss cover within minutes.

Good companions for cypripediums in open beds are ferns. One of the best displays for hardy slipper orchids is a rockery planted with non-invasive ferns such as *Athyrium filix-femina* and *Dryopteris filix-mas.* *Matteucia struthiopteris* should be avoided because the need to remove its strong runners can injure nearby cypripediums, yet if not removed they overgrow everything. Groups of *Cypripedium calceolus,* *C. macranthos,* and *C.* × *ventricosum,* for example, in full flower in front of the young green of recently unfolded fronds, give an impressive display. Enough room should be left between the fern stems and the cypripediums because in summer the fully developed adult ferns can reach enormous dimensions.

Some moisture-tolerant species like *Cypripedium reginae* and *C. parviflorum* var. *parviflorum* can also be grown in artificial bogs. To some degree they can tolerate high moisture, but they do not need it in cultivation. In North America the so-called Holman bog is sometimes used. This is constructed like a small garden pond but filled with substrate. In the centre a mound of compost is created to offer different levels of moisture, from wet at the base to mesic at the top. This hummock should be the growing site of the cypripediums. Such an artificial bog does not provide the optimal conditions for growing them in the garden, but it helps to keep the compost moist when the grower is absent for a longer period in summer.

PLANTING

Usually cypripediums are offered and shipped in autumn or early spring, when the old growth has died and the new one is still in bud. Newly purchased specimens, or plants for repotting, have to be checked for rotting parts, recognizable by decaying tissue. These have to be cut out with a clean and sharp knife, down into the healthy part. The wound should be powdered with charcoal. Spraying with a fungicide (see "Pests and Diseases") can be beneficial.

The rhizome should now be held in position (the tips of the buds have to be upright) in a hole made in the growing bed or in the container, and the compost filled around the roots. The rhizome should be covered by 2–4 cm of compost. In open beds the buds should also be covered by the soil, but the tips must be just below the surface and never deeper than 2 cm. With pots in the greenhouse or under lights the buds, if overwintered frost-free, should stay at the surface. Make sure that mulch is not too high and dense to avoid burying the buds too deeply so that they subsequently rot.

If the cypripediums are to be planted in pots or containers (window boxes are suitable), choose a smaller, not a larger, one. With tropical orchids "no overpotting" is the motto, but just the opposite is true for cypripediums. For a cluster with five to six growths of a bigger species, such as *Cypripedium calceolus, C. henryi,* or *C. parviflorum* var. *pubescens,* a 10-litre pot should be taken; for smaller species a 5-litre pot is sufficient. The bigger the pot, the more constant are the growing conditions in the substrate and this helps to keep the plants healthy. Most growers use plastic pots, but some prefer clay pots. Prosperous growth can be obtained in plastic or clay. An interesting alternative is wooden boxes made from untreated wood. These can be used for a couple of years until the wood begins to decay. Any container for cypripediums needs sufficient drainage holes. These should be protected from being sealed with compressed compost by applying a layer of coarse drainage material at the bottom.

The need for repotting depends upon the condition of the compost. High-organic composts demand yearly repotting. Composts well balanced between organic and non-organic compounds should be removed about every three to five years, depending upon the condition of plant and compost. Fully inert materials such as gravel can be used for longer periods of time, but if a plant, growing in such a substrate for a couple of years, is declining in the number of growths, it should be repotted. If a plant in any compost is looking unhealthy for no apparent reason, it should be repotted immediately. This can be problematic for a new plant in its establishment phase: if the problems are not due to the compost, repotting may further weaken the plant.

COMPOST

The soil in which a terrestrial orchid is rooted gives support to the plant and provides water, air, and minerals to be taken up by the roots. Even the most diverse soils in which cypripediums grow have to fulfill these demands. The same is true for the artificial composts in which hardy slipper orchids are grown. Two growers may recommend two extremely different mixtures for the same species, but this means that, under the given conditions encountered by the two growers, the composts provide similar amounts of mineral release, water retention, aeration, and so forth. For a third grower both composts may fail because too much or too little water is provided, or the sun may be shining on the compost and heating it up.

A soil that has supported a cypripedium in the wild can become harmful to the same specimen under artificial conditions. For example, a particular specimen of *Cypripedium parviflorum* var. *parviflorum* grows in a fen with soil consisting of about 50 percent organic material, that is, black, finely structured, and with a high water content. Undisturbed, this soil is sufficiently aerated and its organic material is in a biochemically steady state. It is ecologically well balanced. Removed and put in a plastic bag, however, it decomposes quickly, starts to rot, stinks terribly within a few days, and would kill the *C. parviflorum* immediately if used now. If growers use materials high in organics they have to make sure that the organics decompose slowly and do not release too much nutrient at once. It is safer to use soils that are low in nutrients than those that are too high. Rich, highly organic soils tend to promote rots and are often too water-retentive.

The physical condition of a compost is very important because it has to maintain an open structure for a long time. In nature even a fine-structured soil supporting cypripediums is well aerated by biological processes (by the activities of worms, micro-organisms that "glue" together the particles, and so forth), while in cultivation the artificial composts host highly active agents, resulting in decomposition and compression. Growers have to take countermeasures, like repotting yearly, if the compost is rich in organics. In general, any recommendation of a certain compost has to be judged against the given growing conditions. Experienced growers test a new compost carefully under the local conditions before over-enthusiastically following a recommendation. Beginners should start with recommended species that can tolerate a greater span of composts and will be more forgiving of faults.

Table 3 presents formulae for 10 mixes used successfully by different growers. The formulae should be taken as hints; new growers should take them as guidelines. Other mixes might also be adequate and should be prepared with the requirements of cypripediums in mind. Each mix can be used in pots as well as in beds.

Compost Materials

Drainage material. Drainage aims primarily to provide an open compost that allows the water to run right through. It also provides a coarse layer at the base of the compost that collects surplus water from rain or heavy watering. Drainage material avoids a compression of the compost at the base of the bed or a blockage of the drainage holes in a pot. Most inert materials such as small pebbles, gravel, coarse sand, perlite, burned clay particles, or styrofoam chips (less admirable in the garden) are good for drainage. Organic materials are not recommended because they decompose eventually, hence promoting the compression of a given compost. After a year or so bark, for example, will rot and lose its suitability for drainage.

Loam. This is a problematic term in horticulture. There are as many different opinions of what is meant by the word as growers involved in the discussion. Some understand fibrous loam to mean composted sods of turf from a clay-rich soil, while others think of pure loam as rich in fine roots from surrounding shrubs and trees. Scientifically, loam is a mixture of clay (25 percent), silt (35 percent), and sand (40 percent). It is sticky, does not transport water, and solidifies composts if applied in high percentages, no matter how perfectly open and loose the mixture might have been in the beginning. This results in loss of roots and the weakening or death of the cypripediums. On the other hand, clay minerals are excellent ingredients for a compost. They store nutrients and release them when needed by the roots. In doing this they work like a buffer for nutrients, something lacking in composts of pure gravel or other inert materials.

While some of the North American cypripediums grow in organic-rich soils in nature, most Eurasian species grow in those which are mineral-rich with a certain amount of clay. Cypripedi-

Table 3. Formulae for mixes used successfully by different growers of cypripediums.

Mix	Formulae
Mix A	*One part* loam pellets, *one part* Seramis® (or comparable materials like pumice gravel), *one part* rotten wood, and *one part* coarse sand.
Mix B	Pure washed pumice gravel or lava gravel 3–8 mm diameter.
Mix C	Pure ungraded pumice gravel (unwashed).
Mix D	*Four to five parts* fine dune sand (from inland dunes) and *one part* fen soil (muck). Add just enough fen soil to make the sand dark grey. With calcareous-growing species, if lime-free sand is used, powder with agricultural lime (preferably dolomitic) over the surface every autumn.
Mix E	*Three parts* coarse, fibrous pine duff, *two parts* coarse sand, and *one part* crushed oyster shells.
Mix F	*Three parts* pumice gravel and *one part* loam pellets.
Mix G	*Three parts* beech leaf mould (sieved through a 5-mm / ¼-inch mesh), *three parts* fine chipped pine bark (available for tropical orchids), *two parts* John Innes No. 3®, and *one part* coarse grade perlite. Repot yearly!
Mix H	*One part* medium grade bark, *one part* fine grade bark, *one part* flaky leaf mould, *one part* perlite, and *½ part* coarse sand. Repot regularly!
Mix I	*Four parts* Seramis® and *one part* compost for ornamentals based on decomposed bark and without peat (or probably John Innes No. 3®).
Mix J	*Two parts* gravel, *one part* perlite, and *one part* fine fir bark. To lift the pH into the neutral range, if needed, add *½ part* oyster shells.

ums have never been found growing in Europe and eastern Asia in leaf mould, but always under a sparse organic layer in the upper mineral-rich soil consisting of clay-humic pellets. These pellets are stabilised by a compound of degraded organic material and clay minerals. The pellets have a diameter of about 0.5–1 cm and form what is termed *a good crumb structure*. This material is very useful as an ingredient for a loam-based compost. It can be found everywhere in the temperate zones in deciduous woods on hills and lower mountains. The bedrock may consist of limestone (this soil is called *rendzina*), or may be of volcanic origin (called *ranker* in soil science). Probably this is what is referred to by some authors as coarse or fibrous loam or "woodland soil". However, the material is here referred to as "loam pellets" and is strongly recommended for loam-based composts. In lowland areas, without bedrock near the surface, this type of soil does not usually occur in the woods. Silty loam from a riverbank or fresh raw loam from other places is not recommended as an ingredient for a *Cypripedium* compost because it tends to solidify the mix.

Sand. Sand consists of small particles finer than gravel and coarser than silt. Usually its main component is quartz. If it is free of lime particles, it can be rather acidic. A simple method to test whether it contains lime is to add a few drops of a weak solution of hydrochloric acid to a sample. If it produces foam and bubbles, the sand contains lime. Both acidic as well as calcareous sand are good bases for certain mixes. Plenty of coarse sand can be used to open a soil that is rich in clay. The particle size of coarse sand is 1–3 mm, that of fine sand is less than 1 mm.

Gravel. Different types of gravel are recommended for cypripediums. They can be used as additives or unblended and pure. Pumice gravel is one of the best materials for *Cypripedium* cultivation. However, there are different qualities, probably depending on origin and/or preliminary treatment. It can be used screened and washed, or ungraded with all sizes included. It is an excellent compound for many mixes. In Japan and Germany growers also use it unblended as a stable compost for a couple of species. After some years the pumice appears to build up some salt deposits and/or hold back some important trace elements. So, after about three years, plants should be repotted and the old pumice rejected. Lava gravel can be used like pumice. However, finer grades may sometimes promote rotting. Quartz gravel and grit are usually not used pure because of their low porosity, resulting in low water retention. On the other hand, they are good bases for a mix.

Burned clay pebbles. This type of artificial gravel, widely used in hydroponics, is recommended as a compound of *Cypripedium* composts. A special variant in Europe is Seramis®, a foamy, burned clay with high water retention within the material, even though the surface of the particles is only moist, not wet. It is a supreme compound in composts. Pure, it can be problematic, because the contrast between too much nutrient by precipitation on the particle surface and too little nutrient by leaching through watering seems to be too wide for cypripediums. Horticulturists in Japan and South Korea sometimes use a material from slightly burned clay that seems to be comparable to Seramis® in some respects.

Perlite. This glassy rock is a compound of various composts used by different growers. The white colour is a disadvantage in garden beds, but the usual mulch will cover it.

Vermiculite. This mineral is another additive sometimes used in *Cypripedium* composts. It can be too-water retentive, but works for certain species under suitable conditions.

Pine needle humus or pine duff. This is the organic layer found under the freshly fallen needles in a pine wood. It includes pieces of bark and composted needles. It is free of loam or lime and has a low pH (that is, it is acidic).

Pine needles. Non-composted, fallen dry needles of different pine species are a suitable mulch for *Cypripedium* beds. The stiff needles of *Pinus nigra* and *P. sylvestris* (Europe) or *P. rigida* (North America) are to be preferred.

Fen soil. The black organic soil from fens (not peat) is called *muck* in soil science and *Niedermoorerde* in Germany. The term is used for organic soils, usually calcareous, which are so thoroughly decomposed that they are black and without obvious plant parts. Fens have contact with ground water, and at least in limestone regions the pH is around 7. The use of pure fen soil is not recommended, but it is an excellent ingredient in a sand-based compost if added in low amounts, just sufficient to make the sand "dirty".

Oyster shells. The broken shells of oysters and mussels are offered for poultry farming. This material is recommended as a mild and easy way to lime a compost, loosening it up at the same time.

Leaf mould. This is the layer of rotten leaves found under the leaf litter in deciduous woodlands. Sometimes it is recommended for cypripediums, especially by English growers who use it successfully as an ingredient. However, it cannot be generally recommended here because it usually decomposes very fast, producing a rapid release of nutrients that weakens the cypripediums and supports pathogenic fungi and bacteria, destabilising the structure of the compost. It is also highly water retentive, and this alone can cause rotting. Some experience and yearly repotting are necessary when using leaf mould to create a well-balanced mix.

Leaf litter. Dry fallen leaves from deciduous trees, especially from beech (*Fagus sylvatica*), can be used as a mulch. This is beneficial, especially with species preferring calcareous soils. Not too deep a layer must be added to avoid a dense rotting mat around the base of the stems. One disadvantage is that leaf litter is easily blown away by wind.

Bracken peat. Bracken peat consists of the decomposing fronds of bracken (*Pteridium aquilinum*) and is found as a more or less thick layer in bracken thickets. Some British growers use it as a component of compost for terrestrial orchids.

Peat. Peat plays a minor role in *Cypripedium* cultivation because it is too water retentive. Some growers use it, but the peat usually decomposes rapidly in open mixes and holds too much water, hence it can do more harm than good.

Wood. Wood seems to have some positive influence on the growth of cypripediums and can be used as rotten wood, bark, or even as saw dust (in moderate amounts). Rotten wood is found in old trunks lying on the ground or under heaps of old timber; it consists of foamy, decomposed wood, non-decomposed wood-fibres, and some bark. Wood, however, is only used as a minor component in composts.

Sphagnum. Sphagnum moss is a traditional material in orchid cultivation. Consequently, it is also listed in literature for use in *Cypripedium* cultivation. It is a problematic component, however, if used in soil mixes because it holds too much water and causes rot. There is no need to use sphagnum and it is, therefore, not recommended here. On the other hand, living sphagnum has some advantages in stabilizing injured, weak rhizomes that have been subject to desiccation. These can be grown in fresh (but not wet) sphagnum for a couple of weeks and then subsequently repotted into a regular sub-

74

strate. Divisions of rhizomes, free of active growth buds, sometimes produce new growths from reserve buds if placed in a plastic bag with living sphagnum. This does not work with every species, and the divisions should be strong and healthy to survive in the slightly moist sphagnum for a few months.

Commercially available composts. A great variety of composts is offered in garden centres and supermarkets, mostly for ornamentals. In the British Isles the best for wildflowers such as alpines are the John Innes® mixes, the different blends marked by different numbers. Peat-based mixes such as Levingtons® in the United Kingdom or the TKS mixtures in Germany are not recommended as ingredients for *Cypripedium* composts. New mixes based on decomposed bark are less water retentive and more open and therefore of interest for the *Cypripedium* grower. Generally, all mixes high in organic ingredients should be used with restraint.

FERTILISER

Every green plant needs water, light, carbon dioxide, and minerals uptaken by the roots and leaves to live and grow. Parasitic plants, and those growing in strong symbiosis with other organisms, may have reduced requirements for some of these basic growth factors. The symbiosis of orchids with fungi is often stressed in the literature, and for many authors this is especially true regarding the cultivation of terrestrial orchids. However, cypripediums seem to have little need for a fungal symbiont the first year following germination. Two-thirds of all higher plants have a symbiosis with fungi, and horticulturists do not concern themselves with this when planting ornamentals, shrubs, or trees. They just try to provide the best growing conditions. The roots may already be in a state of symbiosis or, subsequently, a suitable fungus will find its way to the plant. If not, except for semiparasites or parasites, there is no problem in cultivation because the grower, by fertilizing the plant, will substitute the role of the fungus completely. All this is true for cypripediums. Do not grow the fungus, grow the orchid!

Many composts are low in nutrients, so fertilizing the plants is necessary. Inorganic fertilisers are perhaps easier to use because it is simpler to control their application. Organic fertilisers often include a lot of high-molecular-weight compounds, which have to be decomposed by microorganisms to release the minerals subsequently taken up by the orchids. Sometimes these compounds may cause too high an activity on the part of the soil microorganisms, which might then attack the orchid! On the other hand fish emulsion or liquid guano are ideal for cypripediums because their dosage and application are safe and easy.

Each of the common inorganic fertilisers available for ornamentals (cheap) and orchids (usually more expensive) is recommended for cypripediums. They have to be diluted in water and applied by watering. Slow-release fertilisers to be mixed into the compost are problematic because the grower has to be very accurate with the dosage. Such stable fertilisers can cause concentrations of nutrients in the compost, resulting in the burning of the root tips and the depression of root development.

The amount and strength of fertiliser depends upon the compost in use. If a mix with leaf mould is used, no fertiliser is recommended because the rotting compost releases enough minerals to satisfy any cypripedium (and would probably kill it if the mix was not well balanced). On the other hand, if a compost of pure gravel or any other inert material is used that does not release minerals, regular fertilizing with every watering is necessary. This watering should be reduced during winter. In dry periods, with a higher frequency of water applications, it is enough to fertilise inert composts with every second watering. Water sufficient to wash out a possible build-up of salts from earlier applications must be applied. The fertiliser must contain all necessary trace elements, and its concentration should be between one-quarter and the full recommended strength (see the label on the package). The grower has to watch the plants. If leaf tips burn, then the concentration of fertiliser must be reduced. Pale, yellowish leaves require heavier fertilizing. Too much light can also result in a pale colour, but a lack in fertiliser often causes a pale colour around the edges of the leaves.

Sand-based composts also require regular fertilization, but not with every watering if the sand is mixed with materials rich in humus or clay. The more of these materials used, the less fertiliser is necessary. Depending upon the mix, the strength should be between one-quarter and one-tenth the dose recommended for houseplants. The frequency should fall between one application per month to one or two per growing season. If clean, pure sand is used, fertilizing has to be done with each or every second watering as with gravel.

Loam-based composts do not need much fertilizing. If the mix is fresh, little or none is necessary. One or two applications per growing season (one-quarter to one-tenth the recommended dose) are enough. As the compost ages the frequency should be increased until repotting is necessary.

WATERING

If the local tap water is of sufficient quality to be applied to houseplants, it can also be used for cypripediums, except for those species such as *Cypripedium acaule,* which need rainwater or deionised water.

When the plants enter dormancy in autumn, watering should be reduced. In winter a certain moisture in the compost of pot-growing plants has to be maintained. It should be slightly mesic, not dry, and certainly not wet. In the garden, most acclimatised species do not need protection from too much moisture in frost-free periods. With species from southwestern China, however, a cover allowing free air movement but no access for rainwater is appropriate (at least for the spotted-leaved species).

In spring, watering has to be increased. Do not let the compost become dry in summer. In hot spells, spraying in the morning and late afternoon is beneficial. Again it must be emphasised that the compost has to be free-draining and not too water-retentive. Even with the frequent watering of water-loving species, the compost must not become wet. When watering, the grower has to take into account the composition and constitution of the compost. Pots of 5- to 10-litre (1- to 2-gal.) capacity, filled with pumice or lava gravel, standing in an open greenhouse in central Germany (northern border of viniculture), need watering once a week in the growing season. Loam-based composts or organic-rich composts need to be watered once or twice a month. These treatments reflect average conditions in central Europe. Different weather conditions and different regions will need modifications in watering frequency.

A technical device to decide when to water is a tensiometer. This is a manometer attached to a tube filled with water. The bottom of the tube is sealed with a special water-permeable ceramic, and this is plunged into the compost. The grower can read the suction force of the compost (directly affecting the water uptake of the roots) on the manometer. A suction force of about 70 mbars is optimal, but with a reading of 120 mbars the grower has to water.

PROPAGATION

Vegetative Propagation

An easy way of propagating cypripediums is to divide a clump, if it has a reasonable number of growths. The more growths, rootstock mass, and roots each division has, the better. Also, a single growth can be cut from the clump. Such a division needs at least two or three scars showing former growths to ensure that enough food reserves and roots are provided for the separated growth. For species with compact growing rhizomes, the new division should have at least 3 cm of rootstock remaining before the bud. For species with creeping rhizomes (such as *Cypripedium formosanum*), the new division should be about 15–25 cm in length. In general, it is wise to let a specimen grow into a clump rich in stems. Such a specimen plant makes a better show, is usually much stronger, and develops more flowers.

When dividing an old rhizome in the autumn, the back part can be treated like the back bulb in tropical orchids. If it is cut (make sure that the division is not too small), reserve buds will often start to grow. This can be promoted by putting the back part in living sphagnum moss, wrapped in a plastic bag, for a few months.

Divisions should be made with a clean, sharp knife. The cut can be powdered with charcoal to dry it and protect it from infections. Some growers recommend that the cut be allowed to dry in the air before replanting. If this is done, it is necessary to protect the roots from drying out. Other growers immediately plant the divisions in the new compost without special treatment for the cuts to avoid too much disturbance for them.

With tropical orchids, the best time to divide a plant is before the start of the new year's growth. The same is true for cypripediums. Immediately after flowering the new growth hardens up, the food reserves have been depleted from the roots to a maximum extent, and the new food reserves are moving down again from the leaves. The new roots are starting to grow at this time. Hence, the division will establish itself quickly. The divisions have to be replanted immediately to ensure water supply and avoid wilting of the leaves. If the remaining root system is too small in comparison with the leaf system, cutting off the top half of the stem (with half the leaves) can be beneficial.

Division in autumn is the standard technique with commercial growers because these divisions can be shipped. However, division in autumn does not permit establishment of the plant until the following summer, so there can be a long period during which problems may develop.

Micropropagation

Propagation of cypripediums from seed is routine today. However, it is not very easy and needs some hands-on experience and technical equipment. In this chapter only some general information can be given. Details are available in the orchid literature, an excellent starting point being the articles "Growing *Cypripedium reginae* from Seed" and "Large scale seedling production of North American *Cypripedium* species" by William K. Steele (1995, 1996) and Hanne Rasmussen's detailed account in her book *Terrestrial Orchids from Seed to Mycotrophic Plant* (1995).

As in tropical orchids the seeds are sown on a sterile medium without symbiotic fungi. Certainly the deflasking would be easier with symbiotically raised seedlings but, at present, no reliable symbionts of *Cypripedium* species are available. Seedlings often have different symbionts from mature plants, and this makes the matter difficult.

Two different methods of harvesting and sowing the seeds are available. One, the green pod method, is to take immature seeds in green capsules, sterilise the capsule, and take out the sterile seeds. They have not developed any inhibition to germination (necessary to survive the winter in nature) if harvested at the right time and will germinate quickly. Depending upon the species, condition of the specimen, and climatic influence, the right time lies between 5 and 12 weeks after fertilization. At this time the embryo is still attached to the placenta and comprises between 9 and 12 cells. Werner Frosch in central Germany recommends the following times to harvest green pods: *Cypripedium calceolus* and *C. reginae*, 6 weeks; *C. kentuckiense*, *C. parviflorum* var. *parviflorum*, and *C. parviflorum* var. *pubescens*, 8 weeks; *C. macranthos*, 10 weeks; and *C. formosanum*, 12 weeks. A change in the local average temperature of about 2°C can mean a change of an entire week to harvest the capsules!

The other method is to use mature seeds. If the seeds are not sterile, they have to be sterilised with a weak sodium-hypochlorite solution. Mature seeds are usually dormant and this has to be overcome, either with hormone treatment or by storing the seeds near freezing for at least two, but preferably four, months. In some cases only a short treatment (such as with sulphuric acid of 2 to 4 percent for a few minutes) helps to destroy the inhibitors located in the inner integument (called carapace) of the seed capsule. The seeds are sown on a jelly-like medium stabilised with agar. The jelly constitution has to be very weak and not as strong as with tropical orchids. The components of a typical medium are sugar, minerals, vitamins, and other complex organic compounds. The literature offers many different formulae (see Arditti and Ernst 1993, H. Rasmussen 1995).

Planting out seedlings and growing them to maturity is nearly as problematic as producing the seedlings in flasks. First of all, *Cypripedium* seedlings do not produce leaves unless they have had a cold treatment, the so-called vernalization (like the adult plants, which need this vernalization every winter). This is done in the refrigerator with temperatures of about 4°C for at least three months. After this the seedlings can planted out in pots or other containers. They can be grown in the same compost as the mature plants. However, the seedlings are very susceptible to droughts and rots and the right conditions are not always achieved in a compost suitable for mature plants. Werner Frosch in Germany uses mix I (see Table 3) for seedlings. However, some skills and experience are necessary before it is possible to grow deflasked *Cypripedium* seedlings successfully to flower.

If optimal conditions are given, a cypripedium can be grown from seed to flower within three years. Usually it takes four to five years. If conditions are good, this is probably the same time needed for a cypripedium in the wild to reach flowering size. Ehrenfried Lucke in Germany (unpublished) has sown *Cypripedium calceolus* seed in nature and found the first flowers five years later. In the older literature it is said that this species requires 12 years to flower. Certainly this long period is based on guesswork. It is not confirmed by the results of propagation in cultivation nor by Lucke's experiment.

PESTS AND DISEASES

Diseases in cypripediums are currently not well understood. Consequently, there is a dearth of adequate remedies that can be applied successful. Cypripediums are not drought-tolerant, and humidity should be in the upper ranges at their growing sites. The degree of moisture of composts also needs to be above the dry range, yet this attracts fungi and bacteria. If cypripediums become weak through poor environmental conditions, either too moist or too dry, the plants can be attacked by pathogens.

Rot at the base of the stem of a plant that seems to be healthy at the first glance is a symptom of too damp a compost. During periods of high temperature with very high humidity, leaf spotting (in North America, apparently *Cercospora cypripedii*) can develop. This causes blackish spots about one cm across, which can become abundant and kill a leaf or growth. Sometimes leaftip die-back may also be a problem, and occasionally it continues down the stem and kills the whole plant. It is usually better, therefore, to cut off the growth than to permit the downward spread of the disease.

In some individuals of *Cypripedium reginae*, North American growers have observed reddish-brown streaks that may extend up the stem into the lower leaves from below the ground. This too seems be due to a fungal problem and can be fatal. Here, probably inadequate water supply might be a reason, but in Germany the same condition was seen with *Epipactis* in adequate water conditions. Once the problem starts, it may be too late and even large clumps may be killed over a period of years. Digging up the plants, washing the roots, and replanting them in a new spot can help.

Another problem sometimes observed in established plants as well as in newly purchased ones is that the roots shrivel and turn black, eventually affecting the whole rootstock. Occasionally it has been observed after a massive leaf-spot outbreak, but it is unknown whether it is related. It probably arises from excessive water.

For all these problems, spraying with fungicides or bactericides recommended for orchids can be tried. Because there are no international standardised pesticides and also because pathogens can differ, no brands nor substances can be recommended here. Growers have to inform themselves at local institutions and in the literature pertinent to the particular country. The best precaution is to maintain good air-movement around the plants and provide free-draining and open composts.

A problem with cypripediums not yet frequent in the Western Hemisphere, but reported from Japan, is virus infestation. There is no remedy for it. The affected plants have to be removed immediately and burned or placed with domestic rubbish to prevent a spread of the infestation.

Less dramatic but also very serious are various pests. In northeastern North America, slugs and snails seem to be less of a problem than, for example, in Europe, where a continuous battle between the grower and the little beasts is not uncommon. Usually the slugs have the upper hand. It takes only minutes for a slug to destroy an emerging growth in spring. Collecting the gastropods with a torch at night or trapping them in plunged glasses half-filled with beer helps to control the pest. However, in greater collections in the open garden this can be hopeless and only pellets of metaldehyde, thinly spread around the plants to kill the gastropods, can effectively control the pest.

Among insects a few minor lepidopteran pests eat leaves, but they rarely occur on cypripediums. A serious pest in North America is a small weevil. The larvae bore holes in the stems, but do not seem to get into the rhizome nor cause any real damage to the stem. The adults, however, severely damage the leaves and stems. In years with cold springs, the adults appear before the plants and then eat the growths as they appear, causing great deformation, often killing them outright. These pests are easy controlled by foliar spraying with acephate (in the United States available as Orthene® and in this product completely safe for cypripediums as long as recommendations on the label are followed).

Sometimes rabbits bite off a stem without eating it. Digging animals such as squirrels, moles, or scratching blackbirds can harm the plants with their activities. Mice can eat the buds in winter if they find a shelter under too thick a layer of mulch.

CULTURAL RECOMMENDATIONS FOR THE SPECIES AND HYBRIDS

Not all cypripediums are yet available in cultivation. At least 32 species and natural hybrids are grown worldwide. About 17 artificial hybrids of flowering size and many more that will be in flower in the coming seasons complete the list. Some cultural comments on the cypripediums (listed in alphabetical order) are given below. These cannot be exhaustive and will probably not be true for every growing condition, but hopefully will help the grower to cultivate cypripediums. The mixes referred to are described in Table 3.

Artificial hybrids. Most of the hybrids produced so far are easy to cultivate. They are usually morphologically intermediate between their parents and also in their requirements for cultivation. Often they are less demanding than either of the parents, hence most of them are choice plants for the beginner, who will have prosperous clumps within a few years. Usually all mixes can be recommended; however, if parents with special demands are involved, the compost for the hybrid should be close to that of the more difficult parent.

Cypripedium acaule. This species is a real extremist regarding soil. It does not forgive any deviation from its demand of growing in very acidic, poor compost, but if some simple rules are followed, it grows easily, as long as the compost stays acidic and does not decompose too much. It grows in a pH range between 3 and 4.5, in soils very low in nutrients. A pH above 5 will kill it within one or two seasons. It is not too difficult to accommodate this demand. To prepare a growing bed, dig out a hole of sufficient diameter to a depth of 40 cm. Make sure that drainage is good. Insulate the walls (not the bottom) with plastic and fill the hole with pure acidic sand, absolutely lime-free and preferably collected in a coniferous forest. It should have almost no nutrients and a pH of 4.5 or less. The hole has to be filled with sand to about 5 cm below the surrounding soil surface. Place the rhizomes flat on the sand. Roots that grow naturally downwards should be pushed into the sand; those that grow horizontally should be left on the surface of the sand. Cover the rhizome and the roots with highly acidic pine humus, which is coarse and well-aerated, but fine enough to maintain moisture around the roots. The base of the bud is also covered, but if it is a large bud, the top may emerge from this humus. Above the humus layer less-well decomposed conifer material is placed that should have more needles, bark chips, decomposed cones, and so forth. The buds have to be covered with this material and the hole completely filled, forming a slight mound. A top dressing with a layer of pine needles, similar acidic conifer needles or oak-leaves, completes the bed. Water only with rainwater or distilled water. Never use water with any minerals. Never use fertiliser. Keep the bed slightly moist and allow it to dry. It must never stay wet and is much better too dry. When established the plant is very drought tolerant and usually should not be watered, even in abnormally dry years. *Cypripedium acaule* can also be grown on the hummock of an artificial raised bog with a similarly acidic and poor substrate that can become rather dry in summer. It is more difficult, however, to establish a plant in such a growing site because of an unpredictable water regime in the compost. In Europe, slugs like the fleshy leaves very much, hence some prevention is necessary. *Cypripedium acaule* will grow and flower as long as the necessary growing conditions are maintained.

Cypripedium × andrewsii. This natural hybrid of *C. candidum × C. parviflorum* grows easily in a variety of composts. It forms choice plants, even for beginners. Mixes A–J.

Cypripedium arietinum. This is one of the dwarf species and, lacking good food reserves, will usually not be able to recover after a heavy loss of roots or growth, things that often happen with pest attacks or too much water. The species is difficult to establish and is subject to all sorts of rots. Once it has become acclimatised it grows easily. It prefers a pH of around 6 and some open shade. It is not a beginner's plant. Mix D.

Cypripedium bardolphianum. This dwarf specimen from southwestern China is not known to be in cultivation. Certainly it needs a very delicate moisture balance, hence it is very prone to either drought or rot. It starts growth late in the season, has high demands of moisture in early summer, and needs very reduced water in autumn and winter. It grows in the wild in alkaline soil over tufa. This is not a beginner's plant. Nothing is known about composts for this species, but they should probably be similar to those for *C. margaritaceum.*

Cypripedium calceolus. This species has been in cultivation longer than any other slipper orchid, but it is not one of the easiest of the hardy ones. In the wild the European clones prefer calcareous, clayey soils that must not be compressed. In Manchuria the plants even grow on volcanic or granitic bedrocks together with the other local cypripediums. A fantastic growth of the European form can be seen in the garden of Otto Möller of Hanover, Germany. He has grown a clump for more than twenty years in a bed with the drainage of a limestone scree. The compost consists of perfect crumbly calcareous clay with sand-like limestone particles and coarser limestone grit, covered with beech leaf litter. The bed receives morning sun and is protected by a coniferous shrub. In May 1995 the clump developed 200 stems, most of them with two flowers. Such a masterpiece is not easy to achieve, and some experience is needed to meet the demands of *C. calceolus.* Some clones react positively to gravel-based mixes. In Manchuria the species is not restricted to limestone and prefers slightly drier sites than does *C. macranthos.* With the European clones, the compost should have a pH around 7 with lime added and be of mesic condition, while the Manchurian plants accept lime-free composts with a pH of 6, still mesic, but with reduced watering requirements. This is not usually a beginner's species. Mixes A, B, C, F, and J.

Cypripedium californicum. This is generally said to be a rather difficult species, but English growers have not had much of a problem in growing it. Barry Tattersall of Middlesex has grown it in his compost (mix G) for a couple of years. The specimens stay in pots, plunged in a frame in front of a north-facing wall. Kath Dryden also grows it in an organic-rich compost. She placed live sphagnum and perlite in the bottom of the pot and fills it with mix H. The species likes plenty of moisture during the growing season, but does not tolerate cold wet winters and should be kept in a frost-free greenhouse. In nature it grows in company with *Darlingtonia californica* above lime-free bedrock. In the milder parts of the British Isles it has been successfully grown outside in a peat bed in a humus-rich mix. If established in time it can form large clumps. However, it is probably not a beginner's species.

Cypripedium candidum. This species is very slow to establish, but it grows very strongly afterwards. It must have nearly full sun, but for the first years it wilts in the heat. It should have some protection by companion plants such as sedges and grasses that do not shade the plant (this would be harmful), but give it some protection from the full sun and promote a microclimate like in a meadow. Indeed *C. candidum* is a plant of mesic meadows, which in former times were abundant in the prairies of North America but for a hundred years or so have been destroyed by the plough. The species needs good watering at first, but is subject to stem rots below the ground line. It does best in a rather clay-rich soil that has to be strongly structured with good pellet formation, as it is sometimes found on marl. After the plant is established, it does very well with little water. It is not a wet-site plant, despite what the literature says. In nature, the growing sites dry out later in the season. The plant is easy to kill with too much water. The pH should be between 7 and 8. In pot cultivation, this species needs bright light but no direct sun around noon. It is not a beginner's plant. Mixes A (with extra lime added) and F.

Cypripedium × *columbianum*. Mainly as a result of new habitats created by logging, the two parents, *C. montanum*, from open sites in montane woods, and *C. parviflorum* var. *pubescens*, from valley regions, have been able to grow in the same locality, subsequently producing this hybrid. The hybrid clones are often attractive plants, with some specimens tending morphologically to one parent, others to the other. The hybrid grows freely in mix E, a compost useful also for other species and clones of the western North America. The pH should be neutral. Hopefully the hybrid will become available soon from horticultural origin. This artificial remake has to receive the same name as the natural hybrid, but with the different spelling *Cypripedium* Columbianum (the same is true for *C.* × *andrewsii* and *C.* × *ventricosum*). With some reservation, it is recommended for beginners. Mix E.

Cypripedium cordigerum. Although imported in quantity some 20 years ago, few clones survived and have adapted to conditions under cultivation. From these specimens a stable garden plant can be produced by micropropagation. Occasionally new introductions appear on the market, unfortunately ripped out of the wild and smuggled to the West. About 98 percent of them die in the first season. The old, established plants grow in open, loam-based composts with a neutral pH. They are fully hardy and start to grow late in the season. They flower about two weeks later than most other cypripediums. Novices should refrain from trying to grow this species until they have had some experience with others. Mixes A, B, C, F, and probably G and H.

Cypripedium debile. Another dwarf species, *C. debile* does not forgive faults in cultivation. Although it is not difficult to grow, it is not easy to maintain for a period of years because, like a delicate seedling, it needs constant conditions. The compost should never dry out nor become wet. *Cypripedium debile* is a plant for pot cultivation and too delicate for the garden. In Japan it is sometimes grown in live sphagnum, but this can easily result in rot at the base of the stem. It should be grown in slightly acidic conditions. A cover of living moss (not sphagnum) can be beneficial. Mixes A, E (without oyster shells), G, H, I, and J.

Cypripedium dickinsonianum. As for *C. irapeanum*, which see.

Cypripedium elegans. This species is closely related to *C. debile* and probably needs the same conditions. It is not known if it is or has been in cultivation.

Cypripedium fargesii. As for *C. lichiangense,* which see.

Cypripedium farreri. This species is closely related to *C. calceolus* and *C. fasciolatum,* but has a more restricted distribution in limestone areas in southwestern China. In cultivation for a few years, this hardy species seems to grow well in calcareous loam-based composts of relative coarse structure. It needs to be watered freely in early summer, with a declining amount towards autumn. In winter, watering has to be reduced to a minimum. The pH should be around 7. Mixes A, B, C, F, and perhaps J (with oyster shells).

Cypripedium fasciculatum. This dwarf species, related to *C. debile,* grows in relatively poor soils in the dry climates of western North America. Nothing is known about a successful cultivation. Seldom-offered seedlings can probably be tried in a layer of coarse acidic sand over conifer humus and watered normally, with a summer/fall drying-off. The species cannot be generally recommended for cultivation.

Cypripedium fasciolatum. This species probably should be treated like *C. farreri* and *C. henryi.* No reliable reports of its cultivation are known so far.

Cypripedium flavum. This close Chinese relative of the North American *C. reginae* grows in calcareous soils, probably rich in humus, and needs more care than its North American cousin. It is fully hardy in central Europe (but must not stay wet in winter). Gerd Sieckkötter of Germany grows it successfully in a mix of three parts quartz gravel (2–4 mm), one part fine limestone chippings, and one-half part fine-graded peat, with a cover of chopped beech leaf-litter. In this compost it grows in the open garden and increases in number of growths from year to year. The compost must not hold too much moisture, because the roots and rhizomes of *C. flavum* are subject to rot. Mixes C, F, and probably D.

Cypripedium formosanum. This attractive orchid is a close relative of *C. japonicum,* but is much easier to grow. In its native Taiwan it occurs in the mountainous north of the island, growing near seepages on schists, in light shade and in the open. In cultivation it can also be grown in calcareous soils; however, it will grow most vigorously in a heavier substrate with frequent watering. Grow it in mix F modified with 60 to 80 percent loam pellets, a pH of 7, and with an extra drainage layer in the bottom of the pot. In this mix two single shoots in a pot developed 80 shoots over an eight-year period, despite the removal of 25 shoots for propagation during that time. When growing well, *C. formosanum* needs to be heavily fertilised, lack of nutrients being indicated by the leaves turning prematurely yellow at the margins. Healthy growth also depends on a regular supply of water, but standing water in the compost will cause instant rot. In the glasshouse, the plant will remain green until November and start into growth in February or March. It is hardy in central Europe and New York State, but needs protection from warm spells to ensure an undisturbed dormancy. In southern Britain it also needs some protection against too much damp in the winter. However, in winter the compost should not be allowed to dry out too much as this will affect the flower buds. When growth resumes, copious watering and constant mild temperatures are necessary to prevent the flower buds dropping. The species requires a pH from slightly acidic to neutral. It is recommended for beginners. Mixes A–J.

Cypripedium forrestii. This species is not known in cultivation, but its requirements should be the same as those of *C. margaritaceum,* which see.

Cypripedium franchetii. Specimens, probably falling within the boundaries of this species, have been in cultivation for some years now. They were, however, mistakenly distributed under the name *C. fasciolatum.* They are treated like *C. macranthos* and are not normally difficult to grow. The pH should be neutral. Mixes A, B, C, and F.

Cypripedium guttatum. This exciting species is native from arctic to temperate zones. It roots in the upper part of mineral-rich soil, just under the organic layer. The rhizome breaks very easily, hence transplanting a specimen usually harms it severely. At least three internodes of the creeping rhizome are necessary (about 20 to 30 cm long) to establish the plant successfully. In Manchuria it grows in the same soil and under the same conditions as the other local cypripediums, but preferring pronounced mesic conditions. In Alaska, Charles Sheviak of the New York State Museum, found it growing together with *C. parviflorum* var. *pubescens* ("planipetalum"-like form) and *C. passerinum* on limestone. Excellent drainage and constant mild moisture are necessary, as for most dwarf cypripediums. It is important to grow it in a cool humid place in the garden. However, strict control of pests such as slugs and digging animals is necessary for successful cultivation. Established and well protected, it grows easy and flowers regularly. The pH should be between 6 and 7. The species is not recommended for beginners. Mixes A (with some extra bark) and D.

Cypripedium henryi. This species with its inconspicuous greenish flowers is a Chinese relative of *C. calceolus* and prefers mineral-rich soils with a pH around 7. Most clones are hardy in Germany, England, and New York State and are not difficult to grow. Special protection in winter is not necessary if no extremes occur. Within a few years a plant can form a nice clump with multiflowered stems, the flowers substituting lack of colour for a strong, sweetish-spicy odour. This species is recommended for beginners. Mixes A–J.

Cypripedium himalaicum. This species occasionally grows together with *C. tibeticum* and is probably to be treated like it. No reliable reports on a successful cultivation are available at present. Perhaps it will do like *C. farreri.*

Cypripedium irapeanum. The yellow lady's slippers from Mexico, *C. dickinsonianum, C. irapeanum,* and *C. molle* are not hardy. It is not unusual to find some cool-growing epiphytic orchids on the oak trees in the same habitats. Nothing is known about cultivation of the plants in composts. Stirling Dickinson from Mexico grows them exclusively in the original soil, the best results obtained if grown in the undisturbed sod, placed in a big pot. Its seems that *C. irapeanum* and its relatives are adapted to so-called ferrasols, namely, the red laterite typical of tropical and subtropical regions and consisting of weathered clay minerals that have lost their capacity to store nutrients. The physical conditions around the roots are nearly like those in clayey soil, but the chemical conditions are very different. Laterite is rich in iron and aluminum, but poor in other minerals. Probably the Mexican cypripediums cannot stand the aggressive edaphic organisms that develop in richer composts. An artificial mix for these species should consist of laterite, mixed with coarse inert materials to keep it open and free-draining. Laterite is sometimes available in pet shops as an additive for aquarium gravel. In this it works as a depot fertiliser of iron for the aquarium plants. In the Tertiary this soil was also formed in Europe and today can be found in some localities such as in central Hessen, Germany. Otherwise laterite is found worldwide in the tropics. All attempts to grow the plants in other composts has failed so far. From autumn to spring it is very dry in the natural growing sites of *C. irapeanum*. The plants appear after the first rains in late spring to early summer and flower in July and August. In cultivation watering the plants has to be reduced to a minimum in winter and early spring. Dickinson recommends the application of a little water around the edge of the pot once a month. Regular watering with rainwater should start in late April or early May. Temperatures in winter should not fall below 10°C. In summer they can be much warmer than for other cypripediums. The Mexican species of *Cypripedium* are subjects for the cold department of a glasshouse for tropical orchids, or a Mediterranean house, but like the other species they cannot stand high soil temperatures. These species are not recommended for beginners or growers without adequate soil.

Cypripedium japonicum. This species is commonly cultivated in Japan. In Europe, however, it has the reputation of being very resistant to any attempt at cultivation over a long period. Without doubt it must be classed amongst the species that are difficult to grow. Perhaps the plant needs a low pH. It seems to need adequate watering when in growth. In South Korea it is grown in garden beds or large pots. The compost consists of woodland soil (probably humus-rich loam pellets) mixed with peat (3:1). The Koreans also find it difficult to establish. It is not recommended for beginners. Mix D (lime-free).

Cypripedium kentuckiense. This is a spectacular species with the biggest flowers within the genus. An 80-cm tall specimen, growing in the open, with flowers 16 cm in diameter makes a spectacular impression. It is the only North American species that grows in alluvial forests. Natural soils mainly consist of sand with some humus (leaf litter). In cultivation this showy species is easy if some advice is followed. It needs a sand-based compost with a pH around 6. It does not like loam-based composts or too much organic material in the mix. In spring it can stand higher rates of watering, but in summer it has to be kept rather dry or it is prone to rot. It is fully hardy in England, Germany, and New York State. It forms big clumps over time. Propagation by division and from seed is rather successful, and seedlings will soon be available on a regular basis, at least in Germany. It is recommended for beginners if instructions are followed. Mix D (the fen soil can be substituted by leaf mould or not-too-acidic pine humus).

Cypripedium lichiangense. The spotted-leafed cypripediums are of interest to growers worldwide. They are, however, difficult to grow for a long period because they seem to be adapted to a rather narrow ecological range. Most experience in cultivation has been had with *C. lichiangense*, often mistakenly identified as *C. margaritaceum* in the past. (Usually articles on cultivation of *C. margaritaceum* were published with illustrations of *C. lichiangense*, until recently also mistakenly known as *C. daliense.*) *Cypripedium lichiangense* and probably also its relatives are hardy in Germany and New York State. In the garden the fleshy leaves are often eaten by slugs, so pot cultivation seems to be safer. The species starts to grow very late in the season. When the leaves begin to unfold, plants needs regular watering, especially with excellent drainage conditions and without water-retentive materials in the compost. This water regime has to be continued over the summer with a lot of fresh air provided. Too high temperatures with very high humidity are problematic and may cause rots such as leaf spotting. In late summer, watering has to be reduced, and in autumn plants have to be watered very carefully, just to prevent the compost from drying out. The same is true for winter and early spring. When the bud starts to develop, moisture can be increased step by step. In nature this species grows on limestone, hence the compost should have a pH between 6 and 7. It is not recommended for beginners. Mixes A, B, C, D, or perhaps I.

Cypripedium macranthos. This species was once a problematic species for most growers, although Charles Clément (1886) found it grew easy in his well-balanced mix (mix A) of coarse sand, crumbly loam, rotten wood (sometimes with some leaf-mould added), and potsherds. If water flows directly through it, the right loam has been chosen, but if loam holds water, even for a few moments only, reject the mix and try a better loam. Too much loam, even if it is rather

91

coarse and free-draining, usually seems to be problematic for *C. macranthos* in cultivation. The compost has to be well balanced with inert ingredients, or may even consist of pure gravel-like pumice. The different *macranthos* types are hardy, at least when established, and need no special protection in winter. In late winter and early spring, however, protection from warm spells can be beneficial to avoid too early a start in growth. Established specimens will develop into considerable clumps over years. If grown in mix C, even the beginner may try it. The pH should be between 6 and 7. Mixes A, B, C, D (to be prepared with coarse sand), F, I, J, perhaps also G and H.

Cypripedium margaritaceum. As for *C. lichiangense,* which see.

Cypripedium micranthum. Like *C. bardolphianum,* this species belongs to the *C. margaritaceum* group. Probably it has to be treated like its very close relative *C. bardolphianum.* Without doubt, it is not a beginner's plant.

Cypripedium molle. As for *C. irapeanum.* Not known to be in cultivation outside of Mexico.

Cypripedium montanum. In North America this species has the reputation of being difficult to cultivate. Certainly it is not a species to be grown in sand and muck mixes that work so well for most other American species. Most European growers have also experienced a lot of problems with this species, but there are exceptions. A successful cultivation with regular flowering each season was achieved in a pot plunged in a sheltered spot with open shade in the garden of J. and P. Poweleit in northern Germany. The specimen grows in a mix of equal parts of lava gravel, burned clay pellets, "Einheitserde P" (fine graded peat- and clay-based mix for repotting immature ornamentals), redwood bark, oyster shells, and some coarse sand. In the wild it grows in calcareous soils as well as in lime-free substrates. The climates where it is native are diverse, from humid to Mediterranean (California, Oregon). Even if growing in the drier climates, however, the plants will have their roots in moist soil while the surface is dry in nearly rainless late summer and autumn. The specimen growing in northern Germany survives rainy summers without a problem in its well-drained compost. It is not recommended for beginners.

Cypripedium palangshanense. Closely related to *C. debile* and probably with the same demands, this species is not in cultivation.

Cypripedium parviflorum var. *parviflorum.* In nature this variety grows under trees and amongst shrubs in fens and wet forests. The soils are rich in organics and minerals, with a pH around 7. In cultivation var. *parviflorum* prefers mesic conditions and does not need a simulated bog or fen. In not too organic-rich composts with sufficient drainage it will increase its number readily and form impressive clumps, while in the wild in fens it usually has only a single shoot or forms rather small clumps. Most of the clones belong to the easiest and most rewarding of the genus, growing in any compost provided it is loose. However, Salisbury when he described it in 1791, used a cultivated specimen that had originated in Virginia as type, in a region where the usual wet-growing var. *parviflorum* of the North does not occur. This southern variety is morphologically very close to var. *pubescens* and grows in acidic and rather dry places, in contrast to the other North American yellow lady's slippers. The usual *C. parviflorum* var. *parviflorum* is recommended for beginners. Mixes A–J.

Cypripedium parviflorum var. *pubescens.* Like var. *parviflorum,* var. *pubescens* is an easy plant to grow. In nature it does not occur in wet but in mesic sites. It is a very variable cypripedium that grows from arctic Alaska to the warm temperate southeastern United States. Especially in the North it prefers limestone areas. In woodlands, it is a tall plant with more or less heavily twisted petals, growing in open situations between shrubs and on clearings. In the meadow-like situations of limestone barrens and in the open tundras of its northern-most occurrence, it grows as a very sturdy plant with nearly or fully untwisted petals. Some of these forms will change to the usual tall plant if grown under woodland conditions, others will retain their dwarf stature. If var. *pubescens* receives enough light and grows in a rich soil, it forms considerable clumps even in the wild. The pH should be between 6 and 7. Like var. *parviflorum* it is easy to grow, but more care has to be taken over good drainage because it is not as water tolerant as the variety from fens. Therefore, it can be harmed by the usual beginner's fault of overwatering. However, it is recommended for beginners. Mixes A–J.

Cypripedium passerinum. This species from the boreal regions of North America cannot stand much heat in summer. The soil has to stay cool. In nature the species usually occurs on riverbanks and near creeks. Again, this habitat should not be duplicated in cultivation, but good mesic conditions have to be provided in the compost. To fulfill the demands of this small and delicate species of the North is rather difficult. A long undisturbed dormancy and cold humid conditions in summer are needed. In Canada, where it grows in the wild, it has the reputation of being an easy species that grows anywhere, in any compost. Not so in more temperate regions. In New York State it has been grown in mix D, staying more or less alive. In a mix of fine-grade vermiculite and perlite (3:1) and kept moist, it grew better. Perhaps not only temperatures, but daylength as well could be a problem for this northern lady's slipper. It probably needs a longer period of daylight to form new buds. It is not recommended for beginners.

Cypripedium plectrochilum. This is the Chinese counterpart of the North American *C. arietinum,* also growing on limestone, often in limestone rubble in more open situations. In cultivation it is better to grow it in pots, plunged in a sheltered bed in summer and well protected from pests and inhospitable weather, but with enough light. Perhaps it is better placed in an alpine house for the entire year. It is not a beginner's plant. Mixes A, D, and J.

Cypripedium reginae. The queen lady's slipper is one of the showiest species and engages the interest of horticulturists with its relative ease of cultivation. It does not like a loamy compost but grows vigorously in mix D. Organic-rich, well-balanced mixes also are acceptable. The species needs a lot of nutrients when established. In pure inert material it can easily show deficiency symptoms if the grower does not feed it regularly (emerging growths become very pale and growths become smaller compared with the previous season). With the years it can grow into massive clumps of very tall, often double-flowered stems. In nature it grows in calcareous fens; even if the surface is covered by sphagnum, the roots are in contact with mineral-rich water with a pH around 7. As with the other fen species, *C. reginae* does not prefer wet conditions in cultivation, but well-drained, mesic composts. It never should become dry. It is recommended for beginners. All mixes, loam, however, should only be added carefully because it is easily compressed with higher rates of watering.

Cypripedium segawai. This species is closely related to *C. henryi* and probably originated as an alpine form, evolving in the mountains of Taiwan. It is less vigorous than its cousin from the Asiatic continent and increases very slowly in cultivation, but it is not particularly difficult to grow. It accepts the same conditions as *C. henryi,* but because of its dwarf stature it should not be planted in the open garden. It is in better hands if grown in a pot. Established, well-grown plants usually develop two flowers of deep golden yellow per stem. Due to the small stature of the plant, the grower should be prepared to give it more care than *C. henryi.* Mixes A–J, but be careful with too much organics.

Cypripedium shanxiense. This relatively new species grows under the same conditions as *C. calceolus* and *C.* × *ventricosum* in Manchuria. In cultivation it grows in a mix of two parts lava gravel, one part Seramis®, and one part loam pellets (from a basaltic mountain) with a pH of 6.5. It should also do well in mixes A, B, C, F, or J. Subject to rots, especially if divided, it is not recommended for beginners.

Cypripedium smithii. As for *C. tibeticum,* which see.

Cypripedium subtropicum. This species is completely unknown in cultivation (sometimes Chinese *Epipactis* species are offered under its name). Judging from the literature, it should have demands similar, in some respects, to those of *C. irapeanum,* at least regarding hardness.

Cypripedium tibeticum. Together with its close relatives, this species replaces *C. macranthos* in southwestern China and the Himalayan region, and requires growing conditions similar to the latter in some respects. It differs in being more adapted to continental highmountain regions. Hence it needs some protection in winter, especially during frost-free periods, to maintain dormancy. Also, it should not receive too much rain in winter. In summer it needs constant watering and a fresh and cool atmosphere while receiving full light (avoid the burning sun around noon). It can acclimatise in the garden, but will not grow into big clumps nor become as persistent as *C. macranthos.* In the wild it is found growing in grassland on limestone and should have a compost with a pH between 6 and 7. It is not a beginner's species. Mixes A, B, C, D (made with coarse sand and some oyster shells), and J.

Cypripedium × ventricosum. This is the natural hybrid between *C. macranthos* and *C. calceolus.* In Siberia it is rather uniform in shape and colour, but in Manchuria it shows a breathtaking variability. Plants from this origin are amongst the finest in the genus. In Manchuria this hybrid grows in the open shade of oak forests in a "loam-pellet soil" with a pH around 6.5. It is not difficult to grow, but until selected clones are available, beginners should be cautious in trying it. Mixes A–I, probably.

Cypripedium wardii. As for *C. flavum,* which see.

Cypripedium wumengense. As for *C. lichiangense,* which see.

Cypripedium yatabeanum. This species needs the same treatment as *C. guttatum.* However, it seems to acclimatise easier and is more persistent. A strong-growing clump was achieved in mix D with pine humus added instead of the fen soil, mulched with pine needles and grown in a bed in front of a north-facing wall, situated in New York State. It requires subacidic to neutral conditions. The species is not recommended for beginners. Mix D (with pine humus).

Cypripedium yunnanense. As for *C. tibeticum,* which see.

ARTIFICIAL HYBRIDIZATION

The promiscuity of *Paphiopedilum* and *Phragmipedium,* where just about any species will hybridise successfully with any other in the same genus, suggests that a similar situation might prevail in *Cypripedium.* The widest successful crosses to date between *C. acaule* and *C. formosanum, C. candidum* and *C. yatabeanum,* and *C. reginae* and *C. lichiangense* do nothing to contradict this idea.

The first artificial hybrid to be registered was by the American grower Carson Whitlow in 1987. Since then he and Werner Frosch in Germany, have raised and registered several artificial hybrids in *Cypripedium.* Improved methods of asymbiotic culture have allowed seed to be germinated more readily, and the success in raising artificial hybrids has grown commensurately. Frosch (pers. comm.) has been successful in flowering seedlings grown asymbiotically in three years from harvesting seed. These plants exhibit some hybrid vigour and may prove to be easier to grow than the wild species.

A list of grexes (all progeny of the same parentage) registered by the Royal Horticultural Society, the international registrar for orchid hybrids, is given in Table 4. To date 19 hybrids have been registered involving 15 taxa. New hybrid grexes are published bimonthly in the *Orchid Review* and consolidated in *Sander's List of Orchid Hybrids,* published to date in five yearly supplements.

The success of artificial crosses, such as *Cypripedium parviflorum* and *C. macranthos,* will help confirm the identity of natural hybrids.

Table 4. Hybrid grex registrations of *Cypripedium* up to 1995. For registration purposes, *C. parviflorum* var. *pubescens* = *C. pubescens,* and *C. speciosum* is treated as distinct from *C. macranthos.*

Grex name	Parentage	Registrant & date
Genesis	*C. reginae* × *C. pubescens*	Whitlow 1987
Promises	*C. formosanum* × *C. acaule*	Whitlow 1988
Karl Heinz	*C. calceolus* × *C. cordigerum*	Frosch 1990
Ingrid	*C. parviflorum* × *C. cordigerum*	Frosch 1990
Rascal	*C. kentuckiense* × *C. parviflorum*	Whitlow 1990
Carolin	*C. parviflorum* × *C. speciosum*	Frosch 1991
Hank Small	*C. parviflorum* × *C. henryi*	Whitlow 1991
Maria	*C. parviflorum* × *C. speciosum*	Frosch 1991
Otto	*C. calceolus* × *C. pubescens*	Frosch 1991
Fantasy	*C. reginae* × *C. lichiangense*	Whitlow 1992
Carson	*C. parviflorum* × *C. formosanum*	Frosch 1992
Kathleen Anne		
Green	*C. kentuckiense* × *C. henryi*	Whitlow 1992
Gisela	*C. parviflorum* × *C. macranthos*	Frosch 1992
Chauncey	*C. parviflorum* × *C. segawai*	Whitlow 1993
Emil	*C. calceolus* × *C. parviflorum*	Frosch 1993
Gidget	*C. candidum* × *C. henryi*	Whitlow 1993
Werner	*C. yatabeanum* × *C. candidum*	Whitlow 1993
Ulli	*C. pubescens* × *C. cordigerum*	Frosch 1994
Princess	*C. reginae* × *C. lichiangense*	Whitlow 1995

TAXONOMY OF
CYPRIPEDIUM

The genus *Cypripedium* was established by Linnaeus in his *Genera Plantarum* (1737), in his *Flora Lapponica* in the same year, and in the first edition of his *Species Plantarum* in 1753. He based it on *C. calceolus* and *C. bulbosum*, the latter now transferred to the monotypic genus *Calypso*. Most slipper orchids were included within the concept of *Cypripedium* until 1888 when Ernst Pfitzer separated the tropical species, the tropical Southeast Asian conduplicate-leaved species into *Paphiopedilum* and all the tropical American species into *Selenipedium*, a genus established by H. G. Reichenbach in 1854. Rolfe (1896) developed Pfitzer's ideas further and surveyed all the described species of slipper orchid. He recognised four genera, *Cypripedium, Paphiopedilum, Selenipedium,* and *Phragmipedium,* the last described as new. He also provided a key to their separation, the tropical American genera distinguished by the unilocular ovaries, *Selenipedium* having long stems, plicate leaves, and vanilla-scented pods with characteristic hard-coated seeds, *Phragmipedium* having short stems and conduplicate leaves, *Cypripedium* and *Paphiopedilum* having trilocular ovaries, the former having pleated leaves and often long stems, the latter conduplicate leaves and short stems.

Despite the attempts of Rafinesque (1819, 1838) and others to divide *Cypripedium,* in the currently accepted sense, into several smaller segregates, there has been almost unanimous support for a broader circumscription of the genus in recent times. Atwood (1984) suggested the reinstatement of *Criosanthes* for *C. arietinum* and *C. plectrochilum,* based on their separate lateral sepals which never form a synsepal. This has not been followed by other authors because in all other features these species agree with *Cypripedium.*

Cypripedium is the most widespread genus of slipper orchids, with a circumboreal distribution extending south to Guatemala in the Americas and to the Himalayas and southwestern China in Asia. At its northernmost extension it reaches the northern ranges in Alaska and equivalent latitudes in Siberia. The centre of diversity of the genus is China where 30 of the 45 species have been reported. Within China, the richest provinces are undoubtedly Sichuan and northwestern Yunnan. The second richest area is North America with about a quarter of the species. The evolution of *Cypripedium* and its relationship with other slipper orchids is discussed in an earlier chapter.

GENERIC DESCRIPTION

Cypripedium *L.*, Sp. Pl. ed.1, 2: 951 (1753); Pfitzer in Engler, Pflanzenr. IV, 50 (Heft 12), Orchid. Pleonan.: 28 (1903); Keller & Schlechter, Monogr. Iconogr. Orchid. Eur. 2: 11 (1930); S.C.Chen & Xi in Proc. 12th World Orch. Conf., Tokyo: 145 (1987). Type species: *Cypripedium calceolus* L. (lectotype selected by R. Salisbury, Parad. Lond. 2: t. 89, 1807)

Calceolus Mill., Gard. Dict. abr. ed. 4: Calceolus (1754); Adanson, Fam. Pl. 2: 70 (1760). Type: *Calceolus mariae* Dodoens.

Calceolaria Heist. ex Fabr., Enum. Meth. Pl. ed. 2: 37 (1763). Based on *Calceolus marianus* of Dodoens and *Elleborine ferruginea Daleschampii* of Daleschamp.

Criosanthes Raf. in J. Phys. Chim. Hist. Nat. 89: 102 (1819); Atwood in Selbyana 7: 129-247 (1984). Type: *Cypripedium arietinum* R.Br.

Arietinum Beck, Bot. North. Midl. States: 352 (1833). Type: *Arietinum americanum* Beck

Sacodon Raf., Fl. Tellur. 4: 46 (1838). Types: *C. macranthos* Sw. & *C. ventricosum* Sw.

Corisanthes Steud., Nomencl. Bot. ed. 2, 1: 474 (1840), sphalm. pro *Criosanthes* Raf.

Hypodema Rchb., Deut. Bot. Herb.-Buch: 56 (1841). Type: not designated.

Fissipes Small, Fl. SE. United States: 311 (1903). Type: *Fissipes acaulis* (Aiton) Small.

DESCRIPTION. Small to large terrestrial herbs with elongate, fibrous roots arising from a short to elongate rhizome. Erect shoots leafy, clustered or well spaced, hairy, glandular or glabrous, the base enclosed by two to four sheathing sterile bracts, one- to several-leaved above. Leaves one to several, usually plicate, prostrate, spreading or suberect, lanceolate, ovate, elliptic, oblong or cordate, obtuse to acute or acuminate, green, spotted with blackish maroon in some species, glabrous or hairy, ciliate or not on the margins. Inflorescence terminal, one- to many-flowered; rhachis terete, hairy, glandular or glabrous; bracts usually leaf-like but smaller than the uppermost leaf, rarely linear. Flowers usually showy, concolorous or bicoloured; pedicel obscure to elongate, elongating after fertilisation in some species; ovary trilocular, three-ribbed, glabrous, hairy or glandular. Dorsal sepal erect to hooded over lip, ovate, lanceolate or elliptic, obtuse, acute or acuminate, glabrous or pubescent on the outer surface, rarely pubescent within, ciliate or not. Lateral sepals usually fused to form a concave synsepal that is similar to the dorsal sepal, but free and linear-lanceolate in section *Criosanthes*. Petals free, spreading, incurved or clasping the sides of the lip, elliptic, ovate, lanceolate, linear-lanceolate or subpandurate, rounded, obtuse, acute or acuminate, often pubescent in basal half within, usually ciliate. Lip deeply pouched and inflated, slipper-shaped or urn-shaped, with incurved side lobes and front margin, hairy within especially on lower surface, glabrous or hairy on outer surface. Column short, stalked, porrect; anthers two, bilocular, borne on short obtuse to acute filaments; pollen powdery or glutinous; staminode terminal on column, sessile or stalked, oblong, ovate, cordate or linear, flat, convex or conduplicate, glabrous to papillose or finely pubescent, ciliate or not; stigma stalked, dependent, tripartite, more or less papillose. Capsule erect to pendent, three-ribbed, cylindrical to almost ellipsoidal.

DISTRIBUTION: A genus of about 45 species widespread in Europe, temperate Asia across to Japan and north, central, and western China and the Himalayas, Sakhalin, the Kurile and Aleutian Islands, North America and Central America south to Guatemala.

INFRAGENERIC CLASSIFICATION

A summary of significant infrageneric treatments of *Cypripedium* is provided in Table 5 on page 110. The first treatment was published by Lindley (1840) at a time when all slipper orchids, including the hard-leafed tropical species, were included in the genus. For the species now retained in *Cypripedium* (sensu Rolfe 1896), Lindley recognised four groups based on morphological characters: *Foliosa* group, including *C. calceolus* and its allies, *C. irapeanum*, *C. macranthos*, *C. molle*, and *C. reginae* and allies; *Arietinum* group, with *C. arietinum*; *Bifolia* group, with two species *C. japonicum* and *C. guttatum*; and *Acaulia* group, with a single species *C. acaule*.

These groups have been more or less retained by most subsequent authors, but at varying ranks and with varying compositions (see Table 5). Morren (1851), for example, recognised five sections: *Calceoli*, *Olocolli*, *Arietinum*, *Bifolia*, and *Acaulia*, the last including *C. acaule* but also other species now attributed to *Paphiopedilum* and *Phragmipedium*. Pfitzer (1903) recognised 28 species in three series: *Arcuinervia*, *Retinervia*, and *Flabellinervia*. Within *Arcuinervia* he recognised four sections: *Eucypripedium*, *Enantiopedilum*, *Trigonopedilum*, and *Criosanthes*, the first being subdivided into two subsections.

Brieger (1973) more or less followed Pfitzer's groupings within the genus. He recognised at subgeneric rank all but subsection *Obtusipetala* of section *Eucypripedium*, which he subsumed in subgenus *Cypripedium*.

The most recent infrageneric treatment of the genus has been that of Chen and Xi (1987), who used palynological data to support their classification of the 38 known species. They recognised seven sections: *Subtropica*, *Cypripedium*, *Calceolus*, *Retinervia*, *Bifolia*, *Criosanthes*, and *Trigonopedium*, the typical section being subdivided into four subsections.

The classification of *Cypripedium* suggested here incorporates morphological, palynological, anatomical, and molecular data. The genus is divided into 10 sections, of which the typical one is further subdivided into two as follows:

1. Section **Subtropica** S.C.Chen & K.Y.Lang. Type species: *C. subtropicum* S.C.Chen & K.Y.Lang. Species nos. 1–2.
2. Section **Irapeana** Cribb. Type species: *C. irapeanum* La Llave & Lex. Species nos. 3–6.
3. Section **Obtusipetala** (Pfitzer) Cribb. Type species: *C. reginae* Walt. Species nos. 7–9.
4. Section **Cypripedium.** Type species: *C. calceolus* L. Species nos. 10–27.
   Subsection **Cypripedium**. Species nos. 10–20.
   Subsection **Macrantha** (Kränzl.) Cribb. Type species: *C. macranthos* Sw. Species nos. 21–27.
5. Section **Enantiopedilum** Pfitzer. Type species: *C. fasciculatum* Kellogg ex S.Watson. Species no. 28.
6. Section **Arietinum** C.Morren. Type species: *C. arietinum* R.Br. Species nos. 29–30.
7. Section **Flabellinervia** (Pfitzer) Hennessy ex Cribb. Type species: *C. japonicum* Thunb. Species nos. 31–32.

8. Section **Acaulia** (Lindl.) C.Morren. Type species: *C. acaule* Aiton. Species no. 33.
9. Section **Bifolia** (Lindl.) C.Morren. Type species: *C. guttatum* Sw. Species nos. 34–35.
10. Section **Retinervia** (Pfitzer) S.C.Chen. Type species: *C. debile* Rchb.f. Species nos. 36–38.
11. Section **Trigonopedia** Franch. Type species: *C. margaritaceum* Franch. Species nos. 39–45.

Analysis of the molecular data from 31 taxa by Cox (1995) and of morphological data of 44 species (excluding *Cypripedium ludlowii,* which may be of hybrid origin) by Cribb and Simpson (in prep.) has allowed the resolution of several problems in previous classification schemes (see Figs. 7 and 8). Neither of the two species, *C. subtropicum* and *C. wardii,* which are basal in the morphological analyses were sampled for the molecular dataset. Intriguingly, both come from the same area of southeastern Xizang (Tibet) in China. The morphological analysis suggests that Chen and Lang (1986) were correct in suggesting that *C. subtropicum* was the most "primitive" *Cypripedium,* having many features more typical of *Selenipedium.* Chen and Xi (1987) suggested that *C. wardii* was possibly closest to *C. flavum,* but here it is the sister species of *C. subtropicum* and the two form a sister clade to *C. flavum* and its allies. It is inappropriate to continue to include *C. flavum* and its allies in section *Cypripedium,* and therefore subsection *Obtusipetala* is raised to sectional rank but restricted for the use of this group.

Although superficially similar to *Cypripedium subtropicum, C. californicum, C. dickinsonianum, C. irapeanum,* and *C. molle* form a distinct clade, which is here given formal sectional rank as section *Irapeana.* The morphological resemblance of *C. irapeanum* and *C. subtropicum* has been commented upon by others and, based on the morphological evidence, they appear to be members of sister clades.

Cypripedium calceolus and its Asiatic allies form a sister clade to that containing the North American species allied to *C. parviflorum,* although the degree of resolution here is low. *Cypripedium macranthos* and *C. calceolus* and their allies are shown to be monophyletic. The hybridization of these species in the wild in Russia is frequent, and this relationship is, therefore, not unexpected. *Cypripedium macranthos* and its allies nest within the clade containing *C. calceolus* and its allies. However, it is useful, I believe, to distinguish at subsectional

103

level *C. macranthos* and the other purple-flowered species with glabrous or hairy to villose ovaries from those species morphologically similar to *C. calceolus* which have shortly glandular ovaries.

The nesting of *Arietinum* (*Criosanthes*) within *Cypripedium* in both morphological and molecular analyses suggests that there is no substance to Atwood's suggestion that it be resurrected as a distinct genus.

Cypripedium acaule is a sister clade to *C. japonicum* and *C. formosanum* in the morphological analysis and to section *Retinervia* in the molecular one. It is, therefore, removed from section *Cypripedium* and placed in its own section. As Brieger (1973) had intimated in placing it in its own subgenus, it is a unique and highly evolved species.

ARTIFICIAL KEY TO THE SPECIES OF CYPRIPEDIUM

1. Lateral sepals divided to the base, linear 2
   Lateral sepals more or less united into an ovate to lanceolate synsepal 3
2. Lip conical and pointed; petals ciliate ...... **29. C. arietinum**
   Lip obliquely conical with a blunt apex; petals ciliate in basal part only, hairy on inner surface in basal half and at apex .. .. **30. C. plectrochilum**
3. Inflorescence four- or more-flowered 4
   Inflorescence one-, two- or rarely three-flowered 9
4. Leaves 2; inflorescence drooping; flowers bronze-coloured or brownish .... **28. C. fasciculatum**
   Leaves 4 or more; flowers yellow or olive and white 5
5. Flowers white with olive sepals and petals; flowers produced simultaneously on an elongated inflorescence axis .... **6. C. californicum**
   Flowers yellow, produced successively, never more than three open at a time 6
6. Petals oblong, narrower than the dorsal sepal, eciliate; staminode vestigial, linear, somewhat sigmoid towards apex .... **1. C. subtropicum**
   Petals ovate, as broad as the dorsal sepal, ciliate; staminode cordate or ovate 7

7. Flowers large, usually more than 5 cm broad; dorsal sepal more than 3.4 cm long; petals more than 4.8 cm long, 4.3 cm wide; lip more than 4 cm long; staminode 1-1.5 cm long with a long tapering apex . . . . **3. C. irapeanum**
Flowers smaller, usually less than 5 cm broad; dorsal sepal less than 3.4 cm long; petals less than 3.8 cm long; lip 3.4 cm long or less; staminode less than 9 mm long 8

8. Flower out-crossing; dorsal sepal 2.9-3.4 cm long; petals 3.2-3.8 cm long; lip obovoid, 2.4-3.4 cm long, side lobes marked with red; staminode 7-9 mm long and wide . . . . **4. C. molle**
Flower self-pollinating; dorsal sepal 1.4-1.8 cm long; petals 1.9-2.1 cm long; lip urn-shaped, 1.9 cm long, side lobes not marked with red; staminode wider than long, 5 mm long . . . . **5. C. dickinsonianum**

9. Leaves 3 or more on an elongated stem 10
Leaves one or two on a short to long stem 33

10. Petals oblong, more or less obtuse; flowers usually solitary . 11
Petals tapering to an acute or acuminate apex, often twisted; flowers one or two 13

11. Flower lemon yellow or butter yellow, sometimes marked with red on inside of sepals and petals, rarely spotted on outside of lip with red . . . . **7. C. flavum**
Flower white or pink, especially on lip 12

12. Plants large, usually more than 50 cm tall; flower white or pale pink with a pink lip; dorsal sepal 3 cm or more long; lip 2.5-5 cm long . . . . **8. C. reginae**
Plants usually less than 40 cm tall; flower with pale greenish or yellow green sepals and petals and a white lip; dorsal sepal less than 2 cm long; lip less than 1.5 cm long . . . . **9. C. passerinum**

13. Ovary glandular; glands short and dense 14
Ovary glabrous or pubescent but never glandular 25

14. Flowers with a white lip 15
Flowers with a pale yellow, yellow, brown or purplish lip . . 17

15. Petals and sepals green; petals oblong-lanceolate, flat and untwisted . . . . **14. C. cordigerum**
Petals and sepals yellow-green suffused with brown or purple-maroon; petals spirally twisted 16

16. Leaves lanceolate, 1.5-4 cm wide, suberect; flowers always solitary; sepals and petals dull greenish-brown, sometimes suffused with brown; sepals about equal to lip in length; dorsal sepal 2-3 cm long; petals 2.5-4.5 cm long . **20. C. candidum**
Leaves elliptic to ovate, 3-8 cm wide, spreading; flowers 1 or 2 rarely 3; sepals and petals maroon; sepals much longer than the lip; dorsal sepal 3-6.5 cm long; petals 4.5-7 cm long . . . .
. . . . **19. C. montanum**

17. Flowers more or less concolorous; sepals, petals and lip green, yellow, ochre, brownish bronze or purple 18
Flowers more or less bicoloured; sepals and petals pale yellow, more or less striped or spotted brown, purple or maroon; lip yellow 20

18. Flowers ochre, brownish bronze or purplish . . . .
. . . . **13. C. shanxiense**
Flowers yellow or green 19

19. Flowers usually two or three, green, rarely with a yellowish lip; petals tapering from base to tip, often spirally twisted . . . . .
. . . . **11. C. henryi**
Flower usually one, yellow, rarely with fine red spotting on the lip; petals linear-oblanceolate, more or less flat . . . .
. . . . **12. C. segawai**

20. Dorsal sepal and petals boldly striped on veins with deep purple
. . . . 21
Dorsal sepal and petals lacking boldly marked veins 22

21. Flowers large; petals 5.8-7.1 cm long; lip ovoid, very inflated, 4-7.3 cm long . . . . **15. C. fasciolatum**
Flowers smaller; petals 2.3-4.2 cm long; lip obovoid, fluted around the mouth, 2.4-3.3 cm long . . . . **16. C. farreri**

22. Staminode oblong-obovate, broadest in apical half, white marked with red spots . . . . **10. C. calceolus**
Staminode trullate to triangular-ovate, broadest in basal half, yellow marked more or less with red 23

23. Lip creamy white to pale yellow, 5-7 cm long, with a mouth almost as wide as the lip; dorsal sepal very long and acuminate, curved forwards over lip, 6.5-11 cm long; petals almost pendent, 7-9 cm long . . . . **18. C. kentuckiense**
Lip yellow, 1.5-5.4 cm long, with a mouth much smaller in diameter than the lip; dorsal sepal suberect or erect, 2-8.5 cm long; petals deflexed at about 45 degrees, usually 3-7 cm long
. . . . 24

24. Flowers small; lip 1.5-3.4 cm long; sepals and petals usually densely and minutely spotted with dark reddish brown or madder and appearing uniformly dark; bracts sparsely or densely pubescent ... **17a. C. parviflorum** var. **parviflorum**
Flowers usually large; lip usually 3-5.4 cm long, rarely as small as 2 cm long; sepals and petals unmarked or spotted, striped, and reticulately marked with reddish brown or madder, rarely extensively blotched . . . .
. . . . **17b. C. parviflorum** var. **pubescens**
25. Staminode vestigial; lip white spotted with purple within; petals ovate, rounded at apex, glabrous and eciliate . . **2. C. wardii**
Staminode trullate or triangular; lip purple or rarely pale yellow or white; petals lanceolate or ovate lanceolate, acute or acuminate 26
26. Ovary villose or densely covered with long hairs 27
Ovary glabrous or sparsely pubescent 28
27. Lip ellipsoidal, often slightly dorsiventrally flattened with a small circular mouth; staminode purple or white and purple . . . . **26. C. franchetii**
Lip obovoid, with a wide fluted mouth; staminode yellow spotted on edges with purple . . . . **27. C. himalaicum**
28. Ovary glabrous 29
Ovary sparsely hairy 30
29. Flowers purple or blackish purple; lip with a white margin to orifice, lacking obvious windows at the back . . . .
. . . . **24. C. tibeticum**
Flowers a rich plum colour, lacking a white margin to the orifice . . . . **25. C. smithii**
30. Flowers light greenish yellow; petals slightly undulate on margins . . . . **23. C. ludlowii**
Flowers purple; petals with straight margins 31
31. Flowers drying dark blackish purple with strongly picked out veins and cross veins on the petals . . . . **24. C. tibeticum**
Flowers drying paler, the veins not boldly picked out on the petals 32
32. Flowers small, lip usually less than 3 cm long; stem glabrous; leaves conduplicate at first, strongly pubescent all over; flowers purple or pink . . . . **22. C. yunnanense**
Flowers larger; lip usually more than 3.5 cm long; stem pubescent; leaves more or less glabrous; flowers purple, pink or rarely white or cream . . . . **21. C. macranthos**

43. Pedicel, ovary and outside of sepals strongly pubescent ......
.... **40. C. micranthum**
    Pedicel and outside of sepals glabrous, ovary subglabrous to
    pubescent 44
44. Ovary glabrous .. **39a. C. bardolphianum** var. **bardolphianum**
    Ovary rather densely pubescent ....
    .... **39b. C. bardolphianum** var. **zhongdianense**
45. Petals less than 2 cm long, eciliate and glabrous ....
    .... **43. C. forrestii**
    Petals more than 2.2 cm long, ciliate and pubescent or glab-
    rous 46
46. Dorsal sepal ovate, acute, 4-7 cm long, larger than the synsepal,
    red-brown or finely spotted with red-brown; petals cream-
    coloured, spotted with purple; staminode trullate, more
    than 15 mm long .... **42. C. lichiangense**
    Dorsal sepal elliptic, concave, shortly apiculate, 2-4.5 cm long,
    as long as the synsepal; petals yellow, streaked and spotted
    with maroon; staminode more or less oblong, less than 10
    mm long 47
47. Petals glabrous with ciliate margins; lip warty all over ....
    .... **45. C. wumengense**
    Petals shortly pubescent or villose; lip warty in front only or
    smooth 48
48. Petals usually more than 4 cm long, densely villose, covered in
    long white hairs on outer surface, longly ciliate ....
    .... **44. C. fargesii**
    Petals usually less than 4 cm long, shortly pubescent on veins of
    outer surface, shortly ciliate .... **41. C. margaritaceum**

Table 5. Infrageneric classification of *Cypripedium*.

Lindley 1840	Morren 1851	Pfitzer 1894	Kränzlin 1901
Foliosa group		*Eucypripedium* *Multiflora*	Sect. *Calceolaria* *Calceolus* group
		C. californicum	*C. californicum*
	Sect. *Calceoli*	*Eucypripedium* *Pauciflora*	
C. irapeanum	*C. irapeanum*	*C. irapeanum*	*C. irapeanum*
	Sect. *Olocolli*		
C. molle	*C. molle*		
	Sect. *Calceoli*		
C. calceolus	*C. calceolus*	*C. calceolus*	*C. calceolus*
			C. henryi
C. cordigerum	*C. cordigerum*	*C. cordigerum*	*C. cordigerum*
	Sect. *Olocolli*		
C. parviflorum (incl. *C. pubescens*)	*C. parviflorum* (incl. *C. pubescens*)	*C. parviflorum* (as *C. pubescens*)	
C. candidum	*C. candidum*	*C. candidum*	*C. candidum*
	Sect. *Calceoli*		
C. montanum	*C. montanum*	*C. montanum* (incl. *C. occidentale*)	
			C. fasciolatum

Pfitzer 1903	Brieger 1973	Chen & Xi 1987	Cribb 1996
		Sect. *Subtropica* *C. subtropicum*	**Sect. *Subtropica*** *C. subtropicum* *C. wardii*
Series *Arcuinervia* Sect. *Eucypripedium* Subsect. *Obtusipetala*	**Subgenus *Cypripedium***	**Sect. *Cypripedium* Subsect. *Obtusipetala***	**Sect. *Irapeana***
C. californicum	*C. californicum*	*C. californicum*	*C. californicum*
C. irapeanum	*C. irapeanum*	*C. irapeanum*	*C. irapeanum*
			C. molle *C. dickinsonianum*
Series *Arcuinervia* Sect. *Eucypripedium* Subsect. *Acutipetala*		**Sect. *Cypripedium* Subsect. *Cypripedium***	**Sect. *Cypripedium* Subsect. *Cypripedium***
C. calceolus	*C. calceolus* (incl. *C. microsaccos*)	*C. calceolus*	*C. calceolus*
C. henryi	*C. henryi*	*C. henryi* *C. shanxiense*	*C. henryi* *C. shanxiense* *C. segawai*
C. cordigerum	*C. cordigerum*	*C. cordigerum*	*C. cordigerum*
C. parviflorum (incl. *C. pubescens*)	*C. parviflorum* (as *C. pubescens*)	*C. parviflorum* (incl. *C. pubescens*)	*C. parviflorum* (incl. *C. pubescens*)
C. candidum	*C. candidum*	*C. candidum*	*C. candidum*
C. montanum	*C. montanum*	*C. montanum*	*C. montanum*
		Sect. *Cypripedium* Subsect. *Obtusipetala*	
C. fasciolatum		*C. fasciolatum* *C. farreri*	*C. fasciolatum* *C. farreri*

(continued)

Table 5. Continued.

Lindley 1840	Morren 1851	Pfitzer 1894	Kränzlin 1901
			Sect. *Calceolaria* *Macrantha* group
C. macranthos	*C. macranthos*	*C. macranthos* (incl. *C. thunbergii*)	*C. macranthos*
			C. corrugatum
			Sect. *Calceolaria* *Calceolus* group
		C. fasciculatum	*C. fasciculatum*
Foliosa group	Sect. *Olocolli*		Sect. *Calceolaria* *Obtusiflora* group
			C. flavum (as *C. luteum*)
C. reginae (as *C. spectabile*)	*C. reginae* (as *C. spectabile*)	*C. reginae* (as *C. spectabile*)	*C. reginae* (as *C. spectabile*)
C. passerinum		*C. passerinum*	*C. passerinum*
Acaulia group	Sect. *Acaulia*		
C. acaule (as *C. humile*)	*C. acaule* (as *C. humile*)	*C. acaule*	*C. acaule*

Pfitzer 1903	Brieger 1973	Chen & Xi 1987	Cribb 1996
		Sect. *Cypripedium* Subsect. *Cypripedium*	Sect. *Cypripedium* Subsect. *Macrantha*
C. *himalaicum*	C. *himalaicum*	C. *himalaicum*	C. *himalaicum*
		Sect. *Cypripedium* Subsect. *Obtusipetala*	
C. *macranthos* incl. C. *thunbergii*)	C. *macranthos*	C. *macranthos*	C. *macranthos*
	C. *tibeticum*	C. *tibeticum*	C. *tibeticum*
C. *corrugatum*	C. *corrugatum*		C. *corrugatum*
			C. *smithii*
C. *yunnanense*	C. *yunnanense*		C. *yunnanense*
			C. *ludlowii*
			C. *franchetii*
eries *Arcuinervia* ect. *Enantiopedilum*	Subgen. *Fasciculata*	Sect. *Cypripedium* Subsect. *Enantiopedilum*	Sect. *Enantiopedilum*
C. *fasciculatum*	C. *fasciculatum*	C. *fasciculatum*	C. *fasciculatum*
eries *Arcuinervia* ect. *Eucypripedium* ubsect. *Obtusipetala*			Sect. *Obtusipetala*
C. *flavum* as C. *luteum*)	C. *flavum* (as C. *luteum*)	C. *flavum*	C. *flavum*
C. *reginae*	C. *reginae*	C. *reginae*	C. *reginae*
C. *passerinum*	C. *passerinum*	C. *passerinum*	C. *passerinum*
		C. *wardii*	
eries *Arcuinervia* ect. *Eucypripedium* ubsect. *Acutipetala*	Subgen. *Acaulia*	Sect. *Calceolus* Subsect. *Obtusipetala*	Sect. *Acaulia*
C. *acaule*	C. *acaule*	C. *acaule*	C. *acaule*

(continued)

113

Table 5. Continued.

Lindley 1840	Morren 1851	Pfitzer 1894	Kränzlin 1901
	Sect. *Bifolia*		***Bifolia* group** ***Bracteosa* subgroup**
			C. elegans *C. debile*
***Bifolia* group**			
C. guttatum	*C. guttatum*	*C. guttatum*	*C. guttatum*
		***Diphylla* group**	
C. japonicum	*C. japonicum*	*C. japonicum*	*C. japonicum*
***Arietinium* group**	**Sect. *Arietinum***	***Arietinum* group**	***Arietinia* group**
C. arietinum	*C. arietinum*	*C. arietinum* *C. plectrochilum*	*C. arietinum*
		***Trigonopedilum* group**	***Bifolia* group *Ebracteata* subgroup** *C. micranthum*
		C. margaritaceum	*C. margaritaceum*
			C. fargesii (as *C. ebracteatum*)

114

Pfitzer 1903	Brieger 1973	Chen & Xi 1987	Cribb 1996
Series *Retinervia*	Subgen. *Retinervia*	Sect. *Retinervia*	Sect. *Retinervia*
		C. palangshanense	*C. palangshanense*
	C. elegans	*C. elegans*	*C. elegans*
C. debile	*C. debile*	*C. debile*	*C. debile*
Series *Arcuinervia* Sect. *Eucypripedium* Subsect. *Obtusipetalum*	Subgen. *Guttata*	Sect. *Bifolia*	Sect. *Bifolia*
C. guttatum	*C. guttatum*	*C. guttatum*	*C. guttatum*
	C. yatabeanum		*C. yatabeanum*
Series *Flabellinervia*	Subgen. *Flabellinervia*	Sect. *Cypripedium* Subsect. *Flabellinervia*	Sect. *Flabellinervia*
C. japonicum	*C. japonicum*	*C. japonicum*	*C. japonicum*
			C. formosanum
Series *Arcuinervia* Sect. *Criosanthes*	Subgen. *Cypripedium*	Sect. *Criosanthes*	Sect. *Arietinum*
C. arietinum	*C. arietinum*	*C. arietinum*	*C. arietinum*
		C. plectrochilum	*C. plectrochilum*
Series *Arcuinervia* Sect. *Enantiopedilum*	Subgen. *Ebracteata*	Sect. *Trigonopedium*	Sect. *Trigonopedia*
C. micranthum	*C. micranthum*	*C. micranthum*	*C. micranthum*
	C. bardolphianum	*C. bardolphianum*	*C. bardolphianum*
Series *Arcuinervia* Sect. *Trigonopedilum*			
C. margaritaceum	*C. margaritaceum*	*C. margaritaceum*	*C. margaritaceum*
			C. forrestii
			C. lichiangense
		C. wumengense	*C. wumengense*
C. fargesii (as *C. ebracteatum*)	*C. fargesii* (as *C. ebracteatum*)	*C. fargesii*	*C. fargesii*

SECTION SUBTROPICA

Cypripedium sect. **Subtropica** *S.C. Chen & K.Y. Lang* in Acta Phytotax. Sin. 24(4): 317 (1986). Type species: *C. subtropicum* S.C. Chen & K.Y. Lang.

Stems elongate, three- to many-leaved; leaves well-spaced on stem, lanceolate, elliptic, or ovate, with linear veins, pubescent; flowers usually five or more, opening successively or simultaneously, predominantly yellow or white; ovary bearing elongate multicellular trichomes and glands; lip ovoid, with obscure side lobes and spotted with red or purple within; synsepal present; petals often as broad as sepals and usually similarly coloured; staminode vestigial, hooked.

A section of two species.

1. CYPRIPEDIUM SUBTROPICUM

This extraordinary species is known only from the type collection. The description is based on the original one, the accompanying drawing of the type, and from examination of the type sheets in the Beijing Herbarium of the Academia Sinica (PE). When they described it, Chen and Lang (1986) suggested that *Cypripedium subtropicum* closely resembled the South American genus *Selenipedium* in habit, inflorescence, and column, and must be considered a primitive species in the genus. It differs, however, from *Selenipedium* in having a unilocular ovary, fruits that are not *Vanilla*-scented, and seeds that are fusiform and have a thin testa. In *Selenipedium* the seeds are globose and have a thick sclerotic testa.

The type was collected in a remote part of SE. Xizang (Tibet) in the valley of the Tsangpo River. This region has been visited by very few botanists and is still a restricted zone because of its proximity to the Indian border.

Cypripedium subtropicum is similar to *C. irapeanum* La Llave & Lex. from Central America in size, habit, and flower colour, but it differs in having a much reduced staminode. The species flowers in mid-July (19th) according to information with the type collection.

116

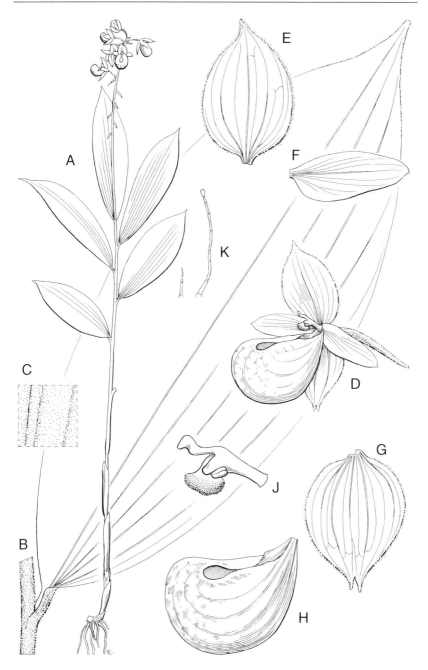

Figure 9. Cypripedium subtropicum. A, habit, ×0.2; B, leaf, ×0.66; C, leaf surface detail, ×6; D, flower, ×0.66; E, dorsal sepal, ×1; F, petal, ×1; G, synsepal, ×1; H, lip, ×1; J, column, ×2; K, hairs from ovary, ×15. All drawn from the holotype by Eleanor Catherine.

117

Cypripedium subtropicum *S.C. Chen & K.Y. Lang* in Acta Phytotax. Sin. 24(4): 317 (1986). Type: China, SE. Xizang (Tibet), Medog, Hajin, *B.S. Li et al.* 11188 (holo. PE!, iso. PE!).

DESCRIPTION. A large terrestrial herb to 1.5 m tall; rhizome short; roots fleshy, 2–3 mm in diameter. Stem to 1 cm in diameter, pubescent, 9- to 10-leaved, densely pubescent, covered below by several sheaths, 2.5–9.5 cm long, pubescent. Leaves erect-spreading, slender, elliptic-lanceolate or oblong-elliptic, acuminate, 21–33 cm long, 7.7–10.5 cm wide, glabrous above, pubescent on and between the veins beneath, margins more or less ciliate, gradually narrowing into a 1–2 cm long petiole but not articulated to the sheathing base. Raceme terminal, seven-flowered; peduncle c. 21 cm long; rhachis reddish hairy, c. 15 cm long; bracts erect-spreading but later reflexed, lanceolate, acute, 1–2.8 cm long, 0.15–0.3 cm wide, reddish hairy. Flowers showy, yellow with a purple-spotted lip; pedicel and ovary c. 4.5 cm long, densely glandular and brownish pilose. Dorsal sepal ovate-elliptic, cuspidate-acuminate, 3.5–3.9 cm long, 2.2–2.5 cm wide, reddish hairy on outer surface; synsepal ovate-elliptic, bifid at apex, a little wider than the dorsal sepal, ciliate, reddish hairy on outside. Petals spreading, suboblong-ovate, acute or apiculate, 3–3.6 cm long, 0.9–1.1 cm wide, nine-veined, the base of the outside and the veins inside reddish hairy, basal margins ciliate. Lip slipper-shaped, slightly dependent-porrect, obovoid-ellipsoidal, 4–4.6 cm long, c. 3 cm wide, glabrous on outside, pilose within at the base, the side lobes oblong, incurved, the mouth suboblong. Column 1.3 cm long; staminode stalked, ligulate-spathulate, obtuse, stipitate at the base, slightly upcurved at tip, 0.5 cm long, 0.15 cm wide. FIGURE 9.

DISTRIBUTION. China (SE. Xizang (Tibet) only). See map p. 205.

HABITAT. In *Alnus* (alder) woodland; 1400 m.

2. CYPRIPEDIUM WARDII

Cypripedium wardii is superficially similar to *C. guttatum* because of its small solitary white flower marked with purple on the lip. It differs, however, in having three or four pubescent leaves with sheathing bases, unspotted sepals and petals, a subglobose lip with incurved margins rather than a pitcher-like one, and a different staminode. It also dries pale brown rather than black. Chen and Xi (1987) sug-

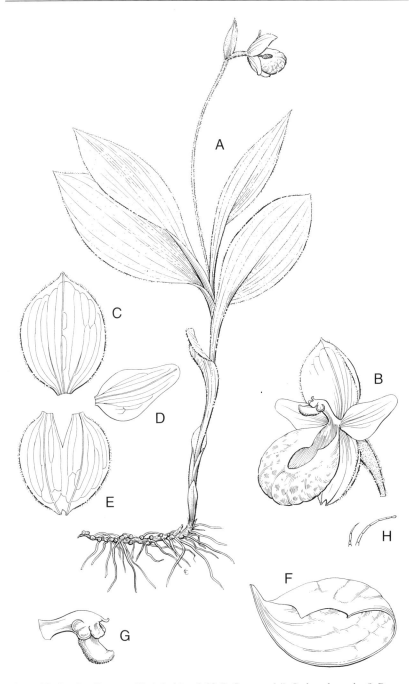

Figure 10. Cypripedium wardii. A, habit, ×0.66; B, flower, ×1.5; C, dorsal sepal, ×2; D, petal, ×2; E, synsepal, ×2; F, lip longitudinal section, ×2; G, column, ×3; H, hairs from ovary, ×15. All drawn from the type by Eleanor Catherine.

119

gested that the species is possibly more closely related to *C. flavum;* however, in my view it seems most closely related to *C. subtropicum,* which grows in the same region. Certainly they appear to be sister species in the morphological cladogram. Pradhan (1976, 1986) treated it as a variety of *C. guttatum* and also mistakenly gave one of its localities as the Debi Valley in the western Himalaya. It is quite clear, however, that Kingdon-Ward collected his no. 8366 (K) in the Debi Valley (28°21'N, 96°37'E), which is in SE. Xizang (Tibet).

Cypripedium wardii *Rolfe* in Notes Roy. Bot. Gard. Edinburgh 8: 128 (1913). Type: China, SE. Xizang (Tibet), Kun-a-tong, above Salween River, *Kingdon-Ward* 145 (holo. E!).
C. guttatum Sw. var. *wardii* (Rolfe) P. Taylor in Pradhan, Indian Orchids. Guide Ident. Cult. 1: 45 (1976) and in Orchid Digest 50(3): 85–91.

DESCRIPTION. A terrestrial plant with a long creeping rhizome, 7 cm or more long. Stems erect slender, pubescent, to 9 cm long. Leaves three or rarely four, elliptic-ovate, acute to somewhat acuminate, 4.5–10 cm long, 2.2–3.5 cm wide, sheathing at the base, hairy above and below, especially on the veins, ciliate. Inflorescence one-flowered; peduncle slender, pubescent; bract foliaceous, ovate-lanceolate, acute, 2–3 cm long, pubescent and ciliate. Flower small, globular, fragrant, creamy white with purple spots on inside of lip and around its rim on the outside; pedicel and ovary 1–1.3 cm long, densely reddish pubescent. Dorsal sepal ovate, obtuse or shortly apiculate, 1.2–1.7 cm long, 0.7–1 cm wide; synsepal elliptic-ovate, shortly bifid and apiculate, 1–1.6 cm long, 0.7–1 cm wide. Petals oblong-ovate, obtuse to rounded at apex, 1–1.3 cm long, 0.5–0.7 cm wide. Lip subglobose, 1.3–1.6 cm long. Column 4 mm long, clearly stalked; staminode 0.15 cm long. FIGURE 10.

DISTRIBUTION. China (SE. Xizang (Tibet) and W. Yunnan only).

HABITAT. Growing on steep grassy limestone cliffs in the shade of dense forest trees in temperate rain forest; 2500–3500 m. Flowering in June and July.

SECTION IRAPEANA

Cypripedium sect. **Irapeana** *Cribb* **sect. nov.** caulis elongatis, foliis pluribus, floribus numerosis simultaneis aperientibus, petalis ellip-

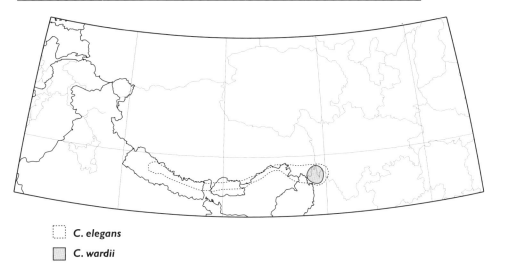

☐ *C. elegans*

☒ *C. wardii*

ticis vel oblongis, labello flavis vel albis ad basin purpureo-notatis, sta-minodio convexo distinguenda. Typus: *C. irapeanum* La Llave & Lex.

Stems elongate, many-leaved; flowers many, opening succes-sionally or more or less simultaneously, yellow or olive and white; lip inflated, subsphaerical, marked with purple spots at the base of the side lobes; staminode convex, heart-shaped, or transversely ovate, with or without marginal cilia.
A section of four species.

3. CYPRIPEDIUM IRAPEANUM

Until recently it was widely accepted that the genus *Cypripedium* was represented by a single species, *C. irapeanum,* in Mexico, Guate-mala, and Honduras. However, the description of another species, *C. dickinsonianum,* from Chiapas in southern Mexico, by Eric Hág-sater (1984), the proposal of *C. luzmarianum* by Gonzalez Tamayo and Ramirez (1992), and reports that *C. irapeanum* in Oaxaca was consistently smaller in habit and size of flower than elsewhere (Dickinson and Greenwood pers. comm.) have suggested that a reappraisal of *C. irapeanum* and its allies was needed.
Cypripediums do not make good herbarium specimens, and res-urrection of flowers using traditional methods is difficult. The lip and staminode in particular are usually distorted so much that in-

121

terpretation of their original shapes is difficult. Access to living material and collections preserved in spirit has clarified matters
greatly. Living plants have been examined in the collection of Stirling Dickinson at San Miguel de Allende and also in the field in
Oaxaca and Chiapas.

An analysis by Cribb and Soto (1993) has shown that, in habit,
the plants of this alliance examined fall into three categories: those
with stems 80–150 cm long and broad and with elliptic-ovate leaves;
those 40–60 cm tall with narrower lanceolate leaves; and those with
stems to 30 cm tall, and smaller narrow, oblong-lanceolate leaves.
Leaf shape is rather variable and overlaps somewhat. In each group
the stems and leaves are hairy all over.

Flower size is variable in this complex, but again it is possible to
distinguish three size classes and these correspond to the vegetative ones. The majority of the specimens examined have large flowers in which the dorsal sepal ranges from 3.4–6 cm long, the petals
4.8–7 cm long, the lip 4–7 cm long, and the staminode 1–1.5 cm
long; the second group have smaller flowers with the dorsal sepal
2.9–3.4 cm long, the petals 3.2–3.8 cm long, a relatively smaller lip
2.7–3.4 cm long, and a staminode 0.7–0.9 cm long; the third group
have very small flowers with a dorsal sepal 1.4–1.8 cm long, petals
1.9–2.1 cm long, a rather differently shaped lip c. 1.9 cm long, and
a staminode 0.5 cm long. Staminode shape is variable in each
group, but in the largest-flowered group it is usually ovate-cordate
with a long tapering pointed apex; in the middle-sized group it is
ovate-cordate to oblong-elliptic and usually a little longer than
broad or about as long as broad; and in the smallest-flowered group
it is transversely elliptic and shorter than broad with a very short
apical point. The scatter diagram of petal versus lip length in Cribb
and Soto (1993) is typical of many that can be drawn.

The type of *Cypripedium irapeanum* falls within the range of the
first group of tall plants with large flowers; the type of *C. molle* falls
within the second group with intermediate-sized flowers; and the
type of *C. dickinsonianum* falls within the range of the third group of
small-flowered specimens. Apart from size, the flowers in each
group are remarkably similar in colour, being golden yellow. The
two groups with larger flowers have a lip with distinctive red marks
on the inturned side lobes, but these marks are absent in the smallest-flowered specimens. The lip in all groups is inflated and has
many tear-shaped translucent "windows" on its surface. The lip in
the smallest group is somewhat cylindrical and less inflated than in

122

the other two. The two types of hairs, glandular and trichome-like, on the ovary are found in each of the groups. The hairs on the sepals and petals and the pattern of hairs within the lip are also similar.

Cribb and Soto (1993) have treated each group as distinct at specific rank whilst suggesting that further field work is necessary to clarify the relationships of the three entities. Plants in the first two groups do not differ substantially in critical features such as tepal shape, staminode shape, pubescence, and vegetative morphology. The differences that do exist are mainly of relative organ size. Plants with large flowers (first group) are widely distributed throughout Mexico from Durango south to Chiapas and also in Guatemala and Honduras. In contrast, plants with medium-sized flowers (second group) are confined to the state of Oaxaca in Mexico. Their geographical separation, the marked differences in plant and flower size, and the relative size of the lip to the sepals and petals suggest that these are best treated as distinct from *Cypripedium irapeanum*. Those with the smallest flowers (third group) are known from only a very small area in southern Chiapas in Mexico. Stirling Dickinson (pers. comm.), who first recognised the latter as distinct, says that it grows in an area where the large-flowered plants are also to be found. The small-flowered plants are distinct in lip and staminode shape as well as plant size, and no intermediates have been found there. It seems unlikely, therefore, that the small and large-flowered plants hybridise in the area. Furthermore, they are also thought to be self-pollinating (Hágsater 1984). Although undoubtedly similar to *C. irapeanum* and doubtless derived from it, I consider *C. dickinsonianum* sufficiently distinct to warrant specific status.

Cypripedium irapeanum was originally described by the Mexican botanists Pablo de la Llave and Juan Lexarza in 1825 based on a collection from the mountains of Irapeo near the city of Morelia in Michoacan, Mexico. The species is still found in the surrounding mountains, for example, near Uruapan, and the plants there are characteristically tall with large flowers. The type specimen of *C. irapeanum* is in Geneva, the only other La Llave and Lexarza type which has been located being that of *Alamania punicea*. Cribb and Soto (1993) have selected a Hartweg specimen in the Lindley Herbarium at Kew as neotype, this specimen having been collected at Irapeo in 1840. A duplicate of this can be found in the main herbarium collection at Kew. *Cypripedium irapeanum* is no longer to be found in the type locality, the habitat having been destroyed.

In 1839, Scheidweiler described two species, *Cypripedium lexarzae* and *C. splendidum,* from Mexico. The types, both of which have been examined, are similar and cannot be distinguished from *C. irapeanum.* The type of *C. lexarzae* may indeed have been part of Lexarza's collection upon which *C. irapeanum* itself was based. *Cypripedium splendidum* is stated to have been collected at Urumbaro and Uruapan, typical *C. irapeanum* being still found near the latter town. Williams (1951) mentioned both as probable synonyms of *C. irapeanum,* a judgement hard to challenge.

Cypripedium turgidum was published in 1890, but was actually collected by Sessé and Moçiño on the Royal Botanical Expedition to New Spain in 1787–1803, near Chilpancingo in Guerrero, Mexico. Material of this species, which may represent the type collection, is preserved in the Herbarium of the Royal Botanic Garden in Madrid and in the Delessert Herbarium in Geneva. A drawing by one of the expeditions's artists is housed in the Hunt Institute for Botanical Documentation, Pittsburgh, Pennsylvania, and this was reproduced by McVaugh (1985) in *Flora Novo-Galiciana.* Copies of this illustration can be found in botanical libraries at Geneva, Missouri, Mexico, and probably elsewhere. *Cypripedium turgidum* has flowers about as large as *C. irapeanum.* Another plate, a copy of which I have seen in MEXU, made by an artist on the expedition, is labelled *C. acuminatum,* an unpublished name, and represents the plant treated here as *C. molle.*

Finally, the described *Cypripedium luzmarianum* of Gonzales Tamayo and Ramirez (1992) is based on a collection from the borders of Michoacan and Jalisco. The authors distinguished it from *C. irapeanum* on its caespitose habit, elliptic-apiculate staminode, indumentum of the lip base and ovary, and anther size. They also stressed that it grows in subtropical forests of *Nolina* rather than in pine forests. I have seen specimens from this region and cannot agree that *C. luzmarianum* is distinct. It seems to fit within the range of variation of *C. irapeanum* in all its critical features. The form of its elliptic, shortly acuminate staminode, which is most distinctive in the drawing of the type, is stated in the type description of *C. luzmarianum* to be ovate-cordate when flattened.

Cypripedium irapeanum is a widespread orchid, but is rather scarce nowadays as many of its former habitats have been destroyed. It can be locally plentiful where it does occur, but its showy flowers have made it vulnerable to collectors and to local children who play with the flowers. Luer (1975) said that "children pop the lips when they are slapped between the hands; but these practices are too painful to dwell upon". Children also use these orchids as whistles. The local names "flor de pelicano" and "pichuhuaxcl" vouch for popularity of this species in Mexico.

Cypripedium irapeanum has proved to be a difficult orchid to grow. Stirling Dickinson has grown it for some years at San Miguel de Allende, but only when he has transferred it with soil from a natural habitat. He considers the mycorrhizal fungus to be important for the survival of this orchid, so that removal of the soil leads inevitably to loss of the fungus. The same applies to *C. molle* and *C. dickinsonianum*. Seed of *C. irapeanum* has been successfully germinated in asymbiotic *in vitro* culture by horticulturists in both the United States and Europe.

Cypripedium irapeanum *La Llave & Lex.*, Nov. Veg. Descr. Orch. Opusc. Fasc. 2: 10 (1825); McVaugh, Fl. Novo-Galiciana Orchid.: 74 (1985). Type: Mexico, Irapeo, *Lexarza* (holo. G!).
C. lexarzae Scheidw. in Allg. Gartenzeitung 8: 265 (1839). Type: Mexico, *Lexarza* (holo. W!).
C. splendidum Scheidw. *op. cit.* 266 (1839). Type: Mexico, from Urumbaro and Uruapan, *Scheidweiler* s.n. (holo. W!).
C. turgidum Sessé & Moç., Pl. Nov. Hisp.: 143 (1890). Type: Mexico, *Sessé & Moçiño* (holo. MA!, iso. Herb.Delessert, G!).
C. luzmarianum R. Gonzales & R. Ramirez in Inst. Bot. Guadalajara 1(2): 64, fig.1 (1992). Type: Mexico, Jalisco-Michoacan border, Los Arcos, 10 km east of Tizapan, *Tamayo, Reyna & Flores* 987 (holo. IUBG; iso. AMO!, MEXU!).

DESCRIPTION. A tall terrestrial herb to 1 m tall, with solitary or less commonly clustered, erect stems growing from a stout short underground rhizome. Stems stout, terete, densely coarsely hairy, leafy along length. Leaves to 20 or more, plicate, ovate to ovate-lanceolate, acute to acuminate, sheathing at the base, 5–18 cm long, 2–6 cm wide, ciliate, hairy on both surfaces. Inflorescence to 10 cm long, to six-flowered, the flowers produced singly in succession; bracts leaf-like, lanceolate to elliptic-ovate, acuminate, 5–10 cm long, hairy. Flowers large, bright yellow with red marks on the staminode and on the incurved basal margins of the lip; pedicel and ovary 3–5 cm long, densely coarsely hairy and glandular. Dorsal sepal erect, elliptic, 3.4–6 cm long, 2–3.5 cm wide, ciliate, finely densely glandular hairy on outer surface. Synsepal similar to the dorsal sepal but oblong-elliptic, 3–6 cm long, 2–3 cm wide. Petals

125

Figure 11. Cypripedium irapeanum. A, habit, ×0.66; B, lip cross section, ×0.66; C, staminode from front, ×1.5; D, column side view, ×1.5; E, column view from below, ×1.5; F, ovary transverse section, ×5; G, hairs from ovary, ×15. All drawn from *Salazar* 865 by Eleanor Catherine.

spreading-incurved, oblong-elliptic, acute, 4.8–7 cm long, 2.3–3 cm wide, ciliate, glandular hairy on inner surface especially near base. Lip deeply saccate, obovoid-globose, 4–7 cm long, 3.5–4.5 cm across, the margins incurved around the broad mouth, with translucent windows all over the surface. Column 1.1–1.5 cm long; stalk glabrous; staminode convex, cordiform to trullate, acute to apiculate, 1–1.5 cm long, 1–1.2 cm wide, ciliate. PLATES 14, 71–73; FIGURES 5, 11.

DISTRIBUTION. Mexico (Chiapas, Durango, Guerrero, Nayarit, Jalisco, Mexico, Michoacan, Morelos, Oaxaca, Sinaloa, Vera Cruz), Guatemala, Honduras.

HABITAT. In *Pinus-Quercus* (pine-oak) forest or grassy banks on clayey soils and amongst rocks, often in volcanic areas; 600–2250 m.

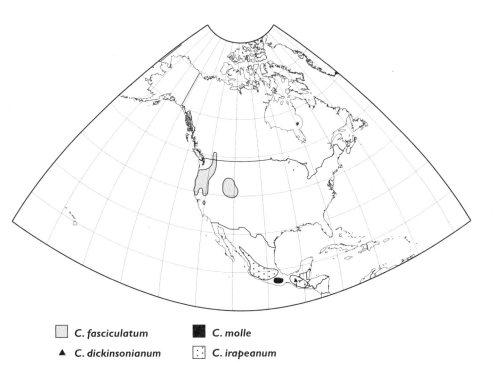

■ C. fasciculatum   ■ C. molle
▲ C. dickinsonianum   ⬚ C. irapeanum

4. CYPRIPEDIUM MOLLE

John Lindley described *Cypripedium molle* in 1840 based on a collection made by Theodore Hartweg from near Oaxaca in Mexico. The type collection, preserved at Kew, is of a smaller plant with markedly smaller flowers than in typical *C. irapeanum. Cypripedium molle* has been sunk into synonymy in *C. irapeanum* by most subsequent authorities (Pfitzer 1903, Williams 1951, Luer 1975) or conveniently ignored (McVaugh 1985, Wiard 1987).

All the collections of *Cypripedium* that I have seen from Oaxaca can be referred to this species except for one specimen (*Ghiesbrecht* s.n.). The type was collected by Hartweg at San Miguel Sola, which is almost due south of the city of Oaxaca. It is a local plant found in suitable habitats on the mountains around the city of Oaxaca, growing in pine-oak forest and scrub on steep banks in a reddish clayey soil.

Some plants can form sizeable clumps with a dozen or more stems which, when in flower, are a memorable sight. When contrasted with *Cypripedium irapeanum*, this species differs most notably in its smaller size and the relative proportions of the lip to the sepals and petals. The leaves are usually lanceolate or ovate rather than elliptic and often less hairy. This species is undoubtedly cross-pollinated and Soto (in Cribb and Soto 1993) has twice collected small bees bearing pollen on their backs from the lip of flowers in the wild.

Cypripedium molle *Lindl.* in Benth., Pl. Hartw.: 72 (1840). Type: Mexico, *Hartweg* 517 (holo. K!, iso. FI!, G!, K!, P!, W!).

DESCRIPTION. A terrestrial herb with clustered erect stems arising from a short subterranean rhizome. Stems 22–60 cm tall, terete, hairy, leafy along length. Leaves plicate, to 18, the lowermost 8 or so sheathing, the others elliptic to lanceolate, 3–13 cm long, 2–5 cm wide, ciliate, hairy on both surfaces. Inflorescence to five-flowered, the flowers appearing singly in succession with rarely up to three open at a time; bracts leaf-like, elliptic-ovate to lanceolate, acute to acuminate, to 10 cm long, 4.5 cm wide, ciliate, hairy on both surfaces. Flowers yellow with red marks on the staminode and on the incurved base of the lip; pedicel and ovary 2.5–3.5 cm long, densely hairy and glandular. Dorsal sepal elliptic, shortly apiculate, 2.9–3.4 cm long, 1.5–1.8 cm wide, ciliate, glandular-pubescent on outer surface. Synsepal similar, elliptic, bifid at apex, 2.5–2.9 cm long, 1.6–1.9 cm wide, ciliate, glandular-pubescent on outer surface. Petals spreading-incurved, 3.2–3.8 cm long, 1.7–2.4 cm wide, ciliate, pubescent on both surfaces. Lip deeply saccate, 2.4–3.4 cm long, 1.7–2.4 cm across, with incurved margins to the broad mouth, densely pubescent in basal part within; side lobes gently rounded.

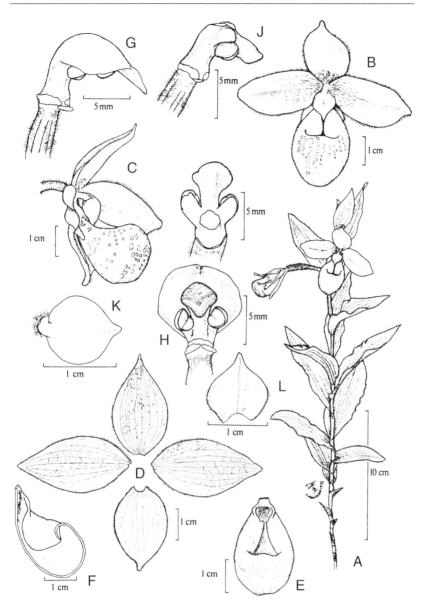

Figure 12. Cypripedium molle. A, habit; B, C, flower front and side views; D, sepals and petals; E, lip from above; F, lip longitudinal section; G, column side view; H, column from below; J, column with staminode removed; K, L, staminode views. All drawn from *Soto 6270* by R. Jiménez.

129

Column 0.6 cm long; stalk glabrous; staminode convex, obovate, shortly apiculate, 0.7–0.9 cm long and wide, ciliate. PLATES 86, 87; FIGURE 12.

DISTRIBUTION. Mexico (Oaxaca only). See map p. 127.

HABITAT. In dryish *Pinus-Quercus* (pine-oak) forest in red clayey soils; 1750–2050 m.

5. CYPRIPEDIUM DICKINSONIANUM

Cypripedium dickinsonianum was described by Eric Hágsater in 1984 based on a collection made by Stirling Dickinson near Comitan in Chiapas, Mexico, in August 1983. It is the smallest of the three Mexican species, plants reaching 30 cm tall and flowers only 2.5–3.2 cm. Hágsater suggests that this species is autogamous, based on the observation that all the flowers in each inflorescence set seed. Little is known of the status of this species in the wild but it must be a rare plant. Its flowers are too showy to be easily overlooked, yet it known to have been collected only twice. It differs from *C. irapeanum* in being a much smaller plant and in having smaller autogamous flowers, which lack red marks on the side lobes of the more cylindrical lip, and which have a small, transversely elliptic, shortly apiculate staminode that is wider than long.

Cypripedium dickinsonianum *Hágsater* in Orquidea (Mexico) 9(2): 204 (1984). Type: Mexico, Chiapas, Comitan, *Dickinson* s.n. (holo. AMO!).

DESCRIPTION. A terrestrial herb to 30 cm tall; rhizome subterranean. Stem terete, elongate, 25–30 cm long, densely hairy, leafy along length. Leaves plicate, narrowly oblong-lanceolate, acute to acuminate, 2.5–5 cm long, 1–2 cm wide, hairy. Inflorescence laxly to six-flowered, with the flowers produced in succession one at a time; bracts leaf-like, 2.5–3 cm long, hairy. Flowers butter-yellow, the lip flushed red inside below the column, 2.5–3 cm tall; pedicel and ovary to 2 cm long, densely hairy. Dorsal sepal elliptic, acute or shortly apiculate, 1.4–1.8 cm long, 1–1.1 cm wide, ciliate, finely shortly hairy on outer surface. Synsepal similar to the dorsal sepal but narrower, 1.4–1.7 cm long, 0.9 cm wide, ciliate, shortly hairy on outer surface. Petals spreading-incurved, elliptic-lanceolate, obtuse, 1.9–2.1 cm long, 0.9 cm wide, sparsely hairy on both surfaces, cili-

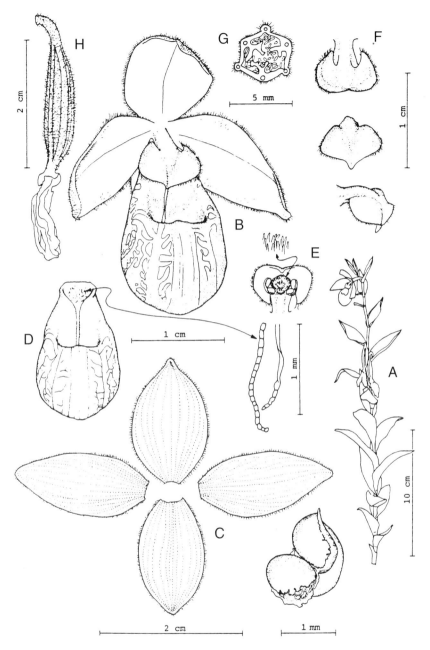

Figure 13. Cypripedium dickinsonianum. A, habit; B, flower from front; C, sepals and petals; D, lip from front; E, column from below; F, staminode, various views; G, ovary cross section; H, fruit. All drawn from the holotype by R. Jiménez.

ate. Lip an inflated obovoid pouch with incurved margins to the mouth, c. 1.9 cm long, 1.2 cm across, with large translucent windows over the surface, hairy within with a dense tuft of hairs at the base; side lobes incurved, blunt. Column short; stalk glabrous; staminode shiny, convex, transversely elliptic or cordiform, shortly apiculate, 0.5 cm long, 0.7 cm wide, ciliate. PLATES 51, 52; FIGURE 13. DISTRIBUTION. Mexico (S. Chiapas only). See map p. 127. HABITAT. In *Juniperus* (juniper) forest; 1500 m. Flowering in late July and August.

6. CYPRIPEDIUM CALIFORNICUM

This elegant orchid is one of the most distinctive in the genus. It usually grows in clumps and each stem can bear up to a dozen charming little flowers with a distinctive white lip shaped like a dove's egg. *Cypripedium californicum* is one of the most restricted species in its distribution, confined to the mountains of southwestern Oregon and northern California, usually at elevations between 450 and 1600 m. There it frequents the margins of mountain streams and damp places in open coniferous woodland and often grows in quite sizeable colonies, a frequent companion being the carnivorous cobra plant, *Darlingtonia californica*.

The individual flowers of *Cypripedium californicum* resemble those of *C. passerinum*, but the latter species is a much smaller plant and always one-flowered. The flowers of *C. californicum* are also distinct in being pubescent on the outer surface of the sepals, having tapering petals and a convex broad staminode. *Cypripedium californicum* is probably most closely related to the Central American species *C. irapeanum* and its allies. It is, however, readily distinguished by its more numerous, smaller flowers with a distinctive colour and all open at the same time.

This pretty orchid was introduced into cultivation in the British Isles before 1890 (Correll 1950), and it can thrive in appropriate conditions grown in a clay pot in a cold frame or alpine house (Dryden pers. comm.). Surprisingly, Correll (1950) quoted the horticulturist Edgar Wherry as saying that there are no records of its successful cultivation in North American gardens up until then.

Cypripedium californicum *A. Gray* in Proc. Amer. Acad. 7: 389 (1868); Correll, Native Orchids North Amer.: 27, t.4 (1950); Luer,

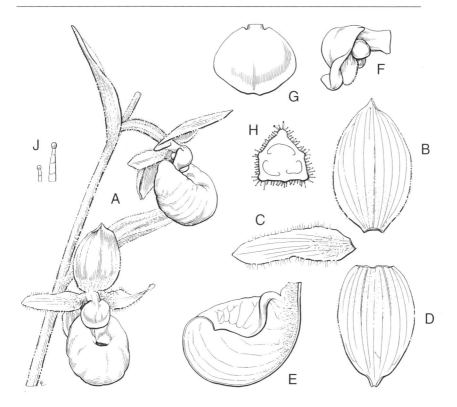

Figure 14. Cypripedium californicum. A, flowers, ×1; B, dorsal sepal, ×2; C, petal, ×2; D, synsepal, ×2; E, lip longitudinal section, ×2; F, column, ×3; G, staminode, ×3; H, ovary transverse section, ×3; J, hairs from ovary, ×20. All drawn from Kew Spirit Collection no. 59736 by Eleanor Catherine.

Native Orchids U.S.A. and Canada: 62, t.11 (1975). Type: U.S.A., California, Mendocino County, *Bolander* 6474 (holo. GH!, iso. BM!, W!).

DESCRIPTION. A clump-forming terrestrial herb 50–120 cm tall, growing from a short stout rhizome. Stems erect, leafy, glandular-pubescent. Leaves 5–10, elliptic to elliptic-lanceolate, acute to acuminate, 5–15 cm long, 2–6 cm wide, pubescent on veins above and below, glandular-ciliate. Inflorescence racemose, laxly four- to twelve-flowered; peduncle and rhachis glandular-pubescent; bracts foliaceous, the largest at the base to 10 cm long, ciliate and pubescent. Flowers developing from the base upwards, small, nutant, with pale yellow-green sepals and petals, and a white lip with yellowish

133

base blotched with brown inside and with lilac lines, the staminode white with green marks, scented like *Cyclamen persicum* or *Convallaria majalis;* pedicel and ovary 1.3–2 cm long, densely shortly glandular-pubescent, the pedicel distinct and slender. Dorsal sepal erect, flat, elliptic-ovate, acute, 1.4–2 cm long, 0.7–1.3 cm wide, pubescent on outer surface, glandular-ciliate; synsepal elliptic, minutely bifid at tip, 1.2–2 cm long, 0.7–1.5 cm wide, pubescent on outer surface, glandular-ciliate. Petals obliquely spreading, lanceolate, acute, 1.4–1.7 cm long, 0.3–0.4 cm wide, pubescent at base and ciliate on upper margin. Lip globose, 1.5–2 cm long, 1–1.4 cm wide, with infolded margins. Column 0.5–0.6 cm long; staminode strongly convex, broadly ovate, obtuse, 0.8–0.9 cm long, 0.6 cm wide; filaments short, blunt. PLATES 5, 41–43; FIGURE 14.

DISTRIBUTION. U.S.A. (California, Oregon).

HABITAT. In wet marshy places by steep mountain streams and by springs, often growing in shade with *Darlingtonia californica* (California pitcher plant) and amongst the *Calocedrus decurrens* (incense cedar); 450–1000 m. Flowering in late May to July.

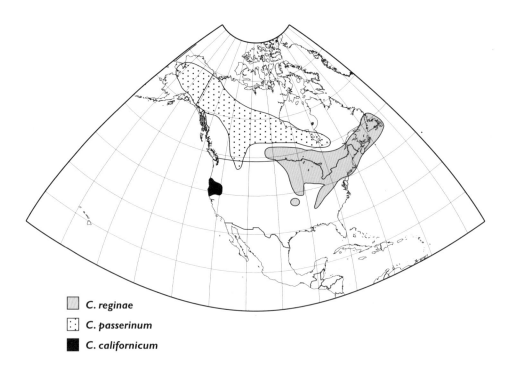

▨ *C. reginae*

▢ *C. passerinum*

■ *C. californicum*

SECTION OBTUSIPETALA

Cypripedium sect. **Obtusipetala** (*Pfitzer*) *Cribb* **stat. nov.** Type species: *C. reginae* Walt.
Cypripedium sect. *Eucypripedium* subsect. *Obtusipetala* Pfitzer in Engler, Pflanzenr. IV, 50 (Heft 12) Orch. Pleonan.: 29 (1903).

Stems elongate, glandular-pubescent, many-leaved; leaves well-spaced on stem, elliptic or ovate, parallel-veined, pubescent; inflorescences usually one-flowered; flowers unicolourous; ovary glandular or villose; lip ovoid, shaped like a dove's egg, glabrous or hairy on outside in basal part, spotted red within; synsepalum present; petals untwisted, oblong or oblong-lanceolate, obtuse; staminode flat or somewhat longitudinally canaliculate, glabrous, spotted or blotched with red or purple.
A section of three species.

7. CYPRIPEDIUM FLAVUM

On four recent visits to southwestern China in 1987, 1990, 1992, and 1996, I have had the opportunity to see large populations of *Cypripedium flavum*, a species endemic to the region and a plant that can still be found in some quantity where it survives. This is the plant referred to by Reginald Farrer (1916, 1925) as "Proud Margaret", a wonderfully evocative name for the clumps of erect stems topped by yellow flowers the size of ping-pong balls.

I remember with particular pleasure seeing this orchid growing in the wild for the first time in 1987 in the Gang Ho Ba valley on the flanks of Yulongxueshan near Lijiang in northwestern Yunnan. I stumbled upon a large colony growing on a grassy bank just below some shrubs at about 3100 m altitude as I entered the valley over the terminal moraine. More than a hundred plants in full flower were scattered over the slope and amongst them were occasional specimens of three other *Cypripedium* species, *C. tibeticum, C. plectrochilum,* and *C. margaritaceum.* In June 1992 I chanced upon a magnificent population growing amongst and on great boulders in one of the valleys of the Min Shan range at Jiuzhaigou in northern Sichuan. Shaded by tall conifers, some of the colonies numbered fifty or more plants in full flower. The flowers of this population were attractively flushed with red on the sepals and petals. Farrer (1925) called these concentrations "sudden outbursts" and that is a fitting description.

Cypripedium flavum is still relatively little known outside China, but it was introduced into cultivation as early as April 1911 by the famous plant collector E. H. Wilson. Despite a six-month journey from China to the Arnold Arboretum in Massachusetts, U.S.A., plants from this introduction flowered for the first time in cultivation on the 6th May 1911 (Wilson 1911). More recently plants have begun to appear in cultivation more frequently, particularly in Japan. It therefore seems timely to reassess the taxonomic history of *C. flavum* and its variability.

This attractive orchid was discovered in June 1869 by the French missionary Père David at Mupin in western Sichuan and was described by the French botanist M. A. Franchet in 1887 as *Cypripedium luteum*. Unfortunately, as pointed out by Peter Hunt and Victor Summerhayes (1966), the name *C. luteum* had already been applied to a North American species by C. S. Rafinesque in 1828. Despite *C. luteum* of Rafinesque now being considered to be a synonym of *C. parviflorum* Salisbury, the Chinese species required a new name, which it was duly given by Hunt and Summerhayes as *C. flavum*.

Cypripedium flavum is an entirely appropriate name for this delightful orchid, one of the most common species in the mountains of western and southwestern China. Its tall hairy stems bear several pubescent elliptic leaves and a single terminal flower with an ellipsoid or globular inflated lip looking rather like a dove's egg. The pale to butter-yellow flower can be variously marked on the segments with red or maroon. In fact, the flowers of this species show a remarkable variation in size, the ground colour of the segments, the degree of marking on the sepals and petals, the spotting on the lip, and the colour of the staminode. Farrer (1925), never one to undersell a plant, remarked on this, noting that the species had

comely round flowers . . . of a clear yellow, with a waxen sulphur lip. The segments are sometimes mottled with a few fleshy stains, the lip is freckled within, and the staminode in some forms, but not in all, is, or goes, of a rich chocolate which gives Proud Margaret her look of well-fed intelligence.

The most common form I have seen, for example, plants near Lijiang in northwestern Yunnan, has pale lemon-yellow flowers with a dark maroon staminode. Occasional plants in that region have flowers with a dorsal sepal and petals that are more or less red- or red-brown-flushed and streaked on the inner surface. The lip is usually pale yellow but occasionally has red or purple spots on the outside near the base. In northern Yunnan around Chungtien (Zhongdian), the red-flushed forms of *Cypripedium flavum* are more frequent. Further north in western Sichuan in the Wolong Reserve set aside to protect the panda, *C. flavum* is a taller plant and has richer yellow flowers with a butter-yellow lip, spotted with maroon on the outside in some specimens. This spectacular form, also with a butter-yellow staminode, is also found in northwestern Sichuan at Jiuzhaigou. However, at Jiuzhaigou and in the nearby valley Huang Long Si, a shorter form with a hooded dorsal sepal flushed with red inside, red-flushed petals, and a pale yellow lip is much more common. In these plants the staminode is commonly dark maroon, but plants with bicoloured maroon and yellow staminodes are not infrequent. Some of these variants are shown in Plates 57 to 60.

The closest ally of *Cypripedium flavum* is probably *C. reginae*, widespread in eastern and central North America, which has flowers of a similar shape but of a pale to rich pink and borne on taller stems. *Cypripedium reginae* is a plant of the margins of marshes and bogs with the roots in fairly neutral soils beneath acid sphagnum moss (Luer 1975). In contrast, *C. flavum* is found in damp woods, woodland margins, and grassland or on rocky boulders, often in limestone regions. These areas, nevertheless, often have rather acidic soils and rhododendrons and other ericaceous plants thrive in the same conditions.

Ernest Wilson (1911) described the species in its habitat around Songpan in northwestern Sichuan as

abundant in thin woods of Spruce and Silver Fir, growing near the margins of certain glacial torrents, which are surcharged with petrifying limestone. Nevertheless, having seen it growing in a variety of soils one would hesitate to say that a calcareous soil is necessary. A cool situation and plenty of leaf soil, would seem the essentials.

The places referred to by Wilson lie in the southern Min Shan mountains, where *Cypripedium flavum* is still to be found in places in

137

some abundance, usually growing with the purple-flowered species *C. franchetii* and *C. smithii,* but also occasionally with the rarer *C. bardolphianum.* The soils in which it grows are shallow and rich in leaf litter but also damp with moisture.

Cypripedium flavum *P.F. Hunt & Summerh.* in Kew Bull. 20: 51 (1966). Type: based on same type as *C. luteum* Franch.
C. luteum Franch. in Nouv. Arch. Mus. Hist. Nat. II, 10: 88 (1887), non *C. luteum* Raf. Type: China, Sichuan, *David* s.n. (holo. P!).

DESCRIPTION. A terrestrial herb with solitary or clustered, erect, shortly pubescent, leafy stems, 17–60 cm long; rhizome stout, short or elongate. Leaves 6–10, well-spaced along the stem, ovate-elliptic to lanceolate-elliptic, acute to acuminate, the largest in the upper part of the stem 9–17.5 cm long, 4.2–12 cm wide, the lowermost three to four sheathing, shortly ciliate, pubescent on both sides. Inflorescence one-flowered; peduncle 3.5–14 cm long, pubescent; bract leafy, lanceolate or elliptic, acute, 4.5–7.9 cm long, 2–2.2 cm wide, pubescent. Flower pale to butter yellow, sometimes flushed with red on the dorsal sepal, petals and/or lip, spotted with maroon inside the lip, sometimes spotted on the outside of lip; pedicel and ovary 3–4 cm long, very pubescent with rusty hairs. Dorsal sepal elliptic- or ovate-oblong, obtuse, (1.6–)3–4.2 cm long, 1.2–3.8 cm wide, shortly ciliate; synsepal elliptic, obtuse, (1.7–)2.8–3.4 cm long, (1–)1.7–2.6 cm wide, glabrous. Petals spreading or recurved, obliquely oblong-lanceolate, obtuse, (1.5–)3.2–3.8 cm long, (0.7–) 1.2–1.5 cm wide, pubescent in basal part only, shortly ciliate. Lip globose-ellipsoidal, (1.8–)2.9–4.7 cm long, with the apical margin acutely infolded. Column 1–1.1 cm long; staminode longitudinally concave, broadly ovate or subcordate, obtuse, 6–6.5 mm long, 5 mm wide, yellow, yellow with black-maroon marked apex, or maroon. PLATES 57–60; FIGURE 15.
DISTRIBUTION. China (SE. Xizang (Tibet), NW. Yunnan, Sichuan, W. Hubei, S. Gansu).
HABITAT. In open woodland and scrub, on the edges of coniferous and mixed coniferous and broadleaf forest and on margins of glacial torrents; 2700–3700 m.

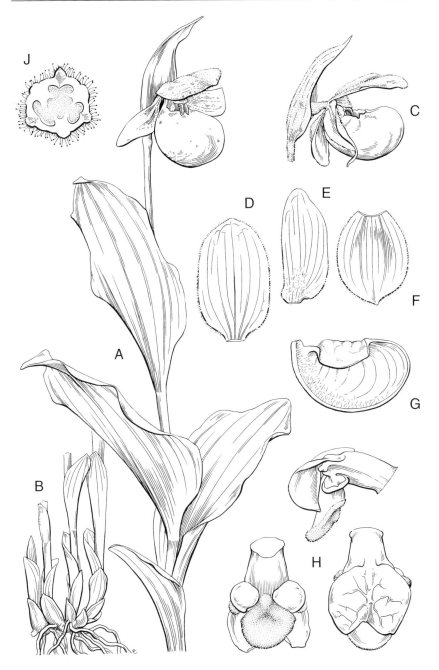

Figure 15. Cypripedium flavum. A, habit, ×0.66; B, base of plant, ×0.66; C, flower, ×0.66; D, dorsal sepal, ×1; E, petal, ×1; F, synsepal, ×1; G, lip longitudinal section, ×1; H, views of column, ×3; J, ovary cross section, ×4. All drawn from Kew Spirit Collection no. 59738 by Eleanor Catherine.

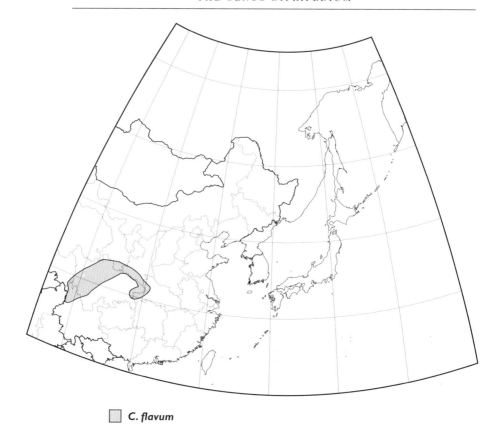

☐ *C. flavum*

8. CYPRIPEDIUM REGINAE

The QUEEN or SHOWY LADY'S SLIPPER ORCHID is one of the most attractive in the genus and a desirable garden plant that has suffered depredation in the wild as a result. Indeed, the earliest record of its cultivation dates back to 1731 when Philip Miller grew it at Chelsea (Brown 1813). However, it was known in Europe much earlier than that having been first named by J. P. Cornut (1635) as "*Calceolus marianus canadensis*". Linnaeus (1753), in the first edition of his *Species Plantarum,* based his *Cypripedium calceolus* var. γ on this early reference and another by Morison (1699). It has been argued by House (1905) that the earliest post-Linnaean name for this species is *C. hirsutum* Miller (1768), based on the fact that Miller stated that the plant "rises to a foot and a half high". In my opinion, the description fits better *C. acaule,* more frequently referred to as the MOCCASIN FLOWER, and having hairy leaves and a "large reddish brown flower marked with a few purple veins", which it usually produces in May. *Cypripedium reginae* usually flowers later.

Cypripedium reginae was first described at specific rank by Walter in 1788 based on his own collection from North Carolina. Walter described the plant as having "flore albo magno". It has been re-described twice since then as *C. spectabile* and *C. album*, both long recognised as synonyms. The type of *C. album* was certainly a plant with white flowers with no trace of the normal pink colouration on the lip. Such plants can be found infrequently in colonies throughout the range. Correll (1950) recorded the species as also found in China, but that report is certainly an error for the closely related *C. flavum*, which when pressed and dried is difficult to distinguish.

This beautiful orchid, considered by many to be the finest in the genus, is the most moisture-loving of all the North American species. Morris and Eames (1929) fetchingly described its habitat at Bonaparte Lake in the Adirondacks: "[W]e went exploring down through the woods till we came to a glorious spring; venturing out a little way into the sphagnum, we suddenly came upon great clumps of the royal flower . . . filling every space about us." In favourable localities, where the plants are left undisturbed, a single plant can exceptionally produce 200 or more flowering stems, truly as spectacular a botanical sight as one could ever hope to see.

The coarse glandular hairs of the stems and leaves have long been known to cause contact dermatitis, similar to that caused by poison ivy, *Rhus toxicodendron* (see MacDougal 1895, Correll 1950). Apparently, the effect increases as the plant matures and reaches its maximum as the capsules are set. This probably protects the plant from predation.

Monstrous flowers in which, for example, the lip is replaced by a petal, have been reported occasionally (Hill 1878, Bastin 1881).

Cypripedium reginae *Walt.*, Fl. Carol.: 222 (1788); Correll, Native Orchids North Amer.: 39, t.10 (1950); Luer, Native Orchids U.S.A. and Canada: 56, t.8 (1975). Type: U.S.A., Carolina, *Walter* (holo. BM!, iso. G!).
C. calceolus L. var. γ L., Sp. Pl. ed.1, 2: 951 (1753). Based on "*Calceolus marianus canadensis*" of J.P.Cornut's *Canadensium Plantarum*

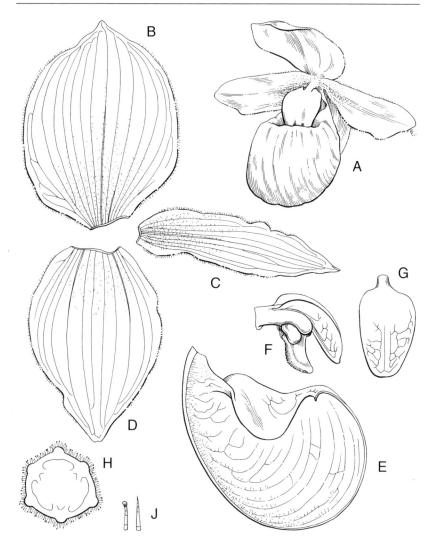

Figure 16. Cypripedium reginae. A, flower, ×0.66; B, dorsal sepal, ×1.5; C, petal, ×1.5; D, synsepal, ×1.5; E, lip longitudinal section, ×1.5; F, column, ×1.5; G, staminode, ×1.5; H, ovary cross section, ×4; J, hairs from ovary, ×20. All drawn from Kew Spirit Collection no. 19473 by Eleanor Catherine.

Historia (1635) and *"Helleborine flore majore purpureo"* of R. Morison's *Plantarum Historia universalis Oxoniensis* (1699).

C. album Aiton, Hort. Kew. 3: 303 (1789). Type: Hort. Kew, *W. Young* (holo. BM!).

C. spectabile Salisb. in Trans. Linn. Soc. 1: 78, t.3, fig.3 (1791). Type: U.S.A., Pennsylvania, *Bartram* (holo. BM!).

C. canadense Mich., Fl. Bor.-Amer. 2: 161 (1803). Types: Canada, *Michaux* (syn. P!) & U.S.A., Alleghenies, near Knoxville, Tennessee, *Michaux* (syn. P!).

C. reginae Walt. var. *album* (Aiton) Rolfe in Orchid Rev. 19: 208 (1911).

Calceolus reginae (Walt.) Nieuwl. in Amer. Midl. Naturalist 3: 117 (1913).

Cypripedium hirsutum Mill. forma *album* (Aiton) Hoffman in Proc. Boston Soc. Nat. Hist. 36: 246 (1922).

DESCRIPTION. A tall erect herb, often forming colonies, with a leafy stem that is glandular hairy, 35–85 cm tall, growing from a short stout rhizome. Leaves strongly ribbed and plicate, three to seven, ovate to elliptic-lanceolate, acute to acuminate, 10–24 cm long, 6–15 cm wide, sheathing at the base, with veins and margins strongly hairy. Inflorescence one- or rarely two- to four-flowered; peduncle villose and glandular hairy; bracts leafy, oblong-elliptic to ovate-lanceolate, 6–13 cm long, 2.5–6 cm wide. Flowers large, showy, white with a rose-pink or rarely a white lip, the staminode white with a yellow margin, spotted with red, in the apical half; pedicel and ovary 3–6 cm long, villose and glandular hairy. Dorsal sepal erect or ascending, flat, elliptic to ovate-orbicular, obtuse or rounded at apex, 3–4.5 cm long, 2.5–4.5 cm wide, hairy on both surfaces, ciliate; synsepal entire, concave, ovate-orbicular, obtuse, 3–4.2 cm long, 2–3.7 cm wide, hairy on outer side, ciliate. Petals spreading oblong to elliptic-lanceolate, obtuse or rounded at apex, 2.5–4.7 cm long, 1–1.7 cm wide, pubescent in basal half of inner surface, glandular-ciliate. Lip subglobose, 2.5–5 cm long, 1.5–3.5 cm across, the margins incurved, longitudinally shallowly furrowed on outer surface. Column 1–1.5 cm long; staminode ovate-trullate, blunt or emarginate, longitudinally concave, 1–1.7 cm long, 0.7–1.4 cm wide; anther filaments blunt, broad, and rounded at apex. PLATES 22, 23, 101, 102; FIGURES 3, 16.

DISTRIBUTION. Canada (Miquelon Island, Nova Scotia, Newfoundland, New Brunswick, Prince Edward Island, Quebec and Ontario across to Saskatchewan), U.S.A. (New England, New York State, New Jersey south to North Carolina and west to Michigan, Wisconsin, Minnesota and North Dakota). See map p. 134.

HABITAT. Found, usually on the margins, in swamps of *Abies* (balsam), *Larix* (tamarack), *Picea* (spruce), *Juniperus* (cedar), or *Thuja* (arborvitae), or in upland bogs and swamps, prairies, meadows, and mossy wooded slopes, often in large colonies of several thousand plants, usually in wet neutral or calcareous soils; sea level to 500 m. Flowering in May to August.

9. CYPRIPEDIUM PASSERINUM

The popular name of this plant is the SPARROW'S-EGG SLIPPER ORCHID, an appropriate one which reflects the small ovoid lip with spotting inside that resembles the spotting of a sparrow's egg. It has also been called FRANKLIN'S SLIPPER ORCHID after Sir John Franklin, the famous Arctic explorer, upon whose expedition the type was collected by Dr. Richardson. It grows further north than any other American species and can be found within the Arctic Circle in northern Canada and Alaska almost reaching the North Shore.

It is related to *Cypripedium reginae,* but is unlikely to be confused with that species, which has much larger flowers that are characteristically flushed with pink on the lip. Catling (1983) reported this species to be self-pollinating.

Frank Morris and Edward Ames (1929) describe its habitat near Jasper in Alaska thus:

The plants were growing on a steep slope beside our trail. Above and beyond them rose rough walls of cliff, overlooking the cotton-wood swamp along whose edge we were walking. The slope was dry and somewhat bare, with only a few scattered trees by way of cover. But there was abundant evidence of springs: the mountain peak was white with snow; poplar and alder flourished a few rods away; the hollows at the cliff-base were filled with sphagnum; and better still, on the sun-baked slope itself, we found Grass-of-Parnassus and some quite sturdy plants of Blunt-leafed Habenaria. Till the end of May at least, these slopes must be well fed with surface springs. The plants [of *C. passerinum*] were very numerous—200 at least.

The
PAINTINGS

Plate 1

Cypripedium acaule   WILLIAM CURTIS

Plate 2

Cypripedium arietinum

MARY GRIERSON

Plate 3

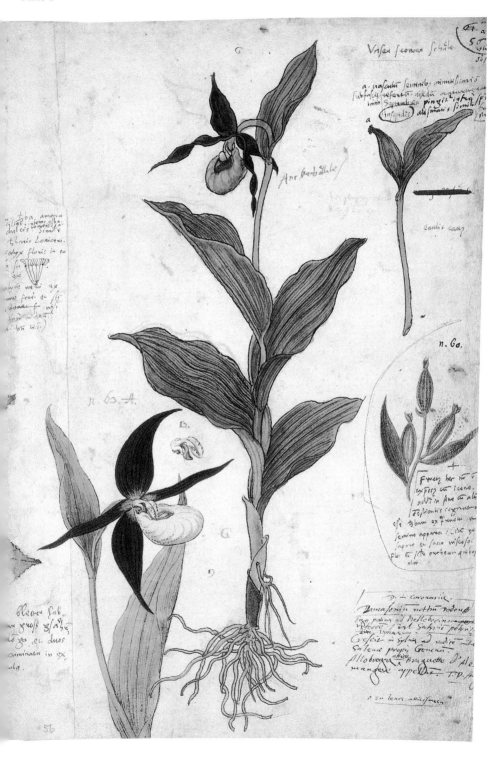

Cypripedium calceolus   CONRAD GESNER

Plate 4

Cypripedium calceolus   FLORENCE WOOLWARD

Plate 5

Cypripedium californicum   MARY BATES

Plate 6

Cypripedium candidum

WALTER FITCH

Plate 7

Cypripedium cordigerum

MARY BATES

Plate 8

Cypripedium debile   MARY BATES

Plate 9

Cypripedium fasciculatum   MATILDA SMITH

Plate 10

Cypripedium formosanum

VALERIE PRICE

Plate 11

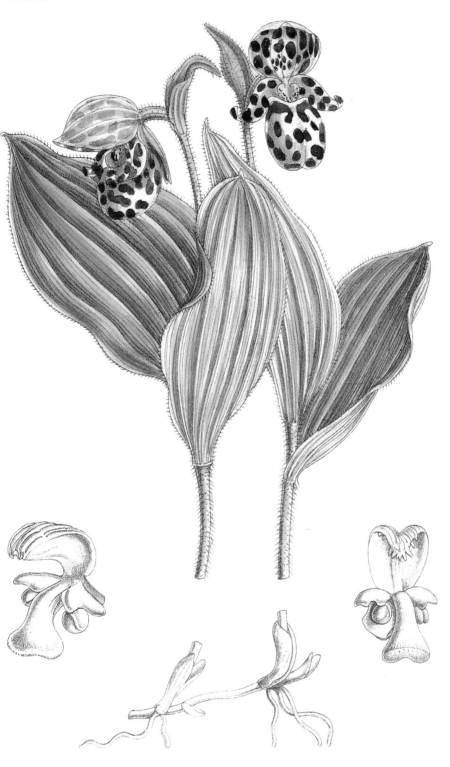

Cypripedium guttatum   MATILDA SMITH

Plate 12

Cypripedium henryi

Plate 13

Cypripedium himalaicum

LILIAN SNELLING

Plate 14

Cypripedium irapeanum

Plate 15

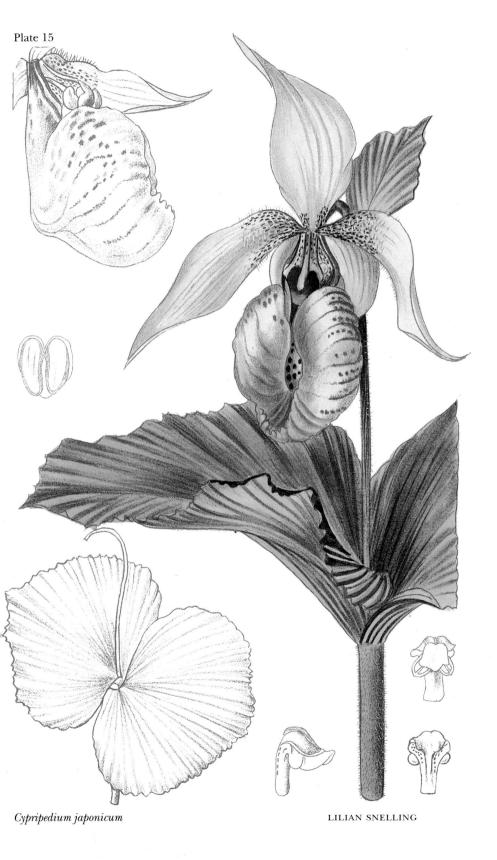

Cypripedium japonicum

LILIAN SNELLING

Plate 16

Cypripedium macranthos

PANDORA SELLARS

Plate 17

Cypripedium macranthos

MARY BATES

Plate 18

Cypripedium macranthos f. *albiflorum*   PANDORA SELLARS

Plate 19

Cypripedium montanum

MATILDA SMITH

Plate 20

Cypripedium parviflorum var. *parviflorum*

MARY BATES

Plate 21

Cypripedium parviflorum var. *pubescens* (top) & *C. calceolus*   MARY BATES

Plate 22

Cypripedium reginae

JAMES SOWERBY

Plate 23

Cypripedium reginae

Plate 24

Cypripedium segawai

SUSIE RAY

Plate 25

Cypripedium tibeticum

MATILDA SMITH

Plate 26

Cypripedium × ventricosum

LILIAN SNELLING

Some of the plants they found had the synsepal split to the base as in *Cypripedium arietinum*. One such plant is illustrated in Correll (1950).

Examination of the type of var. *minganense* suggests that it represents a dwarf ecotype; it does not differ otherwise from the typical variety.

Cypripedium passerinum *Richardson* in Franklin, J. Polar Sea, Bot. Append. quarto ed.2: 762 (1823); Correll, Native Orchids North Amer.: 37, t.9 (1950); Luer, Native Orchids U.S.A. and Canada: 60, t.10 (1975); Case, Orchids Western Great Lakes: 81 (1987). Type: Canada, *Richardson* (holo. BM!, iso. AMES!, K!).
C. passerinum Richardson var. *minganense* Vict. in Proc. & Trans. Roy. Soc. Canada III, 22: 168, t.1–3 (1929). Type: Canada, Quebec, Mingan Islands, Île Nue, *Marie-Victorin & Rolland-Germain* 24332 (holo. MT, iso. GH!, K!, P!).

DESCRIPTION. A small erect herb with villose pubescent leafy stems 12–38 cm tall arising from a short stout creeping rhizome. Leaves three to five, obviously pleated, elliptic, ovate-lanceolate or elliptic-lanceolate, obtuse to acute, 5–16 cm long, 1.5–5 cm wide, pubescent on both sides, ciliate, sheathing at the base and subtended by two sheaths. Inflorescence one- or rarely two-flowered; peduncle 7–12 cm long, villose-pubescent; bract erect, ovate-lanceolate to elliptic, acute, 3–8 cm long, 1–2 cm wide, pubescent. Flower small, the size of a small dove's egg, with pale green or yellow-green sepals, white petals and a white lip, spotted inside with purple, the staminode white with a yellow apex spotted with purple; pedicel and ovary densely villose, pedicel distinct. Dorsal sepal hooded over lip, orbicular to orbicular-ovate, shortly apiculate, 1.5–2 cm long, 1–1.5 cm wide, pubescent on outer surface and ciliate; synsepal appressed to lip, elliptic-orbicular, bifid at apex, 1–1.5 cm long, 1–1.3 cm wide, ciliate, the lateral sepals sometimes free to base. Petals flat, spreading-decurved, linear-oblong, rounded at apex, 1.2–2 cm long, 0.3–0.4 cm wide. Lip small, obovoid-subglobose, 1.2–2 cm long, 0.8–1 cm across, glandular within and outside at the base. Column short; staminode ovate-cordate to ovate-oblong, retuse at apex, longitudinally grooved, 0.6 cm long, 0.4–0.5 cm wide. PLATES 97, 98; FIGURE 17.

DISTRIBUTION. Canada (Quebec, Ontario, and Manitoba across to British Colombia and the Yukon), U.S.A. (Montana, Alaska). See map p. 134.

145

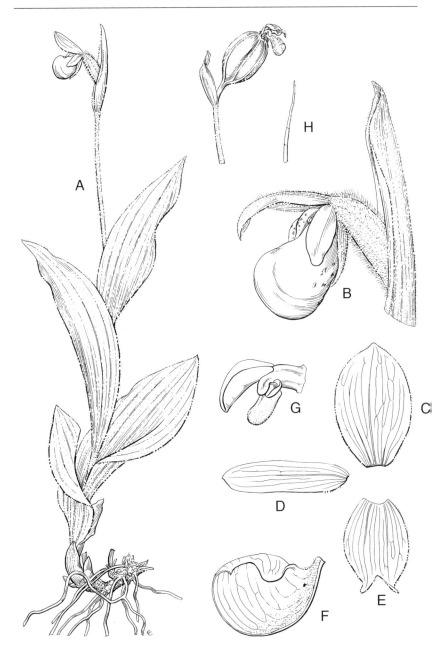

Figure 17. Cypripedium passerinum. A, habit, ×0.5; B, flower, ×2; C, dorsal sepal, ×2; D, petal, ×2; E, synsepal, ×2; F, lip longitudinal section, ×2; G, column, ×3; H, hair from ovary, ×15; fruit, ×0.66. All drawn from *Williams* 1584 by Eleanor Catherine.

HABITAT. Usually found in rich moist coniferous woodlands, in deep ravines, in tundra, and on the edges of streams and lakes, on gravel outwashes, dunes, and talus slopes, usually on neutral or acidic soils, in limestone gravel, moderately acid coniferous humus (Correll 1950), or sphagnum (Morris and Eames 1929); to 2200 m in British Colombia. Flowering in June and early July.

SECTION CYPRIPEDIUM

Stems clustered, short to elongate, pubescent, with three or more leaves; leaves well-spaced on stem, lanceolate, ovate, or elliptic, pubescent, parallel-veined; inflorescences erect, one- to three-flowered; ovary glandular hairy or with multicellular trichomes or rarely glabrous; lip ovoid or obovoid, with marked side lobes; synsepal present; petals linear and tapering to apex and often spirally twisted; staminode oblong, ovate, cordate or trullate, flat, conduplicate or canaliculate, glabrous, often spotted in the apical half with red or purple.

A section of 18 species in two subsections.

SECTION CYPRIPEDIUM
SUBSECTION CYPRIPEDIUM

Cypripedium sect. **Cypripedium** subsect. **Cypripedium**. Type species: *C. calceolus* L.

Stems elongate, with three or more leaves; leaves pleated, green, pubescent; inflorescences one- to three-flowered; ovary hexagonal in cross section, densely clothed with short glandular hairs; lip yellow, green, or white, ellipsoidal to obovoid, may be slightly bilaterally or dorsiventrally compressed; the dorsal sepal similar to the synsepalum, the latter being only slightly bifid at the apex; petals linear-tapering, spreading, eciliate, usually spirally twisted to some degree, borne more or less at an angle of 45° below horizontal; staminode linear, oblong, obovate or trullate, yellow, green, or white, usually spotted with red or purple, longitudinally somewhat conduplicate, concave in the apical part.

A subsection of 11 closely related species.

147

Specific delimitation within this group has been problematic, with few species having marked morphological characters that allow them to be easily identified. This is particularly true of herbarium material where provenance, ecological information, and good flower colour notes are needed in many cases to allow certain identification. A few species, such as the Himalayan *Cypripedium cordigerum* and the Chinese *C. fasciolatum* and *C. farreri* are relatively readily recognised. However, the complex of taxa around *C. calceolus*, including the North American yellow-lipped *C. parviflorum* and *C. kentuckiense*, the white-lipped *C. candidum* and *C. montanum*, and the Asiatic *C. henryi*, *C. segawai*, and *C. shanxiense*, have proved taxonomically intransigent and have received varying treatments by different authors. Discussion of the problems can be found under each taxon of the complex treated here.

10. CYPRIPEDIUM CALCEOLUS

The LADY'S SLIPPER ORCHID of Europe is one of the best known and most widely illustrated of all flowering plants. The earliest record of this fine orchid is Gesner's fine watercolour illustration of 1541, which was sadly not published until the eighteenth century by Camerarius. The LADY'S-SLIPPER ORCHID was first reported as a native European plant by the herbalists Dodoens (1568, 1583), L'Obel (1576), and Clusius (1583). The fine woodcuts in their works are an immediately recognisable likeness, so much so that they were reproduced many times over the succeeding years, Dodoens's appearing unchanged in John Gerard's herbal of 1597.

Linnaeus named *Cypripedium calceolus* in his *Species Plantarum*, the species selected as the type of the genus, based on Dodoens's "*Calceolus marianus*". A detailed discussion of its typification is provided by Baumann et al. (1989). Their selection of a lectotype (Dodoens, *Fl. coron. hist.*: 77, 1568) is mistaken because it is not cited by Linnaeus. The citation by Jarvis et al. (1993) of Dodoens, *Stirpium Historiae Pemptades* ed.2: 180, f.1 (1616) is correct.

Cypripedium calceolus is one of the most widely distributed of all species, ranging from Spain, the British Isles, and Scandinavia in western Europe across to northeastern China, eastern Siberia, and Sakhalin Island. It may also occur on Honshu in Japan (Masamune 1987). In Europe, it is a widespread plant but, in parts of its range,

148

its beauty has proved costly because it has been dug up in quantity by gardeners and botanists. In Greece it is now extinct and is an endangered plant in several other countries, the best-documented case being that of England where a single plant has persisted in splendid but sad isolation in Yorkshire for more than 60 years. Nevertheless, in parts of central and northern Europe and Asia it can still be seen in some numbers in suitable habitats, but in most of these it needs the protection of the law and of local enthusiasts, who guard it carefully.

In its more sizeable populations, the variability of this species can be assessed. Many variants have received taxonomic recognition at both specific and infraspecific rank. Keller and Sóo (1930) have recognised the following variants, mostly either at the rank of variety or form:

- subvar. *album* with a white perianth
- var. *atsmori* with narrow leaves and narrow sepals; dubiously distinct
- forma *biflorum* with two flowers
- forma *flavum* with a yellow perianth
- forma *fulvum* with yellow flowers washed with "rouille"
- var. *helveticum* dubiously distinct
- forma *ochroleucum* with brown-purple sepals and petals and a pale yellow-white lip
- forma *triflorum* with three flowers
- forma *variegatum* with the bracts spotted with brown
- forma *viridiflorum* with green or greenish sepals and petals
- forma *viridifuscum* with yellow-green flowers spotted and streaked with purple

Camus (1929) listed most of these, but I feel that, if at all, they should, by and large, be recognised at the rank of form. Despite this variation, *C. calceolus* is much less variable than its North American relatives, such as *C. parviflorum* and *C. kentuckiense*.

Until recently, the North American yellow-lipped slipper orchids have been included by most authors within *Cypripedium calceolus*, either at subspecific or varietal rank. Atwood (1985), however, considered the North American plants to be distinct species from the Eurasian one. Bergstroem et al. (1992) have shown that the floral fragrance spectrum of *C. calceolus* is distinct from that of *C. parviflorum* var. *parviflorum* and var. *pubescens*. Molecular data from Cox

149

(1995) supports this, suggesting that *C. calceolus* may be closer to its Asiatic allies, *C. henryi* and *C. segawai*, than to the North American ones. I have therefore followed Atwood here. *Cypripedium calceolus* can be relatively easily distinguished from them by its dark maroon sepals and petals, the latter being 3.5–6 cm long and only moderately twisted, the obovate white staminode, which is U-shaped in cross-section rather than V-shaped, and the small lip.

Most of the several synonyms listed here are superfluous names based on *Cypripedium calceolus* and/or its pre-Linnaean names. Morren described *C. atsmori* in 1851 and its identity has remained somewhat enigmatic, the epithet having been taken from the Japanese. However, the illustration that accompanied the description is certainly of *C. calceolus*, which is recorded only from Rebun Island off the coast of Japan, the nearest other localities being in Sakhalin and on the adjacent Asian mainland.

The name *Cypripedium microsaccos* has been the cause of some confusion since Kränzlin described it in 1913. The type specimen in the St. Petersburg herbarium has been carefully examined by Perner (pers. comm.), and I have seen a colour photograph of it. It has a yellow lip and undoubtedly represents a small-lipped form of *C. calceolus*. Unfortunately, *C. microsaccos* has been used for plants now referable to *C. shanxiense*, which has flowers of a similar size to the type specimen of *C. microsaccos* but of a different colour, the lip being bronze coloured.

Cypripedium calceolus *L.*, Sp. Pl. ed.1, 2: 951 (1753); Keller and Sóo, Feddes Rep. Sp. Nov. Sonderb. A: 11 (1930). Lectotype: Dodoens, Stirp. hist. pempt., ed. 2: 180, fig.1 (1616).
Calceolus marianus Crantz, Stirp. Austr. Fasc. 6: 454 (1769), *nom. superfl.*
Cypripedium boreale Salisb., Prodr.: 10 (1796), *nom. superfl.*
C. ferrugineum Gray in Nat. Arr. Brit. Pl. 2: 203 (1821), *nom. superfl.*
C. atsmori C. Morren in Belg. Hort. 1: 171, t.21 (1851). Type: Japan, *Siebold*, cult. Jardin Botanique Gand (illustration cited here).
Cypripedilum calceolus Asch., Fl. Brandenberg: 700 (1864), sphalm. pro *Cypripedium calceolus.*
Cypripedium cruciatum Dulac, Fl. Hautes-Pyrénées: 128 (1867). Type: France, *Saint-Amans* (not located).
Calceolus alternifolium St.-Lag. in Ann. Soc. Bot. Lyon 7: 62, 124 (1880), *nom. superfl.*
Cypripedilon marianus (Crantz) Rouy in J. Bot. (Morot) 8: 58 (1894).

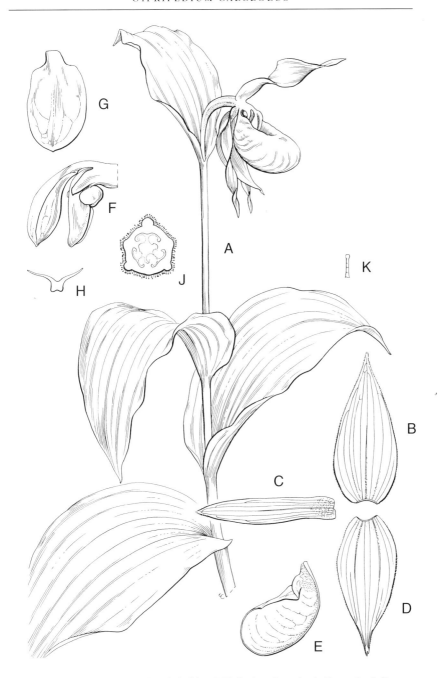

Figure 18. Cypripedium calceolus. A, habit, ×0.66; B, dorsal sepal, ×1; C, petal, ×1; D, synsepal 1; E, lip longitudinal section, ×1; F, column, ×2; G, staminode, ×2; H, staminode transverse section, ×2; J, ovary transverse section, ×4; K, gland from ovary, ×30. All drawn from cult. Kew s.n. by Eleanor Catherine.

C. calceolus L. var. *atsmori* (C. Morren) Pfitzer in Engler, Pflanzenr. IV, 50 (Heft 12) Orch. Pleonan.: 37 (1903). *C. microsaccos* Kränzl. in J. Russe Bot. 1913: 54 (1913). Type: Siberia, *Palczewsky* s.n. (holo. LE, photo of holo.!).

DESCRIPTION. A terrestrial herb 15–60 cm tall, with a short stout creeping rhizome and fibrous roots, often forming clumps. Erect stems glandular-pubescent, terete, leafy above. Leaves three to four, suberect-spreading, strongly pleated, often with upcurved sides, elliptic to ovate, rarely lanceolate, acute to acuminate, 6–18 cm long, 3–9 cm wide, green. Inflorescence one- or less commonly two-flowered; bracts leaf-like, lanceolate to ovate or elliptic-ovate, acuminate, 1–6 cm long. Flowers showy, the sepals and petals maroon or rarely green, the lip yellow spotted within with red, the staminode yellow spotted with red; pedicel and ovary c. 3 cm long, shortly glandular-pubescent. Dorsal sepal suberect, elliptic-lanceolate or ovate, acuminate, 3.5–5 cm long, 1.5–2 cm wide, rarely slightly twisted towards apex, ciliate. Synsepal elliptic-lanceolate or lanceolate, acuminate and bidenticulate at apex, 3.5–5 cm long, 1.5–1.8 cm wide, the sides recurved somewhat, ciliate. Petals deflexed at c. 45° to horizontal, spirally twisted one to three times, linear-tapering, acute or acuminate, 3.5–6.5 cm long, 0.5–0.7 cm wide, pubescent at base within. Lip glossy, ellipsoidal to obovoid, 3–5.3 cm long, 2.5–3 cm wide, the margins smoothly incurved with a fold at the base on each side. Column c. 1 cm long; staminode shortly stalked, longitudinally channelled, slightly concave at apex, obovate with a cordate base, blunt, 1–1.2 cm long, 0.7–0.9 cm wide; filament extending beyond anthers, acute. PLATES 3, 4, 21, 35–40, 118; FIGURES 1, 2, 4, 18.

DISTRIBUTION. Europe (from northern England and Scandinavia, eastern France, NE. Spain, Germany, N. Italy and N. Greece (now extinct)) and eastern Europe eastward to European Russia, Siberia, N. Sakhalin, Korea, NE. China (Heilongjiang, Jilin, Nei Monggol), and Japan (Rebun Isl., *fide* S. Kawahara pers. comm.).

HABITAT. In partial shade in open woodland and scrub under conifers, species of *Quercus* (oak), *Fraxinus* (ash), and *Corylus* (hazel), in lime-rich soils over limestone, rarely in full sunlight at higher elevations; sea level to 2500 m. Perner (pers. comm.) reports that in eastern Siberia it is found growing in neutral or slightly acidic (pH 6) conditions.

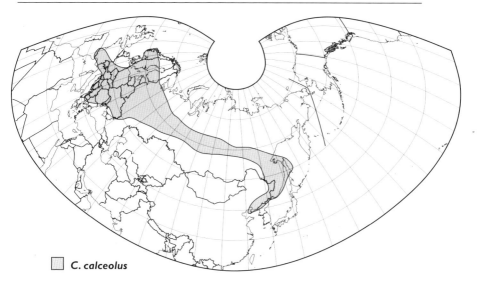

☐ *C. calceolus*

11. CYPRIPEDIUM HENRYI

Cypripedium henryi and *C. segawai* have appeared in cultivation in increasing numbers in recent years and have been confused with each other. *Cypripedium henryi* was described by Robert Rolfe in 1892 based on a collection made by Augustine Henry under the number 5391. In fact, Henry made four separate collections, each from a different locality, under this number, and these are distinguished by the suffixes A to D. The specimen used by Rolfe as a type appears to have been *Henry* 5391A from Hubei Province, China, which has the additional annotation "= *Henry* 5391". Two years later M. A. Franchet described *C. chinense* based on three collections, *Henry* 5391C and D and *Farges* 1036. These do not differ from *C. henryi*, and it could be argued that Rolfe's citation of *Henry* 5391 as the type of *C. henryi* includes all Henry's collections under that number. Therefore, Franchet's *C. chinense* is a superfluous name for this species.

Cypripedium henryi resembles superficially the widespread *C. calceolus*, but can be readily distinguished by its usually two- or three-flowered inflorescence, smaller green or yellow-green flowers, untwisted petals, small glossy lip, and anther filaments that are not covered by the staminode. Its distinction from the Taiwanese *C. segawai* is given under that species.

Cypripedium henryi is named after the Irish botanist Augustine

153

Henry, one of the most prolific but little-known collectors in China. At the time he collected this species, Henry was employed as an assistant medical officer by the Chinese Maritime Customs based, between 1882 and 1889, at Ichang in Hubei Province at the lower end of the famed Yangtse Gorges. His relative eclipse from fame by Wilson and the rest lies in his concentration upon collecting herbarium specimens rather than living material.

Cypripedium henryi *Rolfe* in Bull. Misc. Inform. Kew 1892: 211 (1892) and in Gard. Chron. III, 12: 364 (1892). Type: China, Hubei, *Henry* 5391 A (holo. K!, iso. AMES!, BM!, E!).
C. chinense Franch. in J. Bot. (Morot) 8: 230 (1894). Types: China, Sichuan, *Farges* 1036 (syn. P!, isosyn. K!), *Henry* 5391C (syn. P!, isosyn. AMES!, BM!, K!) and Hubei, *Henry* 5391D (syn. P!, isosyn. AMES!, BM!, E!, K!).

DESCRIPTION. A terrestrial herb 30–55 cm tall, with clustered pubescent stems. Leaves four to five, elliptic to elliptic-lanceolate, acuminate, ciliate, 10–21 cm long, 4.6–8.5 cm wide, glabrous above and below, subtended by three sheaths. Inflorescence usually two- to three-flowered; peduncle glandular-pubescent; bracts lanceolate, acuminate, 4.5–11 cm long, 1–3 cm wide, ciliate. Flowers entirely greenish yellow, green or yellow with a glossy yellow lip marked with red on the veins within and towards the base; ovary 2.5–4 cm long, densely glandular hairy. Dorsal sepal lanceolate, acuminate, 3.2–4.5 cm long, 1–1.5 cm wide; synsepal ovate, bifid and acuminate at the apex, 3.3–4 cm long, 1–1.5 cm wide. Petals not twisted, linear-lanceolate, acuminate, 3.7–5 cm long, 0.5–0.8 cm wide, pubescent on the mid-rib of the outer surface, villose at base on inner surface. Lip ellipsoidal, indented on main veins, 1.5–2.7 cm long, 1.4–1.7 cm in diameter, and a small orifice; side lobes obliquely oblong. Column 6–9 mm long; stigma oblong, obtuse, obscurely papillose; staminode stalked, oblong-elliptic, obtuse or slightly apiculate, 6–7 mm long, conduplicate with the lateral margins incurved somewhat, yellow or green with red marks towards the apex. PLATES 12, 67, 68; FIGURE 19.
    DISTRIBUTION. W. China (Guizhou, NW. Yunnan, Sichuan, Hubei, S. Gansu, S. Shaanxi). See map p. 161.
    HABITAT. In deciduous and mixed deciduous woods and on scrubby slopes and grassland; 1800–2800 m.

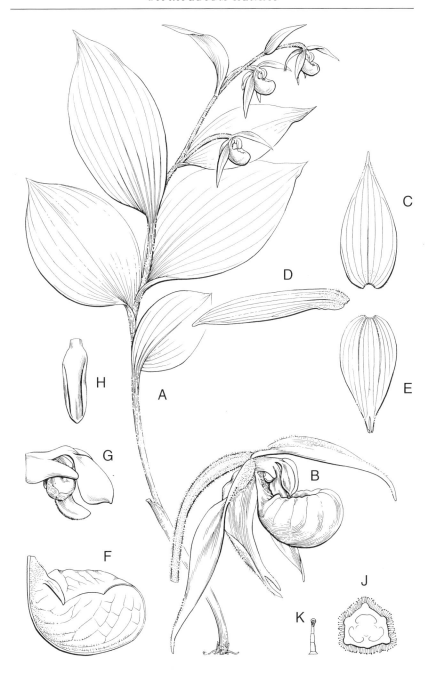

Figure 19. Cypripedium henryi. A, habit, ×0.33; B, flower, ×1.5; C, dorsal sepal, ×1; D, petal, ×1; E, synsepal, ×1; F, lip longitudinal section, ×2; G, column, ×3; H, staminode, ×3; J, ovary transverse section, ×5; K, hair from ovary, ×20. All drawn from *Chien* 5552 by Eleanor Catherine.

155

12. CYPRIPEDIUM SEGAWAI

I have received photographs of cultivated plants from Switzerland, Sweden, and the British Isles of yellow-flowered slipper orchids over several years and these have either been unidentified or named as *Cypripedium segawai* or *C. henryi*. The former name puzzled me because, in the standard *Flora of Taiwan* account (Su 1978) and in Chen and Xi (1987), it has been considered a synonym of the well-known *C. macranthos* whilst, in a more popular account (Ying 1977), it was treated as a variety of *C. guttatum*, a species not known to occur in Taiwan. In contrast, *C. henryi* is a relatively well-known and well-defined species from western China, the stamping ground of many famous plant hunters such as Ernest Wilson, George Forrest, and Reginald Farrer.

When he described *Cypripedium segawai*, Masamune compared it with *C. guttatum*, which is characterised by having two leaves and a distinctive white flower heavily blotched with purple or brown and with an urceolate lip. *Cypripedium segawai* is by no means closely related and it seems likely that Masamune was misled by the single-flowered inflorescence and lip which is sometimes finely spotted with red. *Cypripedium segawai* differs markedly from *C. guttatum* in many features, including having more leaves and a predominantly yellow flower with an almost globose lip, trullate staminode, and glandular-pubescent ovary. Nevertheless, Ying (1977) reduced *C. segawai* to varietal status within *C. guttatum*. This is puzzling because, in 1969, Masamune had published a drawing of *C. segawai* together with a floral dissection. It seems likely that this had escaped Ying's notice.

Cypripedium segawai has also been reduced into the synonymy of *C. macranthos* by Su (1975, 1978). It differs, however, in many features, notably flower size and colour, lip shape and the lack of a pinched margin on the lip orifice, in petal and staminode shape, and in its glandular hairy ovary.

Cypripedium segawai is most closely allied to the Chinese species *C. henryi*, both being related to the widespread *C. calceolus*. Like *C. henryi*, it has greenish yellow flowers with a small lip and linear-lanceolate untwisted petals, but it differs in being usually a smaller plant with a one- or, less commonly, two-flowered inflorescence. The larger flower usually has yellow or greenish yellow sepals and petals and a bright yellow lip, the latter occasionally being finely spotted with red. The margin of the orifice of the lip is often toothed.

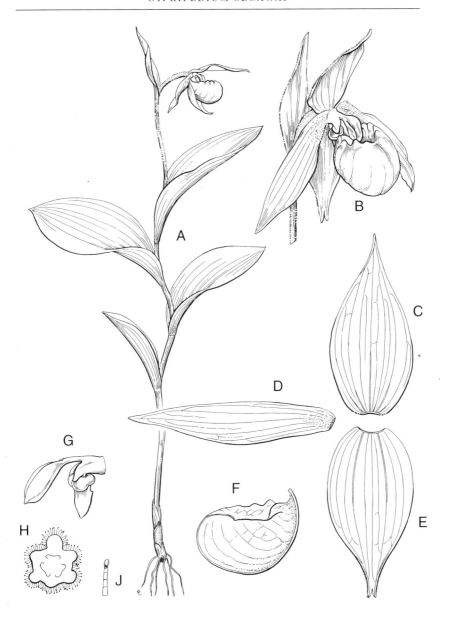

Figure 20. Cypripedium segawai. A, habit, ×0.33; B, flower, ×1; C, dorsal sepal, ×1.5; D, petal, ×1.5; E, synsepal, ×1.5; F, lip longitudinal section, ×1.5; G, column, ×2; H, ovary transverse section, ×4; J, hair from ovary, ×30. All drawn from cult. Kew s.n. by Eleanor Catherine.

I have only located two herbarium collections of *Cypripedium segawai*, one in Japan and the other in Taiwan. It seems likely, therefore, that the species is rare in the wild in its native Taiwan, made more so because wild plants have been exported in some quantity and can be currently found in collection in Japan, the United States, and Europe.

Cypripedium segawai *Masam.* in Trop. Hort. 3: 31 (1933) *nomen;* in Trans. Nat. Hist. Soc. Formosa 23: 209 (1933); and in J. Geobot. 17(3): t.152 (1969). Type: Taiwan, *Segawa* s.n. (holo. TIU!).
C. guttatum Sw. var. *segawai* (Masam.) Ying, Coloured Ill. Indig. Orch. Taiwan 1: 442 (1977).

DESCRIPTION. A terrestrial herb with erect, leafy, glandular, pubescent stems. Leaves suberect, three to four, elliptic-lanceolate, acute, 5–10 cm long, 1.5–3 cm wide, pubescent on both surfaces, subtended at base by one to two sheathing bracts. Inflorescence one-flowered; peduncle slender, elongate, glandular-pubescent, to 12 cm long; bract leaf-like, lanceolate, 2.5–3.5 cm long. Flower small for the genus, with yellow or yellow-green sepals and petals and a yellow lip, rarely finely spotted with red; pedicel and ovary glandular-pubescent. Dorsal sepal lanceolate, acuminate, 2–4 cm long, 0.8–1.4 cm wide, glabrous; synsepal ovate, shortly bifid at apex, 1.8–3.5 cm long, 1.1–1.6 cm wide, glabrous. Petals untwisted, linear-lanceolate, acuminate, 2.3–4 cm long, 0.6–0.8 cm wide, densely pubescent at base on inner side. Lip small, subglobose, 2–2.5 cm long, 1.5–1.7 cm wide, with a very small mouth often edged by teeth. Column 6–7 mm long; staminode trullate, obtuse, 0.6–0.7 cm long, conduplicate and deeply concave in apical half, yellow spotted with red. PLATES 24, 103, 104; FIGURE 20.
DISTRIBUTION. Taiwan only. See map p. 161.
HABITAT. In montane forest of *Juniperus formosana* (Taiwan juniper). Flowering in late March to late April.

13. CYPRIPEDIUM SHANXIENSE

Cypripedium shanxiense is a rather drab species clearly allied to *C. henryi* and *C. segawai* with which it shares the pubescent ovary, staminode structure, and linear untwisted or scarcely twisted petals and small lip. According to Chen in the original description (1983), it differs in having smaller purple or purplish flowers, a brown-spotted purple staminode, and capsules that are glabrescent at maturity. In the latter, at least, I suspect that it does not differ from its allies. It also has a rather wider, untoothed, smooth mouth to the lip. These differences are small, and the species' relationship to *C. henryi* needs investigation. The type collection by K. Liou was made in Shanxi Province, after which the species has been named. However, the species is much more widely distributed across northern China, Korea, and far eastern Russia.

I have recently examined material collected by Holger Perner and photographs of plants from the vicinity of Vladivostok, which confirm the species' presence in Russia. The flowers range from ochre to deep dull bronze with characteristic greenish tips to the sepals and petals. Perner found scattered plants growing in mesic deciduous woodland of *Quercus mongolica*, with *Cypripedium macranthos, C. calceolus*, and *C. guttatum* in the vicinity (Perner and Averyanov 1995). The dull colouring of *C. shanxiense* makes it difficult to find plants in the lush woodland and, consequently, the species has been undercollected. It seems certain that it has been reported from this region by Russian botanists under the name *C. microsaccos;* the type specimen of *C. microsaccos*, which has a short globose rather than ellipsoidal lip, is referable to *C. calceolus.*

Coloured photographs of plants published by Slyusarenko (1981) from Sakhalin Island and by Kanda (1984) from Hokkaido in Japan seem to me to be referable to *Cypripedium shanxiense*, thereby extending the range of the species considerably. I have not, so far, been able to trace herbarium specimens from these islands. If these illustrations do indeed represent *C. shanxiense*, and they fit nothing else, then the flower colour of this species is purplish brown with darker veins on the lip and other segments. The purplish brown seems to overlay a yellow base. The staminode is brownish yellow with red spotting. The petals are spreading at perhaps 20° below horizontal and are half twisted rather than truly flat.

Cypripedium shanxiense is self-pollinating in Primorsky, E. Siberia, according to Averyanov and Perner (pers. comm.), the pollen being like treacle and oozing onto the stigma. All flowers set seed in the specimens examined by them.

Cypripedium shanxiense *S.C. Chen* in Acta Phytotax. Sin. 21(3): 8 (1983); Perner and Averyanov in Die Orchidee 46: 196 (1995).

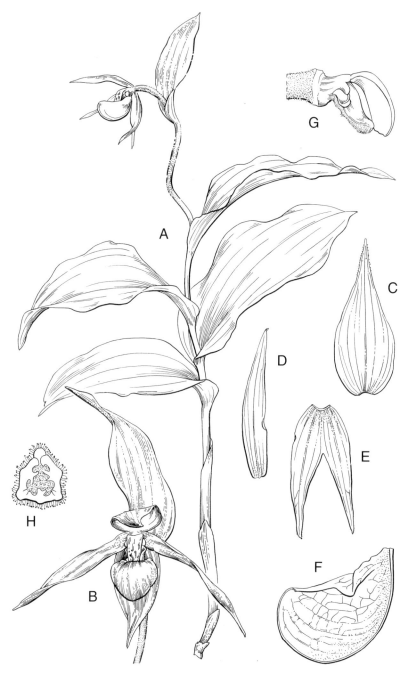

Figure 21. Cypripedium shanxiense. A, habit, ×0.5; B, flower, ×1; C, dorsal sepal, ×1; D, petal, ×1; E, synsepal, ×1; F, lip longitudinal section, ×1.5; G, column, ×2; H, ovary transverse section, ×4. All drawn from *Perner* s.n. by Eleanor Catherine.

160

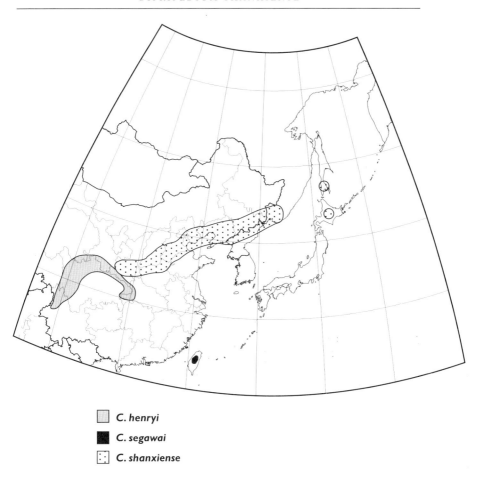

C. henryi
C. segawai
C. shanxiense

Type: China, Shanxi, Qin Yuan, *K.M. Liou* 1423 (holo. PE!, photo of holo. K!).
C. microsaccos auct. non Kränzl.
C. indet.: Slyusarenko in Amer. Orchid Soc. Bull. 50: 779 (1981).
C. calceolus var. *parviflorum* sensu Kanda, Wild Orchids Japan: t.49–51 (1984).

DESCRIPTION. A terrestrial herb 40–55 cm tall with an erect pubescent stem, covered below by three to five sheaths each 2–6 cm long. Leaves three to four, sheathing at the base, elliptic to ovate-lanceolate, acuminate, 7–15 cm long, 4–8 cm wide, somewhat pubescent to glabrescent at the base on the underside, ciliate. Inflorescence one- to three-flowered but usually two-flowered; peduncle and rhachis pubescent; bracts leaf-like, 5.5–10 cm long, 1–3(-4) cm wide, with pilose veins on both surfaces. Flowers brown, purple or purplish, small, about 4 cm across; pedicle and ovary 3.5–5 cm long, densely glandular-pubescent. Dorsal sepal lanceolate, more or less cordate-acuminate, 3–3.5 cm long, 1 cm wide; synsepal subsimilar but shorter, 2.5–3 cm long, bifid at apex, the free tips 5–10 mm long. Petals untwisted, narrowly lanceolate or linear-lanceolate, acuminate, 3–3.5 cm long, 0.4 cm wide, almost glabrous. Lip small, subglobose, 1.6–2 cm long, c. 1.3 cm across, hirsute within towards the base, the side lobes inflexed, subtriangular. Column short; anthers subglobose, with slender 1–2 mm long curved filaments; staminode purple with brown-purple spotting in the basal part, oblong-elliptic, biauriculate at base, subacute and more or less mucronate, c. 0.7 cm long, 0.35 cm wide. PLATES 105, 106; FIGURE 21.

DISTRIBUTION. China (Shanxi, Hubei, Ningxia, Gansu, Qinghai). Possibly also in Japan (Hokkaido) and Russia (Sakhalin Island).

HABITAT. In somewhat shaded places in deciduous and mixed deciduous woodland and in grassland; sea level to 2500 m. Flowering in May and June.

14. CYPRIPEDIUM CORDIGERUM

Cypripedium cordigerum was described by David Don in 1825 based on a collection made by Nathaniel Wallich in Nepal. Jacquemont collected the species several times between 1829 and 1832 during his Indian travels, and an excellent illustration is given in Decaisne's account of Jacquemont's collections.

The distribution of *Cypripedium cordigerum* extends from one end of the Himalayas in northern Pakistan through Kashmir, northern India, Nepal, and southernmost Xizang (Tibet) to Bhutan, where its local name is "dyuma". Although French botanist M. A. Franchet reported it from Abbé Delavay's collections in western Yunnan, examination of those collections has failed to confirm the report.

Cypripedium cordigerum is readily distinguished from other Asiatic species by its distinctive green and white flower borne solitary at the apex of a long, glandular peduncle, the linear-tapering petals that are untwisted, the synsepal that has its apex deeply divided into two slender tapering tips, and the dorsal sepal that is usually a third longer than the synsepal.

As with many *Cypripedium* species, flower size is variable and occasionally plants produce tiny flowers with the sepals and petals less than 2 cm long and the lip only 1 cm long.

Cypripedium cordigerum *D. Don,* Prodr. Fl. Nepal.: 37 (1825); Duthie in Ann. Bot. Gard. Calcutta 9: 203, t.151 (1906); Summerh. in Bot. Mag. 157: t.9364 (1934). Type: Nepal, *Wallich* (holo. K!).

DESCRIPTION. A terrestrial herb 22–60 cm tall, growing from a very short stout rhizome. Stems solitary, slender to stout, to 55 cm long, 3–8 mm in diameter, increasingly pubescent and glandular from the base upwards, with three to four tubular sheaths at the base and two to five leaves well-spaced along its length. Leaves elliptic to broadly elliptic, acute to acuminate, 8–18 cm long, 3.5–10.5 cm wide, glabrous above and below, sparsely ciliate on the lower margins. Inflorescence one- or rarely two-flowered; peduncle 4–15 cm long, glandular especially towards the apex; bract leaf-like, elliptic to lanceolate, acuminate, 6–9 cm long, 1.5–4 cm wide, pubescent on veins of lower side, ciliate. Flower variable in size, sepals and petals green or pale green, rarely white or pale lemon-yellow, lip white spotted with pink within, staminode yellow with red spots; pedicel and ovary (2–)3–4 cm long, densely glandular. Dorsal sepal lanceolate, acuminate, 2.8–6 cm long, 1.4–2 cm wide, pubescent at base on inner side and on outside, ciliate towards apex; synsepal narrowly elliptic, with two free acuminate tips, 3.5–5 cm long, 1–1.7 cm wide, pubescent on outside, ciliate. Petals lanceolate or linear and tapering above, acuminate, 2.8–5.5 cm long, 0.5–1.1 cm wide, pubescent at base within, eciliate. Lip porrect, somewhat ellipsoidal or globose and dorsiventrally flattened, with a small mouth, 2.5–3.5 cm long; side lobes infolded and creased. Column 1–1.5 cm long; staminode oblong-trullate, obtuse, slightly longitudinally concave, 9 mm long, 5 mm wide, glabrous. PLATES 7, 47, 48; FIGURE 22.

DISTRIBUTION. Pakistan, N. India, Nepal, Bhutan, S. Xizang (Tibet). See map p. 165.

HABITAT. In wet and shady woods, open *Abies* (fir) forest on outskirts of forest or in open glades and in *Caragana* (pea shrub) and *Juniperus* (juniper) scrub on south-facing slopes; 2100–4000 m. Flowering in July and August.

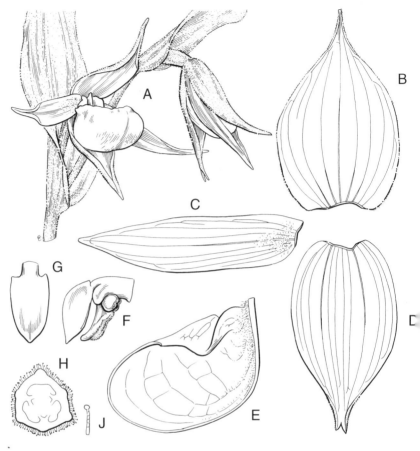

Figure 22. Cypripedium cordigerum. A, flowers, ×1; B, dorsal sepal, ×2; C, petal, ×2; D, synsepal, ×2; E, lip longitudinal section, ×2; F, column, ×2; G, staminode, ×2; H, ovary transverse section, ×4; J, hair from ovary, ×20. All drawn from Kew Spirit collection no. 19474 by Eleanor Catherine.

15. CYPRIPEDIUM FASCIOLATUM

Cypripedium fasciolatum vies with the American *C. kentuckiense* as having the largest flowers in the genus. It was discovered in Sichuan by Père Farges, a French missionary, and was described by M. A. Franchet in 1894. It is a spectacular orchid with large yellow unpleasantly scented flowers marked with maroon on the sepals and petals and with a large bulbous lip. It is also distinguished by its reddish glandular hairy ovary, striped sepals and petals, and a large in-

164

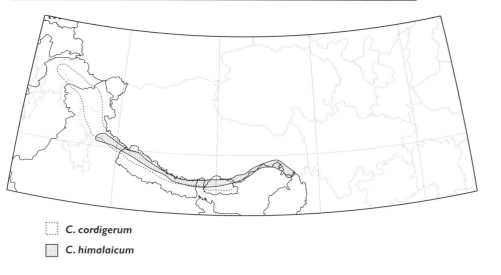

☐ *C. cordigerum*

▦ *C. himalaicum*

flated lip with a small mouth with a toothed margin. It is the finest of all the Chinese species, but is a rarity, recorded only from Sichuan and western Hubei provinces. I have visited Mt. Omei [Emei Shan] and searched for it but without success.

Chen and Xi (1987) treated *Cypripedium wilsonii* as conspecific with *C. fasciolatum*. The specimens of the type collection of *C. wilsonii* (seven sheets at Kew, two at Edinburgh) all have larger flowers than those I have examined of the type collection of *C. fasciolatum* (four sheets at Kew, ten in Paris). However, in their vegetative and floral morphology they are similar, and I am inclined to agree with Chen that these taxa are conspecific, bearing in mind the variation observed in the flower size of other *Cypripedium* species.

It seems probable that *Cypripedium lang-rhoa*, a provisional name given by Jean Gattefossé (in *Revue de la parfumerie moderne* 4: p.53, 1918) and validated by Constantin, is also referable to *C. fasciolatum*. The name was based on a plant that flowered in France from a specimen sent from "district Kien-Tchean dans le province du Sseu-Tchouan [Sichuan]". The text, a copy of which I have been unable to trace, was accompanied by a photograph, the flower being described as having "les petales . . . très longs et trop étroits, beaucoup plus longs que les sepales, tordus en spirale".

It is found on the famous mountains of Erlang Shan and Emei Shan in western Sichuan and again in eastern Sichuan and adjacent Hubei.

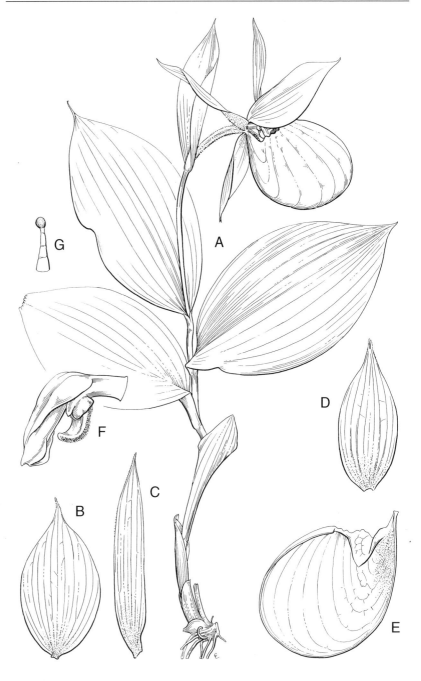

Figure 23. Cypripedium fasciolatum. A, habit, ×0.5; B, dorsal sepal, ×0.66; C, petal, ×0.66; D, synsepal, ×0.66; E, lip longitudinal section, ×0.66; F, column, ×1.5; G, hair from ovary, ×26. All drawn from *Wilson* 4581 by Eleanor Catherine.

166

Cypripedium fasciolatum *Franch.* in J. Bot. (Morot) 8: 232 (1894); Schltr. in Acta Horti Gothoburg 1: 127 (1924); S.C. Chen in Proc. 12th World Orch. Conf.: 144 (1987). Type: China, Sichuan, *Farges* 922 (holo. P!; iso. AMES!, K!).
C. wilsonii Rolfe in Bull. Misc. Inform. Kew 1906: 379 (1906). Type: China, Sichuan, *Wilson* 4581 (holo. K!, iso. E!).
? *C. lang-rhoa* Gattefossé in Rev. Parfum. Mod. 4: 53 (1918), *nom. prov.;* Constantin in Bull. Mus. Hist. Nat. Paris 25: 221 (1919). Type: China, Sichuan, illustration accompanying description.

DESCRIPTION. A terrestrial herb 30–45 cm tall. Stems erect, stout, glabrous or rarely pubescent. Leaves six, the lowermost ones reduced to sheaths, the upper three elliptic to obovate, shortly acuminate, 8–17.3 cm long, 4.5–11.5 cm wide, ciliolate, glabrous on both surfaces. Inflorescence one- or rarely two-flowered; peduncle pubescent below bract; bract leaf-like, elliptic to ovate, acuminate, 7–12.7 cm long, 2.4–7.8 cm wide. Flower large, showy, pale yellow to rose with maroon venation on the sepals and petals and a pale yellow lip spotted with maroon, unpleasantly scented; ovary 2.2–3 cm long, reddish glandular-pubescent. Dorsal sepal ovate, acuminate, 4.7–6.6 cm long, 2.3–3.5 cm wide, margins sometimes undulate; synsepal elliptic-ovate, acuminate and bifid at the apex, 4–6.4 cm long, 1–2.9 cm wide. Petals linear-tapering, acuminate, 5.8–7.1 cm long, 1–1.5 cm wide, ciliate, pubescent in basal half of inner side, untwisted or twisted. Lip deeply saccate and inflated, 4–7.3 cm long, with a toothed margin to the mouth. Column 1.3–1.5 cm long; staminode oblong, obtuse, 1.3–2 cm long, 0.7–1.3 cm wide, with the side margins somewhat incurved. FIGURE 23.
DISTRIBUTION. China (Sichuan and Hubei). See map p. 168.
HABITAT. In woodlands on broken limestone; 1650–2500 m. Flowering early in the season from April to early June.

16. CYPRIPEDIUM FARRERI

Cypripedium farreri is related to *C. fasciolatum*. Based on the limited herbarium material available and a few plants that have recently appeared in cultivation in Europe and Japan, it can be distinguished from *C. fasciolatum* by its daintier habit with only two or three small leaves, subtended by a single sheath, and the smaller flower that has a distinctively pitcher-shaped lip which is creamy or

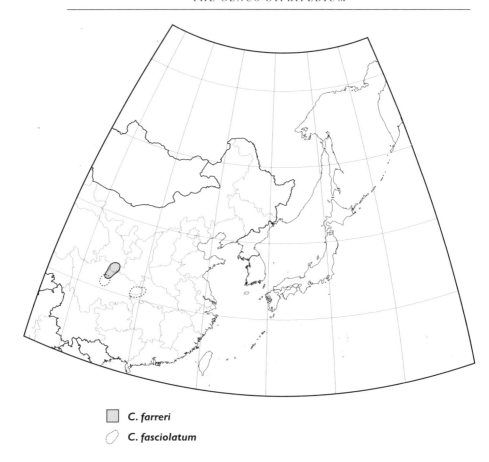

☐ *C. farreri*

◌ *C. fasciolatum*

butter-yellow with purple veins within but lacking the spotting of
C. fasciolatum.

Reginald Farrer is always good value for his evocative descriptions of the plants he collected, which obviously took his fancy. In
the *Gardeners' Chronicle* of 15th May 1915 we read:

> Still rarer is the last Slipper I have this year noted. That is found
> in cool loose woodland soil, in steep cool banks on the shady side
> of deep and precipitous limestone gorges at some 8000 ft. or
> higher. It lives among herbage and very scanty low scrub, evi-
> dently asking its shade of cliff, not plant, and seeks its model
> among the far-away Slippers of America. For here we come back
> to the twisted moustache of *C. calceolus;* the whole plant is similar,
> though much slighter in build—a dainty growth of 6–8 inches,
> with two or three glossy emerald-green leaves to the stem. Usually

only one stem comes up from the slender crown of roots; never more than two. No stem carries more than one flower. These have their cork-screwed petals and pointed sepals of a yellowish green, lined regularly with maroon. The lip is the essential originality of the plant, for it is so curiously pulled in below the mouth as to present a perfect soda-water-bottle shape, and round its rim is cut into the most elegant vandykes that catch the light and shine again. For the Slipper is of the waxiest gloss, and in colour of a very bland palest cream or butter-yellow, through which dimly show the broad bands of maroon with which it is striped on the inside. Finally, the inconspicuous strange charm of the plant is justified and enhanced by its intense and penetrating perfume of Lily-of-the-Valley.

A watercolour painting by Farrer of the type in the field in China and entitled "Cypripedium Sweetlips Siku" is preserved in the archives of the Lindley Library at the Royal Horticultural Society in London and was recently reproduced as plate 12 in Illingworth and Routh (1991). In recent years a few plants of this delightful orchid have appeared in cultivation in Japan and Europe. Photographs of this striking orchid have appeared in the *Wild Orchid Journal* 1992, Part 11: 96 and 1995, Part 1: 98.

Cypripedium farreri *W.W. Sm.* in Notes Roy. Bot. Gard. Edinburgh 9: 102 (1916); Chen and Xi in Proc. 12th World Orch. Conf.: 144 (1987). Type: China, W. Gansu, *Farrer & Purdom* 155 (holo. E!, illustration of holo. Lindley Library!).

DESCRIPTION. A small terrestrial herb 20–25 cm tall, with a glabrous stem. Leaves two or three, the lowermost sheathing, the upper two ovate-elliptic, shortly acuminate, 5.5–7 cm long, 2.2–2.7 cm wide, ciliolate, glabrous. Inflorescence one-flowered; peduncle glabrous below, pubescent below the bract; bract ovate, acuminate, 3.5–4 cm long, 1–1.5 cm wide. Flower fragrant, the sepals and petals green-yellow lined with maroon, the lip waxy, cream or butter-yellow lined inside with maroon; pedicel and ovary 1.8–2.4 cm long, shortly sparsely glandular-pubescent. Dorsal sepal ovate, acuminate, 1.9–3.2 cm long, 1.1–1.5 cm wide, shortly pubescent on outside; synsepal lanceolate, acuminate and bifid at apex, 1.6–3.2 cm long, 0.8–1 cm wide, shortly pubescent on outside. Petals straight or slightly spirally twisted, linear-tapering, acuminate, 2.3–4.2 cm long,

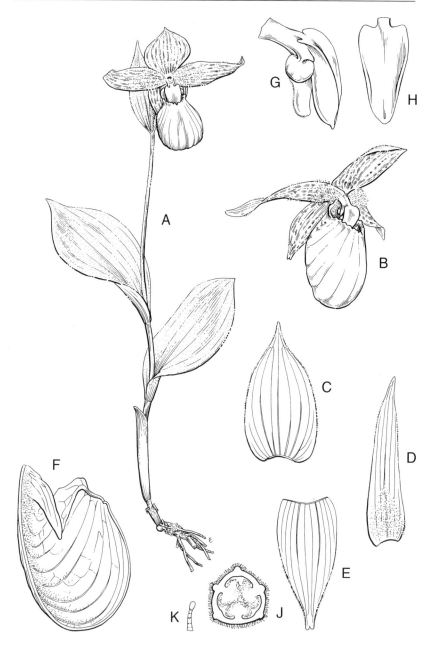

Figure 24. Cypripedium farreri. A, habit, ×0.66; B, flower, ×1; C, dorsal sepal, ×2; D, petal, ×2; E, synsepal, ×2; F, lip longitudinal section, ×2; G, column, ×3; H, staminode, ×3; J, ovary transverse section, ×6; K, hair from ovary, ×30. All drawn from the type collection by Eleanor Catherine.

170

0.5–0.8 cm wide, pubescent in basal part and along mid-vein on outer surface. Lip pitcher-shaped with a dilated mouth, very inflated and with noticeably incised veins, 2.4–3.3 cm long, 1.6–2 cm wide, the margin of the mouth narrow and toothed. Column 0.7–0.8 cm long; staminode shortly stalked, oblong-obovate, obtuse, 1–1.2 cm long, 0.5 cm wide, cucullate at apex, the lateral margins incurved. PLATE 54; FIGURE 24.

DISTRIBUTION. China (S. Gansu and NW. Sichuan only). See map p. 168.

HABITAT. On cool grassy gully sides in deep limestone gorges under shade of cliffs; 2600–2850 m.

17A. CYPRIPEDIUM PARVIFLORUM
VAR. PARVIFLORUM

The taxonomic confusion surrounding the status of this and the following taxon is nothing new. In 1828 C. S. Rafinesque stated: "Many botanists have made two species, *C. pubescens* and *C. parviflorum,* of this, to which the previous and better name *C. lutescens* ought to be restored". Modern studies suggest that Rafinesque was close to the mark in surmising that it was not feasible to recognise more than a single species in this variable group. However, he was wrong in suggesting that *C. lutescens* was the earliest and correct name for it.

Cypripedium parviflorum was described by R. A. Salisbury (1791) based on a plant collected by H. Marshall in Virginia. The type collection has not been traced (see Sheviak 1994), but Salisbury's description is detailed and the accompanying drawing should be considered as the type. *Cypripedium parviflorum* is one of four taxa illustrated by Salisbury and is markedly the smallest-flowered, hence the name "parviflorum". Sheviak commented that the description fits well the plant typical of the eastern woodlands of North America, particularly in flower colour and size. He noted that the staminode is unusual in being sagittate, but that such staminodes are sometimes found in populations.

More or less detailed accounts of the variation within the North American yellow-lipped taxa have been provided by Correll (1950), Atwood (1985), and Sheviak (1992, 1994, 1995). Correll (1950), in his account of this taxon in his *Native Orchids of North America,* included all the North American yellow-flowered slipper orchids in a single taxon, *C. calceolus* var. *pubescens*, based on Willldenow's *C. pubescens*. He distinguished four "ecological entities" within var. *pubescens*, but did not give them formal taxonomic rank. These correspond to *parviflorum*, *planipetalum*, *pubescens* and *kentuckiense*, currently recognised by various authors at either the specific or varietal level. This is understandable when living and preserved specimens are examined. However, a sizeable proportion cannot be satisfactorily assigned to a taxon.

Luer (1975) treated the first three variations at varietal rank within *Cypripedium calceolus*. His var. *pubescens* seems, in the herbarium, to form a bridge between the other three taxa. Atwood himself noted that intermediates of *pubescens* and *planipetalum* are found not uncommonly in Colorado, Michigan, and Wisconsin and variously calls these intergrades and hybrids. Intermediates of *pubescens* and *parviflorum* are, likewise, frequently found as has been mentioned already, and Atwood also comments on these. Finally, the distinctness of *kentuckiense* is often difficult to see in the herbarium material from across the continent. Specimens from Missouri, Tennessee, Arkansas, Louisiana, and Kentucky have very large flowers bearing all the hallmarks of typical *kentuckiense*. However, specimens from Canada and in the northern United States with similar large flowers have been noted in the Kew and other herbaria.

Atwood (1985) distinguished the North American taxa from *Cypripedium calceolus* on the basis of subtle morphological differences, mainly floral. He recognised four taxa in North America, namely, *C. parviflorum*, *C. pubescens* vars. *pubescens* and *planipetalum*, and *C. kentuckiense*. Whilst acknowledging the variation within each taxon, he distinguished them mainly on flower size and colouration: *C. parviflorum* with small flowers, a lip length of 2–2.8 cm, and a mean orifice length of 0.54 cm; *C. pubescens* var. *pubescens* with a lip ranging from 3 to 5.2 cm long (a mean length of 4.2 cm) and a mean lip orifice length of 0.94–1.01 cm; *C. pubescens* var. *planipetalum* with a lip length similar to that of *C. parviflorum* but differing markedly in habit, flower colour, and petal shape and twist; and finally, *C. kentuckiense* with considerably larger flowers with a lip 5–7 cm long and a mean orifice length of 1.5–1.7 cm.

Atwood's separation of the North American taxa from *Cypripedium calceolus* presents a departure from that used by most earlier authorities. I can nearly always distinguish the Eurasian species from the North American ones on the basis of staminode shape and colour, although their affinities through *parviflorum* are obvi-

172

ous and close. The floral fragrance analyses of Bergstroem et al. (1992) confirm that the Eurasian taxon has a distinctive fragrance spectrum from its North American relatives. I have therefore followed Atwood's treatment in distinguishing the Eurasian and North American taxa at specific rank. Atwood's separation of the North American taxa into three species also represents a departure from other recent treatments.

The work of Sheviak (1992, 1994, 1995) has addressed the problems of the *Cypripedium parviflorum–C. pubescens* complex in some detail, based on extensive field and herbarium studies. Sheviak agrees with Atwood in treating the North American taxa as distinct at specific level from the Eurasian *C. calceolus*. He has, however, included all the yellow-lipped North American taxa, except for *C. kentuckiense*, in *C. parviflorum*, recognising three varieties: var. *parviflorum*, var. *makasin*, and var. *pubescens*. Sheviak provides a key to these, distinguishing var. *parviflorum* and var. *pubescens* on flower size and colouration, and var. *makasin* on the sparser indumentum of the young bract and its intense sweet floral fragrance. He also cites distributional and ecological differences: var. *parviflorum* is a plant of the eastern states found in deciduous woodland in drier more acidic sites than var. *pubescens*, whereas var. *makasin* has a more northerly distribution in New England and across Canada, favouring calcareous fens and other wet sites on organic and sandy soils.

Var. *makasin* was first described by Farwell based upon several collections of his own from Michigan. Since then it has mostly been sunk into the synonymy of var. *parviflorum*. Sheviak (1994) in resurrecting this taxon as a variety of *C. parviflorum* has distinguished it from the typical variety by its glabrous uppermost sheathing bract, intensely sweet scent, and habitat preference. In open sites the leaves are characteristically narrow and ascending, but more spreading and broader in shaded places. Var. *makasin* has a more northerly distribution than the typical variety, ranging from New England and adjacent Canada across the continent to the Rockies. In most localities but the last it has dark maroon sepals and petals rather than spotted or blotched ones.

The distinctiveness of vars. *parviflorum* and *makasin* is, I believe, practically impossible to see in herbarium material, and Sheviak's photographic comparison of them is unconvincing. I have, therefore, for the time being included var. *makasin* in a broader circumscription of the typical variety in this treatment.

In summary, in this revision I have adopted a hybrid of the treatments of Atwood, Luer, and Sheviak, recognising two taxa at varietal rank within *C. parviflorum*. Too many intermediates exist for any of these taxa to be considered distinct and discrete species. The recently described forma *albolabium* with a white lip may be better referred to *Cypripedium* × *andrewsii*, despite the authors' disclaimer (Magrath and Norman 1989).

Cypripedium parviflorum *Salisb.* in Trans. Linn. Soc. 1: 77, t.2, fig.2 (1791). Lectotype: Illustration cited here.

var. **parviflorum**

C. bulbosum Mill., Gard. Dict. ed.8, Cypripedium (1768), *non* L.

C. luteum Aiton ex Raf., Med. Fl. 1: 140 (1828).

C. luteum Aiton var. *parviflorum* (Salisb.) Raf., *op. cit.* (1828).

C. bifidum Raf., Atl. J. 1: 178 (1833).

C. hirsutum Mill. var. *parviflorum* (Salisb.) Rolfe in Orchid Rev. 15: 184 (1907).

Calceolus parviflorus (Salisb.) Nieuwl. in Amer. Midl. Naturalist 3: 117 (1913).

Cypripedium bulbosum Mill. var. *parviflorum* (Salisb.) Farw. in Rep. Michigan Acad. Sci. 15: 170 (1913).

C. pubescens Willd. var. *makasin* Farw. in *op. cit.* 18: 198 (1918). Types: Michigan, *Farwell* 418, 418a, 418b, 3402, 4173, 4495 (syn. MICH).

C. makasin Farw., *loc. cit.* (1918).

C. calceolus L. var. *parviflorum* (Salisb.) Fernald in Rhodora 48: 4 (1946); Luer, Native Orchids U.S.A. and Canada: 48, t.5, figs. 1,2 (1975).

C. parviflorum Salisb. var. *makasin* (Farw.) C.J. Sheviak in Amer. Orchid Soc. Bull. 63: 403 (1994).

C. parviflorum Salisb. forma *albolabium* L.K. Magrath & J.L. Norman in Sida 13: 372 (1989). Type: U.S.A., Oklahoma, Tate ranch, *Magrath & Norman* 16847 (holo. OCLA).

DESCRIPTION. A terrestrial herb with a short stout rhizome and fibrous roots, often forming large clumps. Erect stems typically slender, sparsely pubescent, 15–35 cm tall, leafy above covered by three sheaths below. Leaves three or four (rarely five), strongly two-ranked, suberect, commonly conduplicate, sheathing at base, lanceolate or ovate-lanceolate, acute or acuminate, 5–15 cm long, 2–8 cm wide, bluish green, pubescent on veins above and below, ciliate. Inflorescence one- or two-flowered; rhachis slender, glandular hairy; bracts leaf-like, lanceolate, acuminate, 3–8 cm long, 1–3 cm wide, pubescent and ciliate. Flowers small, showy, fragrant, the sepals and petals madder purple to maroon, glossy, the lip yellow with red spotting inside, the staminode yellow with red spotting; pedicel and ovary subsessile 1.5 cm long. Dorsal sepal suberect, lanceolate-ovate, acuminate, 2–4 cm long, 1.5–2.5 cm wide, undulate. Synsepal similar, slightly incurved, bifid at the apex, 2–4 cm long. Petals spirally twisted two to four times, linear-tapering, acute, 3–5 cm long, 0.5–0.8 cm wide, pubescent within in basal half. Lip porrect, obovoid to ellipsoidal, with a small mouth, 1.5–2.8 cm long, 1.2–2 cm wide, the apical margins incurved, the incurved sides with a basal pleat. Column short, 0.6 cm long; staminode subsessile, trullate, blunt, concave in apical half, 0.8–1 cm long, 0.5–0.6 cm wide; filaments extend beyond anthers, blunt to acute. PLATES 20, 90–92, 124; FIGURE 25.

DISTRIBUTION. Canada (British Colombia across Ontario, Quebec and Newfoundland), U.S.A. (New England and southern midwestern States: Maine south to North Carolina and Tennessee and across to Great Lakes and Eastern Rockies). See map p. 176.

HABITAT. In sunny places in damp calcareous fens, non-sphagnous bogs, marshes and meadows with *Mertensia* and skunk cabbage, in "wet prairies where sedge, shrubby cinquefoil, poison sumac and red osier dogwood abound", in marly cedar swamps and in deciduous woodland, favouring drier, often more acidic sites than var. *pubescens*.

17B. CYPRIPEDIUM PARVIFLORUM
VAR. PUBESCENS

Cypripedium parviflorum var. *pubescens* is a widespread and very variable taxon whose status has been the cause of much debate (for a detailed discussion see Sheviak 1995). It is undoubtedly closely allied to var. *parviflorum* and, superficially at least, the small dark coloured forms of var. *pubescens* can be easily confused with var. *parviflorum*. It differs, however, in usually having a larger flower with differently coloured sepals and petals, a longer undulate dorsal sepal, longer and more twisted petals, and a larger more obovoid lip. However, it is very variable in plant and flower size and plants of very different habit and flower size can grow intermingled in colo-

175

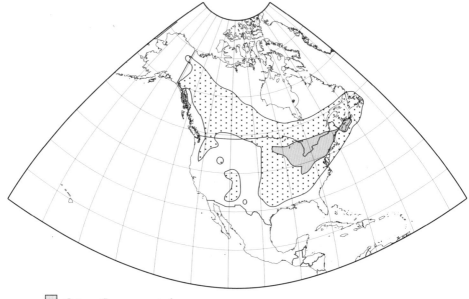

☐ **C. parviflorum var. pubescens**

⊡ **C. parviflorum var. parviflorum**

nies in the wild. Var. *parviflorum* tends to grow in alkaline bogs and marshes and deciduous woods and may hybridise with var. *pubescens* where their range and habitats overlaps. The picture is further confused by many authors referring both to varietal rank within *C. calceolus* of Europe and Asia, which has flowers that more closely resemble those of var. *parviflorum,* but the Eurasian species can be distinguished by the white staminode that is obovate and broadest in the apical half.

The status of var. *pubescens* has been the cause of considerable confusion over the past 240 years. Linnaeus included it within the concept of his *Cypripedium calceolus* by including "*Helleborine virginiana forma calceolus flore luteo majore*" of R. Morison (1699) amongst the citations. A. de Candolle (1802) was the first to recognise it as distinct at specific level, naming it as *C. flavescens* in Redoute's famous folio on *Liliacées.* Two years later Willdenow also gave it specific status as *C. pubescens,* a name that has stuck with it at specific and varietal ranks ever since. If this taxon is ever raised to specific rank again then *flavescens* has precedence over the better known epithet *pubescens.*

The eccentric botanist C. S. Rafinesque had a field day with this taxon. He recognised six varieties of *Cypripedium luteum* Aiton (synonym *C. parviflorum*), all of which are referable to this taxon. In addition he described a further four species, *C. assurgens, C. aureum, C. undatum,* and *C. furcatum,* which can also be attributed here. Another name, *C. veganum* Cockerell & Barker, based on a plant from high elevation in New Mexico, nests within the variable var. *pubescens* and can also be reduced to its synonymy.

Intermediate forms between vars. *pubescens* and *parviflorum* are commonly reported and have usually been interpreted as hybrids (Luer 1975, Case 1987) or as depauperate forms of var. *pubescens* (Whiting and Catling 1986, Sheviak 1995). Herbarium material is usually inadequate to decide which of these is the correct interpretation or if both, on occasion, are correct.

Var. *planipetalum* was described by Fernald (1926) based on his own and Long's collection from Newfoundland. It is a dwarf orchid found in northeastern North America in the tundra of Newfoundland, adjacent mainland Canada, north of the St. Lawrence River, and the northern Rockies. It differs from the other North American yellow-lipped taxa in its diminutive habit and in the flower, which has yellow-green sepals and petals, and flat or scarcely twisted linear-lanceolate petals.

The status of this orchid has been changed four times since it was first described as a variety of *Cypripedium parviflorum* by Fernald. It was raised to specific rank by Morris and Eames in 1929 and then reduced to varietal rank within *C. calceolus* by Marie-Victorin and Rousseau (1940). Correll (1950) included it as a synonym of *C. calceolus* var. *pubescens,* but he distinguished four entities within that variety, the second of these corresponding to *planipetalum.* Atwood (1985) treated it as a variety of *C. pubescens.* Finally, Sheviak (1992, 1994) included it within the concept of his var. *pubescens.* Its affinities with the northern var. *pubescens* are obvious in its floral features and indumentum. Examination of herbarium specimens of var. *planipetalum* suggests that the plants continue to grow as the season progresses and fruit is set so that the fruiting specimens can reach 35 cm in height. The type collection also contains a specimen with twisted petals, and Sheviak (1995) reported that the populations in Newfoundland contain a complete gradation of form. The dwarf plants grow in open tundra and the typical var. *pubescens* in sheltered places with intermediates in between. In cultivation the dwarf habit is often lost, and the plants flower when the leaves are better developed. It seems likely that *planipetalum* is best considered an

177

ecotype of var. *pubescens.* Allozyme work by Case (1993) confirms this interpretation.

Distribution maps such as that given by Luer (1975) suggest that var. *planipetalum* is sympatric with var. *pubescens* in at least part of its range, and I have seen some specimens from the region that might be referable to the latter. Because of these intermediates amongst the herbarium specimens I have examined, I am inclined to follow Sheviak in including var. *planipetalum* in var. *pubescens.*

Some of the observed field variation in var. *pubescens* may also be the result of hybridisation with the closely allied *Cypripedium candidum*, a prairie species that is a smaller plant with narrow, suberect leaves, a solitary flower, greenish sepals and petals, and a white lip. The influence of *C. candidum* can be variable depending upon whether the hybrids are F1s, later generations, or backcrosses (Garay 1953, Klier et al. 1991). Morphological evidence of introgression of *C. candidum* into *C. pubescens* is not always apparent, but isoenzyme studies indicate that introgression is frequent in areas where the two are sympatric. Their hybrids have been described as *C. × favillianum* and *C. × landonii*, now considered synonyms of *C. × andrewsii.*

An interesting property of this variety is the traditional use in North America of a tincture made from the rhizomes for the cure of hysteria and nervous tension. Hopefully, this use is dying out because of the potential damaging effect upon wild populations.

Cypripedium parviflorum *Salisb.* var. **pubescens** *(Willd.) O.W. Knight* in Rhodora 8: 93 (1906); Correll in Bot. Mus. Leafl. 7: 14 (1938) & Native Orchids North Amer.: 24, t.3 (1950); Luer, Native Orchids U.S.A. and Canada: 44, t.3,4 (1975); Sheviak in Amer. Orchid Soc. Bull. 64(6): 606–612 (1995). Type: North America, cult.Berlin Bot. Gard. (holo. WILLD!).

C. calceolus L., Sp. Pl. ed.1, 2: 951 (1753), in part.

C. flavescens DC. in Redouté, Liliacées 1: 20 (1802). Type: illustration cited.

C. pubescens Willd., Hort. Berol. 1: t.13 (1804).

C. luteum Aiton ex Raf. var. *angustifolium* Raf., *loc. cit.* (1828).

C. luteum Aiton ex Raf. var. *biflorum* Raf., *loc. cit.* (1828).

C. luteum Aiton ex Raf. var. *concolor* Raf., *loc. cit.* (1828).

C. luteum Aiton ex Raf. var. *glabrum* Raf., *loc. cit.* (1828).

C. luteum Aiton ex Raf. var. *grandiflorum* Raf., *loc. cit.* (1828).

C. luteum Aiton ex Raf. var. *maculatum* Raf., *loc. cit.* (1828).

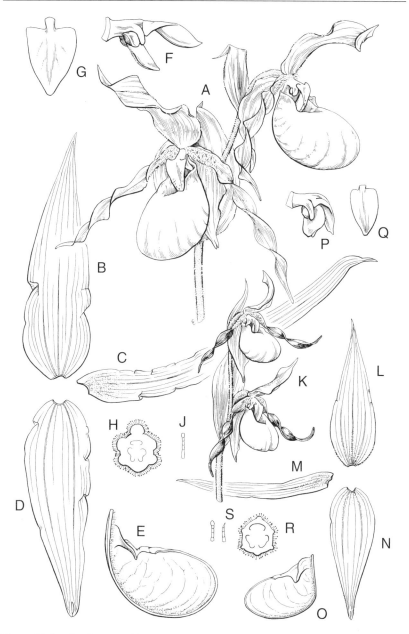

Figure 25. Cypripedium parviflorum var. **pubescens.** A, flowers, ×0.66; B, dorsal sepal, ×1; C, petal, ×1; D, synsepal, ×1; E, lip longitudinal section, ×1; F, column, ×1.5; G, staminode, ×1.5; H, ovary transverse section, ×4; J, hair from ovary, ×20. **Cypripedium parviflorum** var. **parviflorum.** K, flowers, ×0.66; L, dorsal sepal, ×1; M, petal, ×1; N, synsepal, ×1; O, lip longitudinal section, ×1; P, column, ×1.5; Q, staminode, ×1.5; R, ovary transverse section, ×4; S, hairs from ovary, ×20. A–J from Kew Spirit Collection no. 59734; K–S from Kew Spirit Collection no. 62761. All drawn by Eleanor Catherine.

C. luteum Aiton ex Raf. var. *pubescens* (Willd.) Raf., Med. Fl. 1: 142 (1828).

C. furcatum Raf., Herb. Raf.: 76 (1833). [This may be referable to *C. kentuckiense* Reed.]

C. assurgens Raf., *loc. cit.* (1833).

C. aureum Raf., *loc. cit.* (1833).

C. undatum Raf., *op. cit.*: 77 (1833).

C. veganum Cockerell & Barker in Proc. Biol. Soc. Wash. 4: 178 (1901). Type: U.S.A., New Mexico, Sapello Canyon, *Cockerell & Barker* s.n. (holo. US).

C. bulbosum Mill. var. *flavescens* (DC.) Farw. in Rep. Michigan Acad. Sci. 15: 170 (1913).

C. parviflorum Salisb. var. *planipetalum* Fernald in Rhodora 28: 168 (1926). Type: Canada, NW. Newfoundland, *Fernald & Long* 27851 (holo. GH!).

C. planipetalum (Fernald) Morris & Eames, Our Wild Orchids: 8,11 (1929).

C. calceolus L. var. *pubescens* (Willd.) Correll in Bot. Mus. Leafl. 7: 14 (1938).

C. calceolus L. var. *planipetalum* (Fernald) Vict. & J. Rousseau in Contr. Inst. Bot. Univ. Montréal 36: 68 (1940).

C. calceolus L. forma *rupestre* Vict. & J. Rousseau, *loc. cit.*: 67. Type: Canada, Quebec, Île-à-la-Vache-Marine, *Marie-Victorin & Rolland-Germain* 24325 (holo. MT).

C. pubescens Willd. var. *planipetalum* (Fernald) J.T. Atwood in Proc. 11th World Orch. Conf.: 108 (1985).

DESCRIPTION. An erect herb 10–80 cm tall, more or less densely glandular hairy throughout, often forming clumps, with short stout creeping rhizomes with fibrous roots. Erect stems terete, leafy above, covered by three more or less pubescent tubular sheaths below. Leaves pleated strongly, many-nerved, three to five (rarely six), elliptic to ovate or ovate-lanceolate, acute to acuminate, 5–20 cm long, 2.1–10 cm wide, somewhat two-ranked, sheathing the stem below, bright green, pubescent above and below on veins, ciliate. Inflorescence one- or two-flowered; rhachis terete, glandular hairy; bracts leaf-like, ovate-lanceolate, acuminate, 2.9–10 cm long, 0.8–4 cm wide, pubescent and ciliate. Flowers medium-sized to large, showy, the sepals and petals yellow or greenish usually suffused and streaked with rusty brown or dull brown, the lip yellow with magenta spots and streaks within, the staminode yellow with red spotting; pedicel and ovary 2–3.2 cm long, reddish glandular hairy. Dorsal sepal suberect to porrect, lanceolate, acuminate, 2.5–7(-8.5) cm long, 1.4–3.5 cm wide, often undulate and slightly spirally twisted. Synsepal similar but bidentate at apex, 2.3–8 cm long, 1.4–2.5 cm wide, incurved behind lip and with lateral margins somewhat reflexed. Petals spreading-deflexed at 45 to 60° below horizontal, spirally twisted one to three times, rarely untwisted, linear-tapering, acuminate, 3–7(-9) cm long, 0.5–1 cm wide, pubescent on mid-vein and at base within. Lip ellipsoidal, obovoid or subreniform, with a small mouth, 2–5.2 cm long, 1.5–2.5 cm wide; apical margins incurved, incurved sides with a pleat on each side at the base. Column short, c. 1 cm long; staminode subsessile, concave towards apex, conduplicate, triangular-ovate, blunt, 1–1.2 cm long, 0.7–1 cm wide; filaments extending beyond anthers, subacute. PLATES 21, 93–96; FIGURES 3, 25.

DISTRIBUTION. Canada (from the Yukon and British Colombia across to the eastern seaboard and Newfoundland), U.S.A. (from southeastern Alaska, Washington and Oregon across to the eastern seaboard and south to Louisiana, Texas, New Mexico and Arizona). Common in the eastern parts of its range but rarer in the west and south. See map p. 176.

HABITAT. A plant of rich woods growing in heavy damp humus-rich but well-drained soils in partial shade, also on rocky hillsides, along streams, in meadows and clearings, in shallow turfy depressions on treeless limestone barrens and plateau in peaty soil, and in talus of limestone cliffs. It thrives in limestone areas, but the soils are usually neutral to slightly acidic; sea level to 2000 m. Flowers from May to July depending on latitude, habitat, climate, and soils.

18. CYPRIPEDIUM KENTUCKIENSE

This spectacular orchid was illustrated as an aberrant form of *Cypripedium parviflorum* var. *pubescens* by Yarian (1939). It was described as recently as 1981 by Clyde Reed and has elicited a great deal of comment since then. Atwood (1984, 1985) has argued strongly for the distinctiveness of this taxon and its recognition at specific rank. Garay (1982) and Wilson et al. (1982) argued that Rafinesque's name *C. furcatum* should be correctly applied to it. Rafinesque had originally described *C. luteum* var. *grandiflorum* based on a specimen from Tennessee, but subsequently renamed it *C. furcatum*. Garay may well be right that *C. furcatum* and *C. kentuckiense* refer to one and the same taxon. However, I agree with Atwood that this is an assumption that cannot be tested because no type material of *C. furcatum* has been traced. Large-flowered specimens of *C. parviflorum* var. *pubescens* are found in Tennessee and it seems unwise to use the name *C. furcatum* for the large-flowered taxon under discussion. A full review of the literature on *C. kentuckiense* has recently been provided by Brown (1995b).

The discussion of the distinctiveness of *Cypripedium kentuckiense* by Atwood and others is difficult to follow in the herbarium. I have examined many specimens of the North American yellow-lipped slipper orchids and it is apparent that whilst large-flowered specimens with large lips do occur in the central southern United States, they also found well outside the region from Michigan, Wisconsin, Rhode Island, Maine, and Manitoba, Canada. Furthermore, the range of variation in size found in var. *pubescens* seems to overlap with *C. kentuckiense* as much as it does with var. *parviflorum* and var. *planipetalum*. However, Atwood's arguments based on lip colour, shape, and size have been largely accepted by other scientists and horticulturists familiar with this taxon. The molecular evidence of Cox (1995) suggests that *C. kentuckiense* is closer to var. *parviflorum* than to var. *pubescens,* and it seems likely that the debate on its status will continue for the time being until the morphological and molecular profiles of further plants are sampled.

Cypripedium kentuckiense *C.F. Reed* in Phytologia 48: 426 (1981); Atwood in Amer. Orchid Soc. Bull. 53(8): 835 (1984); P.M. Brown in North Amer. Native Orchid J. 1(3): 255 (1995). Type: U.S.A., Kentucky, *Reed* 18141 (holo. Herb.C.F.Reed).
C. daultonii V.G. Soukup in The Mid-American 41(1): 9 (1977), *nom. illeg.*
C. furcatum sensu Garay in Amer. Orchid Soc. Bull. 51(9): 902 (1982), ? non Raf.

DESCRIPTION. A large terrestrial herb with a short stout rhizome. Erect stems 40–71 cm tall, finely glandular-pubescent. Leaves usually five, broadly elliptic-ovate, 14–17 cm long, 5–9.5 cm wide, finely pubescent on the veins on the lower surface, ciliate. Inflorescence one-flowered; bract leaf-like, 6–11.5 cm long, 2.8–4.6 cm wide. Flower showy with the sepals and petals greenish striped and mottled with purple and a creamy white to pale yellow lip, marked

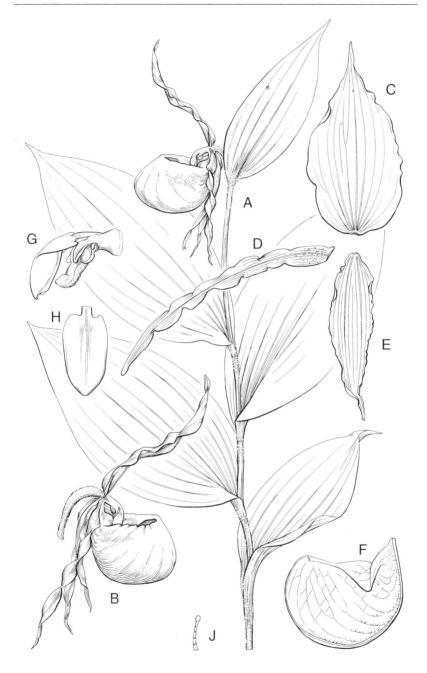

Figure 26. Cypripedium kentuckiense. A, habit, ×0.5; B, flower, ×0.66; C, dorsal sepal, ×1; D, petal, ×1; E, synsepal, ×1; F, lip longitudinal section, ×1; G, column, ×1.5; H, staminode, ×1.5; J, hair from ovary, ×20. A–B from *J. & E. Price* 8083; C–J from *Patrick & Baker* 4261. All drawn by Eleanor Catherine.

within with purple, the staminode pale yellow marked with red; pedicel and ovary 3–5.5 cm long, reddish glandular-pubescent. Dorsal sepal suberect-curving over lip, lanceolate, acuminate, 6.5–11 cm long, undulate on margins, slightly twisted, sparsely pubescent. Synsepal lanceolate, bidenticulate at apex, 5.7–6.3 cm long, 1.1–1.3 cm wide. Petals deflexed-pendent, spirally twisted, linear-tapering, acute, 7–9 cm long, 0.7 cm wide, pubescent within at base and along mid-vein. Lip large, 5–7 cm long, 3.5 cm across, with a broad mouth, 1.5–1.7 cm long and 1.2–1.3 cm across. Column 1–1.4 cm long; staminode conduplicate, ovate. PLATES 76, 77; FIGURE 26.

DISTRIBUTION. U.S.A. (Texas, Mississippi, Kentucky, Ohio, Missouri, Arkansas, Louisiana, Tennessee).

HABITAT. In mesophytic woodland of *Ulmus rubra* (slippery elm), *Acer saccharum* (sugar maple), *Betula nigra* (black birch), *Liriodendron tulipifera* (tulip tree), and so forth, mainly in deep ravines on acid sandstone soils, alluvial terraces and on the banks of streams; sea level to 500 m. Flowering in May to June.

19. CYPRIPEDIUM MONTANUM

The streamlined flowers of *Cypripedium montanum*, strikingly coloured maroon-brown and white, are unlikely to be confused with other American species apart from *C. candidum*, which is a smaller plant with narrower, suberect leaves, a smaller but similarly coloured solitary flower, and a distinct distribution and habitat in the prairies well to the east of the range of this attractive orchid. *Cypripedium montanum* is also closely allied to the widespread *C. parviflorum* and its segregates, differing mainly in its lip colour and distribution.

David Douglas collected the type material of this species in Washington State in northwestern North America and coined the name that John Lindley published with a description in 1840. Watson (1876), apparently unaware of Lindley's publication of the name *Cypripedium montanum* for this species, subsequently published the name *C. occidentale* based on several collections from western North America, citing Hooker's *C. parviflorum* (in part) and Asa Gray's *C. passerinum* as misapplied names for this taxon. Examination of the type material confirms that *C. occidentale* is conspecific with *C. montanum*.

Cypripedium montanum is a relatively uniform species, but two minor variants have received taxonomic recognition: forma *praeter-*

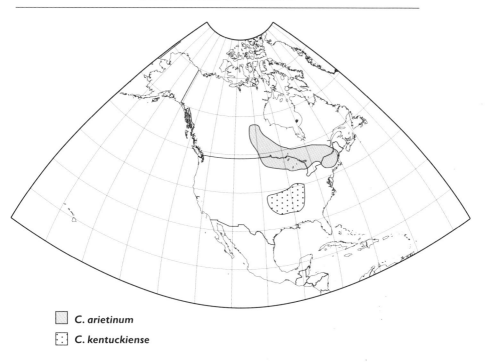

C. *arietinum*

C. *kentuckiense*

nictum Sheviak (1990) lacks anthocyanin in the flowers, which have pale yellowish sepals and petals and a white lip; and forma *welchii* P. M. Brown (1995) has a crimson-edged mouth to the lip.

Cypripedium montanum is widely distributed in western North America from Oregon north to southeastern Alaska. It was cultivated at Kew by William Aiton as early as 1785, and this specimen is preserved now in the Natural History Museum in London.

Cypripedium montanum *Douglas ex Lindl.*, Gen. Sp. Orch. Pl.: 528 (1840); Correll, Native Orchids North Amer.: 35, t.8 (1950); Luer, Native Orchids U.S.A. and Canada: 54, t.7 (1975). Type: U.S.A., Washington, junction of Colombia and Lewis Rivers, *Douglas* s.n. (holo. K!, iso. BM!).

C. occidentale S. Watson in Proc. Amer. Acad. 11: 147 (1876). Types: Western North America, *Tolmie* (syn. AMES!, isosyn. K!), *Burke s.n.*, *Spalding* 334, *Geyer* 513, *Torrey* 513, *Hall s.n.*, *Bolander* 970, *Kellogg & Harford s.n.*, *Gray s.n.*, *Nevius s.n.* (all syn. AMES!).

C. montanum Dougl. ex Lindl. forma *praeternictum* C.J. Sheviak in Rhodora 92: 48 (1990). Type: Canada, British Colombia, Radium, *C.J. & J.K. Sheviak & W.F. Metzlaff* 3109/2 (holo. NYS).

185

Figure 27. Cypripedium montanum. A, habit, ×0.5; B, detail of back of leaf, ×10; C, dorsal sepal, ×1; D, petal, ×1; E, synsepal, ×1; F, lip longitudinal section, ×1.5; G, column, ×2; H, staminode, ×2; J, ovary transverse section, ×6; K, hair from ovary, ×20. All drawn from *Reed & Barkley* 56 by Eleanor Catherine.

C. montanum Dougl. ex Lindl. forma *welchii* P.M. Br. in North Amer. Native Orchid J. 1(3): 198 (1995). Type: U.S.A., Oregon, Lake County, *J. Welch* (photo *loc. cit.* 196).

DESCRIPTION. A terrestrial herb 25–70 cm tall, growing from a short stout rhizome. Stem erect, leafy, somewhat flexuous, covered below by several tubular sheaths, four- to seven-leaved above, glandular-pubescent. Leaves spreading-ascendent, plicate, broadly ovate to elliptic-lanceolate, obtuse to shortly acuminate, 5–16 cm long, 2.5–8 cm wide, glandular-pubescent on the veins, glandular-ciliate. Inflorescence one- to three-flowered; peduncle 6–11 cm long, glandular-pubescent; bracts foliaceous, ovate-elliptic to broadly elliptic, acute to acuminate, 4–8.5 cm long. Flowers showy, with maroon-brown sepals and petals and a white lip, the staminode yellow with red spotting, well-spaced on rhachis; pedicel and ovary 2–3.6 cm long, densely glandular-pubescent. Dorsal sepal ascending-suberect, lanceolate to ovate-lanceolate, long-acuminate, 3–6.5 cm long, 1–1.5 cm wide, the margins somewhat undulate, pubescent on outer surface; synsepal elliptic-lanceolate, bidentate at acuminate apex, 3–6.5 cm long, 0.8–1.5 cm wide, pubescent on outer surface. Petals deflexed at 45° to horizontal, linear to linear-lanceolate, acuminate, 4.5–7 cm long, 0.3–0.6 cm wide, spirally twisted two to three times, pilose on inner surface. Lip obliquely ellipsoidal, somewhat boat-shaped, 2–3 cm long, 1.3–1.7 cm across, pilose within, the mouth small. Column short, c. 1 cm long; staminode ovate-oblong to trullate, subacute, 0.8–1.2 cm long, 0.5–0.6 cm wide, longitudinally conduplicate, glabrous. PLATES 19, 88, 89; FIGURE 27.

DISTRIBUTION. Canada (Vancouver Island, British Colombia, Alberta), U.S.A. (SE. Alaska, Washington, Oregon, Montana, Idaho, Colorado, Wyoming, California). See map p. 237.

HABITAT. In moist and dry open woods, subalpine slopes, and sometimes in scrub oak or swamps, usually at high elevation; to 1600 m. Flowering in April to July.

20. CYPRIPEDIUM CANDIDUM

The SMALL WHITE LADY'S SLIPPER ORCHID was first described by Willdenow in 1805 based on a Mühlenberg collection from Pennsylvania. The name *Cypripedium candidum* was coined but not published by Mühlenberg. It belongs to the group of species around *C. calceolus,* being distinguished by its narrow suberect leaves and solitary white-lipped flowers. It can be confused with *C. montanum,* which also has a white lip, but that is a montane species from western North America whereas *C. candidum* is essentially a prairie plant. The ranges of these two do not overlap. *Cypripedium candidum* is also distinguished by its smaller stature, fewer narrower, conduplicate leaves, and a solitary smaller flower with yellow-green sepals and petals more or less flushed with brown, a smaller lip marked with purple on the margin of the mouth and, a smaller obovate staminode.

Luer (1975) described the plant thus:

[I]n the spring the sturdy, leafy plants rise quickly and the flowers unfold usually before the leaves unwrap from about the stem. The bright green leaves maintain a more or less erect position and usually do not unfurl to expose the stem completely.

In the wild *Cypripedium candidum* often grows in association with *Platanthera leucophaea* and plants of the *C. calceolus* complex. It is perhaps not surprising that this species hybridises with both *C. parviflorum* var. *parviflorum* and var. *pubescens,* the hybrids being respectively known as *C.* × *andrewsii* and *C.* × *favillianum.* The hybrids both have a pale yellowish lip, lacking the glossy pure white lip of *C. candidum.* Introgression to both parents has been reported by Klier et al. (1991), making it difficult at times to determine the identity of these plants.

Cypripedium candidum is not one of the easier species in cultivation. It usually grows with its rhizomes and roots buried in neutral to somewhat alkaline soils under a thick layer of leaf litter and with a constant supply of cool, lime-rich water. It was first grown in the British Isles as early as 1826.

Cypripedium candidum *H.L. Mühl. ex Willd.,* Sp. Pl. ed.4: 142 (1805); Correll, Native Orchids North Amer.: 29, t.5 (1950); Luer, Native Orchids U.S.A. and Canada: 52, t.6 (1975); Case, Orchids Western Great Lakes: 78 (1987). Type: U.S.A., Pennsylvania, *Mühlenberg* s.n. (holo. B!).
Calceolus candidus (Mühl. ex Willd.) Nieuwl. in Amer. Midl. Naturalist 3: 117 (1913).

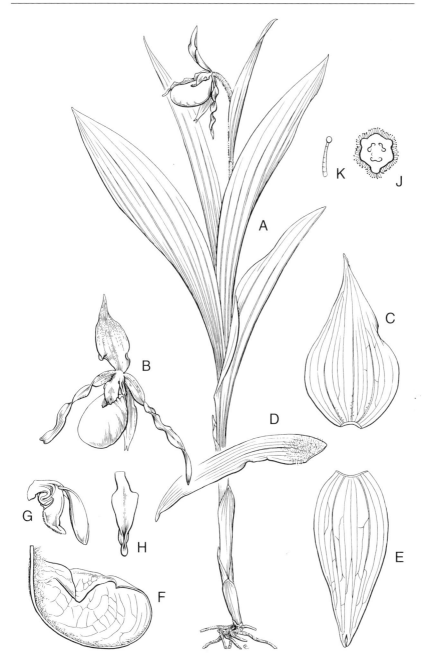

Figure 28. Cypripedium candidum. A, habit, ×0.66; B, flower, ×1; C, dorsal sepal, ×2; D, petal, ×2; E, synsepal, ×2; F, lip longitudinal section, ×2; G, column, ×2; H, staminode, ×2; J, ovary cross section, ×4; K, hair from ovary, ×20. All drawn from *Schwartz* s.n. in Kew Spirit Collection no. 59737 by Eleanor Catherine.

189

DESCRIPTION. A terrestrial herb 12–38 cm tall, with stems often in clusters and with a short rhizome. Stems erect, covered below by about three glabrous, tubular, obtuse sheaths and by leaf sheaths above. Leaves three to four (to five), suberect, often conduplicate, lanceolate or elliptic-lanceolate, acute or acuminate, 6–19 cm long, 1.5–4 cm wide, bright green, glandular-pubescent on the veins above and below, glandular-ciliate. Inflorescence one- or rarely two-flowered; peduncle slender, glandular-pubescent; bract erect, always overtopping the flower, foliaceous, erect, conduplicate, elliptic-lanceolate, acute, 3–10 cm long, densely glandular-pubescent, glandular-ciliate. Flower small, slightly fragrant, with greenish or greenish yellow sepals and petals often flushed, streaked, or spotted with purple-brown, a waxy white lip purple-spotted on the edge of the mouth and purple-streaked within, and a yellow staminode spotted with purple-red; pedicel and ovary 1.5–2.8 cm long, densely glandular-pubescent. Dorsal sepal lanceolate, acuminate, 2–3 cm long, 0.9–1.2 cm wide, undulate and somewhat twisted, glandular on outer surface; synsepal lanceolate or elliptic-lanceolate, bifid at acute apex, 2–3 cm long, 0.8–0.9 cm wide, glandular on main veins. Petals spreading-deflexed at 45° to horizontal, linear-tapering, acuminate, spirally twisted, 2.5–4.5 cm long, 0.3–0.4 cm wide, pubescent at base on inner surface. Lip obovoid, 1.8–2.5 cm long, 1–1.5 cm across, silky pubescent within. Column short, 0.8–0.9 cm long; staminode slenderly stalked, concave in apical half, obovate, obtuse, 0.7–1 cm long, 0.35–0.45 cm wide. PLATES 6, 44–46; FIGURE 28.

DISTRIBUTION. Canada (Ontario), U.S.A. (New York, Pennsylvania, New Jersey west to southern Minnesota, eastern North Dakota, Iowa, northeastern Nebraska and eastern South Dakota and south to Missouri and Kentucky).

HABITAT. In full sunlight in prairies and damp meadows, bogs and fens on limestone and marl, often along railway lines, and in sheltered ravines, limestone barrens, swamps, on the edge of thickets, on dry rocky slopes, in wet woods; sea level to 1000 m. Flowering in April to June.

SECTION CYPRIPEDIUM
SUBSECTION MACRANTHA

Cypripedium sect. **Cypripedium** subsect. **Macrantha** *(Kränzl.)* Cribb **stat. nov.** Type species: *C. macranthos* Sw.

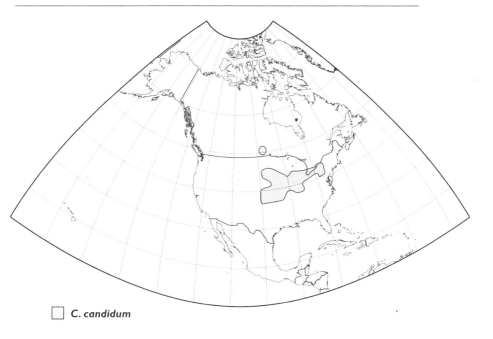

□ *C. candidum*

Cypripedium sect. *Calceolaria* group 2. *Macrantha* Kränzl., Orch. Gen. Sp. 1: 24 (1901).

Stems pubescent, with several leaves; leaves somewhat pubescent, elliptic, the lowermost three or four reduced to sheaths enclosing the stem; inflorescence one-flowered; flowers usually predominantly pink, purple, or maroon but rarely can be white or creamy white; ovary glabrous or coarsely hairy but never glandular; lip large, inflated, often with a wrinkled surface and pinched margin to the small orifice; petals lanceolate or oblong-lanceolate, untwisted; staminode trullate, rather flat, glabrous, pink, purple, or white, in front of visibly protruding acute filaments.

A subsection of seven species.

This complex is the most problematic in the genus from a taxonomic viewpoint and has proved more difficult to resolve that even the *Cypripedium calceolus* complex. At least 18 species and a large number of infraspecific taxa have been recognised in the complex by various authors. However, specific delimitation is difficult, and none of the current classifications is entirely satisfactory. No doubt this is partly because of the distribution of the complex, which ranges from eastern European Russia across northern Asia to east-

191

ern Siberia, Sakhalin Island, and the Kuriles, Japan, northern and western China, Taiwan, northern Myanmar (Burma), northeastern India, Bhutan, and Sikkim. Much of this territory is still poorly collected botanically but, even where botanists have been able to make field observations, it is evident that the taxonomy is far from straightforward.

Part of the problem may be the result of hybridisation and subsequent introgression. *Cypripedium macranthos* is known to hybridise with *C. calceolus* in Russia and eastern Siberia. It might also hybridise with other species in China, such as *C. shanxiense* and *C. smithii*. Likewise, its larger-flowered ally *C. tibeticum* might cross with *C. smithii*, *C. franchetii*, and other allied sympatric species. In my travels in western China I have seen plants that appear to be morphologically intermediate between *C. tibeticum* and *C. franchetii* and *C. tibeticum* and *C. smithii*, but have not been able to analyse these further. I have, however, seen no evidence in China of species in this group hybridising with other sympatric species such as *C. flavum*, *C. guttatum*, *C. plectrochilum*, and *C. margaritaceum* and its allies.

Variability in plants of this alliance in China can be seen in plant size, flowering time, flower colour and size, ovary indumentum, and the relative shape and size of the floral segments. However, it is often difficult in the herbarium to find consistent character sets to distinguish many of the taxa that have been described. I have, therefore, attempted here to distinguish the more distinct entities within this complex. The obscurely distinct I have treated in synonymy where I have seen type material.

21. CYPRIPEDIUM MACRANTHOS

Cypripedium macranthos is distinguished by its large purple or rarely white or pink flower borne on a tall stem. Characteristically the flower has a glabrous ovary, flat lanceolate petals, a large inflated lip with a small crimped mouth, often edged with white, and a trullate almost flat staminode.

The name *Cypripedium macranthos* was based on material collected in eastern Russia by Gmelin. Although in 1800 Swartz made no reference in the original description to a specimen, in 1805 he mentioned Gmelin's collection as the basis for *C. macranthos*. Gmelin's collections are said to be in the Pallas Herbarium, now in the Willdenow Herbarium in Berlin, but the specimens of *C. macranthos* there have no indication on them of their having been collected by Gmelin. There are also two collections in the Swartz herbarium, which might be considered as type material, but again neither is attributed to Gmelin. However, Swartz (1805) cited Gmelin (1747), who included a description and illustration, and this might be better considered the basis of *C. macranthos*. Since there is no confusion over the application of the name and both the specimens and illustration refer to the same taxon, I have followed Swartz in his later publication and selected Gmelin's illustration as the lectotype.

The orthography of the name *Cypripedium macranthos* has been controversial and has not been used by the majority of later authors, who have chosen to use *C. macranthon* (Lindley 1840, Hooker f. 1890) or *C. macranthum* (Pfitzer 1903, Schlechter 1919, Keller and Schlechter 1926, Keller and Sóo 1930). William Stearn (pers. comm.) sees no reason why the Greek form used by Swartz cannot be maintained as has been done by some authors (e.g., Moore 1980) in the influential account of orchids in *Flora Europaea*. The epithet derives from the Greek *anthos* (flower), which is neuter, thus *macranthon* is incorrect. The choice of name is, therefore, restricted to "*macranthos*" or "*macranthum*". Because the former was the original spelling and has come into currency again since the publication of *Flora Europaea* and been used by some recent authors, I have chosen to use it in this treatment.

At the same time as he published *Cypripedium macranthos*, Swartz also published the similar *C. ventricosum,* based according to Swartz (1805) on Gmelin's collection from eastern Siberia. De Candolle (1880) stated that the Pallas Herbarium contained Gmelin's types from Siberia, and it does, indeed, possess two specimens on the single sheet labelled *C. ventricosum,* but neither is attributed to Gmelin. It seems safer, therefore, to treat Gmelin's 1747 illustration as the type of *C. ventricosum.* It differs from *C. macranthos* in having a larger flower with relatively longer narrower petals, longer than the more elongate lip, a concave staminode, and a glabrous ovary. It is worth noting that Gmelin's illustrations of *C. calceolus* on the same page mistakenly are shown as having glabrous ovaries. We now know that plants resembling the types of *C. macranthos* and *C. ventricosum* can be found in close proximity throughout Siberia (Perner pers. comm.), Korea, and northeastern China.

H. G. Reichenbach (1851) was the first to treat *Cypripedium ventricosum* as a variety of *C. macranthos,* and others have followed (Hooker f. 1890, Pfitzer 1903, Keller and Schlechter 1926, Stapf

193

1927). Conversely, Rolfe (1904, 1910) considered *C. ventricosum* to be a hybrid of *C. macranthos* and *C. calceolus*. Stapf (1927) discussed this problem when describing *C. manschuricum,* which is undoubtedly a hybrid of *C. macranthos* and *C. calceolus*. He considered that *C. ventricosum* was conspecific with *C. macranthos* but that plants then in cultivation under the name *C. ventricosum* were referable to his new species, *C. manschuricum.*

Cypripedium macranthos is undoubtedly variable in plant and flower size, petal and lip length, and flower colour, the last ranging from deep plum-coloured to white. Some of the variation can, however, be traced to introgression from sympatric *C. calceolus*. Primary hybrids of *C. macranthos* and *C. calceolus* and plants that look like backcrosses are not infrequent in far eastern Siberia around Vladivostok (Perner pers. comm.), and the backcrosses to *C. macranthos* undoubtedly further confuse specific delimitation. Based on the Gmelin description and illustration and the Pallas specimens in Berlin, I am inclined to follow Rolfe and consider *C. ventricosum* as a hybrid of *C. macranthos* and *C. calceolus* and, therefore, an earlier name for the plants known as *C.* × *barbeyi* and *C. manschuricum.*

Carl Blume (1859) recognised that Thunberg's use of *Cypripedium calceolus* referred to a distinct species which he duly named *C. thunbergii.* Examination of the type material, which is in a rather poor condition, confirms that this species is conspecific with *C. macranthos*. It has a flower rather smaller than the typical plant.

Cypripedium speciosum was described by Robert Rolfe based on a plant sent to Kew for identification by the nursery of Messrs. Bees for whom it flowered in June 1910. Rolfe equated it with the Japanese "So mokou Zusetsu" which he stated to be "widespread in that country". The illustration of the type by Matilda Smith shows that the flower has a pubescent ovary but this is not substantiated by examination of the type specimen. *Cypripedium speciosum* falls within the range of variation of *C. macranthos,* being distinguished only by its attractive pale rose-coloured flowers.

Cypripedium rebunense was named, but not validly described, by Kudo based on a pale cream-flowered plant from Rebun Island off the northwestern coast of Japan which flowered in the garden of Ushijima in Sapporo. It was first validly described by Miyabe and Kudo (1932) as *C. macranthum* var. *rebunense.* This is now relatively common in cultivation and is, consequently, very rare in its original habitat on Rebun Island. It is widely regarded now as a variety or form of *C. macranthos,* differing only in flower colour.

194

Ohwi (1965) recognised three forms of *Cypripedium macranthos* in Japan: forma *macranthos* (including var. *atsmori* and *C. speciosum*), forma *albiflorum* with white flowers, and forma *rebunense* with pale yellow flowers. More recent horticultural treatments recognise four varieties of *C. macranthos* as occurring in that country: var. *macranthos*, var. *speciosum* (pink flowers), var. *hotei-atsmorianum* (very close to the typical variety but with a large, white-rimmed, somewhat dorsiventrally flattened lip), and var. *rebunense*. These names will undoubtedly persist for horticultural purposes, but I am inclined to follow Ohwi and treat them as forms. All these variations also apparently occur in mainland Asia (Averyanov in Okuyama 1995). A very large flowered variant of *C. macranthos* was described by Nakai (1940) as var. *maximum*. The type has sepals to 5.7 cm long and a lip 5.5 cm long. However, the variability in size of *C. macranthos* throughout its range encompasses this specimen, and I have therefore chosen not to recognise formally this variety.

Most of the problems are associated with the Chinese members of this complex, particularly those in western China whence some 12 allied species have been described. Some authors consider all these to be varieties of *Cypripedium macranthos* and have formally recognised some of them, such as *C. macranthos* (as *macranthum*) var. *tibeticum*. I have not followed this approach in this revision (see under *C. tibeticum*). *Cypripedium macranthos,* as understood here, is found in China only in the north, especially in the northeast and around Beijing.

A small-flowered variant has been found in Taiwan and was named *Cypripedium taiwanianum* by Masamune, but this name has never been validated. I have examined herbarium material of Taiwanese origin and compared it with Japanese collections. One of two specimens on a sheet in the Kew Herbarium collected by Tschonoski in Nambu Province in Japan matches *C. taiwanianum* in size, the other specimen being more typical of Japanese *C. macranthos.*

A plant of *Cypripedium macranthos* was sent from the Ukraine by John Prescott to the Horticultural Society's Garden in Chiswick where it first flowered in May 1829. It is illustrated in both Hooker (1829) and Lindley (1832).

Cypripedium macranthos *Sw.* in Kongl. Vetensk. Acad. Nya Handl. 21: 251 (1800). Lectotype: Illustration t.1, f.1 in Gmelin's *Flora Sibirica* 1747, selected here.

Figure 29. Cypripedium macranthos. A, habit, ×0.5; B, flower, ×0.66; C, dorsal sepal, ×1; D, petal, ×1; E, synsepal, ×1; F, lip longitudinal section, ×1; G, column, ×1.5; H, staminode, ×1.5; J, ovary transverse section, ×4. All drawn from Kew Spirit Collection no. 45172 by Eleanor Catherine.

C. calceolus L. var. *rubrum* Georgi, Reise Russ. Reich. 1: 232 (1775). Type not located.

C. calceolus sensu Thunb. in Fl. Jap.: 30 (1794), *non* L.

C. macranthos Sw. var. *vulgare* Rchb. f., Icon. Florae Germ. Helv. Orch.: 210 (1851).

Sacodon macranthos (Sw.) Raf., Fl. Tellur. 4: 45 (1836).

Cypripedium thunbergii Blume, Coll. Orchid.: 169, t.59, f.2 (1859). Type: Japan, ex Yedo, *Thunberg* s.n. (holo. L!).

C. speciosum Rolfe in Bull. Misc. Inform. Kew 1911: 207 (1911) and in Bot. Mag. 137: t.8386 (1911). Type: Japan, cult.Bees (holo. K!).

C. rebunense Kudo in Jap. J. Bot. 2: 251 (1925), *nom. nud.*

C. macranthum Sw. var. *albiflorum* Makino in Jap. J. Bot. 3: 27 (1926).

C. macranthos Sw. var. *speciosum* (Rolfe) Koidz. in Jap. Bot. Mag. 40: 336 (1926).

C. macranthum Sw. var. *maximum* Nakai in Jap. J. Bot. 16: 63 (1940). Type: Japan, Yezo, Sempozi, Kusuri, *Miyake* s.n. (holo. TI!).

C. macranthum Sw. var. *rebunense* (Kudo) Miyabe & Kudo, Fl. Hokkaido 3: 355 (1932). Type: Japan, Rebun Isl., cult. Ushijima, *Tatewaki* s.n. (holo. SAPA!).

C. macranthum Sw. forma *rebunense* (Kudo) Ohwi, Fl. Japan: 342 (1953).

C. macranthum Sw. forma *albiflorum* (Makino) Ohwi, Fl. Japan (in English): 322 (1965).

C. taiwanianum Masam., Native Orchids of Nippon 4: 68 (1987), *nom. nud.*

C. macranthos Sw. var. *taiwanianum* (Masam.) F. Maekwa, Wild Orchids of Japan in Colour: 80 (1971).

DESCRIPTION. A terrestrial herb with an erect, sparsely or somewhat pubescent leafy stem, 15–40 cm tall, base of stem covered by three to four tubular sheaths, occasionally forming large clumps; rhizome short, stout. Leaves three to five, elliptic-ovate or elliptic-lanceolate, acuminate, largest 10–14 cm long, 4–6.5 cm wide, shortly ciliate on margins, usually hairy on veins above and below, sometimes glabrous above. Inflorescence one-flowered; bract longer than the flower, leaf-like, lanceolate, acuminate, 7–14 cm long, 3–5.5 cm wide, ciliate, hairy on veins above and below. Flower purple or pink with darker veins especially on the sepals and petals, rarely white or creamy white; pedicel and ovary 3–4.5 cm long, glabrous. Dorsal sepal elliptic-ovate, acute or apiculate, 3.2–5.3 cm long, 2–3.4 cm wide. Synsepal elliptic-ovate, bifid at acute apex, 2.8–4 cm long, 1.4–2 cm wide. Petals curving forwards either side of the lip, lanceolate, acuminate, untwisted, 3.8–5.7 cm long, 1–2.1 cm wide. Lip deeply saccate, subglobose to subellipsoid, with a pinched margined small mouth, 3–5.5 cm long. Column short; staminode sessile, trullate to oblong-trullate, blunt, not keeled beneath, 10–12 mm long, 7–8 mm wide. PLATES 16–18, 81–83, 118; FIGURES 4, 29.

DISTRIBUTION. European Russia, Asiatic Russia to E. Siberia, Kamchatka, Sakhalin Island, Korea, NE. China, Japan, Taiwan.

HABITAT. In meadows, scrub and forest in damp places and in light shade, often on slopes and banks; sea level to 2400 m.

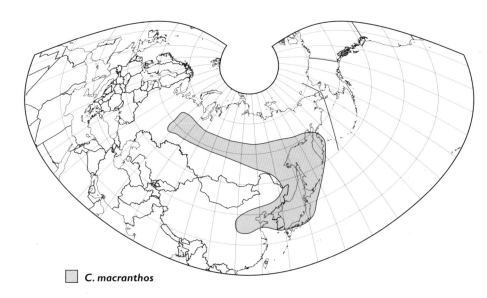

☐ *C. macranthos*

22. CYPRIPEDIUM YUNNANENSE

Cypripedium yunnanense is very closely allied to *C. macranthos*, resembling it in habit, flower shape, and range of flower colour. It differs, however, in having a glabrous stem usually hidden by the leaf bases, leaves which are conduplicate at first and are pubescent all over, and the flower which is smaller in all its parts.

Its range seems not to overlap that of *Cypripedium macranthos*, which is found in northeastern China, but it is apparently sympatric with the closely related *C. tibeticum* and perhaps also with *C. franchetii*. It has much smaller less boldly marked flowers than the former and tends to flower after the stem and leaves have developed.

Its flowers are usually purple, pink, or off-white rather than deep maroon. The latter usually has larger flowers with a very hairy even villose ovary, but its flowers can be otherwise quite similar. It seems possible that *C. yunnanense* is a regional variant of *C. macranthos*, and further study is needed to see if it warrants recognition at specific rank. For the present I have followed Chen and Xi (1987) in recognising it as distinct.

Schlechter (1919) described *Cypripedium amesianum* based on two Wilson collections from western Sichuan. The syntypes in Berlin have been destroyed, but examination of a duplicate of Wilson 1753 in the AMES herbarium suggests that it does not differ significantly from *C. yunnanense* and should be considered conspecific with it.

I have seen *Cypripedium yunnanense* in several localities in northwestern Yunnan, in the region of Lijiang and Zhongdian. Most populations were of purple-flowering plants with ovaries that were glabrous or very sparsely pubescent towards the apex. In one colony just on the outskirts of Zhongdian I found some plants with hairier ovaries and paler flowers, but, in all cases, they were less pubescent than *C. franchetii*.

In northwestern Yunnan, *Cypripedium yunnanense* grows in the wild on north-, northwest-, or west-facing slopes under *Pinus yunnanensis* and the shade of shrubs, such as rhododendrons and sallows, at between 3200 and 3400 m. The substrate is limestone, but the pH usually neutral or even slightly acidic. The plants are usually found growing in small colonies of up to 100 but often fewer plants. Some form clumps of up to 20 shoots.

Cypripedium yunnanense *Franch.* in J. Bot. (Morot) 8: 231 (1894). Types: China, Yunnan, *Delavay* 2480 (syn. P!) and Mo-so-yn, Koutoui, *Delavay* s.n. (syn. P!).
C. amesianum Schltr. in Feddes Rep. Sp. Nov. Beih. 4: 38 (1919). Type: China, Sichuan, Wen Chuan Distr., *Wilson* 1753 (syn. B†, isosyn. AMES!) and SE of Tatsienlu, *Wilson* 1758 (syn. B†).

DESCRIPTION. A slender terrestrial herb 20–37 cm tall, with a short rhizome. Stems leafy, erect, glabrous or sparsely pubescent. Leaves five to six, the lowermost two to three sheathing stem, the uppermost three to four lanceolate to ovate-elliptic, acuminate, conduplicate when young, 6–14 cm long, 1–4.1 cm wide, ciliate, pubescent on lower surface particularly on the veins, sparsely pubescent on the upper surface. Inflorescence one-flowered; peduncle

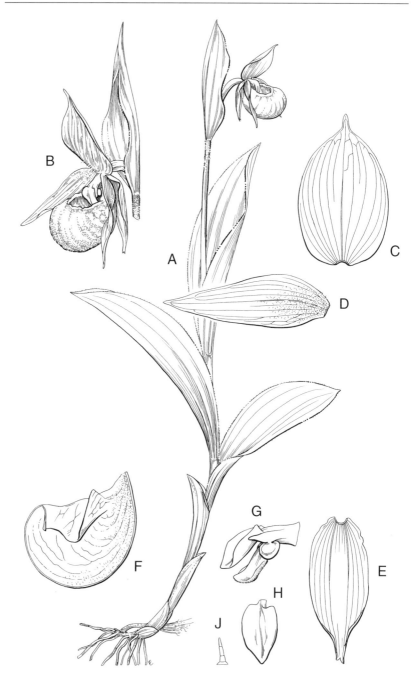

Figure 30. Cypripedium yunnanense. A, habit, ×0.5; B, flower, ×1; C, dorsal sepal, ×1.5; D, petal, ×1.5; E, synsepal, ×1.5; F, lip longitudinal section, ×1.5; G, column, ×2; H, staminode, ×2; J, hair from ovary, ×20. All drawn from *Forrest* 12479 by Eleanor Catherine.

sparsely pubescent below the bract; bract overtopping the flower, lanceolate to elliptic, acute or acuminate, 3.7–7 cm long, 1.7–3 cm wide, ciliate and pubescent. Flower similar to that of *C. macranthos* but relatively smaller, off-white, pink, or red-purple with darker veins, drying brown; staminode usually off-white with a central purple stripe; pedicel and ovary 1.5–4 cm long, glabrous or slightly pubescent towards the apex. Dorsal sepal ovate-elliptic, acute or acuminate, 2.3–3.2 cm long, 1.6–1.7 cm wide. Synsepal half to three-fifths the width of the dorsal sepal, lanceolate, bifid at the tip, 2-3.4 cm long, 0.8–1.2 cm wide. Petals lanceolate acute or acuminate, slightly twisted, 3–3.9 cm long, 0.7–0.8 cm wide, glabrous. Lip ellipsoidal, with a small elliptic mouth with an obscure pinched margin, 2.2–3.5 cm long. Column short; staminode elliptic, cordate at base, 6–7 mm long and wide. PLATES 121, 122; FIGURE 30.

DISTRIBUTION. China (Yunnan, W. Sichuan, SE. Xizang (Tibet)).

HABITAT. Mossy banks and by streams in mixed forest, north-facing slopes in pine forest, shrubberies, and meadows; 2700–3800 m.

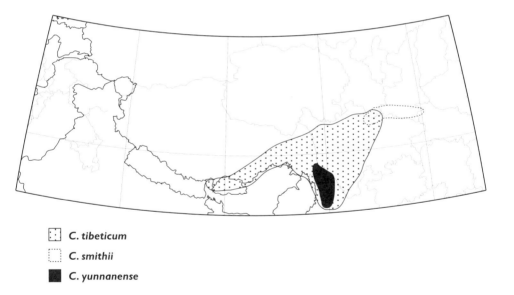

☷ *C. tibeticum*

☐ *C. smithii*

■ *C. yunnanense*

23. CYPRIPEDIUM LUDLOWII

It is with some trepidation that I describe here yet another species in the *Cypripedium macranthos* alliance. *Cypripedium ludlowii* is based on a single collection from the little-known region of Pome in southeastern Xizang (Tibet), visited by Ludlow, Sherriff, and Elliot but by few other botanists. These three made an exemplary collection, the holotype in The Natural History Museum, London, bearing four flowering stems and the isotypes three each. The material is remarkably uniform and differs from other specimens in the alliance that I have examined. In particular, the light greenish yellow flowers are distinctive, albinistic plants of allied species such as *C. macranthos,* having white or pale creamy flowers. *Cypripedium ludlowii* also differs in several less obvious characters: it has very sparsely pubescent ovaries bearing a few hairs and possibly glands at the apex; the flowers are smaller than most specimens of *C. macranthos* I have examined and match most closely in size those of *C. yunnanense;* the lip is shallower than related species, rather resembling that of *C. cordigerum* in shape; and the petals appear to have undulate rather than straight margins.

Pome (now Zhamo) lies just north of the Tsangpo River where it loops south before breaching the Himalayas. *Cypripedium ludlowii* was collected there growing in moist places in forest at considerable altitude. Most of its allies in southwestern China are found in montane grassland or on the edge of forest at rather lower elevations. On balance I consider it better to draw this remarkable collection to the notice of botanists rather than lump it into *C. yunnanense,* which it only superficially resembles.

I surmise that *Cypripedium ludlowii* might be of hybrid origin and cannot dismiss the possibility. The possible sparse glandular hairs on the ovary and undulate petals are similar to those found in *C. × ventricosum.* It is possible that *C. henryi* or even *C. cordigerum* is one parent, given its flower colouration, sparse glands on the ovary, and petal shape. The other parent might possibly be one of the species with more or less glabrous ovaries such as *C. yunnanense* or even small-flowered specimens of *C. tibeticum.* I am not entirely convinced, given that neither *C. cordigerum* nor *C. henryi* has yet been recorded from the region. On balance, I include *C. ludlowii* at specific rank with the caveat that its origins need further study in the field, a possibility as botanists have gained increasing access to southeastern Xizang (Tibet) in recent years.

This orchid is named after Frank Ludlow, an intrepid and prolific plant collector who, with George Sherriff and, on various occasions, other companions, added much to our knowledge of the plant life of the eastern Himalayas.

Figure 31. Cypripedium ludlowii. A, habit, ×0.5; B, dorsal sepal, ×1.5; C, petal, ×1.5; D, synsepal, ×1.5; E, lip, longitudinal section, ×1.5; F, column in side view, ×2; G, staminode, ×2; H, ovary in cross section, ×3; J, hair from ovary, ×20; K, fruiting stem, ×0.5. All drawn from the type by Eleanor Catherine.

Cypripedium ludlowii *Cribb* sp. nov. SE. Tibet *C. macranthei* Sw. et *C. yunnanensi* Franch. affinis sed foliis sparsim pubescentibus, floribus pallide galbinis, petalorum marginibus undulatis, labello ellipsoideo, ovario sparsim pubescenti differt. Typus: SE. Tibet [Xizang], Pome [Zhamo], *Ludlow, Sherriff & Elliot* 15361 (holotypus BM!, isotypi E!, K!).

DESCRIPTION. A terrestrial herb 25–38 cm tall; stems glabrous. Leaves three, elliptic-ovate or elliptic, acuminate or acute, 6–13 long, 3.6–7.5 cm wide, very sparsely glandular pubescent especially at base and towards the apex, sparsely pubescent on the veins, subtended by two to three sheaths. Inflorescence one-flowered; bract ovate to ovate-elliptic, acuminate or acute, 6–8 cm long, 3–4 cm wide, sparsely pubescent. Flower light greenish yellow, glabrous on outer surface; pedicel and ovary 3.5–4.1 cm long, very sparsely glandular pubescent towards the apex. Dorsal sepal ovate-elliptic, acuminate, 3.3–3.8 long, 1.5–1.7 cm wide. Synsepal ovate to lanceolate, acutely bifid at the apex, 3.3–3.8 long, 0.12–1.5 cm wide. Petals spreading, untwisted, somewhat obliquely lanceolate, acuminate, 3–4 cm long, 0.9–1.2 cm wide, pubescent at the base on the inner surface, with somewhat undulate lateral margins. Lip rather shallowly saccate, subellipsoid, 3–3.6 cm long, with marked infolded side lobes. Column 1–1.4 cm long; staminode subporrect, trullate, c. 1 cm long, longitudinally grooved along mid-vein, glabrous; filaments acute. FIGURE 31.

DISTRIBUTION. China (SE. Xizang (Tibet) only).

HABITAT. In moist places in forest; c 4300 m.

24. CYPRIPEDIUM TIBETICUM

I have taken a broad view of what constitutes *Cypripedium tibeticum* because I have been unable to find consistent features that distinguish between the plants which have been ascribed to this and other large-flowered species of this alliance from southwestern China, southeastern Xizang (Tibet), and the eastern Himalayas. Critical characters are lost in herbarium material, and I strongly suspect that field work is needed to assess the merits of the several species in this complex that have been recognised by some authorities.

Cypripedium tibeticum was described by R. A. Rolfe in 1892 based on five collections, four made by Pratt in Sichuan in western China

☐ *C. franchetii*

▲ *C. subtropicum*

＊ *C. ludlowii*

and the fifth in Sikkim by Dungboo, one of Sir George King's native collectors. None of these localities is nowadays considered to be in Xizang (Tibet). As the Pratt specimens form 80 percent of the type material, and for the sake of clarifying future work on this complex, I am designating the best of his Sichuan collections as the lectotype of *C. tibeticum*. The Pratt material differs from the King collection, of which I have seen several specimens, in representing smaller three-leaved plants with a smaller flower, a glabrous ovary, eciliate petals, a smaller staminode, and an ovate dorsal sepal that is sparingly pubescent inside towards the base. In contrast, the King collection has a rather larger flower with a somewhat pubescent ovary, slightly ciliate petals, and a rather hairier dorsal sepal.

Although *Cypripedium tibeticum* usually has a glabrous ovary like *C. macranthos,* it can often bear a few hairs particularly towards the apex, the Himalayan material being hairier than the Chinese and Bhutanese material I have seen. It is distinguished from *C. macranthos* by its flower, which is usually larger and darker maroon with boldly striped sepals and petals, broader 9- to 13-veined petals and lip that has a characteristically corrugated surface. When this species grows in alpine pastures, the flower is characteristically produced as the young leaves develop and the stem is still short. The stem lengthens and leaves grow to maturity as the flower goes over. Plants growing on the edges of woodland or in shade and flowering when the stem is taller and the leaves better developed more closely resemble the larger-flowered forms of *C. macranthos* and can be difficult to tell apart. The flowers can, however, be distinguished when pressed and dried because they are black or deep maroon, and the venation on the sepals and petals is boldly picked out in maroon or deep purple.

The types of *Cypripedium corrugatum* Franch., its var. *obesum* Franch., and *C. compactum* Schltr. agree well with the Sichuan types of *C. tibeticum*, and I consider that they all fall within the range of variation of *C. tibeticum* as it is presently understood. The first two are based on Delavay collections from Yunnan, whilst the last is based on a Limpricht collection from western Sichuan, close to where Pratt's collections were made.

I have seen many plants in the field at several localities in northwestern Yunnan (Lichiang and Zhongdian) and in western Sichuan (Balang Pass, Songpan, Huanglong, and Jiuzhaigou). The Balang Pass plants were flowering just after the snow had melted on alpine pastures above 3300 m. They were very dark maroon, appearing almost black from a distance. They differed from Yunnan and northwestern Sichuan material I have examined in having a darker maroon flower with a slight ridge on the back of the dorsal sepal, narrower petals, and a bract borne at right angles to the peduncle rather than erect and parallel to the ovary. Most of these features are very difficult to see in the preserved material, and my analyses of herbarium specimens have proved inconclusive, largely I suspect because of their poor state of preservation. I have examined the type material of *Cypripedium corrugatum* Franch., collected by Abbé Delavay in western Yunnan, and this agrees best with specimens I have examined from around Lijiang in northwestern Yunnan. In these the flowers are usually very large with a big inflated corrugated lip, the petals are somewhat ciliate and the dorsal sepal is pubescent towards the base on the inner surface. I am reluctant to recognise formally *C. corrugatum* because too many plants are either intermediate or difficult to place in one or another species. Extensive field work in the region is highly desirable and may solve this problem.

A single collection of seven specimens from southeastern Xizang (Tibet) (*Ludlow, Sherriff & Elliot* 15238) may represent a hybrid swarm between *Cypripedium tibeticum* and *C. himalaicum*, judging by the flower size, pubescence, and rather variable lip shape. Some plants have a lip shaped like that of typical *C. himalaicum*, in others the lip is shaped liked that of a small *C. tibeticum*.

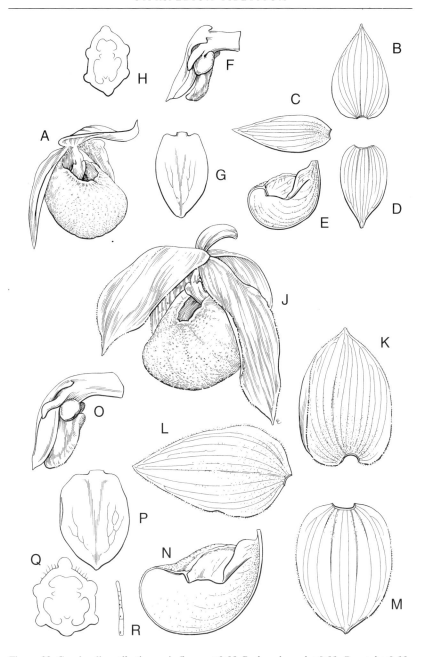

Figure 32. Cypripedium tibeticum. A, flower, ×0.66; B, dorsal sepal, ×0.66; C, petal, ×0.66; D, synsepal, ×0.66; E, lip longitudinal section, ×0.66; F, column, ×1.5; G, staminode, ×1.5; H, ovary cross section, ×4; J, flower, ×0.66; K, dorsal sepal, ×0.66; L, petal, ×0.66; M, synsepal, ×0.66; N, lip longitudinal section, ×0.66; O, column, ×1.5; P, staminode, ×1.5; Q, ovary transverse section, ×3; R, hair from ovary, ×20. A–H from Kew Spirit Collection no. 59740; J–R from Kew Spirit Collection no. 55880. All drawn by Eleanor Catherine.

207

Cypripedium tibeticum *King ex Rolfe* in J. Linn. Soc. 29: 320 (1892). Types: China, Sichuan, Tachienlu (now K'ang-ting), *Pratt 301* (lecto. K! selected here), 14, 42, 736 (all syn. K!, isosyn. BM!) and Sikkim, Chumbi and Phari, *Dungboo in King* s.n. (syn. K!).

C. corrugatum Franch. in J. Bot. (Morot) 8: 251 (1894). Types: China, Yunnan, Ma-eul-chan, *Delavay* 3478 (syn. P!, isosyn. K!) and Yunnan, Yen-tze-kay, *Delavay* s.n. (syn. P!, isosyn. K!).

C. corrugatum Franch. var. *obesum* Franch. *loc. cit.* (1894). Types: China, Yunnan, Lien-yn, *Delavay* s.n. (syn. P!, isosyn. K!) and Koutoui, *Delavay* s.n. (syn. P!, isosyn. K!). (As *C. corrugatum* Franch. var. *obesa* Franch.).

C. macranthum Sw. var. *corrugatum* Franch. *nomen.*

C. macranthum Sw. var. *tibeticum* (King ex Rolfe) Kränzl., Orchid. Gen. Sp. 1: 26 (1897).

C. compactum Schltr. in Feddes Rep. Sp. Nov. Beih. 12: 327 (1922). Type: China, Sichuan, Tatsienlu (now K'ang-ting), *Limpricht* 1647 (holo. B†, iso. K!).

DESCRIPTION. A robust terrestrial herb 13–35 cm tall, with a short creeping rhizome. Stem erect, glabrous, leafy along length. Leaves six, the lowermost three reduced to sheaths around the base of the stem, uppermost round to elliptic-ovate, obtuse to acute, 7–15 cm long, 3.3–7.2 cm wide, ciliate, glabrous on both surfaces except towards the tips. Inflorescence one-flowered, produced usually before the leaves have fully developed; bract overtopping the flower, elliptic, ovate or lanceolate, acute or acuminate, 5–10.5 cm long. Flower nodding, purple or dark maroon, usually with a darker lip with a white-margined rim to the mouth and darker marked veins on the sepals and petals, flower drying black or very dark maroon; pedicel and ovary glabrous or rarely slightly pubescent or papillose towards the apex, 2–3.2 cm long. Dorsal sepal ovate-elliptic, acuminate to shortly mucronate, 3–5.2 cm long, 2.2–3 cm wide, sparsely ciliate. Synsepal elliptic-ovate or oblong-elliptic, bifid at tip, 3–3.5 cm long, 1.8–2 cm wide, sparsely ciliate towards apex. Petals incurved-porrect to subspreading and decurved, lanceolate to oblong-lanceolate, acuminate to acute, 3.6–6 cm long, 1.4–2.5 cm wide, sparsely ciliate, densely pubescent at the base on the inner surface. Lip deeply ventricose, usually broader than deep, 3.5–6 cm long and wide, the margins of the circular to elliptic mouth crimped all round, the outer surface usually wrinkled, hairy within. Column short; staminode subsessile, cordate-trullate, 1.5–2 cm

long, 0.8–1.2 cm wide, more or less flat but somewhat concave at the blunt tip, glabrous. PLATES 25, 110–116; FIGURE 32.
DISTRIBUTION. Sikkim, Bhutan, W. China (Xizang (Tibet), Yunnan, Sichuan, and possibly S. Gansu). See map p. 201.
HABITAT. Open montane meadows, margins of coniferous and mixed woodlands, open limestone ledges and screes; 2300–4200 (4600) m.

25. CYPRIPEDIUM SMITHII

This close ally of *Cypripedium macranthos* differs in having a deep plum-coloured flower, a very deeply saccate lip with prominent translucent windows at the back and lacking a white rim to its mouth, narrowly lanceolate seven-nerved petals, and a sparsely hairy ovary with the hairs borne on the ribs. It characteristically dries very dark purple or even blackish, whereas *C. macranthos* typically dries a paler colour, usually brown or brownish purple.

The species is found in the mountains of central China, but is possibly sympatric with *Cypripedium macranthos* in the northeast and with *C. tibeticum* in the southwestern part of its range. I have found it growing in Jiuzhaigou in northern Sichuan amongst a large colony of *C. flavum* in areas of fallen rocks in conifer forest at 3200 m. In the living state it is easy to distinguish from its close allies, but when pressed the distinctions are less obvious. Plants I have seen varied a lot in plant and flower size, and this may have led Schlechter to describe *C. smithii* and *C. calcicolum*, both based on collections by Harry Smith from Dongrergo in northern Sichuan. *Cypripedium calcicolum* has much smaller flowers than those of the type material of *C. smithii*, but this variation can be seen within a colony, and I therefore consider it to be conspecific with *C. smithii*.

Cypripedium smithii *Schltr.* in Acta Horti Gothoburg 1: 129 (1924). Type: China, Sichuan, Dongrergo, *H. Smith* 3702 (holo. UPS!).
C. calcicolum Schltr. in *op. cit.*: 126 (1924). Type: China, Sichuan, Dongrergo, *H. Smith* 3704 (holo. UPS!).

DESCRIPTION. A terrestrial herb 15–45 cm tall, with a short creeping stout rhizome. Stem erect. Leaves three to four, elliptic, acute to acuminate, 5–16.5 cm long, 4–5.5 cm wide, almost glabrous on both surfaces, shortly ciliate, subtended by two to three sheaths. Inflo-

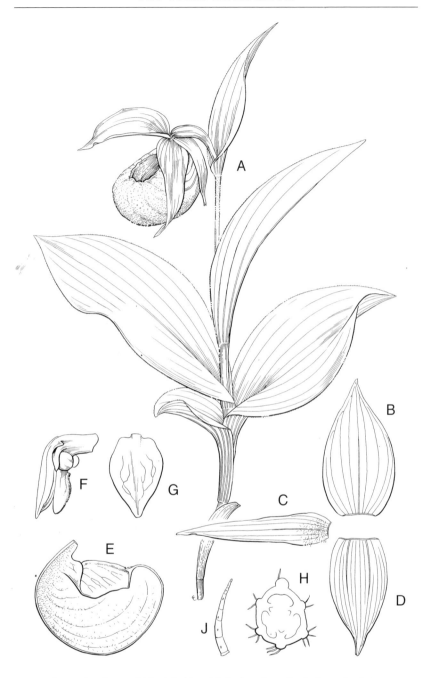

Figure 33. Cypripedium smithii. A, habit, ×0.5; B, dorsal sepal, ×1; C, petal, ×1; D, synsepal, ×1; E, lip longitudinal section, ×1; F, column, ×1.5; G, staminode, ×1.5; H, ovary transverse section, ×4; J, hair from ovary, ×20. A from type collection; B–J from Kew Spirit Collection no. 59739. All drawn by Eleanor Catherine.

210

rescence erect, one-flowered; peduncle pubescent; bract lanceolate, acuminate, to 9.5 cm long, 2.5 cm wide. Flower deep plum-coloured with translucent windows on back of lip; pedicel and ovary 3–3.7 cm long, bearing sparse multicellular hairs, especially towards the top. Dorsal sepal elliptic-ovate, acuminate, 3.5–5 cm long, 1.9–2.2 cm wide. Synsepal elliptic-lanceolate, acute and slightly bilobed at apex, 3.2–4.2 cm long, 1.5–2 cm wide. Petals untwisted, linear-lanceolate, acuminate, 4.4–5.2 cm long, 0.8–0.9 cm wide, pubescent at base on inner side otherwise glabrous, five-veined. Lip deeply saccate, 3.5–4.2 cm long, 2.5–2.8 cm wide, with a pinched raised rim to the orifice, glabrous on the outer surface. Column 1–1.2 cm long, glabrous; staminode trullate, acute, 1.3–1.5 cm long, 0.8–1 cm wide, slightly longitudinally concave but with lateral margins slightly recurved; anther filaments falcate, acute; stigma longly stalked, papillate. PLATES 107–109; FIGURE 33.

DISTRIBUTION. China (Sichuan, Shanxi, NW. Yunnan). See map p. 201.

HABITAT. In mixed deciduous and coniferous forest, amongst rocks in forest, on tufa islands in scrub and low forest in the bed of mountain streams; 2600–3900 m. Flowering in June and July.

26. CYPRIPEDIUM FRANCHETII

Cypripedium franchetii is closely related to *C. macranthos* and *C. tibeticum*, but generally has a smaller flower, a more heart-shaped staminode, and a densely pubescent or villose ovary and stem. This group of generally pink- or purple-flowered species are difficult to distinguish in the field and the herbarium, but the densely hairy ovary always serves to distinguish this species.

I have examined an isotype of *Cypripedium pulchrum*, described by Oakes Ames and Schlechter, based on a collection in western Sichuan by E. H. Wilson, and it agrees well with *C. franchetii* in its floral features. It differs in having only two fully developed leaves, but this is probably insufficient grounds for its recognition as a distinct taxon.

Handel-Mazzetti's *Cypripedium macranthos* var. *villosum*, based on a collection from Hubei Province by E. H. Wilson, also agrees well with *C. franchetii* and is here reduced to its synonymy. I have tentatively placed Schlechter's *C. lanuginosum*, the type of which was destroyed, into the synonymy of *C. franchetii*, based on his detailed de-

211

scription, which states that the ovary is "*perdense lanuginoso*" and the lip "*calceolare oblongoideo, 3 cm long, medio fere 1.5 cm alto, osteo anguste ovali, lamella pluricrenulata lateribus donato*". However, *C. lanuginosum* is from a province where *C. franchetii* has yet to be found, and it may indeed prove to be distinct.

I have seen *Cypripedium franchetii* several times in western and northern Sichuan, growing amongst grasses and small bushes of rhododendron on banks or terraces above fast-flowing rivers at between 2000 and 3000 m elevation. It often grows in small clumps of to ten or more flowering stems.

Cypripedium franchetii *E.H. Wilson* in Horticulture 16(5): 145 (1912); Schltr. in Acta Horti Gothoburg 1: 128 (1924). Type: China, *Wilson* 1754 (holo. AMES!).

C. pulchrum Ames & Schltr. in Feddes Rep. Sp. Nov. Beih. 4: 39 (1919). Type: China, Sichuan, Mupin (Pao Hsing), *Wilson* 1756 (holo. B†, iso. AMES!).

? *C. lanuginosum* Schltr. in *op. cit.*: 38 (1919). Type: China, Kouytcheou (Guizhou), Pin-fou, *Esquirol* s.n. (holo. B†).

C. macranthos var. *villosum* Hand.-Mazz. in Oesterr. Bot. Zeitschr. 85: 227 (1936). Type: China, Hubei, *Wilson* 1884 (holo. W!).

DESCRIPTION. A terrestrial herb 13–35 cm tall, with clustered erect densely villose stems. Leaves three to seven, the lowermost three sheathing, the uppermost ones elliptic to elliptic-ovate, shortly acuminate, 6–17.5 cm long, 3–8.8 cm wide, ciliate, hairy on the veins of both surfaces. Inflorescence one-flowered; peduncle densely villose; bract leaf-like, elliptic to lanceolate, 6–8.5 cm long, 2–3.5 cm wide, ciliate. Flower pink with purple venation on all segments; ovary 2–4 cm long, densely red-villose and glandular. Dorsal sepal elliptic-ovate, acute or shortly acuminate, 4–5.2 cm long, 2.2–2.8 cm wide; synsepal elliptic-lanceolate, bifid at apex, 3.3–4.2 cm long, 1.3–2.5 cm wide. Petals straight or subfalcate, lanceolate-tapering, acute, 3.7–5 cm long, 1.2–1.9 cm wide, pubescent at base on inner surface. Lip deeply saccate, 3.2–5 cm long. Column 1–1.1 cm long; staminode heart-shaped to triangular, acute, 1.2–1.4 cm long, 0.8–0.9 cm wide. PLATES 63, 64; FIGURE 34.

DISTRIBUTION. China (W. Sichuan, S. Gansu, S. Shaanxi, W. Henan, NW. Hubei). See map p. 205.

HABITAT. On grassy banks, in scrub, on the edge of woodland and in forest; 1500–3700 m.

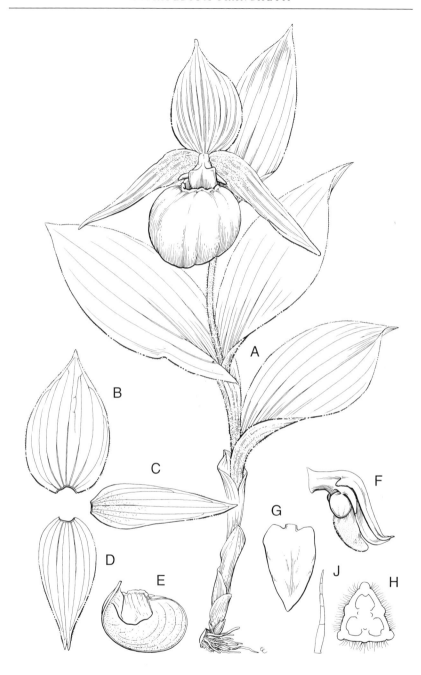

Figure 34. Cypripedium franchetii. A, habit, ×0.66; B, dorsal sepal, ×0.66; C, petal, ×0.66; D, synsepal, ×0.66; E, lip longitudinal section, ×0.66; F, column, ×1.5; G, staminode, ×1.5; H, ovary cross section, ×3; hair from ovary, ×20. All drawn from *Wilson* 1754 by Eleanor Catherine.

27. CYPRIPEDIUM HIMALAICUM

Cypripedium himalaicum was first collected by Joseph Hooker and Thomas Thomson in the Sikkim Himalayas and was described by Robert Rolfe in 1892. It was originally thought to be *C. macranthos* and subsequently has often been confused with the sympatric *C. tibeticum*, which grows in similar places in the Himalayas. However, it is easily distinguished from both in having a smaller flower with a distinctive lip and a densely pubescent ovary, the hairs being multicellular. The flower's most distinctive features are the dorsal sepal, which is much broader than the synsepal, and the lip, which is somewhat bulbous in side view and bilaterally compressed and has a broad mouth with a toothed margin. The staminode is much smaller and coloured bright yellow and has blunt filaments rather than slender tapering ones. Occasional specimens from the Himalayas that have a somewhat pubescent ovary, but otherwise resemble *C. tibeticum*, have been seen in herbaria and may be hybrids of the two species.

Cypripedium himalaicum somewhat resembles *C. farreri* from Gansu and northern Sichuan in its facies and lip shape, but that species has a glandular ovary, pale yellow flower, boldly striped sepals and petals, petals that are usually more twisted and a lip with marked grooves on the outer surface radiating from the mouth.

Cypripedium himalaicum *Rolfe* in J. Linn. Soc. 29: 319 (1892); Curtis's Bot. Mag. 148: t.8965 (1923). Type: Sikkim, *J.D. Hooker & T. Thomson* 317 (holo. K!).

DESCRIPTION. A small terrestrial herb 14–30 cm tall, growing from an elongate rhizome 2–4 mm in diameter. Stems erect, short, 4–20 cm long, sparsely pubescent, with two to three basal tubular sheaths, three- to four-leaved. Leaves closely spaced on stem, elliptic to ovate, acute, 5–10 cm long, 2.4–4.7 cm wide, slightly pubescent on upper surface, glabrous beneath, ciliate. Inflorescence one-flowered; peduncle 3–10 cm long, pubescent especially above; bract lanceolate, acuminate, 3.2–6 cm long, 0.5–1.3 cm wide. Flower very fragrant, claret and green, crimson-purple or reddish chocolate with a yellow column; pedicel and ovary 1.6–2.4 cm long, densely long-pubescent, hairs multicellular. Dorsal sepal ovate or elliptic, shortly acuminate or acute, 2.4–2.8 cm long, 1.8–2 cm wide, glabrous, eciliate; synsepal deeply concave, oblong-lanceolate, acute,

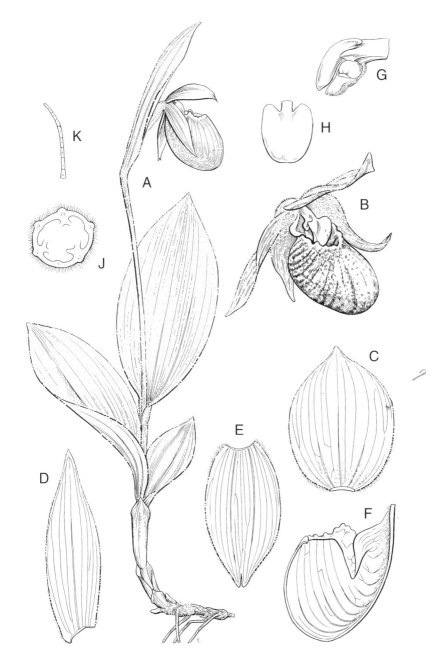

Figure 35. Cypripedium himalaicum. A, habit, ×0.66; B, flower, ×1; C, dorsal sepal, ×1.5; D, petal, ×1.5; E, synsepal, ×1.5; F, lip longitudinal section, ×1.5; G, column, ×2; H, staminode, ×2; J, ovary cross section, ×4; K, hair from ovary, ×20. All drawn from *Schilling* 420a by Eleanor Catherine.

215

1.8–2.2 cm long, one-third as wide as dorsal sepal, glabrous, eciliate. Petals untwisted, lanceolate or linear-lanceolate, acute, 2.3–3.4 cm long, 0.6–0.7 cm wide, pubescent at the base, ciliate. Lip bulbous, broadest towards the apex in side view, bilaterally compressed, 2.8–3.4 cm long, with a small mouth with a toothed margin; side lobes incurved and with a distinct crease. Column 0.7–0.9 cm long; staminode trullate-subcordate, obtuse to truncate, longitudinally concave, 0.7 cm long, 0.55 cm wide. PLATES 13, 69, 70; FIGURE 35.

DISTRIBUTION. N. India, Nepal, Sikkim, Bhutan, SE. Xizang (Tibet). Possibly SW. China. See map p. 165.

HABITAT. Amongst grass-clad limestone boulders, in nooks and crevices, amongst small shrubs on steep hillsides, in pastures, on open rocky slopes, or in *Rhododendron-Cassiope* scrub, growing in partial shade; 2800–4900 m. Flowering in June and July.

SECTION ENANTIOPEDILUM

Cypripedium sect. **Enantiopedilum** *Pfitzer* in Engler, Pflanzenr. IV, 50 (Heft 12) Orch. Pleonan.: 29, 39 (1903). Type species: *C. fasciculatum* Kellogg.
Cypripedium sect. *Cypripedium* subsect. *Enantiopedilum* (Pfitzer) S.C. Chen in Proc. 12th World Orch. Conf.: 145 (1987).

Leaves two, subopposite; inflorescences suberect-nutant, two- to four-flowered; flowers small, bronzy-brown; ovary bearing glandular and multicellular hairs.
A monotypic section.

28. CYPRIPEDIUM FASCICULATUM

This is one of only three species in the genus endemic to western North America, the others being *Cypripedium californicum* and *C. montanum*. Its affinities, however, do not lie with those species but more probably with the Asiatic species *C. elegans, C. debile,* and *C. palangshanense,* particularly with the first of these. It differs from all these one-flowered species in having two or more flowers in a clustered, more or less drooping raceme. It is distinctive and unlikely to be mistaken for any other North American species.

Cypripedium fasciculatum was originally described by S. Watson in

1882 based on collections by Suksdorf from Washington State and by Austin and Bradley from northern California. Robert Rolfe described *C. pusillum* in 1892, based on a specimen that flowered at Kew. The plant was of unknown origin but another specimen, probably from the same importation and sent to him by H. J. Elwes of Cirencester, was said to have been sent from Florida. Plants from Idaho, Wyoming, Colorado, Utah, and Montana are often slightly smaller in habit and flower than those from Washington, California, and Oregon, but Correll (1950) rightly dismissed the idea that this species merited recognition at specific rank and correctly assigned *C. pusillum* to the synonymy of *C. fasciculatum*. Correll (1950) also considered *C. knightiae* to be a synonym. The type material was collected by Knight in the Medicine Bow Mountains of Wyoming. I have seen material labelled as *C. knightiae* and agree with him. An illustration by Kellogg in the Reichenbach herbarium in Vienna and labelled by him "*C. glomeratum*" is undoubtedly of *C. fasciculatum*. *Cypripedium glomeratum* appears to be an unpublished name.

This dwarf orchid grows in coniferous forest in dappled light conditions, usually in subclimax forest. Elliman and Dalton (1995) describe its habitat in Montana as Douglas fir and Ponderosa pine forest which eventually gives way to Grand fir and Western red cedar forest.

Cypripedium fasciculatum *Kellogg ex S. Watson* in Proc. Amer. Acad. 17: 380 (1882); Correll, Native Orchids North Amer.: 31, t.6 (1950); Luer, Native Orchids U.S.A. and Canada: 64, t.12 (1975); Elliman and Dalton in North Amer. Native Orchid J. 1: 59–73 (1995). Types: U.S.A., Washington Territory, White Salmon River, *Suksdorf* s.n. (syn. AMES!, isosyn. BM! K!), California, Plumas County, near Prattville, *Austin* s.n. (syn. AMES!, isosyn. K!) and California, probably mountains of Del Norte County, *Bradley* s.n. (syn. AMES!).
C. pusillum Rolfe in Bull. Misc. Inform. Kew 1892: 211 (1892) and in Gard. Chron. III, 12: 364 (1892). Type: cult. Kew (holo. K!).
C. fasciculatum var. *pusillum* (Rolfe) Hooker f. in Bot. Mag. 119: t.7275 (1893).
C. knightiae A. Nelson in Bot. Gaz. 42: 48 (1906). Type: U.S.A., Wyoming, Medicine Bow Mts., Cooper Hill, *Knight* s.n. (holo. Rocky Mts. Herb.); Utah, Uinta Mts., *Goodding* 1201 (para. AMES!).

DESCRIPTION. A small terrestrial herb with a drooping habit, to 25 cm tall, with a slender short rhizome. Stems one to two, rather weak

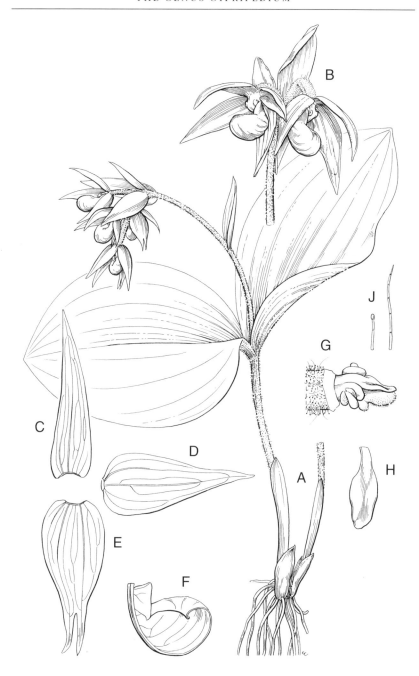

Figure 36. Cypripedium fasciculatum. A, habit, ×0.66; B, detail of inflorescence, ×1; C, dorsal sepal, ×3; D, petal, ×3; E, synsepal, ×3; F, lip longitudinal section, ×3; G, column, ×6; H, staminode, ×10; J, hairs from ovary, ×20. A from *Halliday & Roderick* s.n.; B–J from *Suksdorf* 7221. All drawn by Eleanor Catherine.

218

and arching, terete or grooved longitudinally, 5–15 cm long, 0.2–
0.3 cm in diameter, densely reddish villose, emerging from two to
three papery sheaths in the basal half. Leaves two, opposite at the
apex of the stem, ovate-elliptic, obtuse or rounded, 5–10 cm long,
3.5–7 cm wide, often convex and curved down to touch the ground,
glabrous above and below, prominently three-veined. Inflorescence
arcuate, distantly densely two- to four-flowered; peduncle weakly
arcuate, villose, 2–15 cm long, bearing a sterile lanceolate bract
along length; bracts lanceolate, acute, 1–3.5 cm long, glabrous.
Flowers small, nutant, borne on a short crowded raceme, purplish
brown to greenish, the lip yellow-green streaked and mottled with
purple around the mouth; pedicel and ovary 1–1.8 cm long, shortly
glandular-pubescent. Dorsal sepal lanceolate, acuminate, 1.5–2.6
cm long, 0.3–0.8 cm wide, arching over lip; synsepal similar but
shortly acuminately bifid at the tip, 1.5–2.5 cm long, 0.4–0.9 cm
wide. Petals lanceolate, acuminate, incurving, 1.5–2.5 cm long, 0.6–
1.7 cm wide. Lip small, globose but slightly dorsiventrally flattened,
mouth small, 0.8–1.5 cm long, 0.5–0.9 cm across. Column short,
0.3 cm long; staminode whitish to pale yellow-green, elliptic-trulli-
form, obtuse, much smaller than the stigma, 0.3 cm long, 0.2 cm
wide. PLATES 9, 55, 56; FIGURE 36.

DISTRIBUTION. Western U.S.A. (Washington, Oregon, California, Colorado, Montana, Idaho, Utah, Wyoming). See map p. 127.

HABITAT. Usually found in moist to dry, cool, open coniferous
forest, less commonly in swampy ground and on rocky places under
scrub in montane regions; 900–1400 m altitude.

SECTION ARIETINUM

Cypripedium sect. **Arietinum** *C. Morren* in Belg. Hort. 1: (1851).
Type species: *C. arietinum* R. Br.
Cypripedium sect. *Criosanthes* (Raf.) Pfitzer in Engler and Prantl,
Pflanzenfam. Nachtr. 1: 97 (1897) and in Engler, Pflanzenr. IV,
50 (Heft 12) Orch. Pleonan.: 40 (1903). Type species: *C. arieti-
num* R. Br.
Criosanthes Raf. in Amer. Monthly Mag. & Crit. Rev.: 268 (1818).
Arietinum Beck, Bot. North Middle States: 352 (1833).

Leaves several, well-spaced on stem, elliptic to lanceolate, parallel-veined; inflorescences one-flowered; lateral sepals free to base,

sublinear; lip obconical, hairy around mouth; petals narrow, tapering; staminode convex, glabrous.

A section of two species. Atwood (1985) considered the section distinct enough to be raised to generic level as *Criosanthes*, but for reasons outlined earlier on this has not been followed here.

29. CYPRIPEDIUM ARIETINUM

Commonly called the RAM'S-HEAD SLIPPER ORCHID, *Cypripedium arietinum* is the most distinctive of the North American species, readily recognised by its conical, pointed, hairy lip, and fully divided, linear lateral sepals. It was described by Robert Brown based upon a plant which flowered at Kew that had been introduced from North America in 1808 by Messrs. Chandler and Buckingham.

It is a relatively uniform species, although albino (Luer 1975) and two-flowered forms (Brown 1995a) have been recognised. Its relationship to the closely allied Chinese species, *Cypripedium plectrochilum*, is discussed under that species. The two differ mainly in their lip and staminode shapes and other minor floral features. Morris and Eames (1929) sum up the appeal of *C. arietinum* thus:

> [I]t has . . . a singular beauty of its own; but one that invites the fond look of a lover rather than the hasty glance of some prize-hunting vandal. To be really seen, it must be looked at from a level as the camera looks at it, and preferably in profile.

In other words, it is not a showy orchid.

It is a species with a northerly and easterly distribution in North America and is generally found at relatively low elevations. It prefers hummocks at the base of tamaracks or the shelter of cedar and spruce. It is characteristically a plant of old rich mossy bogs and only rarely is it found in drier areas under conifers. In contrast, its Chinese relative is found in dry rocky places in forests in the mountains of western China.

The names *Criosanthes parviflora, C. borealis,* and *Arietina americana* seem to be superfluous names as they are all based either directly or indirectly on the same type as *Cypripedium arietinum*. The genus *Criosanthes*, established by C. S. Rafinesque, was based on the lateral sepals being distinct and not forming a synsepal. Rafinesque's genus has been largely ignored by later authors writing

220

on North American slipper orchids, but Atwood resurrected it for *C. arietinum* and *C. plectrochilum* based on a phylogenetic analysis which suggested that these taxa were a sister group of the other hardy slipper orchids in the genus *Cypripedium*. By and large this view has been dismissed by others, and cladistic analyses involving molecular and morphological data suggest that *Criosanthes* nests within *Cypripedium* (Cox 1995, Cribb and Simpson in press).

Cypripedium arietinum *R. Br.* in Aiton, Hort. Kew. ed.2, 5: 222 (1813); Correll, Native Orchids North Amer.: 22, t.2 (1950); Luer, Native Orchids U.S.A. and Canada: 42, t.2 (1975). Type: North America, cult.Kew ex Chandler & Buckingham (holo. BM!).
Criosanthes borealis Raf. in Amer. Monthly Mag. & Crit. Rev.: 268 (1818). Nom. nov. pro *Cypripedium arietinum* R. Br.
Arietinum americanum Beck, Bot. North Middle States: 352 (1833). Nom. nov. pro *Cypripedium arietinum* R. Br.
Criosanthes parviflora Raf., Fl. Tellur. 4: 46 (1837). Nom. nov. pro *Arietinum americanum* Beck.
C. arietina (R. Br.) House in Bull. Torrey Bot. Club 32: 374 (1905).
Cypripedium arietinum R. Br. forma *biflorum* P.M. Br. in North Amer. Native Orchid J. 1(3): 198 (1995). Type: U.S.A., Vermont, Windsor County, *P.M. Brown* (photo by Brown in AMES).

DESCRIPTION. A terrestrial herb with one to several clustered stems to 32 cm tall, growing from a short rhizome with fibrous roots. Stems slender, terete, bearing three to four leaves in the apical half, pubescent, covered almost entirely by three to four tubular sheaths. Leaves suberect or ascending, narrowly elliptic-lanceolate, acute, 5–10 cm long, 1–3 cm wide, bluish green. Inflorescence one-flowered, 4–10 cm long; peduncle slender, wiry, densely shortly pubescent and glandular especially above; bract lanceolate, usually longer than the flower, 2–5 cm long. Flower with purple-green sepals and petals, the lip white heavily veined and mottled with purple except around the mouth; pedicel and ovary 0.8–1.5 cm long, densely shortly glandular pubescent. Dorsal sepal narrowly ovate, acuminate, 1.5–2.5 cm long, 0.5–1.1 cm wide, pubescent and ciliate; lateral sepals deflexed, linear-lanceolate, acute, 1.5–2 cm long, 0.2–0.4 cm wide, pubescent and ciliate. Petals porrect or deflexed, linear, acute, 1.3–2.2 cm long, 0.1–0.2 cm wide, ciliate. Lip obliquely conical, pointed, 1.5–2.5 cm long, 1–2 cm across, densely white-pubescent on the incurved margin of mouth, pubescent on front

221

surface. Column short; staminode concave, clawed, suborbicular, c. 5 mm long, 4 mm wide. PLATES 2, 31, 32; FIGURE 37.

DISTRIBUTION. Canada (Quebec and Ontario west to Manitoba), U.S.A. (Maine, Vermont, New Hampshire, Massachusetts, New York, Connecticut, Michigan, Wisconsin, Illinois, Minnesota). See map p. 185.

HABITAT. In cold sphagnum, *Larix* (tamarack), *Thuja* (arborvitae and cedar) swamps and bogs, in damp coniferous forest and on wooded rocky slopes; sea level to 1000 m.

30. CYPRIPEDIUM PLECTROCHILUM

Cypripedium plectrochilum is one of the most distinctive Chinese species with its small flower, slender sepals and petals, and a pointed conical lip. It was discovered by Abbé Delavay in southwestern Sichuan and was described by M. A. Franchet in 1885. It is apparent that Franchet had doubts over the distinctness of his new species. In a letter dated April 1886 he asked Robert Rolfe to check an enclosed Delavay collection against specimens of *C. arietinum* in the Kew Herbarium because "[J]e ne crois pas aujourd'hui être distincte du *C. arietinum* R. Br.".

Certainly, *Cypripedium plectrochilum* and *C. arietinum* are similar and very closely related, so much so that they are difficult to distinguish in herbarium specimens. In the living state, the two can be distinguished by flower colour and pubescence, and lip shape: *C. plectrochilum* has an obliquely conical lip that is white and scarcely veined with pink, with a rather broader blunt yellow-green apex and hairs that concentrate around the mouth, whereas *C. arietinum* has a conical lip suffused and veined with purple, tapering to an acute green or purple point, and with lots of hair both around the mouth and down the front. In the specimens I have examined, *C. plectrochilum* has petals that are scarcely ciliate and sepals that are ciliate but not hairy. In *C. arietinum*, the petals are distinctly ciliate and the sepals hairy and ciliate. The ovary of *C. plectrochilum* is also distinctly less pubescent than that of *C. arietinum*. The staminode seems to provide the best distinctions. In *C. plectrochilum* it is sessile, strongly convex, and pure white, whilst in *C. arietinum* it is stalked, less convex, and purple. The filaments are clearly visible in *C. arietinum* and have distinct elongate apices. Vegetatively they are also close. The bract of *C. plectrochilum* is shorter and broader, usually shorter than or rarely just slightly longer than the flower. In *C. arietinum*, the bract is often linear and always longer than the flower. Perner (1995) provided a detailed discussion of the differences between these species accompanied by excellent diagnostic colour photographs.

Cypripedium plectrochilum *Franch.* in Bull. Soc. Bot. France 32: 27 (1885). Type: China, Sichuan, Houng-li-pin, above Ta-pin-tze, *Delavay* 46 (holo. P!).

DESCRIPTION. A terrestrial herb forming small clumps; rhizome very short. Stems erect, clustered, slender, 5–18 cm long, 0.2 cm in diameter, pubescent, usually with three or rarely with two or four leaves subtended by three, cylindrical, obtuse sheaths. Leaves suberect elliptic to lanceolate, obtuse to acute, 3–8 cm long, 1–3.8 cm wide, very shortly ciliate. Inflorescence erect, one-flowered; peduncle slender, 3.5–9 cm long, shortly pubescent; bract leaf-like, elliptic to lanceolate, acute, 1.7–3.6 cm long, very shortly ciliate. Flower small, with an elusive fragrance, with chocolate-brown or greenish brown sepals and petals and a white lip and staminode, the lip lightly spotted with pink on apical rim; pedicel and ovary 1.5–1.8 cm long, shortly and densely pubescent. Dorsal sepal erect, ovate to lanceolate, acute, 1.8–2.2 cm long, 0.6–0.9 cm wide, slightly pubescent at the base; lateral sepals free to base, falcate, linear-ligulate, acute, 1.2–1.5 cm long, 0.2–0.3 cm wide, slightly pubescent at the base. Petals porrect, falcate, linear-ligulate, acute, 1.6–1.8 cm long, 0.1–0.2 cm wide, pubescent in basal half. Lip saccate, obliquely conical with a blunt apex, 1.6–2.4 cm long, pubescent on front rim. Column 0.6–0.7 cm long; staminode convex, subquadrate-obovate, truncate or slightly notched with a short blunt apicule, 0.5–0.7 cm long and wide, slightly pustular in middle. PLATES 99, 100; FIGURE 37.

DISTRIBUTION. N. Burma, China (SE. Xichang, NW. Yunnan, Sichuan, W. Hubei). See map p. 225.

HABITAT. In stony ground, usually limestone, in semi-shade on margins of and in *Pinus* (pine) and *Picea* (spruce) forest, and in mixed montane forest and scrub; (1570–)2300–3600 m.

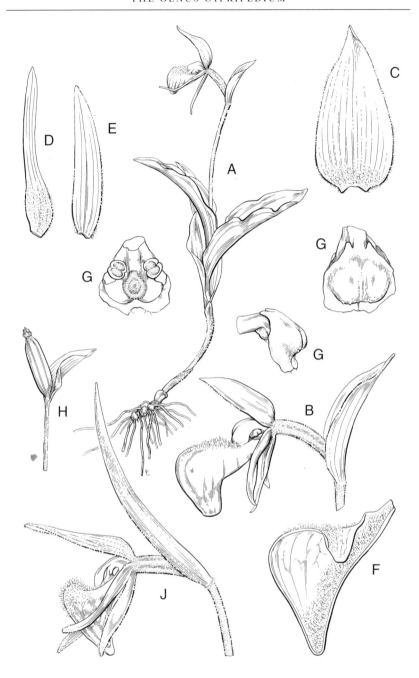

Figure 37. Cypripedium plectrochilum. A, habit, ×0.66; B, flower, ×2; C, dorsal sepal, ×3; D, petal, ×3; E, lateral sepal, ×3; F, lip longitudinal section, ×3; G, column, three views, ×3; H, fruit, ×1. **Cypripedium arietinum.** J, flower, ×2. A–H drawn from Kew Spirit Collection no. 55186; J from photograph. All drawn by Eleanor Catherine.

The
PHOTOGRAPHS

Plate 27. *Cypripedium acaule*, Connecticut, U.S.A. Photo by P. J. Cribb.

Plate 29. *Cypripedium acaule*, cult. R.B.G., Kew. Photo by P. Harcourt Davies.

Plate 28. *Cypripedium acaule*, Maryland, U.S.A. Photo by E. Greenwood.

Plate 30. *Cypripedium acaule* (albino form), Montmorency County, Michigan, U.S.A. Photo by C. Luer.

Plate 31. *Cypripedium arietinum*, Montmorency County, Michigan, U.S.A. Photo by C. Luer.

Plate 32. *Cypripedium arietinum*, Ontario, Canada. Photo by E. Greenwood.

Plate 33. *Cypripedium bardolphianum* var. *bardolphianum*, Huanglong, Sichuan, China. Photo by C. Grey-Wilson.

Plate 34. *Cypripedium bardolphianum* var. *bardolphianum*, Huanglong, Sichuan, China. Photo by P. J. Cribb.

Plate 35. *Cypripedium calceolus*, cult.
W. Frosch, Germany. Photo by
P. J. Cribb.

Plate 36. *Cypripedium calceolus*,
Vercours, France. Photo by
P. Harcourt Davies.

Plate 37. *Cypripedium calceolus*, Bargen, Switzerland. Photo by P. J. Cribb.

Plate 38. *Cypripedium calceolus,* northern England. Photo by P. J. Cribb.

Plate 39. *Cypripedium calceolus,* cult. W. Frosch, Germany. Photo by P. J. Cribb.

Plate 40. *Cypripedium calceolus* f. *flavum,* Donau Eschingen, Germany. Photo by P. Harcourt Davies.

Plate 41. *Cypripedium californicum*, Curry County, Oregon, U.S.A. Photo by C. Luer.

Plate 42. *Cypripedium califor-nicum*, cult. K. Dryden. Photo by P. J. Cribb.

Plate 43. *Cypripedium californicum*, cult. B. Tattersall, Hounslow, U.K. Photo by P. Harcourt Davies.

Plate 44. *Cypripedium candidum*, Livingston County, Michigan, U.S.A. Photo by C. Luer.

Plate 45. *Cypripedium candidum*, Oakland County, Michigan, U.S.A. Photo by C. Luer.

Plate 46. *Cypripedium candidum*, cult. B. Tattersall, Hounslow, U.K. Photo by P. Harcourt Davies.

Plate 47. *Cypripedium cordigerum*, Langtang Valley, Nepal. Photo by S. Miehe.

Plate 48. *Cypripedium cordigerum*, cult. R.B.G., Kew. Photo by P. Harcourt Davies.

Plate 50. *Cypripedium debile*, cult. B. Tattersall, Hounslow, U.K. Photo by P. Harcourt Davies.

Plate 49. *Cypripedium debile*, Wolong, Sichuan, China. Photo by P. J. Cribb.

Plate 51. *Cypripedium dickinsonianum*, type collection, Chiapas, Mexico. Photo by E. Hágsater.

Plate 52. *Cypripedium dickinsonianum*, type collection, Chiapas, Mexico. Photo by E. Hágsater.

Plate 53. *Cypripedium elegans*, Habashan, northwestern Yunnan, China. Photo by C. Grey-Wilson.

Plate 54. *Cypripedium farreri*, cult. Evertse, Netherlands. Photo by W. Evertse.

Plate 55. *Cypripedium fasciculatum*, Larimer County, Colorado, U.S.A. Photo by C. Luer.

Plate 56. *Cypripedium fasciculatum*, Larimer County, Colorado, U.S.A. Photo by C. Luer.

Plate 57. *Cypripedium flavum*, road to Betahei, Yunnan, China. Photo by C. Grey-Wilson.

Plate 58. *Cypripedium flavum*, Jiuzhaigou, Sichuan, China. Photo by P. J. Cribb.

Plate 59. *Cypripedium flavum*, Jiuzhaigou, Sichuan, China. Photo by P. J. Cribb.

Plate 60. *Cypripedium flavum*, Lijiang, Yunnan, China. Photo by P. J. Cribb.

Plate 61. *Cypripedium formosanum*, cult. R.B.G., Kew. Photo by D. Menzies.

Plate 62. *Cypripedium formosanum*, cult. R.B.G., Kew. Photo by P. J. Cribb.

Plate 63. *Cypripedium franchetii*, Wolong, Sichuan, China. Photo by P. J. Cribb.

Plate 64. *Cypripedium franchetii*, Wolong, Sichuan, China. Photo by P. J. Cribb.

Plate 66. *Cypripedium guttatum*, near Palmer, Alaska, U.S.A. Photo by C. Luer.

Plate 65. *Cypripedium guttatum*, near Palmer, Alaska, U.S.A. Photo by C. Luer.

Plate 68. *Cypripedium henryi*, cult. R.B.G., Kew. Photo by P. J. Cribb.

Plate 67. *Cypripedium henryi*, cult. R.B.G., Kew. Photo by P. J. Cribb.

Plate 69. *Cypripedium himalaicum*, Temo la Pass, Tibet. Photo by A. Chambers.

Plate 70. *Cypripedium himalaicum*, Temo la Pass, Tibet. Photo by A. Chambers.

Plate 71. *Cypripedium irapeanum*, Mexico State, Mexico. Photo by C. Luer.

Plate 72. *Cypripedium irapeanum*, Mexico State, Mexico. Photo by C. Luer.

Plate 73. *Cypripedium irapeanum*, cult. S. Dickinson, San Miguel Allende, Mexico. Photo by P. J. Cribb.

Plate 74. *Cypripedium japonicum*, China. Photo by S. C. Chen.

Plate 75. *Cypripedium japonicum*, cult. Hiroshima B.G., Japan. Photo by P. J. Cribb.

Plate 76. *Cypripedium kentuckiense*, cult. F. Case. Photo by J. & B. Cooper.

Plate 77. *Cypripedium kentuckiense*, Louisiana, U.S.A. Photo by J. Atwood.

Plate 78. *Cypripedium lichiangense*, Lijiang, Yunnan, China. Photo by P. J. Cribb.

Plate 79. *Cypripedium lichiangense*, Lijiang, Yunnan, China. Photo by P. J. Cribb.

Plate 80. *Cypripedium* sp. near *C. lichiangense*, said to be from Yunnan, China, or North Vietnam, cult. Germany. Photo by H. Perner.

Plate 81. *Cypripedium macranthos*, cult. K. Dryden. Photo by P. J. Cribb.

Plate 83. *Cypripedium macranthos*, cult. B. Tattersall, Hounslow, U.K. Photo by P. Harcourt Davies.

Plate 82. *Cypripedium macranthos*, cult. K. Dryden. Photo by P. J. Cribb.

Plate 84. *Cypripedium margaritaceum,*
Lijiang, Yunnan, China. Photo by
P. J. Cribb.

Plate 85. *Cypripedium margaritaceum,*
Lijiang, Yunnan, China. Photo by
P. J. Cribb.

Plate 87. *Cypripedium
molle,* Matatán, Oaxaca,
Mexico. Photo by
P. J. Cribb.

Plate 86. *Cypripedium molle,* Matatán, Oaxaca,
Mexico. Photo by E. Greenwood.

Plate 88. *Cypripedium montanum,* Wasco County, Oregon, U.S.A. Photo by C. Luer.

Plate 89. *Cypripedium montanum,* Wasco County, Oregon, U.S.A. Photo by C. Luer.

Plate 91. *Cypripedium parviflorum* var. *parviflorum,* cult. R.B.G., Kew. Photo by P. Harcourt Davies.

Plate 90. *Cypripedium parviflorum* var. *parviflorum,* Oakland County, Michigan, U.S.A. Photo by C. Luer.

Plate 92. *Cypripedium parviflorum* var. *parviflorum*, cult. R.B.G., Kew. Photo by P. J. Cribb.

Plate 93. *Cypripedium parviflorum* var. *pubescens*, Michigan, U.S.A. Photo by J. & B. Cooper.

Plate 94. *Cypripedium parviflorum* var. *pubescens*, Gettysburg, Pennsylvania, U.S.A. Photo by E. Greenwood.

Plate 95. *Cypripedium parviflorum* var. *pubescens*, cult. R.B.G., Kew. Photo by P. Harcourt Davies.

Plate 96. *Cypripedium parviflorum* var. *pubescens* (planipetalum type), Cape Norman, Newfoundland, Canada. Photo by C. Luer.

Plate 98. *Cypripedium passerinum*, north shore of Lake Superior, Canada. Photo by C. Luer.

Plate 97. *Cypripedium passerinum*, Thunder Bay County, Ontario, Canada. Photo by C. Luer.

Plate 99. *Cypripedium plectrochilum,* Lijiang, Yunnan, China. Photo by C. Grey-Wilson.

Plate 100. *Cypripedium plectrochilum,* Lijiang, Yunnan, China. Photo by P. J. Cribb.

Plate 102. *Cypripedium reginae,* cult. E. Grell, Frankfurt, Germany. Photo by E. Grell.

Plate 101. *Cypripedium reginae,* Warren County, Pennsylvania, U.S.A. Photo by C. Luer.

Plate 103. *Cypripedium* *segawai*, cult. K. Dryden. Photo by P. J. Cribb.

Plate 104. *Cypripedium segawai*, cult. K. Dryden. Photo by P. J. Cribb.

Plate 106. *Cypripedium shanxiense*, Primorsky, eastern Russia. Photo by Y. Mokhov.

Plate 105. *Cypripedium shanxiense*, Primorsky, eastern Russia. Photo by Y. Mokhov.

Plate 107. *Cypripedium smithii*, Jiuzhaigou, Sichuan, China. Photo by C. Grey-Wilson.

Plate 108. *Cypripedium smithii*, Jiuzhaigou, Sichuan, China. Photo by P. J. Cribb.

Plate 109. *Cypripedium smithii*, Jiuzhaigou, Sichuan, China. Photo by P. J. Cribb.

Plate 110. *Cypripedium tibeticum*, Lijiang, Yunnan, China. Photo by P. J. Cribb.

Plate 111. *Cypripedium tibeticum*, Lijiang, Yunnan, China. Photo by P. J. Cribb.

Plate 112. *Cypripedium tibeticum*, Huang-long, Sichuan, China. Photo by C. Grey-Wilson.

Plate 113. *Cypripedium tibeticum*, Huang-long, Sichuan, China. Photo by P. J. Cribb.

Plate 114. *Cypripedium
tibeticum*, Balangshan,
Sichuan, China. Photo
by M. Cribb.

Plate 115. *Cypripedium tibeticum,*
Balangshan, Sichuan, China. Photo by
C. Grey-Wilson.

Plate 116. *Cypripedium
tibeticum,* Temo La Pass,
Tibet. Photo by
A. Chambers.

Plate 117. *Cypripedium* × *ventricosum,* Primorsky, eastern Russia. Photo by H. Perner.

Plate 118. *Cypripedium calceolus, C.* × *ventricosum,* and *C. macranthos,* Primorsky, eastern Russia. Photo by H. Perner.

Plate 120. *Cypripedium yatabeanum,* Kodiak Island, Alaska, U.S.A. Photo by C. Luer.

Plate 119. *Cypripedium yatabeanum,* Kodiak Island, Alaska, U.S.A. Photo by C. Luer.

Plate 121. *Cypripedium yunnanense,* Zhongdian, Yunnan, China. Photo by P. J. Cribb.

Plate 122. *Cypripedium yunnanense,* Zhongdian, Yunnan, China. Photo by P. J. Cribb.

Plate 123. Artificial hybrids shown by W. Frosch at the European Orchid Conference and Show, Rome, 1991. Photo by P. J. Cribb.

Plate 124. *Cypripedium acaule* and *C. parviflorum* varieties, R.B.G., Kew. Photo by P. J. Cribb.

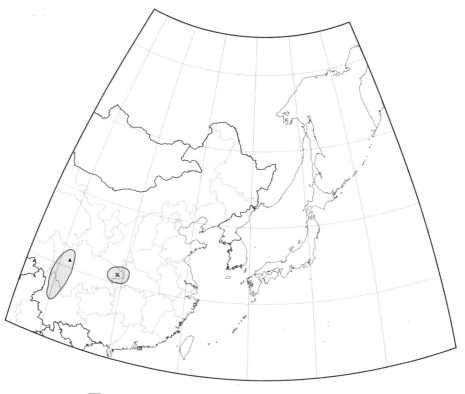

☐ *C. plectrochilum*

× *C. palangshanense*

▲ *C. micranthum*

SECTION FLABELLINERVIA

Cypripedium sect. **Flabellinervia** *(Pfitzer) Hennessy ex Cribb* **stat. nov.**
Type species: *C. japonicum* Thunb.
Cypripedium Ser.II *Flabellinervia* Pfitzer in Engler and Prantl,
   Pflanzenfam. Nachtr. 1: 97 (1897).
Cypripedium Ser.III *Flabellinervia* Pfitzer in Engler, Pflanzenr. IV, 50
   (Heft 12) Orch. Pleonan.: 42 (1903).
Cypripedium sect. *Cypripedium* subsect. *Flabellinervia* (Pfitzer) S.C.
   Chen in Proc. 12th World Orch. Conf.: 145 (1987).

   Stem, pedicel, and ovary lacking glandular hairs; rhizomes elongate; leaves distinctive, opposite, fan-shaped, with radiating vena-

225

tion; inflorescences one-flowered; lip strangely shaped, somewhat L-shaped in side view, with a narrowly pandurate mouth, crimped apex, and lacking distinct side lobes; staminode convex, glabrous.

A section of two closely allied species, *Cypripedium japonicum* from China, Korea, and Japan and *C. formosanum* from Taiwan. The latter is probably the easiest cypripedium to grow in pot culture, providing it is kept frost-free.

31. CYPRIPEDIUM JAPONICUM

This strange orchid was one of the earliest species to be described in the genus. Carl Peter Thunberg, a student of Linnaeus, described it in 1784, based on his own collection made on his seminal visit to Japan. An illustration was later published by Thunberg (1794) as the first plate in his *Icones*. For many years, this species remained an enigma and living plants were not seen in the West until Victorian times.

Cypripedium cathayanum was described in 1930 by S. S. Chien based on a collection by K. K. Tsoong from Zhejiang Province, China. He distinguished it from *C. japonicum* and *C. formosanum* because of its "tomentose stem, longer and broader bract . . . its rather strongly falcate and much narrower petals". However, the author then goes on to say that he had seen material of neither *C. japonicum* nor *C. formosanum*, nor the type description of the former. Examination of the type of *C. cathayanum* and a watercolour painting of the type in the Beijing Herbarium shows that it fits well within the concept of *C. japonicum*, which usually has an equally tomentose stem, broad bract and falcate narrow petals. Therefore, I agree with S. C. Chen and Y. Z. Xi (1987) in considering this concept conspecific with *C. japonicum*. The flowers of Chinese plants are similarly coloured to the Japanese ones and have the same shaped lip, characteristically pinched near the apex. Nakai (1932) was the first to report it from Korea where it had been collected by Hayashi in Keiki Province.

A rare albino form has been illustrated in the *Wild Orchid Journal* (1994 (5): 3). It has green sepals, petals, column, and staminode and a creamy white lip. A variant with a glabrous stem and peduncle has also been formally recognised as var. *glabrum* by Suzuki (1980).

Cypripedium japonicum is closely allied to *C. formosanum*, but is

226

readily distinguished when in flower by its yellow-green to green sepals and petals and by its lip. The latter is somewhat L-shaped in side view, has a crimped apical part that is also strongly grooved, and lacks a triangular apicule at the tip.

Cypripedium japonicum *Thunb.*, Fl. Jap.: 30 (1784) and Icon. Plant. Jap., t.1 (1794); Summerh. in Bot. Mag. 161: t.9520 (1938); S.C. Chen and Y.Z. Xi in Proc. 12th World Orch. Conf.: 145 (1987). Type: Japan, *Thunberg* (holo. UPS!, iso. BM!).

C. cathayanum S.S. Chien in Contr. Biol. Lab. Sci. Soc. China, Bot. Ser. 6: 23 (1930). Type: China, Zhejiang, Tienmu Shan, *K.K. Tsoong* 282 (holo. N, iso. PE!).

C. japonicum Thunb. var. *glabrum* M. Suzuki in Jap. J. Bot. 55: 351 (1980). Type: Japan, Honshu, Hitachi, *M. Suzuki* s.n. (holo. TKB).

DESCRIPTION. A terrestrial herb 25–45 cm tall, with a slender flexuous creeping rhizome, 15–40 cm long, 0.2–0.3 cm in diameter, bearing occasional scales and bunches of roots at intervals. Stems erect, slender, 0.4–0.5 cm in diameter, densely tomentose hairy, enclosed in several obtuse overlapping sheaths in lower part, bearing two subopposite leaves just above the middle. Leaves more or less horizontal, flabellate from a short sheathing base, rounded, obtuse or apiculate at the apex, 8–16 cm long, 7–23.5 cm wide, the margins undulate all round, usually glabrous but sometimes sparsely hairy, with radiating veins which apparently terminate at the margin. Inflorescence one-flowered, erect; peduncle slender, terete, 7–12 cm long, hairy; bract leafy, ovate or lanceolate, acute or acuminate, 3–6.5 cm long, 0.4–5.2 cm wide. Flower nutant, the sepals and petals pale yellow or yellow-green with purple spots at the base, the lip whitish or yellowish pink with carmine or crimson spots and veins, more intense on the inner surface, the staminode purplered with a green or yellow central line; pedicel and ovary 1.4–3 cm long, densely pubescent. Dorsal sepal incurved, lanceolate, acuminate, 4–6 cm long, 1.5–2.5 cm wide; synsepal elliptic-ovate, acuminate and bidentate at apex, 3.5–5 cm long, 1.2–2 cm wide. Petals falcate, lanceolate, acuminate, 3.5–6 cm long, 0.8–1.2 cm wide, hairy at the base on inner side. Lip calceiform, pendent, somewhat L-shaped in side view, with a crimped and grooved apical part, 3.8–6 cm long, 3–3.5 cm across. Column greenish-white, about 1 cm long; staminode convex, ovate or cordate, with two obscure longitudinal

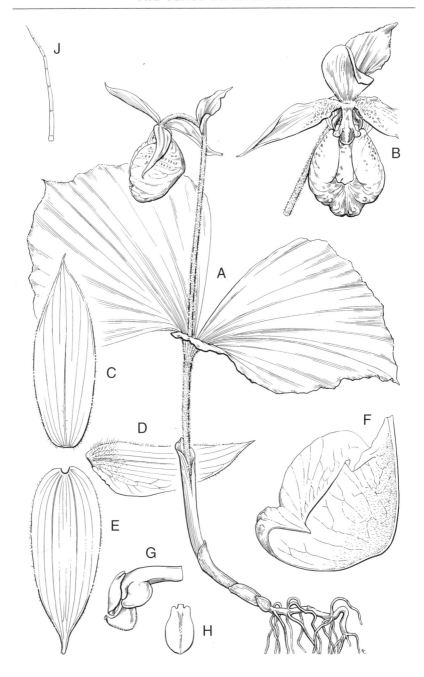

Figure 38. Cypripedium japonicum. A, habit, ×0.4; B, flower, ×0.66; C, dorsal sepal, ×1; D, petal, ×1; E, synsepal, ×1; F, lip longitudinal section, ×1; G, column, ×1.5; H, staminode, ×1.5; J, hair from ovary, ×20. A from *Farges* s.n.; B–J from *Murata et al.* 113. All drawn by Eleanor Catherine.

228

ridges, 1 cm long, 0.8–0.9 cm wide. PLATES 15, 74, 75; FIGURES 6, 38.

DISTRIBUTION. Japan (Awaji, Kyushu, S. Hokkaido, NE. Honshu, Sado, Shikoku), Korea, China (Anhui, Zhejiang, Jiangxi, Hunan, Hubei, S. Shaanxi, Gansu, Sichuan, NE. Guizhou).

HABITAT. In and on edge of bamboo groves and in thin montane forest often near water, in dappled shade; 1000–2000 m. Flowering in May and early June.

☐ C. japonicum
■ C. formosanum

32. CYPRIPEDIUM FORMOSANUM

Cypripedium formosanum is considered by many to be the most beautiful of all the species in the genus. It was discovered at Oiwake in the mountains of Taiwan and described in 1916 by the Japanese botanist B. Hayata. It is endemic to the island where it is found growing in the mountains between 2000 and 3000 m. It is closely related to *C. japonicum* and has been considered by several authorities to be a variety of that species. However, it differs in having a glabrous stem, sparsely pubescent or glabrous peduncle, and a flower with several distinctive features. The flowers are white spotted and flushed with pink, the petals are broader and oblong-oblanceolate, and the lip is fuller without a constriction near the apex. I am, therefore, inclined to give it specific status unless further evidence is presented to show that these differences are not as discrete as they presently appear. Certainly more needs to be discovered about the Chinese specimens assigned presently to *C. japonicum* to see if those from the mainland nearest to Taiwan are at all intermediate between the Japanese and Taiwanese materials.

Despite its being very poorly represented in herbaria outside of Japan and Taiwan, this species is relatively frequently seen in cultivation and is one of the easiest of all the cypripediums to grow. It thrives in an open sandy loam in light shady conditions, but unlike many of its relatives is not hardy in the British Isles where it needs winter protection in a greenhouse.

Cypripedium formosanum *Hayata,* Icon. Pl. Formos. 6: 66, fig.9 (1916); Schltr. in Feddes Rep. Sp. Nov. Beih. 4: 81 (1919); Cheng, Formos. Orch.: 62 (1979). Type: Taiwan, Oiwake, April 1916, *B. Hayata* (holo. TIU!, iso. AMES!, TAIF!).

C. japonicum sensu Hayata, *op. cit.* 2: 136 (1912); Liu and Su in Fl. Taiwan 5: 951 (1978); Su, Nat. Orchid. Taiwan: 171 (1985).

C. japonicum Thunb. var. *formosanum* (Hayata) S.S. Ying in Chinese Flowers 15:33, t.1 (1975): Quart. Bull. Chin. For. 8: 141 (1975); Coloured Ill. Indig. Orch. Taiwan 1: 356, 442, t.52 (1977); J.J. Wood in Kew Mag. 4: 62, t.74 (1987).

DESCRIPTION. A terrestrial herb with erect glabrous flowering stems arising from a creeping, branching rhizome, 0.2–0.3 cm in diameter, bearing remote scales and clustered roots at intervals along the length. Stems 10–25 cm long, enclosed below by five to eight imbricate obtuse sheaths, two-leaved at the apex. Leaves plicate, spreading, flabellate, obtuse, rounded or apiculate at the apex, 10–13 cm long, 7–11 cm wide, ciliate on the entire to erose margin, with 11 to 13 radiating veins. Inflorescence one-flowered, erect; peduncle 10–11 cm long, sparsely pubescent; bract ovate-lanceolate, acute, sparsely pubescent. Flower nutant, white to pink

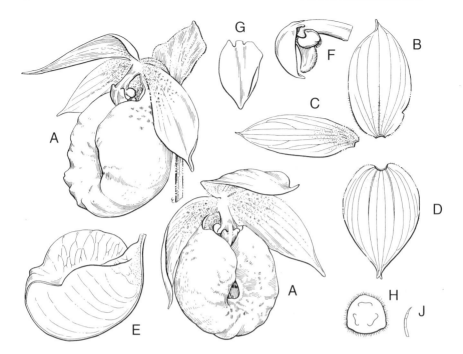

Figure 39. Cypripedium formosanum. A, flower, two views, ×0.66; B, dorsal sepal, ×0.66; C, petal, ×0.66; D, synsepal, ×0.66; E, lip longitudinal section, ×0.66; F, column, ×1.5; G, staminode, ×1.5; H, ovary cross section, ×4; J, hair from ovary, ×20. All drawn from Kew Spirit Collection no. 56277 by Eleanor Catherine.

with crimson spots at the base of the petals and larger spots on the lip especially within, the staminode purple-red with a white tip; pedicel and ovary 1.8–2.3 cm long, densely shortly tomentose. Dorsal sepal curving forwards, ovate-elliptic to narrowly elliptic, acute or acuminate, 4.5 cm long, 2–2.5 cm wide, pilose towards the base, ciliate; synsepal elliptic, naviculiform, acuminate and bidentate at the apex, 4.5–5.2 cm long, 2.5–3 cm wide, pilose towards the base. Petals spreading-deflexed, flat, oblong-oblanceolate, acute or acuminate, 4.8–5.3 cm long, 1.5–1.8 cm wide, pilose towards the base. Lip calceiform, ovoid to ellipsoidal in shape, with a narrowly pandurate mouth, often shortly apiculate at apex, 5.5–6.5 cm long, 4 cm wide, the margins incurved, the veins sunken especially towards the apex, barbate-pubescent within. Column c. 1 cm long, greenish white; staminode convex, ovate-sagittate, cuspidate or blunt at apex, c. 1 cm long, 0.7–0.8 cm wide. PLATES 10, 61, 62; FIGURE 39.

DISTRIBUTION. Taiwan only. See map p. 229.

231

HABITAT. In forest and open, damp places; 2300–3000 m. Flowering in April and May.

SECTION ACAULIA

Cypripedium section **Acaulia** *(Lindl.) C. Morren* in Belg. Hort. 1: (1854). Type species: *C. acaule* Aiton.
Cypripedium group 5. *Acaulia* Lindl., Gen. Sp. Orch. Pl.: 530 (1840).
Cypripedium subgen. *Acaulia* (Lindl.) Brieger in Schlechter, Die Orchideen ed.3, 3 (9–12): 190 (1973).
Cypripedium sect. *Acaulia* (Brieger) Hennessy in Hennessy and Hedge, The Slipper Orchids: 31 (1989).

Stems very short; rhizomes elongate; leaves two, subopposite, glandular-pubescent; inflorescences erect, one-flowered, glandular; ovary glandular; lip very large in proportion to other flower segments, obovoid, bladder-like, with a longitudinal orifice; petals lanceolate, untwisted or very slightly twisted; staminode convex, ovate, hairy.
A monotypic section.

33. CYPRIPEDIUM ACAULE

The MOCCASIN FLOWER or PINK LADY'S SLIPPER ORCHID is the most distinctive of all the North American species. This has not, however, stopped it being described several times. The earliest reference to this orchid is a description and illustration given by Leonard Plukenet in 1700 in his *Mantissa* where he described it as *"Helleborine Calceolus dicta, Mariana, foliis binis e radice ex adverso prodeuntibus"*. Interestingly he uses the name "Mofkasin flower" for his *"Helleborine Virginiana, flore rotundato luteo, purpureis linis striato"*, probably referable to *C. parviflorum* var. *pubescens*. The line illustration appears on plate 418, which also includes line drawings of *C. parviflorum* var. *pubescens* and *C. reginae.*

The earliest post-Linnaean name for this species may be *Cypripedium hirsutum,* used by Philip Miller (1768). However, this has been ignored by most subsequent authors other than Farwell (1917), and House (1905) has argued that the name refers to *C. reginae,* rather than to *C. acaule.* For the reasons stated above under *C. reginae,* I believe that Miller's description of *C. hirsutum* fits this species. I am, therefore, preparing a proposal to reject this little used name which has caused confusion in the past.

Cypripedium acaule was described by William Aiton in 1789 in the first edition of his *Hortus Kewensis* (1789), based on a plant which flowered at Kew and which had been introduced in 1786 by Sir William Hamilton, the husband of Lady Emma. *Cypripedium humile*, described and illustrated by Richard Salisbury in 1793 based on a plant from Nova Scotia collected by Archibald Menzies, is undoubtedly conspecific with *C. acaule*. It has no close allies in the genus, but resembles *C. japonicum* somewhat in the shape of its lip which opens by a narrow slit. Like that species it also has two leaves, but these are ovate and densely pubescent, never flabellate.

Cypripedium acaule grows in large colonies, often of many hundreds of plants, most commonly in moist or dry pine woods, but also in upland open hardwoods, on the edge of swamps, in bogs and in densely shaded woods, particularly under pines, hemlocks, spruces and cedars, or in ericaceous shrubby areas. Correll (1950) stated:

> [I]t is as much at home in the sand hills of the low Coastal Plain of North Carolina and in the pine barrens of New Jersey as it is on the higher mountain slopes of North Carolina, New England and Canada.

White-flowered variants are not uncommon. An excellent photograph of one is provided by Luer (1975) in his *Native Orchids of the United States and Canada*. The name var. *album* was used by Linden and Rodigas (in *Lindenia* 4: 96, 1888) as a *nomen nudum* and has not been validly published. Therefore, Rand and Redfield's forma *albiflorum* (in *The Flora of Mount Desert Island*: 311, 1894) should be applied to this plant. Keenan (1995) has catalogued the variation in *Cypripedium acaule*, the most bizarre form being a semi-peloric form in which the petals are somewhat lip-like. Occasionally, plants can bear two flowers per inflorescence, and Brown (1995) described forma *biflorum*, but this scarcely warrants recognition.

Despite its early introduction into horticulture, this species has proved to be amongst the most difficult to grow, flowering the first year but fading rapidly away in the more usual composts used for slipper orchids. Some success has been achieved by growing plants in pure sphagnum moss.

Cypripedium acaule *Aiton,* Hort. Kew. 3: 303 (1789); Correll, Native Orchids North Amer.: 20, t.1 (1950); Luer, Native Orchids U.S.A. and Canada: 40, t.1 (1975); Case, Orchids Western Great Lakes: 71 (1987). Type: Hort. Kew 1788 (holo. BM!, iso. B-WILLD!).

C. hirsutum Mill., Gard. Dict. ed.8, Cypripedium sp. 3 (1768), *nom. rejec. prop.*

C. humile Salisb. in Trans. Linn. Soc. 1: 79 (1793). Type: Canada, Nova Scotia, *Menzies* (holo. not located).

C. acaule Aiton forma *albiflorum* Rand & Redfield, *Fl. Mt. Desert Isl.*: 311, (1894).

Calceolus hirsutus (Mill.) Nieuwl. in Amer. Midl. Naturalist 3: 117 (1913).

Fissipes acaulis (Aiton) Small, Fl. SE. U.S.: 311 (1917).

F. hirsuta sensu Farw. in Druggists Circular 61: 230 (1917).

Cypripedium acaule Aiton forma *biflorum* P.M. Br. in North Amer. Native Orchid J. 1(3): 197 (1995). Type: U.S.A., New Hampshire, Stafford County, *P.M. Brown* (photo by Brown in AMES).

DESCRIPTION. A terrestrial herb 20–45 cm tall, with a very short erect underground stem, 1–7 cm long, covered by two to three glabrous tubular sheaths and growing from a short underground rhizome. Leaves two, plicate, basal, spreading-suberect, elliptic, 10–28 cm long, 5–15 cm wide, glandular-pubescent, ciliate, glossy bright green. Inflorescence one- or rarely two-flowered; peduncle erect, to 40 cm long, glandular-pubescent; bract arching over flower, foliaceous, lanceolate, acuminate, 4–5 cm long, 1–1.5 cm wide, glandular-pubescent. Flower large, nutant, with yellow-green to maroon sepals and petals and a pink or rarely white lip, the staminode green to pink; pedicel and ovary 1–1.5 cm long, glandular-pubescent. Dorsal sepal often arching over lip, ovate- to elliptic-lanceolate, acuminate, 3–5 cm long, 0.5–1.7 cm wide, glandular-ciliate on basal margins, sparsely glandular-pubescent without and within; synsepal elliptic- to ovate-lanceolate, acute to obtuse, 3–4.5 cm long, 1–2.3 cm wide, sparsely glandular-pubescent without, glandular-ciliate. Petals deflexed at 45°, slightly twisted, slightly falcate, linear-lanceolate to lanceolate, acute, 4–6 cm long, 1–1.7 cm wide, densely pubescent at the base within. Lip ellipsoid-obovoid, longer than the sepals, 4–6 cm long, 2.5–3.5 cm wide, densely pubescent on inner surface at base, pubescent on front margin and around mouth on outer surface, lacking discernable side lobes, the orifice elongate and narrow, the margins incurved except at the apex. Column 1–

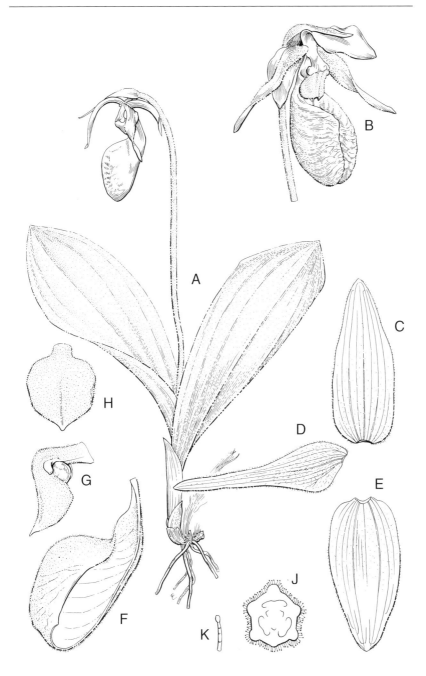

Figure 40. Cypripedium acaule. A, habit, ×0.5; B, flower, ×0.66; C, dorsal sepal, ×1; D, petal, ×1; E, synsepal, ×1; F, lip longitudinal section, ×1; G, column, ×1.5; H, staminode, ×1.5; J, ovary cross section, ×4; K, hair from ovary, ×20. All drawn from Kew Spirit Collection no. 57353 by Eleanor Catherine.

1.2 cm long, pubescent on dorsal surface; staminode convex, sub-orbicular-rhombic to ovoid-deltoid, obtuse to 1.8 cm long and 1.4 cm wide, densely pubescent. PLATES 1, 27–30, 124; FIGURES 3, 40.

DISTRIBUTION. Widespread in North America, most abundantly in the eastern and northeastern parts of its range. Canada (Newfoundland, Nova Scotia, New Brunswick, Prince Edward Island, Quebec, Ontario west to Saskatchewan and Alberta), U.S.A. (New England south to South Carolina, Georgia, Tennessee and Alabama and west to Minnesota, Ohio, Indiana, Kentucky).

HABITAT. In a variety of habitats from wet sphagnum bog to dry *Pinus* (pine) forest, usually in moderate shade where the soil is rich in humus, strongly acidic and thoroughly aerated. Flowering in April to June.

SECTION BIFOLIA

Cypripedium sect. **Bifolia** *(Lindl.)* *C. Morren* in Belg. Hort. 1: (1854) and in S.C. Chen in Proc. 12th World Orch. Conf.: 145 (1987). Type species: *C. guttatum* Sw.
Cypripedium group 4. *Bifolia* Lindl., Gen. Spec. Orch. Pl.: 529 (1838), pro parte.

Stems long, pubescent; rhizomes elongate; leaves two, ovate to elliptic, pubescent; inflorescences erect, one-flowered; flowers white, with a purple- or brown-spotted lip and petals; ovary glandular; lip urn-shaped, without an incurved apical margin; petals sub-pandurate, rounded at apex; staminode conduplicate, glabrous.
A section of two very closely allied species.

34. CYPRIPEDIUM GUTTATUM

Cypripedium guttatum was named by Olof Swartz in 1800 based on a specimen from eastern Siberia collected by Gmelin. Linnaeus (1753) included it as var. δ under his description of *C. calceolus,* referring to two sources: an illustration and description in Johann Amman's *Stirpium rariorum in Imperio Rutheno Icones et Descriptiones* (1739) and a description in J. G. Gmelin's *Flora Sibirica* (1747).

It is a distinctive species recognised by its two leaves and spotted flower with narrowly ovate petals, constricted and rounded at the

236

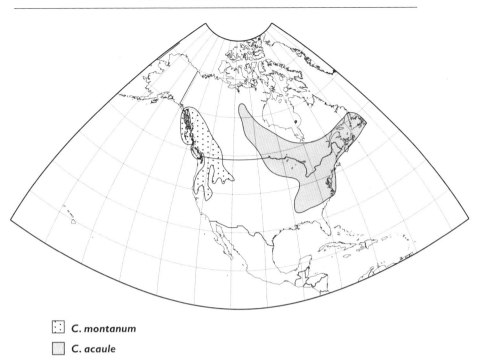

[:·:] *C. montanum*

[▨] *C. acaule*

apex, and a distinctive urceolate lip with a wide mouth, lacking an incurved apical margin but with a fleshy glossy rim. It is one of the most widespread species in the genus, distributed from the Urals across Asia to Siberia, Korea, and Manchuria, and south through China to the Himalayas. It is also found in Alaska.

Cypripedium guttatum is closely related to *C. yatabeanum*, the latter having been treated by many authors as a variety of the former. *Cypripedium guttatum* is distinguished by its short broad lip and brightly coloured flowers that have purple spots on the lip and inner surface of the petals, and petals that are not spathulate or cupped at the tips. Brown (1995a) has named the natural hybrid between *C. guttatum* and *C. yatabeanum* as *C. × alaskanum*, based on material from near Anchorage, Alaska.

Several varieties and forms have been described over the years, but probably do not deserve formal recognition. Var. *redowskii* Rchb. f., with an elongated lip and white flowers, occurs occasionally in populations of the typical form; forma *latifolium* Rouy ex Camus has leaves 5–7 cm wide, but these fall within the range of leaf measurements commonly found in the species; var. *tongolensis*

(Franchet ex U.Pradhan in *Orchid Digest* 50: (1986)) from Xizang (Tibet) has a small lip with an irregular shape and is probably a monstrosity; var. *koreanum* Nakai seems typical of the type.

This pretty orchid grows in colonies in montane grassland in western China and the Himalayas, and in meadows and open woodland in the northern parts of its range. Luer (1975) recorded it as growing in large colonies amongst *Cornus canadensis* on hillsides in open birch forests. I have seen it growing on banks in grassland and scrub in several localities in northwestern Yunnan near the towns of Lijiang and Zhongdian. It usually grows there on north- to west-facing slopes. In more exposed places the plants are particularly small with the leaves borne at ground level, giving the plant the appearance of being stemless. In more sheltered spots, however, the plants develop a distinct stem as they do in eastern Siberia (Frosch pers. comm.). Flower size and colour are variable in the material I have examined from southwestern China, the degree of purple-spotting on the petals and lip and the purple colouration of the sepals and lip varying considerably from plant to plant. It was in full flower in early to mid-June.

Cypripedium guttatum *Sw.* in Kongl. Vetensk. Acad. Nya Handl. 21: 251 (1800); Keller and Schlechter, Monogr. Iconogr. Orchid. Eur.: 17 (1926); Correll, Native Orchids North Amer.: 33, t.7 (1950); Luer, Native Orchids U.S.A. and Canada: 66, t.13 (1975). Type: E. Siberia, *Gmelin* (holo. B!, iso. BM!, W!).
  C. calceolus var. δ L., Sp. Pl. ed.1, 2: 951 (1753). Type: E. Siberia, *Gmelin*, herb.Pallas (holo. B!, iso. BM!).
  C. variegatum Georgi, Reise Russ. Reich. 1: 232 (1775). Type not located.
  C. calceolus L. var. *variegatum* (Georgi) Falk., Beitr. II: t.17 (1786).
  C. orientale Spreng., Syst. Veg. 3: 746 (1826). Based on same type as *C. guttatum.*
  C. guttatum Sw. var. *redowskii* Rchb. f., Tent. Orchidogr. Eur.: 166, t.168, f.3 (1851). Types: Russia, many specimens cited (syn. W!).
  C. guttatum Sw. forma *latifolium* Rouy ex Camus, Monogr. Orchid.: 451 (1908). Type not located.
  C. guttatum var. *koreanum* Nakai *nomen;* T.B. Lee, Ill. Fl. Korea: 232 (1985).

DESCRIPTION. A terrestrial herb 10–38 cm tall, often forming loose clumps; stem 1.5–10 cm long, pubescent, hollow below the

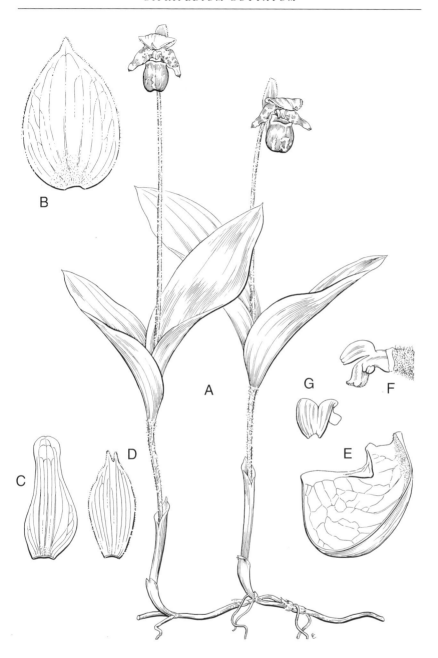

Figure 41. Cypripedium guttatum. A, habit, ×0.66; B, dorsal sepal, ×2; C, petal, ×2; D, synsepal, ×2; E, lip longitudinal section, ×2; F, column, ×2; G, front view of column, ×2. All drawn from *Forrest* 12460 by Eleanor Catherine.

239

leaves; rhizomes slender, long, creeping, the internodes usually more than 5 mm long. Leaves two, subopposite or up to 2 cm apart, lanceolate to ovate, acute to acuminate, 4.5–12.5 cm long, 2.5–5.5 cm wide, lacking a sheathing base, usually drying black, glabrous above, more or less pubescent on the veins beneath, subtended by two tubular sheathes. Inflorescence one-flowered; peduncle 7–13 cm long, densely glandular and pubescent; bract ovate, acute to acuminate, 1.5–3.5 cm long, ciliate. Flower white spotted with purple or brown; pedicel and ovary 0.6–1.8 cm long, glandular-pubescent. Dorsal sepal ovate-elliptic, acute or shortly acuminate, 1.7–2.5 cm long, 1.4 cm wide; synsepal narrowly elliptic, bifid and acute at apex, 1.1–1.5 cm long, 0.5–0.6 cm wide. Petals spreading, ligulate to subpandurate or spathulate, rounded at apex, 1.3–2 cm long, 0.5–0.8 cm wide. Lip pitcher-shaped with a broad mouth, 1.4–2.2 cm long, 1–1.3 cm across, the incurved sides subquadrate. Column 0.5–0.7 cm long; staminode ovate, retuse, with upcurved sides, 0.5–0.6 cm long, 0.4–0.5 cm wide. PLATES 11, 65, 66; FIGURES 41.

DISTRIBUTION. W. North America, E. Europe across to Siberia and Sakhalin, Korea, China, S. Xizang (Tibet), Bhutan.

HABITAT. In small to large colonies in grassland and open woodland; 1000–4100 m at lower altitudes in the north of its range, but to 4100 m in the Himalayas and SE. China. Flowering in late May to July.

35. CYPRIPEDIUM YATABEANUM

This orchid was first described by Makino in 1899 as *Cypripedium yatabeanum*, based on a collection by Ryokichi Yatabe from Mt. Togaksi in Sinano, Honshu. Most subsequent authors have followed Ernst Pfitzer (1903) in treating it as a variety of the widespread *C. guttatum*. I have kept it as a distinct species because of its distinct geographical distribution and the lack of any obvious hybrids amongst herbarium collections I have examined. Nevertheless, Luer (1975) has reported seeing what he interpreted as hybrids in the Aleutian Islands and perhaps they do hybridise at least in part of the range. Brown (1995a) has formally recognised the natural hybrid as *C. ×alaskanum*.

Cypripedium yatabeanum is closely related to *C. guttatum*, but is distinguished from it by its narrower, longer lip, more spathulate tips to the petals and the flower colour, which is yellowish green marked

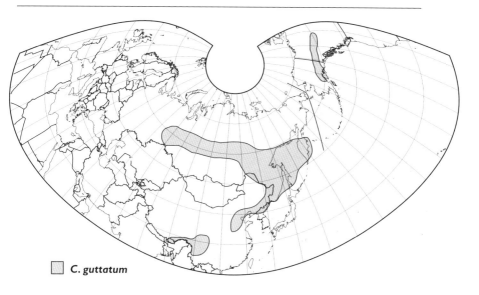

C. guttatum

on the lip and petals with pale brown rather than purple. It is much more restricted in its distribution than *C. guttatum*, being found in an arc from central Japan and Kamchatka in eastern Siberia across the Kuriles and Aleutian Islands to Kodiak Island and the south-western peninsula of Alaska. Luer (1975) reported finding it growing with *Dactylorhiza aristata* on cold, wet, wind-swept meadows facing the sea on Kodiak Island in Alaska.

Cypripedium yatabeanum *Makino* in Bot. Mag. (Tokyo) 13: 91 (1899); Miyoshi, Alpine Pl. Jap.: t.1, fig.3 (1). Type: Japan, Honshu, Mt. Togakushi, *Yatabe* (holo. TI!).
C. guttatum Sw. var. *yatabeanum* (Makino) Pfitzer in Engler, Pflanzenr. IV, 50 (Heft 12) Orch. Pleonan.: 33 (1903); Matsumura, Index Pl. Jap. 2: 241 (1905).
C. guttatum Sw. subsp. *yatabeanum* (Makino) Hultén in Ark. Bot. II, 7: 34 (1968).

DESCRIPTION. A terrestrial herb 20–35 cm tall, with a creeping rhizome. Stems erect, pubescent, two-leaved. Leaves elliptic to elliptic-ovate, acute, 7–14 cm long, 3.5–8 cm wide, ciliate and hairy on veins, especially on underside of leaves. Inflorescence one-flowered, glandular hairy especially towards apex; bract lanceolate or ovate, acute, 2.5–5 cm long. Flower pale yellowish green marked with brown spots on lip and inside of petals, the staminode white with a

241

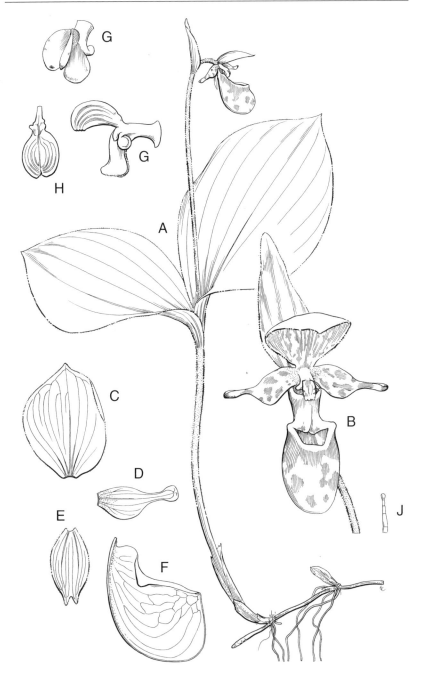

Figure 42. Cypripedium yatabeanum. A, habit, ×0.66; B, flower, ×1.5; C, dorsal sepal, ×1.5; D, petal, ×1.5; E, synsepal, ×1.5; F, lip longitudinal section, ×1.5; G, column views, ×3; H, staminode, ×3; J, hair from ovary, ×20. All drawn from the type by Eleanor Catherine.

242

yellow mark; pedicel and ovary 1–1.5 cm long, glandular-pubescent. Dorsal sepal suberect, elliptic or oblong-elliptic, obtuse, 1.7–2.4 cm long, 1.3–1.8 cm wide. Synsepal narrowly elliptic, distinctly and acutely bifid, 1.1–1.6 cm long, 0.3–0.6 cm wide. Petals spreading, spathulate, rounded and concave at apex, 1.2–1.6 cm long, 0.4–0.6 cm wide. Lip deeply urceolate, 2.2–2.7 cm long. Staminode somewhat subquadrate, conduplicate, curved in side view, 0.4–0.6 cm long. PLATES 119, 120; FIGURE 42.

DISTRIBUTION. Japan (Honshu, Yezo), Sakhalin Island, E. Siberia, the Kamchatka Peninsula, the Kurile and Aleutian Islands, SW. Alaska to Kodiak Island.

HABITAT. On grassy slopes, often in full sun, or under *Betula* (birch) trees; sea level to 1000 m. Flowering in June and July.

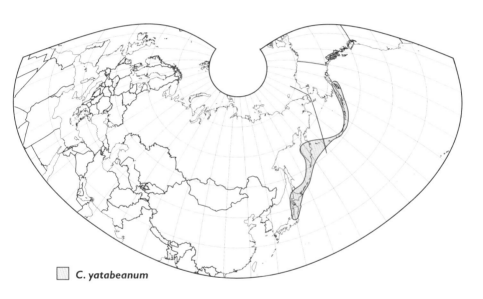

C. yatabeanum

SECTION RETINERVIA

Cypripedium sect. **Retinervia** *(Pfitzer)* S.C. *Chen* in Proc. 12th World Orch. Conf.: 145 (1987). Type species: *C. debile* Rchb. f.
Cypripedium Series II *Retinervia* Pfitzer in Engler, Pflanzenr. IV, 50 (Heft 12) Orch. Pleonan.: 41 (1903).

Stems short, glabrous; rhizomes elongate; leaves two, subopposite, ovate to cordate, with three prominent longitudinal veins, glabrous; inflorescences one-flowered, erect or sometimes nodding; flowers small; ovary pubescent or glabrous; lip small, ovoid to subsphaerical, in *C. elegans* adorned in front with rows of warts; petals linear or lanceolate; staminode convex, papillate.

A section of three small species. *Cypripedium fasciculatum*, which is similar in habit but has two- or more-flowered inflorescences, may also belong here.

36. CYPRIPEDIUM PALANGSHANENSE

Cypripedium palangshanense was described by the Chinese botanists T. Tang and C. W. Wang in 1936 based on a collection made by Wang from Mt. Pa-lang that towers over the town of Wen-chuan in the Min River gorge north of Chengdu in northwestern Sichuan. It is closely related to *C. debile*, but differs in being a shorter plant, with ovate leaves lacking cross veins, a glandular-pubescent peduncle and ovary, an elliptic-ovate bract, different-coloured flower, a distinctive, acuminate, dorsal sepal and petals, and a staminode that is longer than wide. Unlike *C. debile*, it is a narrow endemic known only from northwestern and eastern Sichuan.

Cypripedium palangshanense *T. Tang & F.T. Wang* in Bull. Fan Mem. Inst. Biol., 7: 1 (1936). Type: China, NW. Sichuan, W. Wenchuan Hsien, Mt. Pa-lang, *Wang* 21164 (holo. PE!).

DESCRIPTION. A dwarf terrestrial herb with a slender, creeping, subterranean rhizome. Stems erect, well-spaced on rhizome, 5–7 cm long, subtended by two to three, acute to obtuse sheaths, bifoliate at apex. Leaves spreading, opposite, ovate, acute or obtuse, 4–4.5 cm long, 3–3.6 cm wide, glabrous, unspotted. Inflorescence one-flowered; peduncle slender, possibly arcuate, 4–6 cm long, pubescent; bract lanceolate, acute, 1.2–1.6 cm long, 0.3–0.4 cm wide. Flowers small, nodding, red-flushed or deep purple with a paler lip; pedicel very short; ovary 4 mm long, densely covered by short glandular hairs. Dorsal sepal lanceolate, acute to acuminate, 1.6–1.7 cm long, 0.4 cm wide, glabrous; synsepal similar but bifid at apex, 1.5 cm long, 0.5 cm wide, glabrous. Petals lanceolate, acute to acuminate, 1.4–1.5 cm long, 0.5 cm wide. Lip porrect, saccate, 0.9–1.1 cm long, glabrous on outside, the incurved side lobes oblong to subelliptic. Column 0.4 cm long; staminode lanceolate-ovate, acute, 0.3 cm long. FIGURE 43.

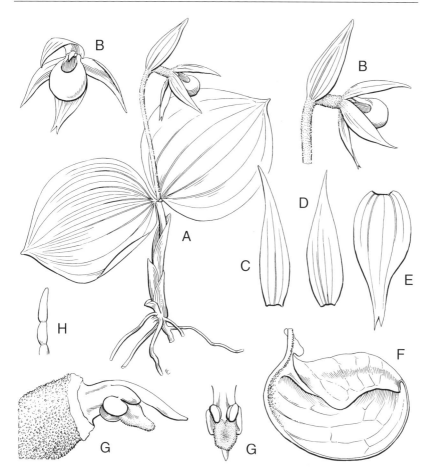

Figure 43. Cypripedium palangshanense. A, habit, ×0.66; B, flower, two views, ×1; C, dorsal sepal, ×2; D, petal, ×2; E, synsepal, ×2; F, lip longitudinal section, ×4; G, column, two views, ×10; H, hairs from ovary, ×60. All drawn from the type by Eleanor Catherine.

DISTRIBUTION. China (NW. and E. Sichuan only). See map p. 225.

HABITAT. In woods and thickets; 2200 m. Flowering in late May (23rd) and early June (4th).

37. CYPRIPEDIUM ELEGANS

This unobtrusive dwarf orchid, one of the least showy of the Sino-Himalayan species of *Cypripedium,* is found in the eastern Himalayas across to southwestern China. It was described by H. G. Reich-

245

enbach in 1886 based on a collection from southeastern Xizang (Tibet) made by one of the native collectors working for Sir George King and was illustrated by King and Pantling (1898). It is characterised by its opposite leaves that have ciliate margins and by its flowers that have claret or green sepals and petals veined with deeper maroon or claret, and a whitish lip with three raised rows of purple warts on the front margin. It seems most closely allied to *C. palangshanense* from Sichuan, but differs in its ciliate leaves, flower colour, and warty lip. It is also allied to *C. debile*, found further east but differs in its ciliate leaves, erect inflorescence, and differently coloured flower with a villose peduncle and ovary and prominent warty ridges on the front of the lip.

It is widespread but local in the Himalayas from eastern central Nepal, Sikkim, and Bhutan across to Hubei Province in China. It is considered endangered in northeastern India, but is probably underreported because of its rather insignificant habit and flower.

Photographs taken on the Alpine Garden Society expedition to northwestern Yunnan undertaken with the Kunming Botanical Institute show that the Chinese form has predominantly green flowers marked with purple, rather than flushed all over with the purple as reported from the Himalayan plants. The expedition found it growing in deep leaf mould in open woodland on limestone in a valley bottom 15 km north of Wengshui (near Geza), north of Zhongdian (Chungtien) and close to Dongcai Snow Mountain on the Sichuan border.

Cypripedium elegans *Rchb. f.* in Flora 69: 561 (1886). Type: China, Xizang (Tibet), Kang Me, native collector in *King* 54 (holo. K!, iso. W!).

DESCRIPTION. A dwarf terrestrial herb with a creeping underground rhizome, 1–2 mm in diameter. Stems erect, 4–11 cm long, red-villose, covered in basal part by two tubular sheaths, bifoliate at the apex. Leaves subopposite, spreading, ovate or oblong-ovate, obtuse, 2.2–8 cm long, 1.6–6.9 cm wide, long ciliate, sometimes pubescent, glossy green above, prominently three-veined beneath. Inflorescence erect, one-flowered; peduncle 1.4–4.7 cm long, villose; bract elliptic to lanceolate, acute, 2–3 cm long, 0.7–0.9 cm wide, as long as the flower and hooded over it, very shortly hairy. Flower small, the sepals and petals dull claret or bright green with claret veins on inner surface, the lip white with three longitudinal rows of

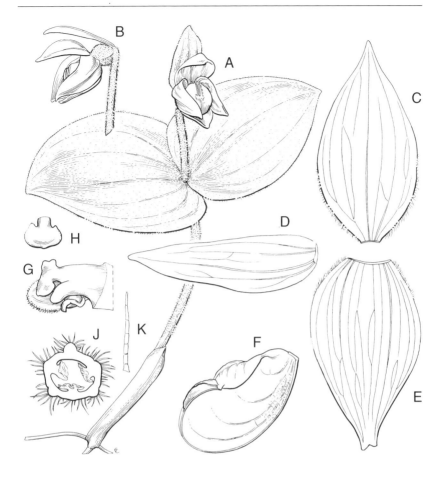

Figure 44. Cypripedium elegans. A, habit, ×1; B, flower, ×1; C, dorsal sepal, ×3; D, petal, ×3; E, synsepal, ×3; F, lip longitudinal section, ×3; G, column, ×6; H, staminode, ×3; J, ovary cross section, ×6; K, hair from ovary, ×20. All drawn from *Bowes Lyon* 15047 by Eleanor Catherine.

purple warts on front; pedicel and ovary short, ellipsoidal, 4–5 mm long, hairy on ribs. Dorsal sepal elliptic-ovate, acute, 1.6–2.1 cm long, 5–8 mm wide; synsepal elliptic, bidentate, 1.6–1.8 cm long, 5 mm wide. Petals lanceolate, subacute at the apex, 1.6–1.8 cm long, 5–6 mm wide. Lip hemisphaerical, with a pinched erect apical rim, 1.2 cm long, upturned at apex to hide mouth, with three longitudinal lines of purple warts on the front. Column 3 mm long; staminode very small, elliptic, rounded at apex, 1.5–2 mm long. PLATE 53; FIGURE 44.

247

DISTRIBUTION. N. India, E. Nepal, Sikkim, Bhutan, China (NW. Yunnan, SE. Xizang (Tibet)). See map p. 121.

HABITAT. At the edge of *Abies* (fir) forest and on steep slopes at the edge of woodland, in clearings in bamboo and *Abies* forest, and under *Juniperus* (juniper) bushes, in valley bottoms in open woodland in deep leaf mould on limestone; 2800–4400 m. Flowering in late May to July.

38. CYPRIPEDIUM DEBILE

The charming and dainty *Cypripedium debile* is a widespread and locally common species in China, Taiwan, and Japan. Despite its size it is commonly cultivated and is certainly one of the most unusual species in the genus, with its pendent inflorescence and flower that hides tantalisingly under the leaves. Farrer's (1919) description of *C. debile* as "a pallid and puny thing . . . so frail that . . . it cannot even bear so much of a burden (as its flower), but declines and flops in a cowardly and disgraceful manner" seems particularly harsh for such a delicate and attractive plant.

It was described by H. G. Reichenbach based on a Japanese illustration he saw in the library of Archbishop Haynald of Kalocsa in Hungary. It is distinguished from all other species in the genus by its glabrous habit, paired heart-shaped leaves borne well above the soil surface, and pendent inflorescence with a small green and purple-marked flower subtended by a linear bract. The leaves have marked main veins with secondary branching veins between them.

Examination of the type material of *Cypripedium cardiophyllum*, described by Franchet and Savatier from material collected by the latter on Mt. Fujiyama in Japan, shows it to be conspecific with *C. debile*.

This diminutive orchid grows in shaded places on banks in montane forest under deciduous trees and conifers. In western Sichuan I have seen it growing in near ridge-top forest at 2600 m., under *Tetracentron sinense* and *Davidia involucrata*, on relatively bare areas in deep shade and leaf litter. On Emei Shan (Mt. Omei) in Sichuan it grows at about 2500 m in montane forest of rhododendrons, *Abies fabri*, and species of *Acer* and *Sorbus*, with *Arisaema* and *Primula* species and *Anemone davidii*.

Cypripedium debile *Rchb. f.,* Xenia Orchid. 2: 223 (1874); Franchet in Bull. Soc. Phil. Paris 7: 136 (1888) and in J. Bot. (Morot) 8:

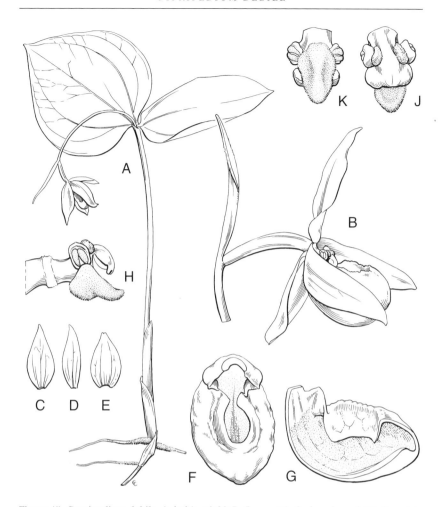

Figure 45. Cypripedium debile. A, habit, ×0.66; B, flower, ×2; C, dorsal sepal, ×1; D, petal, ×1; E, synsepalum, ×1; F, lip, ×3; G, lip longitudinal section, ×3; H, column, side view, ×4; J, column from above, ×4; K, column from below, ×4. All drawn from *Wilson* 4585 by Eleanor Catherine.

(1894); Schlechter in Feddes Rep. Sp. Nov. Beih. 4: 80 (1919); Maekwa, Wild Orchids of Japan in Colour: 84, t.5 (1971); S.S. Ying, Coloured Ill. Indig. Orch. Taiwan 1: 137 (1977); Liu and Su, Fl. Taiwan 5: 951 (1978). Type: Japan, based on a Japanese drawing labelled "Koatsumoriso, *Calypso borealis*" in Soc-mok-dru-sets (Somoku Zusetsu) vol.18, No.85.

C. cardiophyllum Franch. & Sav., Enum. Pl. Jap. 11: 39 (1876). Type: Japan, Mt. Fujiyama, *Savatier* 3475 (holo. P!).

249

DESCRIPTION. A dwarf colony-forming herb with a short rhizome; roots elongate, villose. Stems solitary or clustered, slender, 8–18 cm long, glabrous, subtended by two sheaths at the base, bifoliate at the apex. Leaves subopposite, spreading, heart-shaped, subacute, 3.2–7 cm long, 2.4–5.7 cm wide, strongly three-veined on underside, the margins often undulate. Inflorescence pendent; peduncle arcuate, slender, 1.3–6.5 cm long; bract linear-filiform, acute, 1.5–2.9 cm long. Flower small, hidden under the leaf, pale green with a white lip and marked with maroon at the base of the segments and inside the lip; pedicel and ovary 0.9–1.5 cm long, glabrous. Dorsal sepal elliptic-ovate or ovate-lanceolate, acute, 1.5–1.9 cm long, 5.5–7.5 mm wide; synsepal narrowly elliptic, acute, 1.1–1.4 cm long, 3.5–5 mm wide. Petals curved forwards, lanceolate, acute, 1.4–1.8 cm long, 3–5 mm wide. Lip small, subellipsoid, 1–1.5 cm long. Column 3 mm long; staminode ovate, very small, 1–1.5 mm long, green with a purple apex. PLATES 8, 49, 50; FIGURE 45.

DISTRIBUTION. Western and central China (Sichuan, Hubei), Japan, Taiwan.

HABITAT. In deep shade in leaf litter on banks in temperate mixed forest; 2000–3000 m in China and Taiwan, but down to 1300 m in Japan. Flowering in May and June.

SECTION TRIGONOPEDIA

Cypripedium sect. **Trigonopedia** *Franch.* in L'Orchidophile 8: 368 (1888). Type species: *C. margaritaceum* Franch.

Cypripedium B. *Ebracteatae* series III *Nudiflorae* Franch. in J. Bot. (Morot) 8 (13): 228 (1894.

Cypripedium sect. *Trigonopedilum* (Franch.) Pfitzer in Engler and Prantl, Pflanzenfam. Nachtr. 2: 97 (1897) and in Engler, Pflanzenr. IV, 50 (Heft 12) Orch. Pleonan.: 40 (1903), sphalm. pro *Trigonopedia*.

Stems very short, glabrous, separated by long underground rhizomes; leaf solitary but subopposite a leaf-like bract, glabrous, spotted or unspotted; inflorescences apparently ebracteate; flower solitary; pedicel elongating considerably after fertilisation; ovary triangular in cross section, glabrous or with multicellular hairs; lip dorsiventrally somewhat flattened, glabrous or verrucose; petals which, in most species, curve forwards around the lip; staminode flat to convex, papillose.

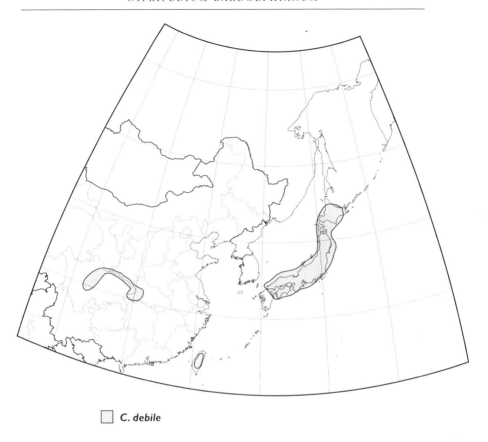

☐ *C. debile*

A section of seven species. This section is the most distinctive in the genus. All its species are endemic to western China in the provinces of Yunnan, Sichuan, Hunan, and Gansu, with one species, *Cypripedium lichiangense,* also reported from northern Myanmar (Burma). It seems probable that the species in this section are fly-pollinated. I have seen flies visiting the flowers of *C. margaritaceum* whilst video filming in northwestern Yunnan. The flower placement, colouration, and scent all point to fly-pollination.

39A. CYPRIPEDIUM BARDOLPHIANUM VAR. BARDOLPHIANUM

This unusual miniature orchid was discovered by Reginald Farrer and William Purdom in southwestern Gansu (Kansu). Farrer (1916) lyrically described it and its habitat:

251

A most curious little plant, running about with single shoots and forming wide colonies in sunny glades and mossy woodland soil of the forest zone in the enormous gorges behind Siku, at about 8000 ft., and often in company with *C. luteum*" [= *C. flavum*].

He named it *Cypripedium bardolphianum* after its warty lip, which is

so grotesque with warts and whelks and bubuckles that it could only make one think of Bardolph's nose . . . though its odour is sweeter than I should imagine that of the swashbuckler (from Shakespeare's Henry V) to have been (Farrer 1917, *On the Eaves of the World*).

However, he had earlier in the *Gardeners' Chronicle* of 1915 described the odour as an "unpleasing aromatic scent . . . that suggests the corruptness of a Catasetum". It was described by W. W. Smith and Farrer in 1916, a note on the type sheet stating that the single flower had not been dissected. The colour of the type has been preserved in drying, and it is apparent that this collection had green sepals and petals and a golden lip.

S. C. Chen and Xi (1987) considered *Cypripedium bardolphianum* to be conspecific with *C. nutans* Schltr., basing their view on the original description but without examining the type of the latter. *Cypripedium nutans* apparently has larger, differently coloured flowers that lack the warty lip of this species. The type material of *C. nutans* I have examined is in fruit with the flower remains still attached at the apex of an elongated pedicel. However, I am inclined to agree with Chen and Xi that the two are conspecific. I have seen flowers in the wild with sepals and petals varying from yellow, heavily speckled with maroon, to dark maroon, and a lip varying from golden-yellow to dull yellow variously flushed and speckled with purple. The lip can have varying degrees of wartiness on its front, although I did not see one as warty as the type of *C. bardolphianum*. The plants also had a red staminode. In contrast, the type of *C. bardolphianum* apparently had green sepals and petals and a golden yellow lip and it is possible that Farrer's collection was an albino.

The habitat in which I have seen *Cypripedium bardolphianum* in northern Sichuan is spectacular, with shallow streams flowing down a valley amongst coniferous woodlands of spruce and fir and over a series of limestone pans and shallow falls in between small islands of shrubby vegetation and trees. *Cypripedium bardolphianum* was growing in small colonies on flattish areas and slopes in shaded places with *C. franchetii*, *C. flavum*, and other orchids such as *Corallorhiza trifida*, *Oreorchis fargesii*, and *Calypso bulbosa*. The small plants of *Cypripedium bardolphianum* bore two ascending glossy bright green leaves, edged with maroon, with the small dark maroon and yellow flower borne between them on an erect maroon-spotted greenish yellow stalk.

Cypripedium bardolphianum *W.W. Sm. & Farrer* in Notes Roy. Bot. Gard. Edinburgh 9: 101 (1916); S.C. Chen in Acta Phytotax. Sin. 23(5): 371 (1985). Type: China, Gansu, Siku, *Farrer & Purdom* 139 (holo. E!).
C. nutans Schltr. in Acta Horti Gothoburg 1: 128 (1924). Type: China, N. Sichuan, Dongrergo, *H. Smith* 3703 (holo. UPS!, iso. GB!).

DESCRIPTION. A dwarf creeping terrestrial herb with a slender elongate subterranean rhizome, to 7 cm long, 1.5 mm in diameter, bearing scattered occasional slender roots, forming large colonies. Stems short, erect, subterranean, bifoliate, 1.6–3 cm long, covered by two sheaths. Leaves spreading or suberect, elliptic, obtuse to shortly apiculate, 5–6.5 cm long, 2.2–2.7 cm wide. Inflorescence erect, 7–8 cm long, one-flowered, ebracteate. Flower small, held clear of the leaves, greenish or reddish with brown stripes, with a golden yellow lip, and a noxious aromatic scent; pedicel slender, 4.5–5 cm long, sparsely pubescent; ovary 0.9–1.1 mm long, sparsely pubescent on ridges. Dorsal sepal elliptic or ovate-elliptic, shortly apiculate or acute, 1.3–2.1 cm long, 0.8–1 cm wide, glabrous; synsepal elliptic to elliptic-ovate, obtuse or shortly apiculate, 1.4–1.8 cm long, 0.8–1 cm wide, glabrous. Petals curved forwards, sometimes clasping the lip, obliquely oblong, acute, 1.4–1.8 cm long, 0.4–0.7 cm wide, glabrous. Lip small, circular from above, dorsiventrally flatted, glossy-waxy, 1.1–1.4 cm long, usually ornamented in front with tubercles. Staminode elliptic-oblong, rounded at apex, 6 mm long, 4 mm wide, minutely papillose. PLATES 33, 34; FIGURE 46.
DISTRIBUTION. China (SW. Gansu, W. Sichuan, NW. Yunnan). See map p. 255.
HABITAT. On banks of mountain streams, in gorges in the forest zone and in sunny glades in woodland, growing amongst mosses; 2400–3600 m. Flowering in June and July.

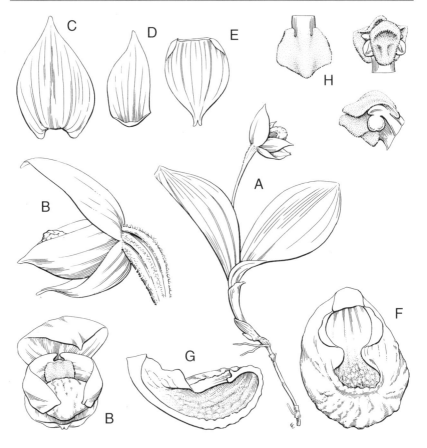

Figure 46. Cypripedium bardolphianum. A, habit, ×0.66; B, flower, two views, ×1.5; C, dorsal sepal, ×1.5; D, petal, ×1.5; E, synsepal, ×1.5; F, lip, ×3; G, lip longitudinal section, ×3; H, column, three views, ×3. A from the type; B–H from Kew Spirit Collection no. 59741. All drawn by Eleanor Catherine.

39B. CYPRIPEDIUM BARDOLPHIANUM VAR. ZHONGDIANENSE

The type material of this variety resembles that of typical *Cypripedium bardolphianum* in its vegetative and floral morphology apart from the features mentioned below. The sepals and petals also appear to be more obviously speckled with maroon than the plants I have seen in the wild. The type was collected in flower in June 1975. Ovary and tepal pubescence are useful diagnostic characters in the spotted-leaved species, and the status of this variety may need to be reconsidered when fresh material is available for analysis.

254

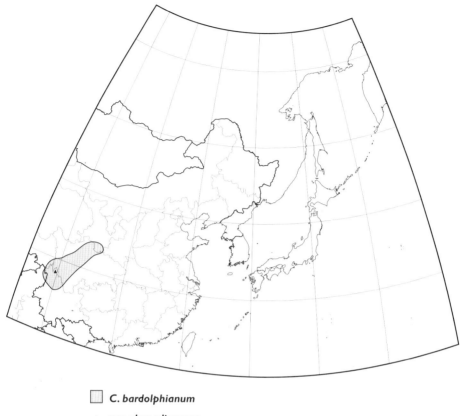

▢ *C. bardolphianum*

▲ **var.** *zhongdianense*

Cypripedium bardolphianum W.W. Sm. & Farrer var. **zhongdia-nense** *S.C. Chen* in Acta Phytotax. Sin. 23(5): 371 (1985); S.C. Chen and Y.Z. Xi in Proc. 12th World Orch. Conf.: 145 (1987). Type: China, NW. Yunnan, Zhong Dian Co., *J.S. Yang* 7487 (holo. and iso. KUN!).

DESCRIPTION. Differs from the typical variety in having an ovary covered entirely with rusty-villose hairs and sepals that are more or less shortly, densely glandular-pubescent on the inner side. See Figure 46.

DISTRIBUTION. China (NW. Yunnan only).

HABITAT. As for the typical variety.

40. CYPRIPEDIUM MICRANTHUM

This dwarf species is known from only three collections, all from eastern Sichuan, two by Farges who collected the type, and one by Wilson. The type collection, however, comprises eight sheets in Paris with another at Kew, so a detailed morphological assessment is possible. The species was described by the French botanist M. A. Franchet in 1894 based on a collection by Père Farges in eastern Sichuan.

Cypripedium micranthum has the smallest flowers in the genus and is distinguished by its densely reddish hairy pedicel and ovary, densely pubescent sepals and very small lip. It is most closely allied to *C. bardolphianum*, but is distinguished by its smaller yellow flower with a tiny lip 6–7 mm long and its dense pubescence on the pedicel, ovary, and exterior surface of the sepals.

Cypripedium micranthum *Franch.* in J. Bot. (Morot) 8: 265 (1894); Schlechter in Feddes Rep. Sp. Nov. Beih. 4: 83 (1919); S.C. Chen in Acta Phytotax. Sin. 23(5): 371 (1985). Type: China, E. Sichuan, Tchen-keou-tin, *Farges* 1286 (holo. P!; iso. AMES!, K!).

DESCRIPTION. A dwarf terrestrial herb with an elongate slender creeping subterranean rhizome, 1.5–2.5 mm in diameter. Stems erect, to 14 cm apart on the rhizome, 2–6 cm long, covered by two acute sheaths, bifoliate at apex. Leaves subopposite, spreading, prostrate on substrate, obovate-elliptic or elliptic, shortly apiculate, 3.3–9 cm long, 2–6.5 cm wide, green, glabrous. Inflorescence erect, one-flowered. Flower yellowish; pedicel 2–3.5 cm long, densely red-villose; pedicel 3–5 cm long, densely reddish pubescent, elongating to 15–25 cm after fertilisation; ovary 0.5–0.6 cm long, densely red-villose. Dorsal sepal ovate, acute, 1.4–1.7 cm long, 0.9–1.1 cm wide, pustular on inner surface, densely villose on outer surface; synsepal elliptic, shortly bifid at the apex, 1.1–1.4 cm long, 0.7–0.8 cm wide, pustular on inner surface and densely villose without. Petals enfolding sides of the lip, obliquely oblong-elliptic, acute, 1.3–1.4 cm long, 0.5–0.6 cm wide, very shortly bristly in apical part. Lip 0.8–1 cm long, papillose in front. Column 0.35–0.4 cm long; staminode oblong, rounded at apex, 0.3–0.35 cm long, 0.3 cm wide, papillose. FIGURE 47.

DISTRIBUTION. China (E. Sichuan only). See map p. 225.

HABITAT. In woods; 2000–2500 m. Flowering in late May and early June.

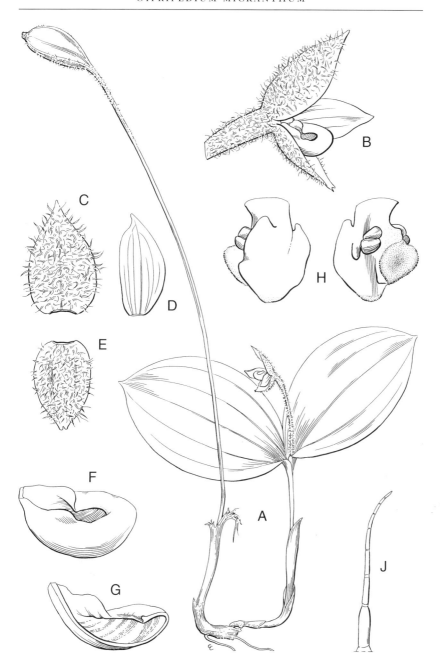

Figure 47. Cypripedium micranthum. A, habit, ×0.66; B, flower, ×2; C, dorsal sepal, ×2; D, petal, ×2; E, synsepal, ×2; F, lip, ×4; G, lip longitudinal section, ×4; H, column, two views, ×6; J, hair from ovary, ×40. All drawn from *Wilson* s.n. by Eleanor Catherine.

41. CYPRIPEDIUM MARGARITACEUM

Cypripedium margaritaceum was described by the French botanist M. A. Franchet in 1888 based on a collection made by a French missionary, Abbé Delavay, on Tsang-chan in western Yunnan. It has two large prostrate leaves that are characteristically spotted all over with dark blackish maroon. However, several other species also have spotted leaves, and examination of living material in the field and preserved specimens has shown that there has been considerable confusion about the application of the name *C. margaritaceum*.

The origins of this confusion can be traced to Franchet, who published a popular account of his new species in *L'Orchidophile*, also in 1888, and this was accompanied by a coloured plate drawn by Jeanne Koch and a line drawing taken from a Chinese encyclopaedia entitled "Ming chi thou kao". In most features, such as flower size, colour, relative proportions of the sepals, and staminode shape, these illustrations do not agree with the Delavay type of *Cypripedium margaritaceum* and are closer, in my view, to the allied species *C. lichiangense,* described by Cribb and Chen (1994). The latter has larger flowers with an reddish, ovate dorsal sepal that is larger than the synsepal, finely spotted petals, and a trullate staminode. An article on this slipper orchid in a Chinese encyclopaedia is reproduced by Franchet in *L'Orchidophile* and it states quite clearly that "le feuille (sepale) supérieure de la fleur est grande; l'inférieure est mince et petit; . . . toutes les feuilles (de la fleur sepales et petales) sont couvert de points rouges très rapproches." Furthermore, it is clear that Jeanne Koch's painting is taken from a dried specimen, possibly the type of *C. margaritaceum,* because the petals are shown to be spreading rather than enfolding the lip, whilst the lip is shown as angled on the sides, another artifact of pressing. It seems possible, therefore, that she took the colouration for her painting from the description of the species illustrated in the Chinese encyclopaedia.

The confusion over the application of this name has been discussed in detail by Cribb (1992). It was no doubt responsible for the publication of *Cypripedium daliense* as a new species, the type of which was collected in the mountains above Dali in northwestern Yunnan, where the type of *C. margaritaceum* was also collected. The type specimens agree well in both floral and vegetative morphology and in flower colour. A photograph of the species has been published by Yang et al. (1993).

Cypripedium margaritaceum is most closely allied to *C. fargesii* from Hubei and eastern Sichuan provinces in China, but differs in having shorter petals lacking the densely villose white hairs on the outside towards the tips. The two taxa are obviously closely allied and Chen's treatment of *C. fargesii* as a variety of *C. margaritaceum* may indeed be reasonable.

In nature the species is often found in small colonies growing in coniferous woodland on limestone slopes in a deep leaf mulch of pine needles. Plants are often found to be joined by long underground rhizomes, and it is probable that most of these colonies originate from a single plant.

Cypripedium margaritaceum *Franch.* in Bull. Soc. Phil. Paris 7, 12: 141 (1888), in L'Orchidophile 8: 368 (1888) and in J. Bot. (Morot) 8: 265(1894). Type: China, Yunnan, Tsang-chan, *Delavay* (holo. P!, iso. PE!).

C. daliense S.C. Chen & Wu in Acta Phytotax. Sin. 29(1): 86, fig.1 (1991). Type: China, Yunnan, Dali, Lan Feng, *H.C. Wang* 1017 (holo. PE!, iso. SCBI).

DESCRIPTION. A terrestrial herb with a stout underground rhizome, 3–4 mm in diameter, bearing many long roots, 1–1.5 mm in diameter. Stems erect, several cm apart on the rhizome, 1–5.5 cm long, covered by two sheaths, bifoliate at the apex. Leaves prostrate on the substrate, subcircular to obovate or broadly ovate, obtuse or shortly apiculate, 7–13 cm long, 5–11.7 cm wide, dark green and heavily spotted with blackish maroon above. Inflorescence one-flowered, ebracteate. Flower yellow marked with maroon stripes on the sepals and petals and spots on the lip, the staminode dark maroon; pedicel glabrous, 4–6 cm long; ovary curved, 1–1.5 cm long, sparsely pubescent on the ridges. Dorsal sepal concave, curved forwards, ovate, obtuse or shortly apiculate, 1.9–4.4 cm long, 1.8–4 cm wide, papillate-ciliate and shortly hairy on veins on outer surface; synsepal elliptic-ovate, obtuse or shortly bifid, 2.4–3.8 cm long, 1.6–2.2 cm wide, papillate-ciliate. Petals curved forwards and enfolding the lip, obliquely oblong-lanceolate, acute, 3–4.2 cm long, 1.5–2.2 cm wide, shortly ciliate and shortly pubescent on the veins on the outer surface. Lip saccate but dorsiventrally flattened, circular from above and with a circular mouth, 2.8–3 cm long, strongly warted on the front face. Column 0.8–1 cm long; staminode subquadrate, 8–9 mm long and wide, papillose. PLATES 84, 85; FIGURE 48.

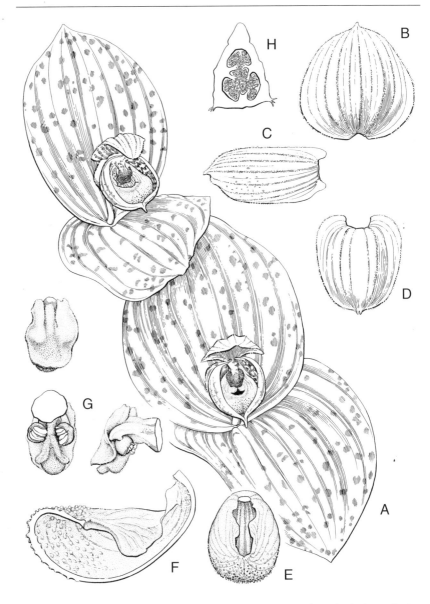

Figure 48. Cypripedium margaritaceum. A, habit, ×0.66; B, dorsal sepal, ×1; C, petal, ×1; D, synsepal, ×1; E, lip, ×1; F, lip longitudinal section, ×2; G, column views, ×2; H, ovary cross section, ×4. All drawn from Kew Spirit Collection no. 55882 by Eleanor Catherine.

DISTRIBUTION. China (NW. Yunnan and SW. Sichuan only).
HABITAT. On grassy slopes and on banks in open woods; 2500–3600 m.

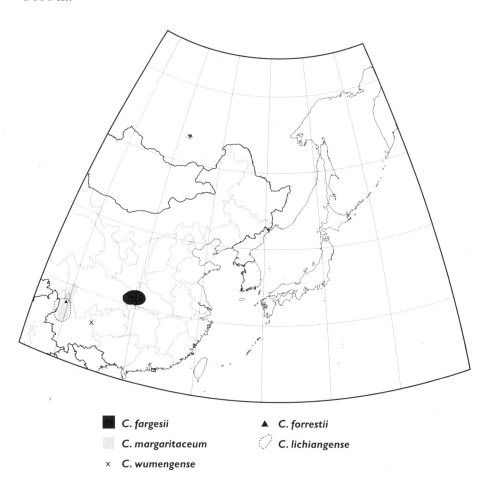

■ *C. fargesii* ▲ *C. forrestii*

▦ *C. margaritaceum* ⟨⟩ *C. lichiangense*

× *C. wumengense*

42. CYPRIPEDIUM LICHIANGENSE

This spectacular orchid, which has the largest flowers of all the species in the group, is closely related to *Cypripedium margaritaceum* and to *C. fargesii,* but differs in having larger, glossy leaves and a differently coloured flower with an ovate-acute dorsal sepal that is larger than the synsepal, longer petals that are shortly pubescent all over on the outer surface, a lip that lacks warts on the front surface, and a longer, trullate staminode. The dorsal sepal is reddish brown or

261

off-yellow and covered with small reddish brown flecks. The petals are reddish yellow and covered with small elliptic maroon spots.

In the wild the species is apparently confined to the mountainous region of northeastern Yunnan and adjacent Myanmar (Burma). At Lijiang (Lichiang), it grows in the same valleys as *Cypripedium margaritaceum*, usually in light to deep shade under bushes, such as rhododendrons, and small trees in limestone rubble and leaf litter on gentle to steep slopes.

I have recently been sent photographs by Holger Perner of a plant that flowered in the collection of a Mr. Möller of Hanover, Germany, in July 1994. It is similar to *Cypripedium lichiangense* in habit, in the leaf size and markings, and in its overall flower shape, the colouration, shape, and attitude of the dorsal sepal, and the petal attitude and indumentum, but it differs in other features of the flower. The ground colour of the petals and lip is white and they are strongly marked with larger maroon spots, rather reminiscent of *Paphiopedilum bellatulum*. The lip appears to be about half the length of the petals, and the petals do not grasp it as closely as in *C. lichiangense*. Indeed the petals are more or less parallel at the apex and well separated rather than touching.

The origin of this plant is unknown, although it was imported from Japan. The literature accompanying the advertisement states that it originated in Vietnam, but I suspect that it must have come originally from China.

Cypripedium lichiangense *S.C. Chen & Cribb* in Orchid Rev. 102: 321 (1994) and in Bull. Alpine Gard. Soc. Gt. Brit. 63(4): 47 (1994). Type: China, Yunnan, Lijiang, *Forrest* 5987 (holo. K!, iso. E!).
C. daliense sensu Cribb in Bull. Alpine Gard. Soc. Gt. Brit. 60(2): 170 (1992), *non* S.C. Chen & Wu (1991).

DESCRIPTION. A terrestrial herb with a stout creeping rhizome bearing numerous long roots, 1.5–2 mm in diameter. Stems erect, short, 3–7 cm long, covered by two tubular sheaths, bifoliate at the apex. Leaves glossy, appressed to substrate, ovate, obovate or subcircular, 8.5–19 cm long, 7–16 cm wide, dark green heavily spotted with black, sometimes with a purplish margin. Inflorescence one-flowered, ebracteate. Flower large, the sepals liver-coloured, the petals and lip dull yellow spotted with maroon, the staminode liver-coloured; pedicel 4–7 cm long, glabrous; ovary curved, 1.2–1.8 cm long, glabrous. Dorsal sepal erect, flat, ovate, acute, 4.2–7 cm long,

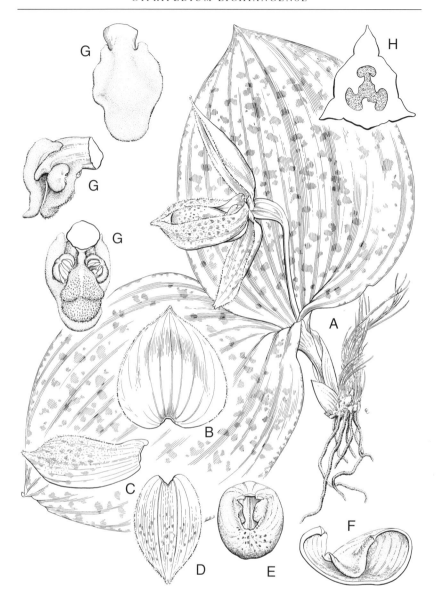

Figure 49. Cypripedium lichiangense. A, habit, ×0.66; B, dorsal sepal, ×0.66; C, petal, ×0.66; D, synsepal, ×0.66; E, lip, ×0.66; F, lip longitudinal section, ×1; G, column, three views, ×2; H, ovary cross section, ×4. A from *Kingdon-Ward* 4278; B–H from Kew Spirit Collection no. 55883 All drawn by Eleanor Catherine.

3.8–6 cm wide, ciliate; synsepal elliptic, subacute, 3.5–5.6 cm long, 2–3.6 cm wide, ciliate. Petals curved forwards enfolding the lip, obliquely oblong-elliptic, acute, 4–6.5 cm long, 1.4–2.1 cm wide, ciliate and pubescent on upper side of outer surface. Lip circular from above but dorsiventrally flattened, 3.3–4 cm long, papillose but not warted in front. Column 1.2–1.4 cm long; staminode trullate, rounded at apex, 1.3–1.5 cm long, papillose. PLATES 78–80; FIGURE 49.

DISTRIBUTION. NE. Myanmar (Burma), China (NW. Yunnan, SW. Sichuan). See map p. 261.

HABITAT. In scrub and open woods, 2600–3500 m.

43. CYPRIPEDIUM FORRESTII

Although only collected twice, *Cypripedium forrestii* is quite distinctive, its nearest allies being the sympatric *C. margaritaceum* and *C. lichiangense*. However, it is readily distinguished from both by its much smaller habit and smaller flowers with a villose pedicel and ovary, glabrous petals with raised patches all over the surface corresponding to the purple spots, and a small oblong, obtuse staminode.

Forrest's type collection, comprising several growths, is in excellent condition, and I have named this strange species in memory of that brave and prolific plant hunter. A second collection by K. M. Fen, made in early June 1939 on the north flank of the Haba Snow Range, was reportedly growing on rocks in pine forest.

Cypripedium forrestii *Cribb* in Bull. Alpine Gard. Soc. Gt. Brit. 60(2): 172 (1992). Type: China, NW. Yunnan, Lijiang Range, *Forrest* 10203 (holo. E!, iso. BM!, K!).

DESCRIPTION. A dwarf terrestrial herb with a creeping subterranean rhizome, 2–2.5 mm in diameter, with scattered slender elongate roots, 1 mm in diameter. Stems erect, borne 3–10 cm apart on the rhizome, 1.5–2.5 cm long, covered by two conical sheaths, bifoliate at the apex. Leaves spreading or prostrate, elliptic or elliptic-ovate, shortly apiculate, 5–6.5 cm long, 2.5–3.6 cm wide, green heavily spotted with black on upper surface. Inflorescence one-flowered, ebracteate. Flower dull yellow finely spotted on all segments with maroon; pedicel 1.7–2.5 cm long, villose; ovary 0.8–1 cm long, vil-

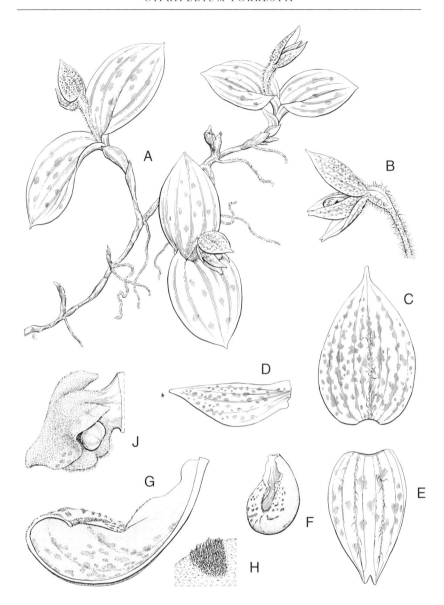

Figure 50. Cypripedium forrestii. A, habit, ×0.66; B, flower, ×1; C, dorsal sepal, ×2; D, petal, ×2; E, synsepal, ×2; F, lip, ×2; G, lip longitudinal section, ×5; H, lip surface detail, ×20; J, column, ×5. All drawn from the type by Eleanor Catherine.

265

lose. Dorsal sepal ovate, apiculate, 2.2–2.4 cm long, 1.4–1.5 cm wide, pubescent at base of outer surface; synsepal ovate-elliptic, bifid and slightly recurved at apex, 1.8–1.9 cm long, 0.8–1 cm wide. Petals curving forwards and enfolding the lip, obliquely ovate, acute, 1.5–1.8 cm long, 0.5–0.6 cm wide. Lip saccate, circular in outline from above, dorsiventrally compressed, 1 cm long, papillose. Column 4–5 mm long; staminode oblong, obtuse, 3.5 mm long, 3 mm wide, papillose. FIGURE 50.

DISTRIBUTION. China (NW. Yunnan only). See map p. 261.

HABITAT. On banks in scrub and open woodland; c. 3500 m.

44. CYPRIPEDIUM FARGESII

Cypripedium fargesii is closely allied to *C. margaritaceum* and has been considered a variety of that species by Pfitzer, Tang and Chen and, more recently, by Chen and Tsi. Although this may eventually prove to be the correct interpretation on *C. fargesii,* I have chosen to keep it distinct at specific level for the time being because of the difficulty of interpreting the limited herbarium material. The long white hairs on the petals of *C. fargesii* are quite distinctive, but the flower colour and patterning are not recorded. Examination of living material has clarified the distinctions between *C. margaritaceum* and *C. lichiangense* and, therefore, I would like to see living material before making up my mind on the true status of this taxon.

Cypripedium fargesii *Franch.* in J. Bot. (Morot) 8: 267 (1894); Chen in Acta Phytotax. Sin. 23(5): 372 (1985); Chen and Xi in Proc. 12th World Orch. Conf.: 145 (1987). Type: China, Sichuan, Tchen-keou-tin, *Farges* 585 (holo. P!, iso. AMES!, K!).

C. *ebracteatum* Rolfe in Bull. Misc. Inform. Kew 1896: 204 (1896). Type: China, Hubei, *Henry* 1404 (holo. BM!).

C. *margaritaceum* Franch. var. *fargesii* (Franch.) Pfitzer in Engler, Pflanzenr. IV, 50 (Heft 12) Orch. Pleonan.: 40 (1903).

DESCRIPTION. A terrestrial herb with a stout, creeping, subterranean rhizome. Stems erect, 3.5–9 cm long, covered by two loose subconical sheaths, bifoliate at the apex. Leaves subcircular, elliptic or obovate, obtuse, 9–19 cm long, 5.5–18 cm wide, green heavily spotted with blackish maroon. Inflorescence one-flowered, ebracteate. Flower dark red or dull yellow marked with maroon spots and dashes; pedicel 2.5–6 cm long, glabrous; ovary 1.2–1.5 cm long, pubescent on the angles. Dorsal sepal ovate, obtuse to shortly apiculate, 2.8–4.5 cm long, 2.3–3.7 cm wide, ciliate and shortly pubescent on veins of the outer surface; synsepal elliptic-ovate, subacute, 3–5 cm long, 2.6–3 cm wide. Petals pointing forwards and enfolding lip, elliptic-oblong, acute, 3.8–5.8 cm long, 1.3–1.8 cm wide, densely longly pubescent on outer surface especially towards the apex, long ciliate. Lip circular from above, dorsiventrally flattened, 2.5–2.7 cm long, warty on front surface. Column 1–1.2 cm long; staminode oblong, rounded in front, 9–10 mm long. FIGURE 51.

DISTRIBUTION. China (E. Sichuan, S. Gansu, W. Hubei). See map p. 261.

HABITAT. Grassy slopes in light open woods. 2000–2200 m. Flowering in May to July.

45. CYPRIPEDIUM WUMENGENSE

Cypripedium wumengense is known only from the type collection, which I have borrowed from the Herbarium of the Institute of Ecology of the University of Kunming. Accompanying the type description is a line drawing that shows some of the critical features distinguishing this species from the closely allied *C. margaritaceum*. In particular, Chen noted that it has glabrous but ciliate petals and that the lip is warty all over. Examination of the type confirms both these features. The suberect leaves may be the result of competition with other vegetation where the type specimen was growing, but it may be that its habit resembles that of *C. bardolphianum*. The relationship of *C. wumengense* to *C. margaritaceum*, to which it is undoubtedly closely allied, needs critical assessment when further material of this elusive species becomes available.

Cypripedium wumengense *S.C. Chen* in Acta Phytotax. Sin. 23(5): 372 (1985). Type: China, Yunnan, Luquan, western parts of Wu Meng Shan, *W.M. Zhu & J.L. Wu* 03447 (holo. HGUY!)

DESCRIPTION. A terrestrial plant to 22 cm tall. Stem to about 10 cm long, covered in three obtuse sheaths, 3–10 cm long, bifoliate at the apex. Leaves suberect-spreading, ovate-elliptic, mucronate, 11–13 cm long, 6.5–7 cm wide, glabrous, green with purple spotting. Inflorescence one-flowered, ebracteate; pedicel a little longer

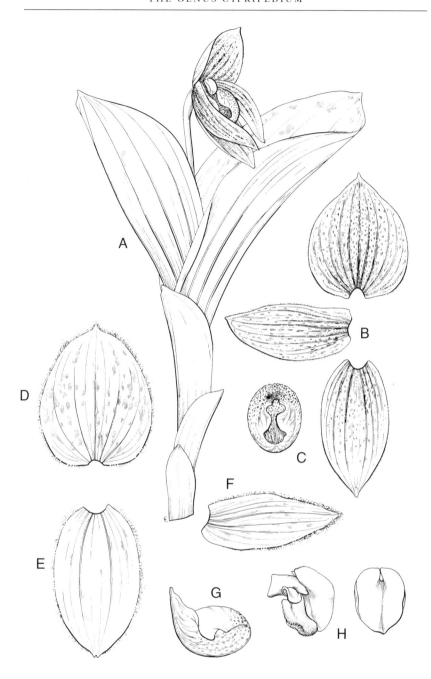

Figure 51. Cypripedium wumengense. A, habit, ×0.66; B, dorsal sepal, synsepal, and petal, ×1; C, lip, ×1. **Cypripedium fargesii.** D, dorsal sepal, ×1; E, synsepal, ×1; F, petal, ×1; G, lip, longitudinal section, ×1; H, column, two views, ×2. A–C from the type; D–H from *Wilson* 4582. All drawn by Eleanor Catherine.

268

than the leaves. Flower 6–7 cm across, covered with purple spotting and stripes. Dorsal sepal broadly ovate, mucronate, about 3.5 cm long, 2.8 cm wide, ciliate, glabrous on both surfaces. Synsepal elliptic, bidentate at the apex, about 4.1 cm long, 2 cm wide, ciliate but glabrous. Petals obliquely subovate-oblong, obtuse-mucronate, about 3.8 cm long, ciliate but glabrous. Lip small, subglobose to slipper-shaped, about 1.6 cm in diameter, glabrous within, the front verruculose. Column short; staminode broadly ovate-orbicular, slightly emarginate at apex, about 5 mm long, 7.5 mm wide. FIGURE 51.

DISTRIBUTION. China (NE. Yunnan only). See map p. 261.

HABITAT. On limestone under *Sinoarundinaria* clumps; 2900 m.

NATURAL HYBRIDS

Natural hybrids of sympatric *Cypripedium* species have been recorded several times. They usually occur where two species that are normally separated by flowering time, pollinator, or ecology chance to meet, for example, in sites disturbed by people or natural disasters such as storms or landslides. Where the parental species are distinct, hybrids are often readily recognised because of their intermediate morphology. Most natural hybrids that have been described fall into this category. Hybridisation between closely allied taxa has been invoked by several authors to explain the confusion of intermediate forms between, for example, the varieties of *C. parviflorum* (e.g., Luer 1975, Case 1987) and between *C. guttatum* and *C. yatabeanum* (Luer 1975, Brown 1995a).

The following natural hybrids have been described and named. Some are reasonably frequently seen in nature and in cultivation.

CYPRIPEDIUM × ALASKANUM

Cypripedium × alaskanum, a hybrid of *C. guttatum* and *C. yatabeanum,* is the most recently described natural hybrid, although it was recognised by both Hultén (1968) and Luer (1975). It was described by R. M. Brown (1995a), using as a basis his own coloured photograph published with the type description. The validity of this hybrid is difficult to judge because no analysis accompanied the description. Hultén suggested that the hybrid is confined to southwestern

Alaska, Kodiak Island, and the Aleutians. The status of these populations needs further examination.

Cypripedium × **alaskanum** *P.M. Br.* in North Amer. Native Orchid J. 1(3): 199, t.6 (1995). Type: U.S.A., Alaska, Anchorage, photo cited here, *P.M. Brown* s.n.

DISTRIBUTION. Alaska. Possibly also in Kamchatka Peninsula.

CYPRIPEDIUM × ANDREWSII

A. M. Fuller described *Cypripedium* × *andrewsii* in 1932 as a hybrid of *C. candidum* and *C. parviflorum* (= *C. parviflorum* var. *parviflorum*), based on material collected near Swan Lake, Wisconsin, U.S.A., by himself and Staffeld. The hybrid was also collected there previously by Dr. E. P. Andrews, after whom it was named.

The same year, *Cypripedium* × *favillianum*, a natural hybrid of *C. candidum* and *C. parviflorum* var. *pubescens*, was described by J. T. Curtis, based on his own and Gale's collection from near Eagle Lake, Wisconsin. Curtis provided a morphological analysis of the hybrid and both parents at the locality. Good photographs of both hybrids are given by Luer (1975).

A third natural hybrid, *Cypripedium* × *landonii*, was described by Leslie Garay in 1953, based on collections from Turkey Point on Lake Erie in Ontario, Canada, by Garay and his colleagues and by Monroe Landon, after whom the hybrid was named. The parentage of these plants is reportedly *C.* × *favillianum* × *C. parviflorum* var. *parviflorum* (as *C. calceolus* var. *parviflorum*). If, however, *C. parviflorum* var. *parviflorum* is considered to belong to the same species as var. *pubescens*, as is the case here, then the correct name for any hybrid of this parentage is *C.* × *andrewsii* (Fuller 1932).

The hybridisation of *Cypripedium parviflorum* var. *pubescens* (as *C. pubescens*) and *C. candidum* in Iowa and Missouri has been studied in some detail by Klier et al. (1991), who examined 31 populations of these taxa and their putative hybrids, 44 morphological and 21 allozyme loci being compared and the results analysed. They convincingly demonstrated that hybridisation and backcrossing occur between these species and that introgression can be detected in both parents even when morphological characters cannot detect it. They suggest that the prairie ecotype of *C. parviflorum* var. *pubes-*

270

cens may have arisen as a result of introgression from *C. candidum,* which is essentially a prairie species.

Cypripedium × **andrewsii** *A.M. Fuller* in Rhodora 34: 100 (1932). Type: U.S.A., Wisconsin, *Fuller & Staffeld* s.n. (holo. MIL, iso. GH!).
C. × *favillianum* J.T. Curtis in Rhodora 34: 241 (1932). Type: U.S.A., Wisconsin, *Curtis & Gale* s.n. (holo. Carroll Coll. Herb., iso. GH!).
C. × *landonii* Garay in Canad. J. Bot. 31: 660–662 (1953). Type: Canada, Ontario, *Soper, Hull & Garay* s.n. (holo. TRT).

DISTRIBUTION. Northern central U.S.A. and adjacent Canada.

CYPRIPEDIUM × COLOMBIANUM

Cypripedium × *colombianum* was described by Sheviak (1992) as a hybrid of *C. montanum* and *C. parviflorum* var. *pubescens,* based on an intensive survey and analysis of wild and herbarium specimens from three localities in the northwestern United States and adjacent Canada. Sheviak suggested that hybridisation has occurred because of habitat disturbance due to logging, allowing plants of the two parents to interbreed. *Cypripedium montanum* is typically a montane species, growing on limestone substrates in spruce-fir forests. It has two or three sweetly fragrant flowers with a white lip, long dark chocolate brown petals, and broad leaves clustered towards the base of the stem, leaving the flowers to stand free of the foliage. *Cypripedium parviflorum* var. *pubescens* is much more difficult to categorise, but is readily distinguishable from *C. montanum* by its flowers which have a musty odour of roses, a yellow lip, paler relatively shorter petals, and leaves that are well spaced along the stem. The hybrids are either intermediate between the parents or have characteristics of each.

Cypripedium × **colombianum** *C.J. Sheviak* in Amer. Orchid Soc. Bull. 61: 546–559 (1992). Type: Canada, British Colombia, *Sheviak & Metzlaff* 3055 (holo. NYS).

DISTRIBUTION. NW. U.S.A. and adjacent Canada (British Colombia).

CYPRIPEDIUM × VENTRICOSUM

Cypripedium calceolus and *C. macranthos* hybridise where their ranges overlap in Russia and across northern Asia to Sakhalin Island (Keller and Schlechter 1926, Keller and Sóo 1930, Slyusarenko 1981, Averyanov 1995, Perner pers. comm.). The hybrid is best known under the name *C. × barbeyi* (Camus 1908). However, I agree with Rolfe (1904, 1910) that the name *C. × ventricosum* is referable to this hybrid and is, therefore, its earliest name. Rolfe considered *C. × ventricosum* to be a hybrid of *C. macranthos* and *C. calceolus*, based on a comparison of plants from western Siberia collected by Edmond Boissier and flowered in Switzerland, with a flowering plant from the artificial hybridisation of *C. calceolus* and *macranthos* made by E. Scapelhorn at the Highgate Nurseries of Messrs. Cutbush and Sons.

Cypripedium × ventricosum from eastern Siberia was described by Olof Swartz in 1800, who in 1805 stated that it was based on Gmelin's collection. De Candolle (1880) indicated that Gmelin's collections were in the Pallas Herbarium, now incorporated in the Willdenow Herbarium in Berlin. Examination of the sheets there has identified two collections labelled as *C. × ventricosum* from the Pallas Herbarium. However, neither is labelled as a Gmelin collection, although it seems likely that both are. I have, therefore, selected Gmelin's clear illustration as the lectotype of *C. × ventricosum* in the absence of any other material that can irrefutably be linked to Gmelin.

Three other names can also be considered conspecific with *Cypripedium × ventricosum*, namely, *C. freynii*, *C. krylowii*, and *C. manschuricum*. All were described as natural hybrids of *C. calceolus* and *C. macranthos*, the last because *C. × ventricosum* was considered by Stapf (1927) to be a variant of *C. macranthos* and conspecific with that species. I have lectotypified it on R. Sweet's illustration in his *British Flower Garden*.

Slyusarenko (1981) also suggested that *Cypripedium macranthos* and *C. × ventricosum* hybridise freely in far eastern Russia to produce many intermediates. Others have interpreted *C. macranthos* and *C. × ventricosum* to be conspecific, extreme variants of a polymorphic species (see under *C. macranthos*). Recent field observations in the Vladivostok area by Perner, Sheviak, Averyanov, and others (pers. comm.) suggest that the variation in *C. macranthos* is extensive. Flowers vary in colour from deep rose-purple through pink to white or cream; petal length is varies in relation to lip size; and lip size and shape vary considerably (Perner pers. comm.). On this basis, *C. × krylowii*, described by Siuzew (1926) as the natural hybrid of *C. × ventricosum* and *C. calceolus*, is considered here to be synonymous with *C. × ventricosum*. Perner and his colleagues found that hybridisation between *C. macranthos* and the sympatric *C. calceolus* was frequent, plants of intermediate nature between the parents being common. They also saw plants that were best interpreted as backcrosses to either parent. These included white-flowered plants that matched well the type of *C. manschuricum* var. *virescens* (Stapf 1927).

Cypripedium × ventricosum *Sw.* in Kongl. Vetensk. Acad. Nya Handl. 21: 251 (1800) and in (1806). Type: Siberia, illustration in Gmelin's *Flora Sibirica*: t.1 (1747), lecto. selected here.
Sacodon ventricosum (Sw.) Raf., Fl. Tellur. 4: 46 (1838).
Cypripedium macranthos Sw. var. *ventricosum* (Sw.) Rchb. f., Icon. Florae Germ. Helv. Orch.: 210 (1851).
C. × freynii Karo in Oesterr. Bot. Zeitschr. 46: 97 (1896). Type: Russia, Nertschinsk, *Karo* (holo. W!).
C. × barbeyi E.G. Camus, Monogr. Orchid.: 453 (1908). Type: cult. Barbey, Lausanne, June 1891 (holo. G!)
C. × krylowii Siuzew in Bull. Inst. Rech. Biol. Perm 4: 435–436 (1926). Type: Russia, *Kryloff* (not located).
C. manschuricum Stapf in Bot. Mag. 152: sub t.9117 (1927). Type: R. Sweet's *British Flower Garden* 4: t.1 (1838), lecto. selected here.
C. manschuricum Stapf var. *virescens* Stapf in *loc. cit.* 152: t. 9117 (1927). Type: E. Siberia, cult. Roy. Bot. Gard. Edinburgh (holo. K!).
C. × kesselringii G. Keller, Monogr. Iconogr. Orchid. Eur. 2: 18 (1940), *nom. nud.*

ILLUSTRATIONS: PLATES 26, 117, 118; FIGURE 4.
DISTRIBUTION. Russia (from the Urals across to eastern Siberia and Sakhalin), Korea, NE. China.

APPENDIX: LIST OF
COLLECTIONS EXAMINED

1. **C. subtropicum.** SE. XIZANG: *B.S. Li et al.* 11188 (PE).
2. **C. wardii.** SW. CHINA: *Kingdon-Ward* 145 (E), 8366 (K), 15018 (BM); *C.W. Wang* 65764 (PE); *T.T. Yu* 8723 (PE).
3. **C. irapeanum.** MEXICO: *Bottieri* s.n. (G); *Bottieri & Dunant* s.n. (G); *Bottieri & Sumichrast* 1242 (P); *Bourgeau* 541 (P), 2666 (K,MO,P), 2808 (G,K,P); *Breedlove* 27069 (MO); cult. *Dickinson* s.n. (K); *Diguet* s.n. (P); *Galeotti* 5162 (G,K,P), 5229 (G,P), 5230 (G), s.n. (K); *Ghiesbrecht* 9 (G), 768 (G,K,MO), s.n. (K,P,W); *Hartweg* s.n. (K,W); *Hinton* 1186 (G,K), 1208 (K,MO), 1438 (K), 4438 (G,K), 9230 (G,K,MO); *Hohenacker* s.n. (G); *Langlasse* 342 (G,K); *Liebmann* 39 (W); *J. Linden* 8 (K,P,W), 8A (G), s.n. (G,W); *McVaugh* 18823 (G); *Nagel* 7302 (SEL); *Nagel & Juan G.* 1302 (MO); *Pringle* 4440 (G,K,P,W,Z); *Purpus* 16450 (K); *Scheidwein* 5230 (W), s.n. (W); *Scott-Gentry* 6567 (MO); cult. *Shuttleworth, Charlesworth & Co.* (K); *Weber* s.n. (P,W). GUATEMALA: *Hamer* A119 (SEL); *J.R. Johnston* 1645 (K); *Klee* s.n. (K); *Ure-Skinner* s.n. (K). HONDURAS: *Ure-Skinner* s.n. (K).
4. **C. molle.** MEXICO: *Andrieux* 90 (K,P,W); *Cribb & Soto* M2 (K); *Cribb & Greenwood* M9 (K); *Greenwood* s.n. (K); *Hartweg* 517 (G,K,P,W); *Karwinski* s.n. (W); *Kenton, Rudall & Howard* 4-18 (K); *Molseed* 266 (MO); *P. Tenorio L.* 11565 (MO).
5. **C. dickinsonianum.** S. MEXICO: *Dickinson* s.n. (AMO,K); *Hartmann* s.n. (MEXU).
6. **C. californicum.** U.S.A.: *Austin* s.n. (K); *Bolander* 6474 (BM,GH,W); *Heller* 13282 (G); *Howell* 13610 (K), s.n. (G); *Lemmon* s.n. (G,P); *H.E. & S.T. Parks* 24008 (G,K,P); *Thompson* 4660a (G,K). MISC.: Hort. K. Dryden, 18 May 1992 (K); Hort. Gumbleton, 14 May 1890 (K); Hort. Kew, 23 July 1909 (K); Hort. J. Mars, 21 March 1977 (K); Hort. Miss Willmott, June 1925 (K).
7. **C. flavum** (selected). CHINA: *Bailey* s.n. (E in part); *Chamberlain et al.* 788 (K), 798 (E); *Ching* 933 (E); *Chu* 2810 (BM,E,W); *Cunningham* 79 (E in part); *David* s.n. (P); *Delavay* 134 (P), 135 (P), 378 (P), 2082 (K,P), 3479 (K,P), s.n. (K,P); *Ducloux* 4574 (P); *Fang* 4160 (E,K,P); *Farges* 134 (K,P), s.n. (K); *Farrer* 138 (E,P), s.n. (E); *Forrest* 2341 (BM,E,K), 2429 (K), 5628 (E,K), 5897 (E), 10118 (BM,E,K,W), 19229 (E,K), 28432 (BM,E), 28478 (BM,E); *J. & C. Gregory* s.n. (BM); *KEY* 194 (E), 444 (E); *Handel-Mazzetti* 3153 (W), 6776 (W); *Hopkinson*

443 (P); *Kingdon-Ward* 3999 (E), 4062 (E), 4788 (E), 5174 (E), 10840 (BM); *McLaren* 14 (BM,E,K), 44 (E,P); *Maire* 431 (E); *Mombeig* 44 (E,K), 252 (E), 1912 (P), s.n. (E,K); *Mussot* 351 (K,P); *Pratt* 263 (K); *Purdom* s.n. (K); *Rock* 3794 (E,P,W), 12536 (E,K), 16189 (E), 23873 (E,K), 24704 (BM,E,K); *Schneider* 1626 (G,E,K); *Schoch* 230 (K); *Sino-British Exp. to Cangshan* 0663 (E), 0664 (K); *H. Smith* 3553 (E,GB,UPS); *Soulie* 413 (K), 575 (P), 576 (P), 979 (P), 1391 (K,P); *Weigold* s.n. (W); *Wilson* 1750 (K), 2417 (E,K,P,W), 4588 (BM,K,P); *Yu* 8604 (BM,E), 17183 (E).

8. **C. reginae** (selected). CANADA: *Cleghorn* s.n. (K); *Dumais* 5020 (W); *Fernald & Wiegand* 3098 (K); *Fyler* s.n. (W); *Gouldie* s.n. (K); *Hooker* s.n. (K); *Louis & Lalonde* 1037 (K); *Lowe* s.n. (K); *Macoun* 1471 (K); *Malte* 392 (W); *Marie-Victorin, Rolland-Germain & Jacques* 44419 (W), 45912 (W); *Roy* 3075 (K), 4312 (K,W); *Scoggan* 9025 (K); *Stewart* s.n. (K). U.S.A.: *Barclay* s.n. (K); *Buker* s.n. (W); *Bush* 410 (K); *Catesby* s.n. (K); *Clarke* 2824 (K); *Coville* s.n. (K); *Dike* s.n. (W); *Fisher* 1391 (K); *Frank* s.n. (K,W); *Geyer* 521 (W); *Jesup* s.n. (K); *McDonough* 1842 (K); *McLouth* s.n. (W); *Pringle* 7 (K); *Seidenberg* 46 (W); *Short* s.n. (K); *Soper* 2026 (K); *Trelease* s.n. (W); *Vasey* s.n. (K); *Webber* s.n. (K); Williams s.n. (K). MISC.: Herb. *Hooker* (K); Hort. Kew, 8 April 1878 (K); Hort. Kew 136.96 (K); Hort. Kew, May '26 (K); Hort. Kew 802-1932 (K); Herb. *Munroe* (K); Herb. *Sartwell* s.n. (K).

9. **C. passerinum.** ALASKA: *Anderson* 5142 (K); *Calder & Kukkonen* 28195 (W); *Cody & Webster* 5257 (W); *Funston* 121 (K,P); *Taylor & Ferguson* 1479 (W); *Went* s.n. (K); *Williams* 1065 (K), 1584 (K), 1771 (K). CANADA: *Calder & Kukkonen* 28265 (K); *Cody* 4044 (K,W); *Cody & Gutteridge* 7389 (W); *Dorrien-Smith* 101 (K); *Haydon* 11 (K); *Lewis* 897 (W); *Lokbrunner* 154 (K); *Macoun* 108 (K), 5983 (K); *McCalla* 2228 (K); *Marie-Victorin & Rolland-Germain* 24322 (K), 28252 (K); *Raup* 2044 (K); *Richardson* s.n. (AMES,BM,K); *Ringius, Kirkby & Wilson* 846 (W); *Schofield* 1166 (W); *Scoggan* 3875 (K), 5336 (K), 6201 (K); Ulke 23 (P). U.S.A.: *Farr* 699 (K); *Lasegne* 345 (G). MISC.: Hort. Kew, 21 June 1883 (K).

10. **C. calceolus** (selected). EUROPE: *Buxbaum* 284 (W); *Fleischmann* s.n. (W); *Fongberg* 20 (W); *Hartner* 756 (W); *K.A. Nilsson* 527 (W); *Preissmann* s.n. (W); *Rechinger* 1127 (W); *Rion* 43 (W); *Svestka* 900 (W); *Topa* 2820 (W); *Vetter* s.n. (W); *Wolfert* s.n. (W). RUSSIA: *Bunge* s.n. (P); *Chaffanjon* 1498 (P), s.n. (P); *Davidov* s.n. (P); *Fedorov et al.* 4805 (BM); *Fischer* s.n. (P); *Freyn* 125 (W); *Jurinsky* s.n. (P); *Karo* 125 (P), 221 (P), 386 (BM,P,W); *Ledebour* s.n. (BM,P); *Maximowicz* s.n. (BM,W); *Stubendorff* s.n. (BM). CHINA: *S.C. Guo* 0024 (PE); *J.H. Hou* 16056 (PE); *Komarov* 439 (BM); *H.W. Kung* 1441 (PE), 1506 (PE); *S.E. Liu* 7180 (PE), 8868 (PE); *L.C. Ma* 39 (PE); *C.Q. Shong* 98 (PE). KOREA: *Komarov* 432 (P,W); *Ohwi* 1136 (PE). JAPAN: Karasawa (sight record).

11. **C. henryi.** CHINA: *Cavalerie* 2087 (E,K,P), 2489 (P), 3985 (K,P), s.n.
(E); *Chien* 5552 (E); cult. Kew s.n. (K); *Farges 1036* (G,K,P), s.n. (K);
Feng 3831 (PE); *K.J. Fu* 5268 (PE); *Henry* 5391A (BM,E,K), 5391B
(BM,E,K,P), 5391C (BM,K,P,W), 5391D (BM,E,K,P); *Z.H. Ji* 0498
(PE); *Y. Liu* 00652 (PE); *T.P. Soong* 306 (PE); *Wilson* 641 (K,P), 893
(K), 4584 (BM,K,P), 5215 (E,K,P); *Y.L. Zhou* 76455 (PE).

12. **C. segawai.** TAIWAN: *Fukuyama* 5987 (TAIF); *Segawa* s.n. (TI); cult.
K. Dryden; cult. Kew.

13. **C. shanxiense.** CHINA: *Z.S. Chang* 2796 (PE); *H.F. Chou* 40678 (PE);
Exp. Dung Lin 264 (PE); *Exp. Flum. Huang.* 2120 (PE), 2451 (PE);
W.Y. Hsia 1186 (PE); *B.Z. Gao* 9173 (KUN,PE); *K.C. Guang & Y.L.
Chen* 548 (PE), 679 (PE); *K.M. Liou* 384 (PE), 1423 (PE), 1488 (PE);
Y. Liu 11728 (PE); *Serre* 2128 (W); *T. Tang* 950 (PE); *Team Nong Yung*
0094 (PE); *Team Zhong Yang* 124 (PE); *H.T. Tsai* 50449 (PE); *C.W.
Wang* 61371 (PE); *T.P. Wang* 3146 (PE). RUSSIA: *Perner* s.n. (K).

14. **C. cordigerum.** BHUTAN: *Bowes Lyon* 3312 (E); *Cooper* 3909 (E); *B.J.
Gould* 64 (K); *R. Bedi* 49 (K). N. INDIA: *C.B. Clarke* 18667 (W), 28667
(K), 28899 (K), 28913 (K), 31098 (K); *H. Collett* 555 (K); *Lady Dal-
housie* s.n. (K,W); Das 201 (W); *Dean* s.n. (K); *Dobremez* 2233 (G);
Drummond 22381 (K), 22727 (G,K); *Duthie* 2058 (W); *Edgeworth* 63
(K); *Falconer* 1074 (W); *Gamble* 4340 (K), s.n. (K); *H. Haines* 2206
(K); *Hartmann* 3050 (G); *F. Kerr* 1248 (K); *Madden* s.n. (K); *Munro*
2123 (K); *Naithani* 47985 (G); *Polunin, Sykes & Williams* 4334 (G);
Rich B249 (K), 281 (K); *Saunders* s.n. (K); *Sharp* s.n. (W); *Stainton,
Sykes & Williams* 984 (G); *Strachey & Winterbottom* 55 (K); *T. Thomson*
318 (K), 1281 (K); *Wallich* s.n. (G,W); *Winterbottom* 427 (K). NEPAL:
G. & S. Miehe 3066 (K). PAKISTAN: *U. Schickhoff* 371 (K), 371A (K).
S. XIZANG: *B.J. Gould* 2091 (K); *E.H. Walsh* 72 (K).

15. **C. fasciolatum.** CHINA: *K.L. Chu* 2408 (PE,W), 2508 (PE,W); *W.P.
Fang* 34013 (PE), 34021 (PE); *Farges* 922 (G,K,P); *K.J. Guang* 460
(PE); *Y. Liou* 588 (PE); *Tien-chuan-hsien* 2408 (E); *C.W. Wang* 65363
(PE); *Wilson* 4581 (E,K); *Yang-guan-hui* 55159 (KUN); *G.H. Yong*
0319 (PE), 55159 (PE).

16. **C. farreri.** CHINA: *Farrer & Purdom* 155 (E); *T.P. Soong* 38878 (PE).

17a. **C. parviflorum** var. **parviflorum** (selected). CANADA: *Bourgeau* s.n.
(W); *Cain* s.n. (W); *Calder* 1387 (W), 7087 (W); *Fernald & St.John*
10815 (W); Hort. Glasgow (K); *Haydon* 34 (K); *Hooker* s.n. (W); *Lubke*
1127 (K); *Macoun* 1469 (K); *Malte* s.n. (W); *Richardson* s.n. (K); *Rosser*
s.n. (W); *Turner* 1293 (W). U.S.A.: *Adams* s.n. (W); *Bebb* s.n. (K); *Ben-
nett* s.n. (W); *Clarke* 2822 (K); *Drummond* 334 (K); *Geyer* 504 (W); *A.
Gray* s.n. (W); *Lawrence & Dress* 301 (W); *Mackenzie* 530 (K); *Paine*
s.n. (W); *Palmer* s.n. (W); *Pittillo* 71 (W); *Pringle* s.n. (K); *Rafinesque*
s.n. (W); *Retz* 1924 (W); *Rugel* s.n. (W); *Sheldon* s.n. (W); *Shriver* s.n.
(K); *Taylor* s.n. (W); *Umbach* 1620 (W).

17b. C. parviflorum var. **pubescens** (selected). CANADA: *Baldwin* 4703 (K); *Baldwin & Breitung* 2450 (K); *Bebb* s.n. (W); *Bourgeau* s.n. (K); *Butler* s.n. (K); *Cain* 830 (W); *Fernald & Long* 27851 (GH); *Fernald, Long & Fogg* 1533 (K), 1535 (K); *Fernald & St.John* 10815 (K); *Gibbs* s.n. (K); *Gouldie* s.n. (K); *Henry* 467 (K); *Hooker & Greville* s.n. (K); *Kennedy & Ganders* 4103 (K); *Loring* s.n. (K); *Macoun* 1470 (K); *Marie-Victorin & Rolland-Germain* 24325 (K); *Paine* s.n. (W); *Richardson* s.n. (K); *Roleau* 122 (K); *Schuette* s.n. (K); *Schweinitz* s.n. (K); *Scoggan* 8530 (K), 10735 (K); *Torrey* s.n. (K); *Welfitt-Nicholls* s.n. (K). U.S.A.: *Adams Fritchey* s.n. (K); *Baplow* s.n. (W); *Bush* 317 (K), 547 (K); Herb. *Carey* s.n. (K); *Chickering* s.n. (K); *Clarke* 2823 (K); *Drummond* 546 (K), s.n. (K); *Eggert* s.n. (K); *A. Gray* s.n. (W); *Hooker* 212 (K), 837 (W); *Kumlein* 83 (W); *Lapham* s.n. (K); *Lowrie* s.n. (K); *Macoun* s.n. (K); *Munroe* s.n. (K); *Olney* s.n. (K); *Pringle* s.n. (K); *Riehl* 176 (W), s.n. (K); *Rugel* s.n. (W); *Sandberg & Leiberg* 125 (K); *Schrenk* s.n. (W); *Schumann* 42 (W); *Sheldon* s.n. (W); *Short* s.n. (K); *Small* s.n. (K); *Sullivant* 43 (W), s.n. (K); *Townsend* s.n. (W); *Woolson* s.n. (K). MISC.: Hort. Glasgow (Bot. Mag. t.3824) (K); Hort. Kew, June 1887 (K); Hort. Liverpool (K).

18. C. kentuckiense. U.S.A.: *Ball* s.n. (AMES); *Boufford, Spongberg, Lang & Wofford* 22884 (AMES); *Brown & Weiss* 7650 (AMES); *Clarke* 3687 (G); *Darche* s.n. (P); *Short* s.n. (K); *Sullivant* s.n. (K); Hort. Kew, June 1909 (K).

19. C. montanum. CANADA: *Bourgeau* s.n. (W); *Crease* s.n. (K); *Geyer* 334 (K), s.n. (K); *Greene* s.n. (K); *Hewitt Bostack* 1801 (W); *Hussey* s.n. (K); *Macoun* 1468 (K), s.n. (K); *Miles* s.n. (K); *Moir* 360 (K); *Warren* s.n. (K). U.S.A.: *Austin* 33 (K), s.n. (K); *Baker* 264 (K); *Barkley* 56 (G); *Bolander* 3911 (K), 4829 (G), s.n. (K); *Cooper* s.n. (K); *Cusick* 96 (G), 1707 (K); *Darlington* 61 (G), 380 (G); *J. Day* s.n. (W); *De Cou* s.n. (W); *Douglas* s.n. (K); *Furnis* 1149 (K); *Geyer* 45 (W), 334 (G,W); *A. Gray* s.n. (W); *A. & E. Heller* 3335 (G); *Hinds* s.n. (K); *Hooker* s.n. (K); *Kellogg & Harford* 970 (G); *Lobb* 271 (K), s.n.; *Lyall* s.n. (K); *MacDougal* 362 (K); *Nuttall* s.n. (K,W); *Reed & Barkley* 56 (K); *St.John* 4559 (K); *Sandberg et al.* 384 (G,K), 572 (K); Steck. s.n. (W); *Suksdorf* s.n. (G,K,W); *Thompson* 4332 (K); *Tolmie* s.n. (K); *Woolson* 373 (G). MISC.: Hort. Elwes, 24 April 1893 (K); Hort. Kew, Aiton, 1785 (BM); Hort. Kew, Johnson, July 1900 (K); Hort. Kew, Kelsey, July 1932 (K).

20. C. candidum. CANADA: *Landon* s.n. (W); *Torrey* s.n. (K). U.S.A.: *Bebb* 387 (W), s.n. (G,K); *Burke* s.n. (K); *Chase* 1323 (G); *Hellmayr* s.n. (G); *Herman* 9445 (K); *Holton* s.n. (K); *Johnson* 4079 (K); *Kumlein* 84 (G,W); *Meadl* s.n. (K); *Munroe* s.n. (K); *Nuttall* s.n. (K); *Pammel* s.n. (W); *Patterson* s.n. (G); *Pitcher* s.n. (K); *Riehl* 127 (G,K,W); *Saunders* s.n. (G); *Schumann* 42 (W); *Short* 50 (W), s.n. (K); *Sullivant* 43 (W); *Vasey* s.n. (K); *Wardmond* s.n. (W); *Wheeler* 10705 (K), 10800 (G).

21. C. macranthos (selected). RUSSIA: *Augustinowicz* s.n. (W); *Baines* 431 (BM); *Besser* s.n. (W); *Brenner* s.n. (K); *Chamisso* s.n. (W); *Desoulavy* 3611 (K,TNS,W); *Ehnberg* s.n. (Z); *Fiedler* s.n. (W); *Fischer* 51 (W), s.n. (BM,K,W); *Freyn* 106 (BM); *Henah* s.n. (K); *Hultén* 2186 (K); *Ivanovski* 3052a (K,W); *Jettmar* s.n. (W); *Karo* 104 (K), 106 (K,W,Z), 435 (K), 436 (BM,W,Z), 3193 (BM,Z), s.n. (K,W,Z); *Klerc* 24 (Z), s.n. (Z); *Komarov* 434 (K), 3873 (W), 3874 (W); *Kuminova* s.n. (K); *Ledebour* s.n. (BM); *Littledale* s.n. (K); *Maack* s.n. (K); *Mameev* 121 (K), 675 (K), 3052b (K,W); *Maximowicz* s.n. (BM,K,W); *Meyer* 832 (K), 875 (K); *Mischta* 3051 (K); *Prescott* s.n. (K); *Price* 409 (K); *Radde* s.n. (BM); *Regel* s.n. (K); *Ross* 54 (K); *Rudmin* s.n. (Z); *Stubendorff* 431 (BM); *Skvortzov* s.n. (K); *Turzaninow* s.n. (K); *Vassiliev* 3611 (BM). SAKHALIN: *R. Conolly* s.n. (BM,W); *Ito* NSM87408 (TNS); *Jegorova* s.n. (W); *Miyake* TNS380032 (TNS), 380033 (TNS), 380034 (TNS), 380035 (TNS), 380036 (TNS), 380037 (TNS), 380038 (TNS), 380039 (TNS); *Nagasawa* TNS380032 (TNS); *Nakano* TSM62543 (TNS), 62544 (TNS); *Nizul* 72 (G). NE. CHINA: *Bodinier* s.n. (K); *Bretschneider* 1968 (BM); *Chaffanjon* 1499 (Z), s.n. (W); *Chu* 2508 (BM); *David* 3 (BM), 2216 (K); *Hugh* 149 (BM), s.n. (BM); *Imperial Museum Tokyo* 1865 (TNS); *James* s.n. (K); *Hancock* s.n. (K); *Komarov* 434 (BM); *Kung* 201 (K); *Licent* 3105 (BM,K), 7596 (BM), 7978 (K), 8675 (BM,K), 8677 (BM,K); *Limpricht* 2504 (K), 2505 (K); *Maximowicz* 2 (BM); *Moellendorf* s.n. (BM,FI,K,W); *Prescott* s.n. (FI); *Purdom* 5 (K); *Sataki* 134 (TSN), 231 (TSN); *Sowerby* s.n. (BM); *Takahashi* 256129 (TNS), 262021 (TNS), 284760 (TNS), 284761 (TNS); *Togashi* 13016 (TNS), 13017 (TNS); *Tschonoski* s.n. (W); *Webster* 34 (K); *Yamatsuta* 3052 (TSN), 3053 (TSN), 3067 (TSN), 3068 (TSN). KOREA: *Chung* 2790 (TSN); *Faurie* 230 (BM,G,W); *Ikuma* 31714 (TNS); *Okamoto* 18730 (TNS); *Ohwi* 228653 (TNS), 228660 (TNS), 228683 (TNS), 228685 (TNS). JAPAN: *Asuyama* TSM41265 (TNS); *Bisset* s.n. (BM,K); *Date* TSM80244 (TNS); *Faurie* 5671 (BM,W), 13141 (G,K); *Fox* s.n. (BM); *Hara* TNS57356 (TNS); *Hiratsuka* TNS546464 (TNS); *Kawamoto* TNS504894 (TNS); *Kubota* TSM71559 (TNS); *Maries* 276c (BM); *Nagasaki & Uemoto* NSM147839 (TNS); *Ogata* NSM137546 (TNS); *Okuyama* TSM87396 (TNS), NSM276990 (TNS); *Satomi* NSM139359 (TNS); *Savatier* NSM190097 (TNS); *Shiobara* TSM40677 (TNS); *Shirai* TSM66020 (TNS); *Sugiyama* IMT4394 (TNS); *Tschonoski* s.n. (BM,K); *Wakana* NSM110877 (TNS); *Watanabe* TSM62539 (TNS); *Yoshiura & M. Hara* 115 (TNS). REBUN ISLAND: near Rebun Falls, 14 June 1927, *Fukai* s.n. (TI); 1926, *Tatewaki* s.n. (SAPA, holo. of var. *rebunense*). TAIWAN: 6 May 1936, *Segawa* s.n. (TI); 7 May 1936, *Segawa* s.n. (TI).

22. C. yunnanense. CHINA: *Cunningham* 79 (E in part); *Forrest* 2429 (BM,K), 5176 (E); *Z.T. Guang* 30-0136 (PE); *S. Jiang* 10103 (PE);

Kingdon-Ward 4115 (E); *Pratt* 748 (BM in part, K); *Rock* 8688 (K), 24697 (E,K), s.n. (W); *Schneider* 1392 (E,K); *Sichuan Forestry Team* 2202 (PE); *Wilson* 1753 (AMES), 4590 (BM,K,PE).

23.   **C. ludlowii.** SE. XIZANG: *Ludlow, Sherriff & Elliot* 15361 (BM,E,K).

24.   **C. tibeticum** (selected). SIKKIM: *Dungboo* s.n. (BM,E,K); *Dungboo* in *King* s.n. (K); *Pantling* 386 (K,Z); *Walsh* 53 (K). BHUTAN: *Bowes-Lyon* 3413 (BM); *Ludlow & Sherriff* 162 (BM), 3233 (BM); *Ludlow, Sherriff & Hicks* 16325 (BM), 18970 (BM), 19123 (BM). CHINA: *Bor & Kirat Ram* 20370 (K); *Butty* 38 (Z); *Chamberlain et al.* 963 (E); *Delavay* 3478 (K), s.n. (K); *Forrest* 157 (E), 2322 (E,K), 5938 (BM,E,K), 19230 (K); *Gould* 477 (K), 2093 (K); *KEY* 95 (E), 433 (E); *Hanbury-Tracy* s.n. (BM); *Handel-Mazzetti* 3987 (W); *Kingdon-Ward* 146 (E), 4408 (E), 5162 (E), 5190 (E), 5795 (K), 7068 (K), 8322 (K), 11656 (BM), 19230 (E); *X. Li* 71074 (PE); *Ludlow & Sherriff* 743 (BM), 1638 (BM); *Ludlow, Sherriff & Elliot* 13139 (BM), 13202 (BM), 13815 (BM), 15084 (BM); *Ludlow, Sherriff & Taylor* 3850 (BM), 4325 (BM); *McLaren* N7 (BM,E,K), 22 (BM), D246 (BM,E,K), V25A (E); *Monbeig* 253 (E), s.n. (K); *Rock* 3773 (E), 12521 (W), 14165 (E,K,PE), 17784 (W), 22255 (E), 23169 (E,K,KUN), 24050 (E); *Schneider* 1637 (E); *Sino-Amer. Bot. Exp.* 419 (E); *Soulie* s.n. (KUN), 953 (K in part); *Wilson* 1748 (K), 4589 (BM,K in part); *Yu* 6128 (PE), 6230 (PE), 6074 (PE), 19079 (E).

25.   **C. smithii.** CHINA: *Giraldi* 7223 (FI), 7224 (FI); *S. Jiang* 9338 (PE); *X.Y. Liu* 20094 (PE); *Rock* 12521 (PE); *Serre* 2044 (W); *H. Smith* 2550 (PE), 3702 (UPS), 3704 (UPS); *T.P. Soong* 2741 (PE); *F.T. Wang* 21173 (PE); *T.P. Wang* 4702 (PE); *Weigold* s.n. (W); *T.T. Yu* 6074 (PE).

26.   **C. franchetii** (selected). CHINA: *Beijing Bot. Inst. Team* 643 (PE); *Chu* 2408 (E); *W.P. Fang* 1240 (PE); *Farges* 134 (K), 509 (K); *Fenzel* 525 (W); *K.T. Fu* 862 (PE); *Giraldi* 6867 (FI), 6869 (FI), 6870 (FI), 6871 (FI), 6873 (FI), 6875 (FI); *Henry* 5391 (K), 6740 (K); *Hopkinson* 445 (PE); *Hugh* 149 (E), s.n. (E); *X.H. Ji* 0316 (PE); *Licent* 5198 (E,K,PE,W), 5333 (K); *T.N. Lion & P.C. Tsoong* 2741 (PE); *Y. Liu* 587 (PE); *P.S. Pen* 456 (PE); *Purdom* 412? (K), s.n. (K); *Sichuan Economic Plant Team* 1020 (PE); *Silvestri* 4235 (FI); *F.T. Wang* 21062 (PE), 21173 (PE); *T.P. Wang* 4632 (PE), 14202 (PE); *Wilson* 1884 (K,W); *G.H. Yang* 58085 (PE); *Yellow River Team* 3187 (PE), 3762 (PE), 4369 (PE), 4553 (PE).

27.   **C. himalaicum.** BHUTAN: *R. Bedi* 383 (K), *B.J. Gould* 483 (K), 546 (K); *Ludlow, Sherriff & Hicks* 16603 (BM), 19131 (BM), 20754 (BM). N. INDIA: *Drummond* 22728 (G,K,P), 23187 (G,K), *Duthie* 192 (BM, FI,G,K), 5994 (BM, G,K); *Rawat* in *Renz* 13666 (Herb. Renz); *Renz & Naithani* 13622 (Herb. Renz). NEPAL: *Bowes Lyon* 2199 (BM), *Gardner* 840 (BM); *Lowndes* 1198 (BM), *G. & S. Miehe* 4008 (K), *E. Morton*

205 (K), *Polunin* 666 (BM), 773 (BM); *Polunin, Sykes & Williams* 292 (BM), 2375 (BM), 2395 (BM), 4374 (BM), 4603 (BM); *Schilling* 392 (K), 420A (K), *Schilling, Sayers & Bisra* 392 (K); *Sharma* E79 (BM); *Stainton* 6353 (BM); *Stainton, Sykes & Williams* 1737 (BM), 3100 (BM), 5804 (BM); *Wallich* s.n. (W). SIKKIM: *Hooker* 13558 (BM), s.n. (G,P,W); *Hooker & Thomson* 317 (K), *Pantling* 373 (BM,FI,K,P,W). S. XIZANG: *Dungboo* (P); *Kingdon-Ward* 7105 (K), 8365 (K), 11872 (BM), *Ludlow & Sherriff* 722 (BM); *Ludlow, Sherriff & Taylor* 5647 (BM); *Younghusband* s.n. (BM,K). MISC.: cult. *Elwes* s.n. (K).

28. **C. fasciculatum.** U.S.A.: *Austin* s.n. (AMES,K); *Churchill* s.n. (BM); *Cockerell* s.n. (K); *Goodding* 1201 (AMES); *Halliday & Roderick* s.n. (K); *Suksdorf* 900 (G,P), 7221 (BM,K), s.n. (W); *Thompson* 6485 (BM); *Wolley-Dod* 246 (K).

29. **C. arietinum** (selected). CANADA: *Calder* 7086 (W); *Erskine* 54.014 (W); *Fernald & Pease* 3247 (K); *Fyles* s.n. (W); *Gouldie* s.n. (K); ex *Lindley* (K); *Macoun* 1472 (K), s.n. (K); *Macrae* s.n. (K); *Savarie & Michel* s.n. (W). U.S.A.: *Bromfield* s.n. (K); *Dike* s.n. (W); *A. Gray* s.n. (W); *Herman* 7474 (K), 22604 (W); *Oakes* s.n. (K); *Pringle* s.n. (K).

30. **C. plectrochilum.** CHINA: *Cunningham* 650 (E); *Delavay* 1020 (G,K); *Forrest* 2198 (E), 5765 (E), 10112 (E), 12526 (E), 19228 (E,K,W); *Handel-Mazzetti* 3090 (W), 6440 (W); *Henry* 5474 (BM,K); *KEY* 212 (E), 506 (E); *Kingdon-Ward* 147 (E), 231 (E), 4039 (E), 5169 (E), 10380 (BM); *Maire* 1478 (BM,E), 6419 (Z), s.n. (G); *Mombeig* 251 (E), s.n. (E,K); *Pratt* 87 (BM,E,K), 763 (BM,K); *Rock* 3810 (E); *Schneider* 1322 (E,G,K), 1323 (E,G,K); *Schoch* 165 (K), 386 (Z); *Soulie* 1392 (K); *Ten* 331 (E); *Tschang* s.n. (E); *Wilson* 4583 (BM,K).

31. **C. japonicum** (selected). CHINA: *W.F. Fang* 1076 (E,K,PE); *Farges* 649 (G,K,P), s.n. (K,P); *Henry* 1404 (BM,K), 3777 (K); Herb. *TI* no. M92-6-25 (TI); *Ho-Ch'ang Chow* 809 (E); *Z.H. Ji* 0888 (PE); *N. Kweichow Team* 405 (PE), 436 (PE); *L.H. Liu* 1946 (PE); *P.S. Pen* 216 (PE); *Plant Res. Expl. Team* D0577 (PE); *K.S. Shen* 0231 (PE); *K.K. Tsoong* 282 (PE); *Wilson* 362 (E,K,P,W), s.n. (K); *Y.G. Xiong* 09925 (PE); *K. Yao* 8929 (K). KOREA: *Yongsok* 6458 (E), 7161 (TNS). JAPAN: *Albrecht* 3 (W); *Bisset* 364 (W), s.n. (K); *Dickins* s.n. (K,P); *Faurie* 411 (K,P), 1038 (G,P), 2636 (P), 3846 (P), 3910 (P), 4029 (P), 8083 (P); *Hiratsuki* TNS546465 (TNS); *Ito* TSM62541 (TNS); *Koidzumi* NSM180220 (TNS); *Kozuma & Masayuki* 31045 (TNS); Herb. *Hong Kong* no. 27860 (K); *Maingay* 785 (K); *Maximowicz* 10648 (BM), s.n. (BM,G,K,P,W); *Mazuda* s.n. (W); *Milne* s.n. (BM); *Murata et al.* 113 (K,P); *Nagasawa* TSM54280 (TNS); *Nikaido* TSM49109 (TNS); *Nomura* NSM210506 (TNS), NSM256248 (TNS); *Okuyama* 10880 (TNS); *Saita* TSM4391 (TNS); *Sakurai* TSM4389 (TNS); *Sasaki* TNS387415 (TNS), TNS387416 (TNS); *Satomi* NSM139361 (TNS), NSM136443 (TNS); *Savatier* 572 (P), 1332 (K,P); *Takeda* s.n. (K); *Ta-*

shiro IMT29907 (TNS), TSM35728 (TNS), TSM49108 (TNS); *Thunberg* s.n. (BM); *Tinakei & Maruyama* NSM84148 (TNS); *Watanabe* TNS54281 (TNS), s.n. (K); *Wright* 11 (K,P); *Yamazaki et al.* 732 (TNS); *Zahlbruckner* 1605 (W). MISC.: Hort. *A. Perry*, May 1916 (K).

32. **C. formosanum.** TAIWAN: *C.C. Hsu* 5871 (TAI,TI), 6095 (TAI,TI); *Chiou & Ho* TFRD 052525 (TAIF); *Fukuyama* 5985 (TI); *Hayata* s.n. (AMES,TI,TAIF); *Hibimo et al.* in Herb. *TAI* no. 032513 (TAI); Hort. Kew s.n. (K); *M.T. Kao* 8615 (TAI); *C.M. Kuo* 5118 (TAI); *Makino* 6659 (TAIF); *Matuda-Eizi* s.n. (TAI); *Nakamura* 5709 (TAI); *Sasaki* 6657 (TAIF), 6656 (TAIF), 6658 (TAIF); *Segawa* s.n. (TI); *Suzuki* s.n. (TAI); *Tamura & Koyama* 23551 (TNS); *J.C. Wang* 4227 (TAI); *Yamazaki et al.* 732 (TI).

33. **C. acaule** (selected). CANADA: *Anselme* s.n. (W); *Baldwin* 5701 (K); *Bourgeau* s.n. (K,W); *Bradford* s.n. (W); *Cain* 570 (W); *Cleghorn* s.n. (K); *Garton* 1388 (W); *S. Gray & Richards* 14534 (W); *Inglis* s.n. (W); *Macoun* 1467 (K), s.n. (K); *Malte* s.n. (W); *Richardson* s.n. (K); *Rousseau* 24319 (K); *Roy* 2443 (K), 3633 (W); *Torrey* s.n. (K). U.S.A.: *Adams* s.n. (W); *Ames* s.n. (K); *Beattie* s.n. (K); *Biltmore* 12116 (W); *Booth* s.n. (K); *Bordo* 28450 (W); *Curtis* s.n. (K); *de Cambrai* s.n. (K); *Drake* s.n. (W); *Forbes* s.n. (W); *Gouldie* s.n. (K); *Graham* 447 (K); *Grant* s.n. (K); *A. Gray* s.n. (W); *Irvine* 161 (K); *Hooker* 837 (K,W); *James* s.n. (K); *Jennings* s.n. (K); *Kitching* s.n. (K); *Lammers* 5065 (K); *Lapham* s.n. (K); *Lawrence, Dress & Kitawaza* 221 (W); *Lester-Garland* s.n. (K); *Mayall & Cormack* 277 (W); *Moldenke* 1262 (K); *Petratz* 236 (W); *Pringle* s.n. (K); *Rugel* s.n. (W); *Schultes* s.n. (K); *Schweinitz* s.n. (K); *Sheldon* s.n. (W); *Short* s.n. (K); *Shriver* 512 (K); *Small* s.n. (K); *Sullivant* 43 (W); *Torrey* s.n. (W); *Watson* s.n. (K). MISC.: cult. M. Masters, 26 April 1879 (K); cult. G. Wilson, 30 May 1888 (K); Herb. *Carey* (K); Herb. *Goodenough* s.n. (K); Herb. *Hooker* s.n. (K); Hort. Kew, 7 July 1900 (K); Herb. *T. Moore* s.n. (K).

34. **C. guttatum** (selected). BHUTAN: *Ludlow & Sherriff* 82 (BM). CHINA: *Bodinier* 2 (K), 6a (P), 317 (E), 347 (P); *Bretschneider* 1967 (BM); *Chanel & Serre* 236 (P), 2032 (P), 3129 (P); *Y.L. Chang et al.* 323 (PE), 375 (PE); *David* 2245 (P); *Delavay* s.n. (P); *W.P. Fan* 36218 (PE); *Fenzel* 227 (W); *Forrest* 12460 (E), 15131 (BM,E,K), 28563 (E); *Hancock* 14 (K); *Handel-Mazzetti* 3177 (W), 8770 (W); *Hemeling* 379 (E), 413 (E); *W.Y. Hsia* 1154 (PE); *Kingdon-Ward* 148 (E), 712 (E); *H.W. Kung* 202 (PE), 1438 (PE); *Licent* 3063 (K,P), 3074 BM,K,P,W), 7978 (BM), 8127 (BM,K), 8671 (BM,K), 10649 (W), 10741 (W), 12886 (P); *Limpricht* 2506 (K); *Liou* 2401 (K); *Y.C. Ma* 65-105 (PE); *Maack* s.n. (P); *McLaren* 43 (BM,E,K,P), 45 (E,P); *Mombeig* s.n. (K); *Pratt* 264 (BM,K); *Przewalski* s.n. (W); *Rock* 23937 (BM,E,K); *Ross* 33 (K); *Schneider* 1627 (E); *Serre* 2032 (W); *Soulie* 311 (P), 327 (P), 328 (P), 2311 (P), 2987 (P), 3495 (P); *T. Tang* 987 (PE); *C.Q. Tsoong* 096

(PE); *F.T. Wang* 21183 (PE); *Z. Wang* 4148 (PE); *Wilson* 4587 (BM,K,P); *Yellow River Team* 1327 (PE); *T.T. Yu* 7136 (PE), 11480 (PE). KOREA: *Mills* 85 (K); *Ohwi* 1145 (PE). RUSSIA: *Augustinowicz* s.n. (K,W); *Chaffanjon* 1497 (P), s.n. (K); *Ehnberg* s.n. (W); *Fischer* s.n. (W); *Freyn* 104 (P,W); *Jettmann* s.n. (W); *Karo* 104 (P), 298 (P), 337 (W), 424 (BM,P,W), 3194 (P,W); *Klementz* 533 (W); *Komarov* 435 (BM,W), 439 (BM); ex Herb. *Kuehlwein* s.n. (BM,W); *Maximowicz* s.n. (BM); *Mischta* 3051 (W); *Radde* s.n. (W); *Rogowicz* s.n. (BM); *Sensinow* s.n. (BM,K); ex Herb. *Shuttleworth* s.n. (BM); *Steven* s.n. (W); *Tronson* 1121 (BM); *Vatke* s.n. (W); *Vessenmeyer* s.n. (W); *Weimann* s.n. (W). SE. XIZANG: *Dungboo* s.n. (BM); *G.X. Fu* 996 (PE); *Ludlow & Sherriff* 1835 (BM); *Ludlow, Sherriff & Elliot* 13912 (BM), 15213 (BM); *Ludlow, Sherriff & Taylor* 5031 (BM). ALASKA: *Calder & Billard* 3228 (W).

35. C. yatabeanum. RUSSIA: *Eyerdam* s.n. (K); *Faurie* s.n. (P); *Hultén* 226 (K), s.n. (K); *Komarov* 3841 (K), s.n. (K,P,W); *Littledale* s.n. (K); *E. & H. Looff* 701 (G). JAPAN: *Yatabe* s.n. (TI). ALASKA: *Besser* s.n. (W); *Chamisso* 45 (W); *Eschscholtz* s.n. (W); *Looff* 701 (W).

36. C. palangshanense. CHINA: *Farges* 1549 (P); *Wang* 21164 (PE).

37. C. elegans. NEPAL: *Bailey's coll.* 99 (BM); *Beer* 8314 (BM); *Gardner* 874 (BM); *Lall Dhwoj* 0452 (BM); *Renz & Naithani* 13623 (Herb. Renz); *Stainton, Sykes & Williams* 1025 (BM,G), 3023 (BM). NE. INDIA: *Pantling* 387 (BM,G,K,P,W); *Pantling* in *Clarke* 46582 (K). BHUTAN: *Bowes Lyon* 3419 (BM), 15047 (BM); *Ludlow & Sherriff* 3193 (BM); *Ludlow, Sherriff & Hicks* 16386 (BM), 19134 (BM). XIZANG: *Brown* 229 (K); *King* 54 (K), s.n. (W); *Ludlow & Sherriff* 1695 (BM). BURMA: *Handel-Mazzetti* 9513 (W).

38. C. debile. CHINA: *X.S. Chang* 0355 (PE), 5206 (PE); *C.H. Chao* 40346 (PE); *K.L. Chu* 2753 (W); *Farges* s.n. (K,PE), 1339 (G,K,P); *T. He* 13307 (PE); *K.J. Guan* 420 (PE); *H.J. Li* 432 (PE); *X. Li* 78662 (PE); *G.L. Qiu* 2753 (E,PE); *Sichuan Economic Plant Team* 00200 (PE); *Sichuan Flora Team* 05343 (PE); *Wilson* 4585 (K); *G.H. Yang* 55181 (PE). TAIWAN: *Fowlie* s.n. (K). JAPAN: *Bisset* 1215 (K), 2489 (BM); *Difret* s.n. (W); *Faurie* 6622 (G,P); *Hayawaka* s.n. (W); Herb. *Hong Kong* 27846 (K); ex *Imperial Univ. Japan* (K); cult. Kew s.n. (K); *Maries* s.n. (BM,K,W); *Savatier* s.n. (K), 3475 (P); *Takeda* s.n. (BM,K); *Watanabe* s.n. (K).

39a. C. bardolphianum var. **bardolphianum.** CHINA: *Farrer & Purdom* 139 (E); *Feng* 1186 (KUN), 1475 (KUN); *Rock* 12499 (E,K,PE); *H. Smith* 3703 (GB,UPS); *Songpan Team* 1475 (PE); *C.W. Wang* 65773 (PE), 65809 (KUN,PE), 68317 (PE); *Z.B. Wang* 14359 (KUN).

39b. C. bardolphianum var. **zhongdianense.** CHINA: Known only from the type.

40. C. micranthum. CHINA: *Farges* s.n. (K,P), 1286 (G,K,P); *Wilson* 2063 (W), 4586 (BM,K,KUN,PE).

41. **C. margaritaceum.** CHINA: *Delavay* s.n. (P,PE); *Forrest* 4855 (BM,E), 7249 (E), 10267 (E,K), 13505 (BM,E); *Handel-Mazzetti* 1178 (K), 6655 (E,W); *Kunming/Edinburgh Yunnan Exp.* 442 (E), 499 (E); *Mission Liotard* s.n. (P); *C.Y. Wu et al.* 1506 (PE).

42. **C. lichiangense.** CHINA: *S.C. Ching* 20454 (KUN); *Forrest* 2264 (E), 5987 (E,K), 18253 (BM,E,K), 23050 (E,K), 28749 (BM,E); *Kingdon-Ward* 4278 (E), 5177 (E); *McLaren* 54 (E), 54B (BM); *Maire* s.n. (P,W); *S.W. Yu* 65064 (PE); *Schneider* 3573 (G).

43. **C. forrestii.** CHINA: *K.M. Fen* 1186 (KUN); *Forrest* 10203 (E,K)

44. **C. fargesii.** CHINA: *Agr. Coll. Sichuan Prov.* 1005 (PE); *Chinese Med. Team* 0261 (PE); *Economic Plant Coll. Team* 1478 (KUN), 3718 (PE); *Farges* 585 (G,K,P); *Henry* 1404 (BM); *Z.H. Ji* 0501 (PE); *X. Li* 78756 (PE); *Z. Qing* 1001 (PE); *Wilson* 2331 (K,W), 4582 (BM,K); *T.T. Yu* 763 (PE).

45. **C. wumengense.** CHINA: *W.M. Lu & J.L. Wu* 03447 (HGUY).

SELECTED BIBLIOGRAPHY

Adanson, M. (1763). *Familles des Plantes.* Vincent, Paris.

Aiton, W. (1789). *Hortus Kewensis.* G. Nichol, London.

Albert, V.A. (1994). Cladistic relationships of the slipper orchids (Cypripedioideae: Orchidaceae) from congruent morphological and molecular data. *Lindleyana* 9: 115–132.

Albert, V.A. & Chase, M. (1992). *Mexipedium:* a new genus of slipper orchid (Cypripedioideae: Orchidaceae). *Lindleyana* 7: 172–176.

Albert, V.A. & Petterson, B. (1994). Expansion of the genus *Paphiopedilum* Pfitzer to include all conduplicate-leaved slipper orchids (Cypripedioideae: Orchidaceae). *Lindleyana* 9: 133–140.

Amman, J. (1739). *Stirpium rariorum in Imperio Rutheno Icones et Descriptiones.* St.Petersburg.

Arber, A. (1986). *Herbals. Their Origin and Evolution.* 3rd ed. Cambridge University Press.

Arditti, J. & Ernst, R. (1993). *Micropropagation of orchids.* J. Wiley & Sons, New York.

Atwood, J.T. (1984). The relationships of the slipper orchids (Subfamily Cypripedioideae, Orchidaceae). *Selbyana* 7: 129–247.

Atwood, J.T. (1985). The *Cypripedium calceolus* complex in North America. In *Proc. 11th World Orchid Conference, Miami*: 10–110.

Balaeva, V.A. & Siplivinski, V.N. (1975). Chromosome numbers and taxonomy of some species of Baikal flora. *Botaniceski Zurnal* 60: 864–872.

Bastin, E.S. (1881). On *Cypripedium spectabile. Bot. Gaz.* 6: 269.

Baumann, H., Kunkele, S. & Lorenz, R. (1989). Die nomenklatorischen Typen der von Linnaeus veröffentlichen Namen europäischer Orchideen. *Mit. Arbeitskreis Heimische Orchid. Baden-Württemberg* 21: 452 (1989).

Belling, J. (1924). Detachment (elimination) of chromosomes in *Cypripedium acaule. Bot. Gaz.* 78: 458–460.

Bentham, G. & Hooker, J.D. (1883). *Cypripedieae. Genera Plantarum* 3: 487–488.

Bergstroem, G., Birgersson, G., Groth, I. & Nilsson, L.A. (1992). Floral fragrance analysis between three taxa of lady's slipper, *Cypripedium calceolus* (Orchidaceae). *Phytochemistry* 31(7): 2315.

Blume, C.L. (1858–1859). *Collection des Orchidees . . . de L'Archipelago Indien et du Japon.* C.G. Sullpke, Amsterdam.

Blunt, W., & Stearn, W. (1994). *The Art of Botanical Illustration.* Antique Collectors' Club, Woodbridge, Suffolk.

Böckel, W. (1972). Ein Ansamungsversuch mit *Cypripedium calceolus. Die Orchidee* 23: 120–123.

Bown, D. (1995). *Royal Horticultural Society Encyclopedia of Herbs and Their Uses.* Dorling Kindersley, London.

Brieger, F.G. (1973). *Cypripedium.* In Schlechter, R., *Die Orchideen.* 3rd ed. 3–4: 185–198.

Brown, P.M. (1995a). New taxa and taxonomic notes. *N. Amer. Native Orchid J.* 1(3): 195–200.

Brown, P.M. (1995b). *Cypripedium kentuckiense:* a retrospective of the literature. *N. Amer. Native Orchid J.* 1(3): 255–266.

Brown, R. (1813). *Cypripedium.* In Aiton, *Hortus Kewensis.* 2nd ed. 5: 220–222.

Brown, R. (1831). On the organs and mode of fecundation in Orchideae and Asclepiadeae. *Trans. Linn. Soc., London* 16: 685–745.

Burgeff, H. (1936). *Samenkeimung der Orchideen.* G. Fischer, Jena.

Candolle A. De. (1802). *Cypripedium flavescens.* In Redouté, P., *Les Liliacées.*

Candolle, A.L.L.P. De. (1880). *La Phytographie.* G. Masson, Paris.

Case, F. (1987). *Orchids of the Western Great Lakes Region.* Cranbrook Institute of Science.

Case, M.A. (1993). High levels of allozyme variation within *Cypripedium calceolus* (Orchidaceae) and low levels of divergence among its varieties. *Syst. Bot.* 18: 663–677.

Catesby, M. (1754). *The Natural History of Carolina, Florida and the Bahama Islands.*

Catling, P. (1983). Autogamy in eastern Canadian Orchidaceae: a review of current knowledge and some other considerations. *Nat. Canad.* 110: 37–45.

Catling, P. (1985). Distribution and pollination biology of Canadian orchids. In *Proc. 11th World Orchid Conference, Miami:* 121–135.

Catling, P. & Knerer, G. (1980). Pollination of the small white lady's slipper *Cypripedium candidum* in Lambton County, southern Ontario. *Canad. Field-Naturalist* 94: 435–438.

Chase, M.W., Cameron, K.M., Hills, H.G. & Jarrell, D. (1994). DNA sequences and phylogenetics of the Orchidaceae and other monocots. In Pridgeon, A. (ed.), *Proc. 14th World Orchid Conference:* 61–73.

Chen, S.C. (1983). *Cypripedium shanxiense. Acta Phytotax. Sin.* 21(3): 43.

Chen, S.C. & Lang, K.Y. (1986). *Cypripedium subtropicum,* a new species related to *Selenipedium. Acta Phytotax. Sin.* 24(4): 317–322.

Chen, S.C. & Xi, Y.Z. (1987). Chinese cypripediums, with a discussion on the classification of the genus. In *Proc. 12th World Orchid Conference, Tokyo:* 141–146.

Clément, C. (1886). Les *Cypripedium* de pleine terre. *L'Orchidophile* 6: 151–157.

Clements, M.A. (1995). *Reproductive biology in relation to phylogeny of the Orchidaceae especially the tribe Diurideae*. Ph.D. thesis, Australian National University, Canberra.

Clusius, C. (1583). *Rariorum aliquot stirpium, per Pannoniam Austriam, et vicinas*. C. Platini, Antwerp.

Cornut, J.P. (1635). *Canadensium Plantarum Historia*. Paris.

Correll, D. (1950). *Native Orchids of North America*. Waltham, Massachusetts.

Cox, A. (1995). *The Utility of 5S r-DNA in Phylogenetic Reconstructions: Development of the Polymerase Chain Reaction in Plant Systematics*. Ph.D. thesis, University of Reading.

Cribb, P.J. (1992). The Chinese spotted-leaved cypripediums. *Bull. Alpine Gard. Soc. Gt. Brit.* 60 (2): 165–177.

Cribb, P.J. & Chen, S.C. (1994). Further thoughts on the Chinese spotted-leaved cypripediums. *Orchid Rev.* 102: 320–323.

Cribb, P.J. & Soto Arenas, M. (1993). The genus *Cypripedium* in Mexico and Central America. *Orquidea (Mexico)* 13(1–2): 205–214.

Curtis, J.T. (1932). A new *Cypripedium* hybrid. *Rhodora* 34; 239–243.

Curtis, J.T. (1943). Germination and seedling development in five species of Cypripedium. *Amer. J. Bot.* 30: 199–206.

Daleschamp, J. (1586). *Historiae Generalis Plantarum*. Paris.

Darwin, C. (1862). *On the Various Contrivances by which British and Foreign Orchids are Fertilised by Insects*. J. Murray, London.

Darwin, C. (1877). *On the Various Contrivances by which British and Foreign Orchids are Fertilised by Insects*. 2nd ed. J. Murray, London.

Daumann, E. (1968). Zur Bestaubbungsoekologie von *Cypripedium calceolus*. *Oesterr. Bot. Z.* 115: 434–446.

Delpino, F. (1867). *Sugli apparecchi della fecondazione nelle plante antocarpee*. Firenze.

Dodoens, R. (1568). *Florum, et coroniariarium odoratumque nonnullarum herbarum historia*. C. Platini, Antwerp.

Dodoens, R. (1583). *Stirpium historiae pemptades sex*. C. Platini, Antwerp.

Don, D. (1825). *Prodromus Florae Nepalensis*. J. Gale, London.

Dressler, R.L. (1981). *The Orchids. Natural History and Classification*. Harvard University Press.

Dressler, R.L. (1983). Classification of the Orchidaceae and their probable origin. *Telopea* 2(4): 413–424.

Dressler, R.L. (1993). *Phylogeny and Classification of the Orchid Family*. Cambridge University Press.

Duncan R. (1959). List of chromosome numbers in orchids. In Withner, C. (ed.), *The Orchids. A Scientific Survey*: pp. 529–587. Ronald Press, New York.

Elliman, E. & Dalton, A. (1995). *Cypripedium fasciculatum* Kellogg ex Watson in Montana. *N. Amer. Native Orchid J.* 1: 59–73.

Farr, E.R., Leussink, J.A. & Stafleu, F.A. (1979). *Index Nominum Generico-rum*. Bohn, Scheltema & Holkema, Utrecht.

Farrer, R. (1916). *Cypripedium bardolphianum. Notes Roy. Bot. Gard. Edin-burgh* 9: 101.

Farrer, R. (1919). *The English Rock Garden*. 2 vols. Nelson & Sons, London.

Farrer, R. (1925). *Cypripedium luteum. English Rock Garden* 2, Appendix: 499.

Farwell, O. A. (1917). *Fissipes hirsuta. Druggists Circular* 61: 230.

Fernald, M.L. (1926). Two summers of botanising in Newfoundland. *Rhodora* 28: 161–178.

Francini, E. (1931). Ricerche embriologische e cariologische sul genere *Cypripedium. Nuovo Giorn. Bot. Ital.* 38: 155–212.

Fuchs, A. & Ziegenspeck, H. (1926). Entwicklungsgeschichte der Axen der einheimischen Orchideen und ihre Physiologie und Biologie I. *Cy-pripedium, Helleborine, Limodorum, Cephalanthera. Bot. Arch.* 16: 360–413.

Fuller, A.M. (1932). × *Cypripedium Andrewsii. Rhodora* 34: 100.

Garay, L. (1953). A new natural hybrid *Cypripedium* from Ontario. *Canad. J. Bot.* 31: 660–662.

Garay, L.A. (1960). On the origin of the Orchidaceae. *Bot. Mus. Leafl.* 19: 57–95.

Garay, L.A. (1972). On the origin of the Orchidaceae. II. *J. Arnold Arb.* 53: 202–215.

Garay, L.A. (1982). Note sub *Cypripedium furcatum* Raf.—a "new" and beau-tiful species in the southern United States. *Amer. Orchid Soc. Bull.* 51(9): 902.

Gerard, J. (1597). *The Herball or General Historie of Plantes.* J. Norton, London.

Gesner, C. (1561). *Horti Germaniae*. Strasburg.

Gill, D.E. (1989). Fruiting failure, pollinator inefficiency and speciation in orchids. In Otte, D. & Endler, J.A. (eds.), *Speciation and its Consequences*: 458–481. Sunderland, Massachusetts.

Gmelin, J.G. (1747–1749). *Flora Sibirica*. St.Petersburg.

Gonzales Tamayo, R. & Ramirez Delgadillo, R.(1992). *Cypripedium luz-marianum. Boletin Inst. Bot. (Guadalajara)* 1(2): 63–69, fig.1.

Gray, A. (1862). Fertilisation of orchids through the agency of insects. *Amer. J. Sci. Arts* 34: 420–429.

Griesbach, R. & Asher, J. (1983). Orchids of the Boundary Waters Canoe Area of northern Minnesota. In Plaxton, E.H. (ed.), *North American Ter-restrial Orchid Symposium* 2. Michigan Orchid Soc.

Guignard, J.A. (1886). Insects and orchids. *Ann. Rep. Ent. Soc. Ont.* 16: 39–48.

Hágsater, E. (1984). *Cypripedium dickinsonianum* Hágsater, a new species from Chiapas, Mexico. *Orquidea (Mexico)* 9(1): 198–213.

Hill, E. (1878). A double-flowered *Cypripedium spectabile. Amer. Natural.* 12: 816.

Hooker, W.J. (1829). *Cypripedium macranthos. Bot. Mag.* 56: t.2938.

Hooker, J.D. (1890). *Flora of British India. Orchideae.* Macmillan, London.

House, H.D. (1905). *Cypripedium hirsutum* Mill. *Bull. Torrey Bot. Club* 32: 375.

Humphrey, L.M. (1932). The somatic chromosomes of eight species of orchids. *Proc. Iowa Acad. Sciences* 39: 137.

Humphrey, L.M. (1933). Somatic chromosomes of *Cyp. hirsutum* and six species of genus *Habenaria. Proc. Iowa Acad. Sciences* 40: 75.

Hultén, E. (1968). *Cypripedium* L. *Flora of Alaska and Neighbouring Territories*: 315–317. Stanford Univ. Press, California.

Hunt, P.F. & Summerhayes, V.S. (1966). Notes on Asiatic orchids IV. *Kew Bull.* 20: 51.

Iinuma, Y. (1874). *Sintei Somoku Dzusetsu.* Tokyo.

Illingworth, J. & Routh, J. (1991). *Reginald Farrer. Salesman, Planthunter, Gardener.* University of Lancaster, England.

Irmisch, T. (1853). *Beiträge zur Biologie und Morphologie der Orchideen.* A. Abel, Leipzig.

Jarvis, C.E., Barrie, F.R., Allan, D.M. & Reveal, J.L. (1993). *A List of Linnaean Generic Names and their Types.* Koeltz, Koenigstein.

Kanda, K. (1984). *The Wild Orchids of Japan.* Seibundo Shinkosha, Tokyo.

Karasawa, K. & Aoyama, M. (1986). Karyomorphological studies on *Cypripedium* in Japan and Formosa. *Bull. Hiroshima Bot. Gard.* 8: 1–22.

Karasawa, K. & Atwood, J. (1988). Karyomorphological observations on *Cypripedium kentuckiense* Reed, Orchidaceae. *Bull. Hiroshima Bot. Gard.* 10: 73–76.

Keenan, P.E. (1995). Diversity in *Cypripedium acaule. N. Amer. Native Orchid J.* 1(3): 201–210.

Keller, G. & Schlechter, R. (1926). Monographie und Inconographie der Orchideen Europas und des Mittelmeergebietes. *Feddes Rep. Sondergebeit* A, 1.

Keller, G. & Sóo, R. von (1930). Monographie und Iconographie der Orchideen Europas und des Mittelmeergebietes. *Feddes Rep. Sondergebeit* A, 2.

King, G. & Pantling, R. (1898). Orchids of the Sikkim Himalaya. *Ann. Roy. Bot. Gard., Calcutta* 8.

Klier, K., Leoschke, M.J. & Wendel, J.F. (1991). Hybridisation and introgression in white and yellow ladyslipper orchids (*Cypripedium candidum* and *C. pubescens*). *J. Heredity* 82: 305–318.

Kränzlin, F. (1901). *Cypripedium* L. *Orchidacearum Genera et Species* 1: 11–86.

de L'Ecluse, C., see Clusius, C.

Lindley, J. (1826). *Orchidearum sceletos.* London.

Lindley, J. (1832). *Cypripedium macranthon. Bot. Reg.* 18: t. 1534.

Lindley, J. (1835). *A Key to Structural, Physiological, and Systematic Botany for the Use of Classes.* Longman et al., London.

Lindley, J. (1840). *Cypripedium*. In *Genera and Species of Orchidaceous Plants*: 525–532. Ridgways, London.

Linnaeus, C. (1737). *Flora Lapponica*. S. Schouten, Amsterdam.

Linnaeus, C. (1753). *Species Plantarum*. L. Salvius, Stockholm.

L'Obel, M. (1576). *Plantarum seu stirpium historia*. C.Platini, Antwerp.

Löve, A. & Löve, D. (1965). IOPB chromosome reports III and IV. *Taxon* 14(3): 86–87.

Löve A.& Löve,D. (1969). IOPB chromosome number reports 21. *Taxon* 18: 310–315.

Löve, A. & Simon, W. (1968). Cytotaxonomical notes on some American orchids. *Southw. Nat.* 13: 335–342.

Lucke, E. (1982). Samenstruktur und Samenkeimung europäischer Orchideen nach Veyret sowie weitere Unterschungen. *Die Orchidee (Hamburg)* 33: 8–14.

Luer, C. (1975). *The Native Orchids of the United States and Canada*. New York.

MacDougal, D.T. (1895). Poisonous influence of various species of *Cypripedium*. *Minn. Bot. Studies Bull.* 9: 450–451.

Marie-Victorin, F. & Rousseau, J. (1940). Nouvelles entités de la Flore Phanérogamie du Canada Oriental. *Contrib. Inst. Bot. Univ. Montréal* 36: 9–74.

Masamune, G. (1984–1990). *Orchids of Nippon*. 6 vols. Tokyo.

McGrath, L.K. & Norman, J.L. (1989). *Cypripedium parviflorum* Salisb. f. *albolabium* J.K. Magrath & J.L. Norman. *Sida* 13: 372.

McVaugh, R. (1985). Orchidaceae. In Anderson, W.R. (ed.), *Flora Novo-Galiciana* 16. Univ. of Michigan Press, Ann Arbor.

Mehra, P.N. & Bawa, K.S. (1970). Cytological observations on some Northwest Himalayan orchids. *Caryologia* 23; 273–282.

Miduno, T. (1955). Karyotypanalyse und differentielle Faerbung der Chromosomen von *Cypripedium debile*. *Jap. J. Genet.* 30: 210.

Miller, P. (1731). *Gardeners Dictionary*. 1st ed.

Miller, P. (1758). *Figures of the most beautiful, useful and uncommon plants figured in the Gardeners Dictionary*.

Miller, P. (1768). *Cypripedium*. Gardeners Dictionary. 8th ed.

Miyake & Kudo (1932). Flora of Hokkaido & Saghalien 3. *J. Fac. Agric., Hokkaido Imp. Univ.* 26(3): 279–387.

Moore, D. (1980). *Cypripedium*. In *Flora Europea* 5: *Orchidaceae*. Cambridge University Press.

Morison, R. (1699). *Plantarum Historiae Universalis*. Oxford.

Morren, C. (1851). Les Soulies de la Vierge Marie des Anciens ou les Sabots de Vénus des Modernes, Monographie des Cypripèdes. *Belg. Hort.* 1: 165–183.

Morris, F. & Eames, E.A. (1929). *Our Wild Orchids*. Scribners, New York.

Müller, H. (1868). *Verh. Naturwiss. Vereins Preuss Rheinl. Westfalens* 25: 1.

Müller, H. (1869). Über die Anwendung der Darwinschen Theorie auf Blumen und blumenbesuchende Insekten. *Verh. Naturwiss. Vereins Preuss Rheinl. Westfalens* 26, *Corr. Bl.:* 43–66.

Müller, H. (1873). Die Befruchtung der Blumen durch Insekten. Engelmann, Leipzig.

Nakai, T. (1932). *Notulae ad plantas Japoniae et Koreae* XLII. *Bot. Mag. (Tokyo)* 66: 603–604.

Nakai, T. (1940). *Notulae ad plantas Asiae Orientalis* XIII. *J. Jap. Bot.* 16: 1–81.

Nilsson, L.A. (1979). Anthecological studies on the lady's slipper, *Cypripedium calceolus* (Orchidaceae). *Bot. Not.* 132: 329–347.

Ohno, R. (1954). Notes on the chromosomes in some species of the phanerogamous plants. *J. Hokkaido Gakugei Univ.* 5: 33–36.

Ohwi, J. (1965). *Flora of Japan* (in English). Smithsonian Inst., Washington.

Okuyama, H. (1995). *Cypripedium* orchids of the Russian Far East (in Japanese). *Wild Orchid J.* 1995 (9): 62–71.

Pace, L. (1907). Fertilisation in *Cypripedium. Bot. Gaz.* 44: 353–374.

Parkinson, J. (1629). *Paradisi in Sole Paradisus terrestris.* H. Lownes, London.

Parkinson, J. (1640). *Theatrum botanicum: The Theater of Plants.* T. Cotes, London.

Perner, H. (1995). Winterarte Frauenschuhe (1): *Cypripedium arietinum* Brown und *C. plectrochilum* Franchet. *Die Orchidee (Hamburg)* 46 (3): 103–108.

Perner, H. & Averyanov, L. (1995). *Cypripedium shanxiense* Chen im Fernen Osten Russlands. *Die Orchidee (Hamburg)* 46: 196–197.

Pfitzer, E. (1886). *Morphologische Studien über die Orchideenblüthe.* C. Winter, Heidelberg.

Pfitzer, E. (1887). *Entwurf einer natürlichen Anordnung der Orchideen.* C. Winter, Heidelberg.

Pfitzer, E. (1889). *Diandrae Cypripedilinae.* In Engler, A. & Prantl, K. (eds.), *Die Natürlichen Pflanzenfamilien* II, 6: 82.

Pfitzer, E. (1894). Beiträge zur Systematik der Orchidaceen. In Engler, A. (ed.), *Bot. Jahrb. Syst.* 19: 1–42.

Pfitzer, E. (1903). *Cypripedium.* In Engler, A., *Das Pflanzenreich IV, 50 (Heft 12) Orchidaceae Pleonandrae.* 28–42.

Plukenet, L. (1696). *Almagestum botanicum.* London.

Plukenet, L. (1700). *Almagesti botanici Mantissa.* London.

Plukenet, L. (1705). *Almatheum botanicum.* London.

Pradhan, U.C. (1976). *Indian Orchids: Guide to Identification and Culture,* vol.1. Calcutta.

Pradhan, U.C. (1986). The Himalayan cypripediums. *Orchid Dig.* 50(3): 84–91.

Procter, M. & P. Yeo. (1973). *The Pollination of Flowers.* Collins, London.

Rafinesque, C.S. (1819). *Criosanthes. J. Phys. Chim. Hist. Nat.* 89: 102.

Rafinesque, C.S. (1828). *Medical Flora; or Manual of the Medical Botany of the United States of North America.* Atkinson & Alexander, Philadelphia.

Rafinesque, C.S. (1838). *Sacodon.* In *Flora Telluriana* 4: 46. Philadelphia.

Rasmussen, F. (1985). Orchids. In Dahlgren, R.M.L. et al. (eds.), *The Families of the Monocotyledons—Structure, Evolution and Taxonomy*: 247–274.

Rasmussen, H. (1995). *Terrestrial Orchids from Seed to Mycotrophic Plant.* Cambridge University Press.

Reed, C.F. (1981). *Cypripedium kentuckiense* Reed, a new species of orchid from Kentucky. *Phytologia* 48(5): 426–428.

Reichenbach, H.G. (1851). *Icones Florae Gemanicae et Helveticae.* Hofmeister, Leipzig.

Reichenbach, H.G. (1854). *Selenipedium* Rchb. fil. *Bonplandia* 2: 116.

Rolfe, R.A. (1896). The *Cypripedium* group. *Orchid Rev.* 4: 327–334, 363–367.

Rolfe, R.A. (1904). *Cypripedium calceolus× macranthos. Orchid Rev.* 12: 185.

Rolfe, R.A. (1910). *Cypripedium× ventricosum. Orchid Rev.* 18: 215.

Schlechter, R. (1919). *Orchideologiae Sino-japonicae prodromus. Feddes Rep. Sp. Nov., Beihefte* 4.

Schlechter, R. (1926). Das System der Orchidaceen. *Notizbl. Bot. Gart. Berlin-Dahlem* 9: 563–591.

Schmiedel, C.C. (1751). *Conradi Gesneri Opera Botanica.* Nuernberg.

Schmiedel, C.C. (1759–1771). *Conradi Gesneri . . . Historiae Plantarum Fasciculus quem ex Bibliotheca Iacobi Trew . . . edidit et illustravit D.C.C.S.* Nuernberg.

Sheviak, C. (1974). An introduction to the ecology of the Illinois Orchidaceae. *Illinois State Mus. Sci. Pap.* 14: 1–89.

Sheviak, C. (1983). United States terrestrial orchids. Patterns and problems. In Plaxton, E.H. (ed.), *North American Terrestrial Orchid Symposium* 2. Michigan Orchid Soc.

Sheviak, C. (1990). *Cypripedium montanum* f. *praeternictum. Rhodora* 92: 48.

Sheviak, C. (1992). Natural hybridisation between *Cypripedium montanum* and its yellow-lipped relatives. *Amer. Orchid Soc. Bull.* 61(6): 558.

Sheviak, C. (1994). *Cypripedium parviflorum* Salisb. I: The small-flowered varieties. *Amer. Orchid Soc. Bull.* 63(6): 664–669.

Sheviak, C. (1995). *Cypripedium parviflorum* Salisb. Part 2. The larger-flowered plants and patterns of variation. *Amer. Orchid Soc. Bull.* 64(4): 606–612.

Siuzew, P.W. (1926). *C.× krylowii. Bull. Inst. Rech. Biol. Perm* 4: 435–436.

Slyusarenko, A.G. (1981). *Cypripedium* L.—the lady's slippers. *Amer. Orchid Soc. Bull.* 50(7): 776–780.

Sokolovskaya, A.P. (1966). Geographicheskoe rasprostranenie poliploidnykh vidov rastenij. *Vestn. Leningradsk Univ. Ser. Biol.* 3: 92–106.

Soto, M.A., Salazar, G.A. & Hágsater, E. (1990). *Phragmipedium xerophyti-*

cum, una nueva especie del sureste de Mexico. *Orquidea (Mexico)* 12: 1–10.

Sowerby, J. (1790). *Cypripedium calceolus. English Botany*, vol.1, t.1. J.Davis, London.

Stace, C. (1991). *New Flora of the British Isles.* Cambridge University Press.

Stapf, O. (1927). *Cypripedium manschuricum virescens. Bot. Mag.* 152: t. 9117.

Steele, W.K. (1995). Growing *Cypripedium reginae* from seed. *Amer. Orchid Soc. Bull.*, April 1995: 382–391.

Steele, W.K. (1996). Large scale seedling production of North American *Cypripedium* species. In C. Allen ed., *North American Native Terrestrial Orchid Propagation and Production.* N. American Native Terrestrial Orchid Conference, Germantown, Maryland.

Stoutamire, W.P. (1963). Terrestrial orchid seedlings. *Austral. Plants* 2: 119–119.

Stoutamire, W.P. (1964). Seeds and seedlings of native orchids. *Michigan Bot.* 3: 107–119.

Stoutamire, W.P. (1967). Flower biology of the lady's slippers (Orchidaceae: *Cypripedium*). *Michigan Bot.* 6: 159–175.

Stoutamire, W.P. (1980). Eastern American *Cypripedium* species and the biology of *Cypripedium candidum.* In Yannetti, R.A. (ed.), *North American Native Terrestrial Orchid Propagation and Production. Conference Proceedings.* Brandywine Conservancy, Mt. Cuba Center & New England Wild Flower Society, Chadds Ford, Pennsylvania.

Su, H.J. (1975). Native orchids of Taiwan. 2nd ed. *Harvest Farm Mag.*, Taipei.

Su, H.J. (1978). Orchidaceae. In Li, H.H. et al. (eds.), *Flora of Taiwan* 5: 950–953.

Summerhayes, V.S. (1951). *Wild Orchids of Britain.* Collins, London.

Summerhayes, V.S. (1968). *Wild Orchids of Britain.* 3rd ed. Collins, London.

Suzuki, M. (1980). *Cypripedium japonicum* Thunb. var. *glabrum* M. Suzuki. *J. Jap. Bot.* 55: 351.

Swartz, O. (1800). *Cypripedium* L. *Kongl. Vetensk. Acad. Nya Handl.* 21: 250–251.

Swartz, O. (1805). Genera et species Orchidearum. *Neues J. Bot.* 1: 1–108.

Tanaka, R. & Kamemoto, H. (1974). List of chromosome numbers in species of the Orchidaceae. In Withner, C. (ed.), *The Orchids. Scientific Studies*: pp. 411–483. J. Wiley & Co., New York.

Tanaka, T. & Kamemoto, H. (1984). Chromosomes in orchids: counting and numbers. In Arditti, J. (ed.), *Orchid Biology. Reviews and Perspectives* 3: 323–410.

Tang, T. & Wang, F.T. (1951). Contributions to the knowledge of eastern Asiatic Orchidaceae II. *Acta Phytotax. Sin.* 1(1): 23–101.

Thunberg, C.P. (1784). *Flora Japonica.* I.G. Müller, Leipzig.

Thunberg, C.P. (1795). *Icones Plantarum Japonicarum.* F. Erdman, Upsala.

Troll, W. (1951). Botanische Notizen II. *Abhandlung Math.-Naturwiss. Kl. Akad. Wiss., Mainz* 1951(2).

van der Pijl, L. & Dodson, C.(1966). *Orchid Flowers. Their Pollination and Evolution.* Miami.

Vermeulen, P. (1966). The system of the Orchidales. *Acta Bot. Neerl.* 15: 224–253.

Vij, S.P. & Mehra, P.N. (1974). Cytological studies in the W. Himalayan Orchidaceae III. *Cypripedieae. Caryologia* 27: 293–300.

Watson, S. (1876). *Cypripedium occidentale. Proc. Amer. Acad. Arts Sci.* 11: 147.

Webster, A.D. (1886). On the growth and fertilisation of *Cypripedium calceolus. Trans. & Proc. Bot. Soc. Edinburgh* 16: 357–360.

Whiting, R.E. & Catling, P. (1986). *Orchids of Ontario.* Coll Foundation, Ottawa.

Wiard, L.A. (1985). *An Introduction to the Orchids of Mexico.* Comstock Publ. Ass., Ithaca & London.

Williams, L.O. (1951). The Orchidaceae of Mexico. *Ceiba* 2.

Wilson, C.L., Maxfield, K. & Livingstone, E. (1982). *Cypripedium furcatum—* a "new" and beautiful species in the southern United States. *Amer. Orchid Soc. Bull.* 51(9): 900–902.

Wilson, E.H. (1911). *Cypripedium luteum* and *C. tibeticum. Gard. Chron.* ser. 3, 49: 402–403, figs. 178, 179.

Xi, Y.Z. & Chen, S.C. (1991). A palynological study of the genus *Cypripedium* (Orchidaceae). *Cathaya* 3: 73–91.

Yang, Z.H., Zhang, Q.T., Feng, Z.H., Lang, K.Y. and Li, H. (1993). *Orchids.* China Esperanto Press, Beijing.

Yarian, N.C. (1939). On the trail of our native orchids. *Amer. Orchid Soc. Bull.* 7: 66–69.

Ying, S.S. (1977). *Coloured Illustrations of Indigenous Orchids of Taiwan,* vol.1. Dept. of Forestry, National Taiwan Univ., Taipei.

Zhu, Y.C. (1989). *Orchidaceae.* In Plantae Medicinales Chinae Bor.-Orient.: 182–185.

Ziegenspeck, H. (1936). Orchidaceae. In von Kirchner, O., Loew, E., & Schroeter, C., *Lebensgeschichte der Blütenpflanzen Mitteleuropas.* Stuttgart.

Zoller, H., Steinmann, M. & Schmidt, K. (1973–1980). *Conradi Gesneri Historia Plantarum facsimile ausgabe. Aquarelle aus dem botanischen Nachlass von Conrad Gesner.* 8 vols. Zurich.

INDEX OF
SCIENTIFIC NAMES

Accepted names are given in **bold** type; synonyms are in *italic* type.

C. californicum A. Gray 26, 28, 39, 41, 42, 43, 44, 56, 85, 103, 104, **132–134**, 274; Fig. 14; Plates 5, 41–43

C. callosum Rchb. f. = Paphiopedilum callosum

C. canadense Michx. = **C. reginae**

C. candidum Mühl. ex Willd. 36, 37, 38, 42, 44, 50, 51, 85, 97, 105, **187–190**, 277; Fig. 28; Plates 6, 44–46

C. cannartianum Hort. = Paphiopedilum philippinense

C. cardiophyllum Franch. & Sav. = **C. debile**

C. caricinum Lindl. & Paxt. = Phragmipedium caricinum

C. Carolin 98

C. Carson 98

C. cathayanum S.S. Chien = **C. japonicum**

C. caudatum Lindl. = Phragmipedium caudatum

C. chamberlainianum O'Brien = Paphiopedilum victoria-reginae

C. chantini Hort. = Paphiopedilum insigne

C. charlesworthii Rolfe = Paphiopedilum charlesworthii

C. Chauncey 98

C. chica Kränzl. = Selenipedium chica

C. chinense Franch. = **C. henryi**

C. ciliolare Rchb. f. = Paphiopedilum ciliolare

C. × **columbianum** C.J. Sheviak 86, **271**

C. compactum Schltr. = **C. tibeticum**

C. concolor Batem. = Paphiopedilum concolor

C. cordigerum D. Don 26, 37, 38, 42, 44, 86, 105, **161–164**, 276; Fig. 22; Plates 7, 47, 48

C. corrugatum Franch. = **C. tibeticum**

C. corrugatum Franch. var. *obesum* Franch. = **C. tibeticum**

C. cothurnum Vell. = Catasetum trulla

C. crossii Morr. = Paphiopedilum barbatum

C. cruciatum Dulac = **C. calceolus**

C. cruciforme Zoll. & Mor. = Paphiopedilum lowii

C. curtisii Richb. f. = Paphiopedilum superbiens var. curtisii

C. czerwiakowianum Kränzl. = Phragmipedium boissierianum

C. daliense S.C. Chen & Wu = **C. margaritaceum**

C. daliense sensu Cribb = **C. lichiangense**

C. dariense Rchb. f. = Phragmipedium longifolium

C. daultonii Soukup = **C. kentuckiense**

C. dayanum Rchb. f. = Paphiopedilum dayanum

C. debile Rchb. f. 20, 25, 26, 27, 28, 29, 35, 37, 38, 42, 43, 44, 48, 86, 103, **248–250**, 282; Fig. 45; Plates 8, 49, 50

C. delenatii (Guillaumin) C.H. Curtis = Paphiopedilum delenatii Guillaumin

C. dickinsonianum Hágsater 26, 35, 41, 42, 45, 55, 56, 86, 103, 105, **130–132**, 274; Plates 51, 52

C. dilectum Rchb. f. = Paphiopedilum villosum var. boxallii

C. dominianum Rchb. f. = Phragmipedium dominianum

C. drurii Bedd. = Paphiopedilum druryi

C. ebracteatum Rolfe = **C. fargesii**

C. elegans Rchb. f. 26, 41, 42, 43, 46, 87, 108, **246–248**, 282; Fig. 44; Plate 53

C. elliottianum O'Brien = Paphiopedilum rothschildianum

C. Emil 98

C. epidendricum Vell. = Eulophia alta

C. ernestianum L. Castle = Paphiopedilum dayanum

C. exul O'Brien = Paphiopedilum exul

C. pereirae Ridley = Paphiopedilum ×
pereirae nat. hybr.

C. petri Rchb. f. = Paphiopedilum
dayanum

C. philippinense Rchb. f. =
Paphiopedilum philippinense

C. pitcherianum Manda =
Paphiopedilum argus

C. planipetalum (Fernald) Morris &
Eames = **C. parviflorum** var.
pubescens

C. platytaenium Rchb. f. =
Paphiopedilum stonei

C. plectrochilum Franch. 27, 28, 33,
42, 44, 45, 94, 99, 104, **222–225**,
280; Fig. 37A–H; Plates 99–100

C. praestans Rchb. f. =
Paphiopedilum glanduliferum

C. Princess 98

C. Promises 98

C. pubescens Willd. = **C. parviflorum**
var. **pubescens**

C. pubescens var. *makasin* Farw. =
C. parviflorum var. **parviflorum**

C. pulchrum Ames & Schltr. =
C. franchetii

C. purpuratum Lindl. =
Paphiopedilum purpuratum

C. purpuratum sensu Wight =
Paphiopedilum barbatum

C. pusillum Rolfe = **C. fasciculatum**

C. Rascal 98

C. rebunense Kudo = **C. macranthos**

C. reginae Walt. 16, 18, 26, 27, 28,
29, 37, 38, 42, 44, 45, 49, 51, 56,
61, 67, 79, 81, 94, 97, 102, 105,
140–144, 275; Figs. 3, 16; Plates
22, 23, 101, 102

C. reichenbachianum Hort. =
Phragmipedium longifolium

C. reichenbachii Bull =
Phragmipedium longifolium

C. reticulatum Rchb. f. =
Phragmipedium boissierianum

C. robinsonii Ridley = Paphiopedilum
appletonianum

C. roebelenii Rchb. f. =
Paphiopedilum philippinense
var. roebelenii

C. roezlii Regel = Phragmipedium
longifolium

C. rothschildianum Rchb. f. =
Paphiopedilum rothschildianum

C. sanderianum Rchb. f. =
Paphiopedilum sanderianum

C. sargentianum Kränzl. =
Phragmipedium sargentianum

C. schlimii Linden ex Rchb. f. =
Phragmipedium schlimii

C. schmidtianum Kränzl. =
Paphiopedilum callosum

C. schomburgkianum Klotzsch ex
Schomb. = Phragmipedium
klotzschianum

C. segawai Masam. 37, 38, 42, 44, 45,
55, 95, 106, **156–158**, 276; Fig. 20;
Plates 24, 103, 104

C. shanxiense S.C. Chen 27, 36, 42,
47, 48, 95, 106, **158–161**, 276; Fig.
21; Plates 105, 106

C. siamense Rolfe = Paphiopedilum
appletonianum × callosum nat.
hybr.

C. sinicum Hance = Paphiopedilum
purpuratum

C. smithii Schltr. 42, 95, 107, **209–
211**, 279; Fig. 33; Plates 107–109

C. socco Vell. = Catasetum sp.

C. speciosum Rolfe = **C. macranthos**

C. spectabile Salisb. = **C. reginae**

C. spicerianum Rchb. f. =
Paphiopedilum spicerianum

C. splendidum Scheidw. =
C. irapeanum

C. stenophyllum Rchb. f. =
Phragmipedium stenophyllum

C. stonei Hook. = Paphiopedilum
stonei

C. subtropicum S.C. Chen & K.Y.
Lang 26, 27, 29, 41, 45, 55, 95,
102, 103, 104, **116–118**, 274; Fig.
9

C. superbiens Rchb. f. =
Paphiopedilum superbiens